Meade and Lee
at Rappahannock Station

The Army of the Potomac's First
Post-Gettysburg Offensive
from Kelly's Ford to the Rapidan,
October 21 to November 20, 1863

Jeffrey Wm Hunt

Savas Beatie
California

Library of Congress Cataloging-in-Publication Data

Names: Hunt, Jeffrey Wm. (Jeffrey William), 1962– author.
  Title: Meade and Lee at Rappahannock Station: The Army of the Potomac's First post-Gettysburg
  Offensive, from Kelly's Ford to the Rapidan, October 21 to November 20, 1863 / Jeffrey Wm Hunt.
Description: El Dorado Hills, CA : Savas Beatie LLC, [2021] | Includes bibliographical references and index. |
Summary: "Hunt's third installment in his award-winning Meade and Lee series is grounded upon
  official reports, regimental histories, letters, newspapers, and other archival sources. It examines the
  intricate command relationships, Lee's questionable decision-making, and the courageous spirit
  of the fighting men" — Provided by publisher.
Identifiers: LCCN 2020057822 | ISBN: 9781611215397 (hardcover) | ISBN: 9781611215403 (ebook)
Subjects: LCSH: Rappahannock Station, 2nd Battle of, Va., 1863 | Virginia–History–Civil War,
  1861-1865–Campaigns. | United States. Army of the Potomac. | Confederate States of America.
  Army of Northern Virginia. | United States–History–Civil War, 1861-1865–Campaigns. |
  Lee, Robert E. (Robert Edward), 1807-1870. | Meade, George Gordon, 1815-1872.
Classification: LCC E475.7 .H86 2021 | DDC 973.7/35–dc23
  LC record available at https://lccn.loc.gov/2020057822

First Edition, First Printing

SB
Savas Beatie
989 Governor Drive, Suite 102
El Dorado Hills, CA 95762
916-941-6896 / sales@savasbeatie.com / www.savasbeatie.com

All of our titles are available at special discount rates for bulk purchases in the United States. Contact us for information.

Proudly published, printed, and warehoused in the United States of America.

For Gill

My Best Friend and Comrade on Many a Field

Table of Contents

Table of Contents (continued)

Illustrations

Illustrations (continued)

Maps

This book is the third in a series of four volumes examining the military actions in Central Virginia during the late summer and fall of 1863. My first work, *Meade and Lee after Gettysburg*, traced the final fortnight of the Gettysburg Campaign; following the armies of Robert E. Lee and George G. Meade over the Potomac and through a two-week duel along the Blue Ridge Mountains. That usually forgotten contest culminated with the Rebels foiling Federal efforts to trap them inside the Shenandoah Valley while simultaneously slipping through the mountains to reoccupy Culpeper County—the very position they had held at the start of their Pennsylvania campaign.

The second volume, *Meade and Lee at Bristoe Station*, explored the months of August, September and October 1863. Despite seeing their armies rebound to pre-Gettysburg strength by the end of August, the two generals spent the last weeks of summer and all of September hobbled by problems ranging from supply shortages to draft riots and intense debate within their respective governments over future strategy. Before either leader could disentangle from these dilemmas, the Federal capture of Chattanooga and Knoxville and subsequent Confederate victory at Chickamauga forced both men to detach significant portions of their armies for western service.

Lee dealt with the reduction of his command better than Meade and launched an offensive that transferred the Virginia Theater's front line from the Rappahannock River nearly to the gates of Washington. Confederate hopes of destroying part of the Union army during the campaign ended in a stinging rearguard defeat at Bristoe Station, though Jeb Stuart's rout of a Yankee cavalry division at Buckland Mills gave an upbeat ending to an otherwise disappointing undertaking.

Misled by bad intelligence Meade sidled his army westward expecting to get a big fight out of Lee near Warrenton, only to discover the Rebels had instead withdrawn behind the upper Rappahannock, thoroughly destroying the Orange & Alexandria Railroad as they went. Since the Army of the Potomac couldn't advance until workmen repaired this vital supply line, the war in Virginia cooled briefly while the Army of the Potomac and Army of Northern Virginia caught their breath preparatory to further exertions.

The work you are holding picks up the story at that point. My original intent was to write a final volume encompassing the months of November and December 1863. Those eight weeks hosted not only the battles at Rappahannock Station and Kelly's Ford, but also the Mine Run campaign and subsequent end of 1863's active operations. As I dove deeper into this period, however, I came to realize that the story was too big for one book and concluded that the complex and fascinating sagas of Rappahannock Station and Kelly's Ford deserved a volume all their own.

My talented and astute publisher, Theodore P. Savas of Savas Beatie, agreed. Ted's keen eye for untold and under-reported stories saw that there is far more to these battles than has been revealed heretofore. Always eager to encourage original research and shed new light on often ignored or misunderstood history, Ted agreed to publish one book on the Rappahannock Station/ Kelly's Ford campaign and another on Mine Run. His literary generosity has allowed me to give these operations the in-depth coverage they deserve but have never received.

Although the late summer and fall 1863 Virginia campaigns have elicited little curiosity among historians, those months' more notable engagements—Bristoe Station and Rappahannock Station—have garnered some attention in magazines, blog posts and the occasional chapter in a biography, regimental history or specialized study. Many of those pieces are well-written and thoughtful. Nonetheless, these necessarily circumscribed efforts seldom afford their authors a chance to delve into great detail or reference much more than the easily accessible source material related to their subject.

Most pieces dealing with these actions and the brief campaign surrounding them rely on the *Official Records of the War of the Rebellion*, a relative handful of well-known printed sources, and a 100-page work written by Martin F. Graham and George F. Skoch entitled *Mine Run: A Campaign of Lost Opportunities. October 21, 1863–May, 1864*, which from the time of its 1987 publication until now has stood alone as the only book-length treatment of this intriguing period.

Graham and Skoch did a fine job of revealing their topic's central themes and story line, but their treatise's brevity renders it more of an outstanding primer than a thorough study. Moreover, in the 30-plus years since *Mine Run's* release a great deal of previously unknown or overlooked material concerning Meade and Lee's November 1863 contest has come to light, some of it appearing in print while other items have surfaced in archives or online. This additional material includes two maps of Rappahannock Station's fortifications, both drawn shortly after the battle, as well as multiple first-person accounts found in diaries, letters and newspapers detailing the assault on that position. Fresh information on the battle at Kelly's Ford has also appeared.

This array of new evidence increases our knowledge of the November 7, 1863 fighting and fills in many of that day's missing details, leaving us with a greatly enhanced understanding of the campaign, the context in which it occurred, the nature of Rappahannock Station's defenses and precisely how the Federals overran them, as well as what happened in the days afterwards.

Consequently, the story found in the following pages differs in many respects from earlier accounts of these battles and the campaign spawning them. Combining this fresh perspective with an intimate understanding of Civil War tactical formations allows a more robust version of Rappahannock Station and its attendant campaign to emerge and, as one might expect, this expanded tale is even more dramatic, compelling and interesting than that previously recorded.

Thanks to new sources, many misperceptions about the battle of the Rappahannock Station and its concurrent campaign can give way to more accurate depictions of those events. This is especially true regarding the assault on Lee's bridgehead. Usually oversimplified as a successful bayonet charge and rare night attack, the operation was far more intricate and its reason for success far more complex than most histories recognize. The role of Emory Upton's brigade in the battle, for example, is very different than has heretofore been brought to light. Not only did it enter the fight from a different direction than is shown on most published maps of the engagement; it undertook a series of maneuvers which reflect far greater credit on Upton and his men than the single bayonet charge most historians recount.

Giving the Rappahannock Station/Kelly's Ford campaign book length treatment also permits a deeper examination of the generalship of Meade, Lee and their respective subordinates. The Confederate general's strategy for holding the Upper Rappahannock and luring the Union army into a dangerous trap came much closer to succeeding than scholars typically believe. Meade, on the other hand, undertook his offensive in a state of high anxiety. Worried that he was walking into a Confederate trap and frustrated with his superiors' refusal to grant him strategic flexibility, he approached the operation with great trepidation. The fighting and maneuvering that ensued is as interesting and exciting as any that grace the larger and bloodier campaigns which have long captivated the reading public. It is my privilege to honor the men populating this drama by bringing the actions of early November 1863 out of the historical shadows they have too long inhabited.

Acknowledgments

One of the most satisfying parts of finishing a book is thanking all the great people who contributed to the final product. I would never have undertaken this project without the inspiration provided by Dr. George Forgie of the University of Texas at Austin. His intriguing thoughts about Gettysburg's role in the Civil War's outcome led me to research the Virginia campaigns that took place in the second half of 1863, an effort that eventually led to this book and the other volumes in my *Meade and Lee* series. I am indebted to Rob Orrison and Mike Block for so generously sharing their expertise and giving so freely of their time in showing me around Fauquier, Madison, Culpeper and Prince William counties. Those trips were not only enlightening but remarkably enjoyable as well. I'd like to thank Bryce Suderow for his encouragement, friendship and suggestions throughout my research; his passion for rigorous scholarship is truly infectious. Charlie Knight, author of *From Arlington to Appomattox: Robert E. Lee's Civil War, Day by Day, 1861-1865*, and Chris Barry, author of *No Flinching From Fire: The 65th New York Volunteer Infantry in the American Civil War*, were kind enough to share some of their research sources with me, for which I am humbled and grateful. Special appreciation is due Mark Ragan and Jonathan Wiley, who plumbed the resources of the National Archives and Library of Congress as well as the North Carolina State Archives and University of North Carolina on my behalf. I owe a special debt to Sara Buehler and Amanda Shields of the Brandywine Museum of Art for their invaluable assistance in securing permission to use the stunning artwork of N. C. Wyeth featured on this book's dustjacket.

A historian's work is only as good as his or her sources and it is with particular delight that I acknowledge the many curators, archivists, librarians, registrars and others who have helped me access the priceless documents preserved by their institutions. Matthew Laudicina, Christine Beauregard and Kaitlin Wolf (New York State Library Manuscripts and Special Collections), Andrew Foster and Jamison Davis (Virginia Museum of History and Culture), Meredith McDonough (Alabama Department of Archives and History), Peter Carini (Dartmouth College), Seth McCormick-Goodhart (Washington and Lee University), Ronald A. Lee (Tennessee State Library and Archives), Virginia Dunn, Megan Townes and Margaret Eastman (Library of Virginia), Ben Tayloe (Thomas Balch Library, Leesburg, Virginia), Helen Tutwiler and Samuel Howes (Maine State Archives), Brooke Guthrie (Duke University), Corinne Nordin (Indiana Historical Society), Linda Thornton (Auburn University), Janet Bloom (William Clements Library – University of Michigan), Leah Weinryb Grohsgal, Teresa Burk and Kathleen Shoemaker (Robert Woodruff Library – Emory University), Joan Wood (Stewart Bell, Jr. Archives, Handley Regional Library, Winchester-Frederick County Historical Society), Blaine Knupp and Theresa

McDevitt (Indiana University of Pennsylvania), Helen Conger (Case Western Reserve University Archives), Katherine Wilkins (Virginia Historical Society), Peiling Li and Alyson Barrett (Gilder Lehrman Institute of American History), Matthew Turi and Emma Parker (Southern Historical Collection, University of North Carolina), Vicki Catozza (Western Reserve Historical Society Library and Archives), Jennifer Coleman, Christina Lucas and Jessica Martinez Kindon (Navarro College), Shannon Schwaller (United States Military History Institute), Emilie Hardman (Houghton Library, Harvard University), the Research & Instructional Services Staff of the Wilson Library (University of North Carolina), and the staff of the Museum of the Civil War (formerly the Museum of the Confederacy).

No book sees print absent a publisher and I am fortunate to work with Savas Beatie, one of the best publishing houses in the history business. Theodore P. Savas, managing director of Savas Beatie, saw merit in my proposal to write about the late summer and fall campaigns of 1863 when other publishers evinced no interest. He has been supportive and encouraging every step of the way. Ted's superb Savas Beatie team make an author feel like family and I am grateful to each of its members for their efforts on my behalf. The same is true of my editor, Tom Schott, and my proofreader, John Foskett (of Westwood, MA), each of whose hard work did so much to improve the final version of this manuscript.

Additionally, I'd like to thank my fellow Civil War reenactors and living historians, with whom I have shared a hobby and a passion for more than 30 years. My experience in their ranks has given me an intimate understanding of 19th Century military tactics and drill that have been vital to my understanding of the events covered in these pages. Foremost among the men I have reenacted alongside is Gill Eastland, my lifelong best friend to whom this volume is dedicated. Talking history and campaigning with him have been one of life's most rewarding experiences.

And then there is my wife, Chris, who I cherish. The maps in this volume are the result of her remarkable talents and the many hours of painstaking, meticulous effort she poured into them. It is safe to say this book is as much hers as mine, for any work on military history lacking outstanding maps is hobbled from the beginning. Moreover, without her love and patience it would have been impossible for me to write a single word. I am lucky to have her at my side.

Jeffrey Wm Hunt
Austin, Texas

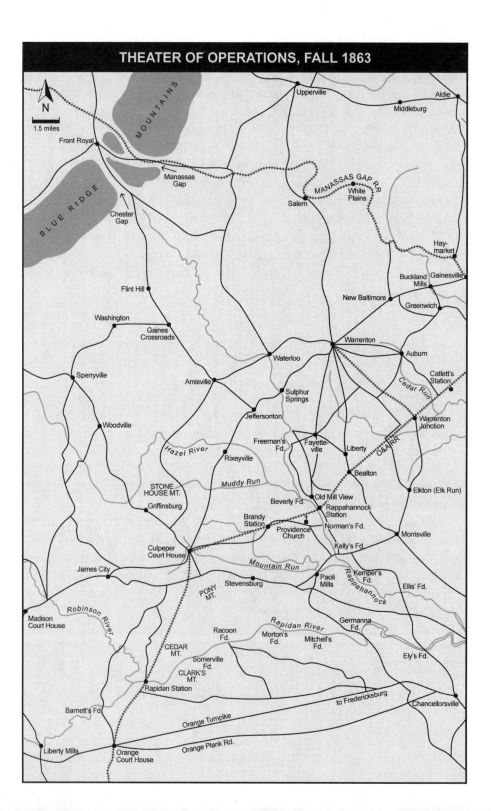

THEATER OF OPERATIONS, FALL 1863

N
1.5 miles

MOUNTAINS

BLUE RIDGE

Upperville

Aldie

Middleburg

Front Royal

Manassas
Gap

Chester
Gap

Salem

MANASSAS GAP RR

White
Plains

Hay-
market

Flint Hill

Washington

Gaines
Crossroads

Buckland
Mills

Gainesville

New Baltimore

Greenwich

Sperryville

Amisville

Waterloo

Warrenton

Auburn

Catlett's
Station

Cedar Run

Sulphur
Springs

Jeffersonton

Woodville

Freeman's
Fd.

Fayette-
ville

Liberty

Warrenton
Junction

O&ARR

Hazel River

Rixeyville

Muddy Run

STONE
HOUSE MT.

Griffinsburg

Beverly Fd.

Bealton

Old Mill View

Rappahannock
Station

Elkton (Elk Run)

Brandy
Station

Providence
Church

Norman's Fd.

Kelly's Fd.

Morrisville

Culpeper
Court House

James City

Stevensburg

PONY
MT.

Mountain Run

Paoli
Mills

Kemper's
Fd.

Ellis' Fd.

Rappahannock

Madison
Court House

Robinson River

CEDAR
MT.

Racoon
Fd.

Rapidan River

Morton's
Fd.

Mitchell's
Fd.

Germanna
Fd.

Ely's Fd.

Somerville
Fd.

CLARK'S
MT.

Rapidan Station

Barnett's Fd

to Fredericksburg

Chancellorsville

Orange Turnpike

Liberty Mills

Orange
Court House

Orange Plank Rd.

"I Am So Anxious and Worried"

July's Aftermath—Dissatisfaction and Disappointment—George Meade—Strategic
Debate—Washington's Expectations—Terrible Strain—Meade's Anxiety

As October 1863 slid toward November the American Civil War neared its thirty-first month with no end in sight. That dreary fact distressed a great many people. In early July, a trio of Union battlefield triumphs at Vicksburg, Mississippi, Port Hudson, Louisiana and Gettysburg, Pennsylvania had hinted at a speedy and climactic end to the conflict. Over optimistic expectations of final victory had faded quickly, however, as the North's rising military tide first faltered and then receded as summer gave way to fall.

In the wake of Vicksburg and Port Hudson, Major General Henry W. Halleck, general-in-chief of all Union armies, dispersed the forces Maj. Gens. Ulysses S. Grant and Nathaniel P. Banks had used to gain complete control of the Mississippi River. Rather than strike toward Mobile, or a similar strategic objective, Halleck reinforced the Trans-Mississippi region and put almost everyone else to garrisoning what Federal forces had won along the great river.

The loss of initiative in the East proved more painful. Unable to prevent General Robert E. Lee's Rebel army from escaping back into Virginia after its Gettysburg defeat, Maj. Gen. George G. Meade's Army of the Potomac (AOP) next failed to trap the Confederates in the lower Shenandoah Valley. In a series of rapid maneuvers Lee outfoxed Meade by slipping through the Blue Ridge Mountains and taking up a position behind the upper Rappahannock River near Culpeper Court House. After pausing briefly to resupply, Meade advanced to the same point only to see his army brought to a six-week halt by President Abraham Lincoln's order to detach 9,200 troops to enforce Northern conscription.[1]

---

1 For a detailed account of the Gettysburg campaign once the armies slipped below the Potomac, see Jeffery Wm Hunt, *Meade and Lee After Gettysburg: The Forgotten Final Stage of the Gettysburg Campaign: July 14–31, 1863* (El Dorado, CA, 2017).

The Confederates took advantage of that pause to detach Lieutenant General James Longstreet's 19,000-man First Corps from Lee's army for service in the Western Theater. Its arrival there bolstered Gen. Braxton Bragg's Army of Tennessee, which in early September had lost the critical railroad junction of Chattanooga to Maj. Gen. William S. Rosecrans' Army of the Cumberland. Hearing rumors of this move, the administration unshackled Meade and ordered him to determine whether Lee had truly sent troops west.[2]

After a tough cavalry fight around Culpeper Court House on September 13, Federal troopers discovered that Lee's infantry had withdrawn below the Rapidan many weeks ago and now occupied a formidable line along the river. Moreover, the Yankee horsemen confirmed that Longstreet's corps had gone elsewhere. As Meade pondered how to deal with Lee's new position, Bragg counterattacked Rosecrans in northern Georgia. Winning the battle of Chickamauga with Longstreet's help, he drove the Yankee army back into Chattanooga and laid it under siege. Meanwhile, Meade sifted about for a way to get at Lee. But before the Federal commander could devise a strategy, Halleck ordered him to detach the AOP's XI and XII Corps for service in Tennessee, where their 13,000 men would play a role in Grant's effort to redeem the Chattanooga situation.

Two weeks after those units departed, the ever-audacious Lee led his Army of Northern Virginia (ANV) out from below the Rapidan in a daring offensive against Meade. The Union general barely avoided falling into disaster, escaping Lee's clutches only by making a rapid 46-mile retreat to Centreville, Virginia. Despite winning a sharp rearguard engagement at Bristoe Station, Meade admitted that Lee had outgeneraled him, leaving the Federals powerless to interfere as the Rebels withdrew unmolested behind the upper Rappahannock, ripping apart the Orange & Alexandria (O&A) Railroad as they went.[3]

At the end of October, Rosecrans remained trapped in Chattanooga without anyone being sure when or if Grant could save the Army of the Cumberland. Meade was relegated to inching south at the pace of repair crews rebuilding his O&A supply line. That endeavor threatened to consume what was left of 1863's campaign season

---

2 *War of the Rebellion: Official Records of the Union and Confederate Armies*, 128 vols. (hereafter cited as *OR*), Volume 29, part 2 (Washington, DC, 1890) 681, 700. Two of Longstreet's Georgia brigades reinforced besieged Charleston, S.C.

3 George G. Meade, Jr., *The Life and Letters of George Gordon Meade: Major-General United States Army*, 2 vols. Meade to Margaret, October 30, 1863, vol. 2, 154.

and likely meant the Union army couldn't do much of importance before winter halted operations.[4]

This course of events lifted Southern fortunes while correspondently depressing those of the North. Although there were valid military reasons for why things had gone as they did, very few people were disposed to accept explanations. Rather, they felt that someone or some combination of persons had fumbled away the bright promise of Vicksburg and Gettysburg. There was no shortage of finger pointing in the press, the army, Congress or the public. Who you blamed depended on your politics, position or point of view. Numerous people laid the mishaps at Halleck's doorstep. Others condemned Lincoln or Rosecrans. Not a few censured Meade who, as they saw things, initiated the entire chain of events by missing his chance to destroy Lee's army after Gettysburg.

The general's mid-July failure to attack the Rebels when he found them trapped against a flooded and unbridged Potomac River had caused extreme displeasure in Washington. When Halleck sent army headquarters word of the president's "dissatisfaction" a row had ensued, with Meade insisting that Lincoln replace him and Halleck having to mollify the general by modifying the term and refusing his demand.

Meade let the matter drop but the passions thus stirred left their mark, sewing doubts in the general's mind about his standing with the administration and the intensity of its future support. Lincoln's habitual sacking of generals who didn't meet expectations was a well-established fact and Meade couldn't forget that he was the fourth commander of the Army of the Potomac in the last 12 months or that the president had replaced six eastern army leaders since 1861. Gettysburg might let him evade his predecessors' fate temporarily, but he knew it was unlikely to do so permanently.[5]

*   *   *

The failure to crush Lee had created reservations about Meade among the powerful and connected in Washington. Lincoln and Halleck would forgive him the missed chance, but they could never forget it. Between August and November the

---

4   For a detailed account of the operations in Virginia during August, September and October of 1863 see Jeffrey Wm Hunt, *Meade and Lee at Bristoe Station: The Problems of Command and Strategy After Gettysburg: August 1–October 31, 1863* (El Dorado, CA, 2019).

5   Meade's predecessors were George B. McClellan, Ambrose E. Burnside and Joseph Hooker. Irvin McDowell had led what would become the Army of the Potomac at Bull Run, but technically never commanded the AOP. John Pope led the Army of Virginia, which included major components of the AOP. Lincoln replaced all of them.

general's inability to deal with Lee to their satisfaction picked at that scab and made Meade's continued tenure uncertain.

In many ways this was most unfortunate for the Union. Of all the men who had led the AOP George Gordon Meade was one of the best, if not the best, to occupy the position. Between graduating from West Point in 1835 and the secession crisis, he had established a solid reputation as a peacetime engineer and a courageous Mexican War officer. After receiving a brigadier general's commission in September,1861 he amassed a commendable record while leading a brigade in the Peninsula Campaign, a division from Antietam to Fredericksburg and a corps at Chancellorsville. Meade ably demonstrated his sense of duty when, after twice being wounded at Glendale in June 1862, he returned to the army before his medical leave expired. The general's steady advancement in rank and responsibility sprang purely from merit, for he lacked political patrons and refused to lobby for promotion.

At 47-years of age, the Pennsylvania-raised Meade was tall, lean and well-educated. A student of linguistics and fluent in French, he gave off something of a patrician air. His brown beard and hair, both speckled with gray, framed a "small compact head" dominated by a large nose. Pronounced bags of skin drooping beneath each eye were his most memorable feature, conveying sadness to some and owl-like wisdom to others. Men commonly said Meade looked like a good family doctor, especially when wearing eyeglasses.[6]

Nonetheless he could cut an exquisite military figure when necessary. A reporter meeting the general in 1863 thought him a "commanding figure and presence," evincing a "pleasant, easy manner" and "much dignity." Usually, however, Meade dressed in the workman-like style of a busy field officer. At the military academy his animosity toward spit and polish had brought him within 32 demerits of mandatory expulsion, but in 1863 it delighted everyone who abhorred pretentious displays of military vanity.[7]

Meade impressed his fellow generals as "the soul of honor" and one of the North's "ablest" leaders. His repute as a "soldier, scholar and gentleman" equaled his well-known bravery and modesty. Many men admired Meade's refusal to curry favor with the press or intrigue for promotion. More noteworthy to some was his lack of

---

6   Robert G. Scott, ed. *Fallen Leaves: The Civil War Letters of Major Henry Livermore Abbott* (Kent, OH, 1992), 189; Frank L. Bryne & Andrew T. Weaver, ed. *Haskell of Gettysburg: His Life and Civil War Papers* (Kent, OH, 1989), 132. The Battle of Glendale was also called the Battle of White Oak Swamp or the Battle of Frayser's Farm.

7   Abbott, *Fallen Leaves*, 189; Isaac R. Pennypacker, *General Meade* (New York, NY, 1901), 3-8; Horace Porter, *Campaigning with Grant* (New York, NY. 1897), 247; Freeman Cleaves, *Meade of Gettysburg* (Norman, OK, 1960), 11.

Maj. Gen. George Gordon Meade
Library of Congress

personal jealousy toward anyone obtaining rank ahead of him—an unusual attribute for old line regular officers.

The general's volatile temper, his least attractive and most commented upon trait, could burst forth with volcanic fury whenever he encountered incompetence or carelessness. Unfortunately, these emotional explosions often came off as heartless, cruel, and demeaning. The Harvard-educated and urbane Colonel Theodore Lyman, a member of the general's staff as well as his close confidant and long-time friend, reflected that Meade "takes things uneasily and. . . has the most singular patches of gunpowder in his disposition, which exploding are then gone." Such outbursts typically occurred during periods of great stress and served to relieve the general's anxiety. He sometimes joked to lessen their impact, but more often did nothing to smooth ruffled feathers, thus leaving the objects of his displeasure hurt and resentful. While some subordinates recognized that Meade intended no offense, many saw his temper as beyond the pale.[8]

The general's relationship with his troops remained a work in progress. When he assumed overall command some men praised his leadership. Others, despising his harsh discipline and hot temper, called him a "damned old goggle-eyed snapping turtle." Initially most of the army greeted him with a cool wait-and-see attitude. Victory at Gettysburg didn't change much. Meade earned only conditional confidence and scant enthusiasm as a result, perhaps because the troops suspected that their own fighting qualities rather than anyone's generalship had won the battle. His failure to attack the well-entrenched Rebels trapped against the Potomac River ten days later hardly helped. Though most of Meade's officers thought he had acted wisely on that occasion, many common soldiers disagreed.[9]

8 David W. Lowe, ed. *Meade's Army: The Private Notebooks of Lt. Col. Theodore Lyman* (Kent, OH, 2007), 49; Porter, *Campaigning with Grant*, 247; Alan Nevins, ed., *Diary of Battle: The Personal Journals of Colonel Charles S. Wainwright* (New York, NY, 1962), 116.

9 Wainwright, *Diary of Battle*, 116; J. Gregory Acken, *Inside the Army of the Potomac: The Civil War Experience of Captain Francis Adams Donaldson* (Mechanicsburg, PA, 1998), 113, 289; Cleaves,

Throughout August and September, the army remained tepid toward its new general. The October campaign, on the other hand, altered countless opinions. At its start Meade proved indecisive, in part because he knew Washington was looking over his shoulder. Uncertain of Rebel intentions he awkwardly deployed half his army for offensive action and the other half for defense before realizing that Lee was circumventing the AOP's right flank. At almost the last minute, Meade declined battle on unfavorable ground around Culpeper Court House and withdrew north of the Rappahannock. This surprised his subordinates, but not as much as did his sending half the army back to Culpeper the next day after concluding the Rebels weren't trying to get between him and the capital.

That was a mistake. Lee was already swinging wide to the west, outflanking Meade by crossing the river well upstream and stealing a day's march. Upon discovering this fact the general reacted in clear-headed and resolute fashion, ordering a rapid retreat northward along the O&A to the defenses of Centreville. It proved a close-run race, but Meade beat the Rebels to the finish line, his II Corps inflicting a painful rearguard reverse on the enemy at Bristoe Station along the way. By and large the army's soldiers believed their commander had displayed outstanding generalship during the campaign. Unlike previous leaders he hadn't fallen into a cunning Rebel trap, instead bringing them through great danger without much harm, although admittedly with much hardship. Savvy veterans appreciated that accomplishment and Meade's stock rose with the troops.[10]

*   *   *

It did not rise in Washington. His failure to seek combat greatly irritated the administration along with most of the press. As the retreating Federals neared the capital, Halleck told Meade that his army ought to fight rather than run away since it badly outnumbered Lee. As he had in July, Meade responded to criticism he perceived as unfair by angrily insisting that the administration replace him. Halleck once again refused with halfhearted apologies for hurting Meade's feelings.

The Army of the Potomac's inability to effectively pursue the Confederates exacerbated the already strained relationship between Meade and his superiors. After the Rebels inflicted a humiliating drubbing to Federal cavalry at Buckland Mills, bad intelligence convinced the general that Lee was hovering near Warrenton and ready to

---

Meade of Gettysburg, 128; Scott, *Fallen Leaves*, 189; Thomas Carpenter to Parents, July 7, 1863, Missouri Historical Society (MHS); Hunt, *Meade and Lee After Gettysburg*, 3-23.

10 Hunt, *Meade and Lee at Bristoe Station*, 438.

fight. Meade shifted his entire army toward that spot only to discover that enemy infantry wasn't there and never had been. Returning to the O&A as they moved south, Yankee troops confronted their foe's complete destruction of the railroad.[11]

This led Meade to surmise that Lee's offensive had been aimed at the O&A's annihilation, which would prevent a Union advance until work crews repaired the line all the way to the Rappahannock, thus using up the last campaigning weather and allowing the Confederates to transfer more troops to Bragg. In light of that analysis Meade suggested pulling his army back to Washington's outskirts for the winter. This would shorten its supply line drastically and free up men to counter the supposed shift of Rebel units to the looming battles around Chattanooga.

Although everyone in the high command had toyed with this proposal back in September, Meade's suggestion so shocked the administration that it called him in for consultation. The ensuing two-hour October 22 conference accomplished little. The president made clear his disappointment that no battle had occurred during the recent campaign. He agreed with Meade that the O&A's destruction probably precluded offensive action before winter set in. The conclave discarded the idea of retiring the army to Washington and shipping more troops westward, but no one put an alternative proposal on the table. Meade knew that Halleck and Lincoln believed it was "very urgent that something should be done" but complained that neither had any useful suggestions as to what the army should do.[12]

That evening Meade read newspaper accounts damning his recent retreat alongside claims he had ignored imperative War Department orders to fight rather than withdraw. The general feigned indifference to these accounts, but in fact they infuriated him, not only because they were false, but because they assaulted Meade's most tender spot: his reputation.

The general's letters frequently referenced a concern for his standing as a solider. Meade's feelings in this regard were so strong that several weeks before becoming army commander he described that post as "more likely to destroy one's reputation than to add to it" and therefore an honor "not to be desired or sought." Indeed, upon reading Lincoln's directive giving him that job, Meade tried to decline the appointment and accepted it only because the order was "unquestionable and peremptory."[13]

---

11 The Battle of Buckland Mills was fought on Oct. 19. For a detailed account, see Hunt, *Meade and Lee at Bristoe Station*, 397-428.

12 Lyman, *Meade's Headquarters*, 37; Lyman, *Meade's Army*, 38-40; Meade to Margaret, October 30, 1863, *Life and Letters*, vol. 2, 154. Meade admitted he too was disappointed at the lack of a battle.

13 Cleaves, *Meade of Gettysburg*, 118; Charles F. Benjamin, "Hooker's Appointment and Removal," *Battles and Leaders of the Civil War*, Vol. 3 (New York, NY, 1956), 239-240; Meade to

The general's protestations against a desire for supreme command were not convincing, however. Following the Battle of Chancellorsville he had admitted "great gratification" upon learning his fellow corps commanders wanted him to replace Maj. Gen. Joseph Hooker as the army's leader. While "unambitious of the distinction," he couldn't help lamenting that a dearth of "political influence" and a refusal to intrigue made it "hardly probable" Lincoln would offer him the job.[14]

It was true that Meade lacked a lust for rank and bore no ill will against those who advanced above him. But it was also true that he cared deeply about the prerogatives of seniority. When, in November 1862, Maj. Gen. Ambrose E. Burnside gave V Corps command to an officer junior in grade to Meade, the latter felt "a right to complain" and did. Taking his case to Burnside he laid out the facts without rancor or making a demand for the job denied him. Meade stressed that he held no animosity to the person placed over him. Despite this gentlemanly approach Meade expected and desired his superiors to correct their mistake, which they did by giving him command of the V Corps not long after the Battle of Fredericksburg.[15]

This incident shone a different light on Meade's oft-referenced humility, which wasn't always what it seemed. Cortlandt Parker, a longtime friend, asserted that the general's modesty was the "outcome of a lofty pride." As a "well-trained, thoroughly cultured gentleman" he could no more "shirk duty" than "claim credit for its discharge." But he very much wanted others to recognize his accomplishments, talents, difficulties and sacrifices. "No man loved appreciation more" Parker said of Meade, "no man longed for it more ardently, no man, in his heart, more demanded it as a right; no man more carefully forbore to complain" when it did not come.[16]

There is no doubt that Meade desired the distinction that went along with earning higher posts. That included army command and prior to getting it he sometimes pondered how "nice" having the job would be, despite all the difficulties it entailed. However, rank and position weren't ends in themselves for Meade. Utterly devoted to the Union cause, he was willing to do whatever was best for the country. Claiming no

---

Margaret, May 10, 1863; Margaret to Meade, May 20, 1863. Meade Papers, Historical Society of Pennsylvania.

14 Meade to Margaret, May 10 and June 25, 1863, *Life and Letters*, vol. 1, 373, 388-89.

15 Meade, *Life and Letters,* vol. 1, 329, 332-33; Lyman, *Meade's Headquarters*, 36. Maj. Gen. Daniel A. Butterfield, the officer in question, would go on to become Hooker's chief of staff and serve Meade in that capacity at Gettysburg. Best remembered for composing the bugle call Taps, Butterfield left the AOP after receiving a July 3 wound at Gettysburg. On July 14, 1863 Meade formally assigned Maj. Gen. Andrew A. Humphreys to replace Butterfield as the army's chief of staff.

16 Isaac R. Pennypacker, *General Meade* (New York, NY, 1901), 6-7. Parker was a distinguished and influential New Jersey lawyer.

"special capacity" entitling him to army command, on multiple occasions he expressed a sincere willingness to surrender his post to someone more able, so long as the change occurred in a manner not damaging to his soldierly reputation.[17]

The Battle of Gettysburg was the pinnacle of Meade's career so far. Regrettably, whatever satisfaction he gained from that considerable success proved short lived. From the moment Lee escaped across the Potomac on July 13 to the start of November, Meade's reputation outside the army took a beating. The press called him to account for failing to crush the Rebels above the Potomac, for failing to advance on Lee since Gettysburg, for failing to keep the Confederates from transferring troops to Tennessee, and for retreating to the outskirts of Washington instead of fighting in October.

The capital's political class was just as critical. Not only were members of the president's cabinet dissatisfied with Meade; the Joint Committee on the Conduct of the War was casting an eye in his direction. The Radical Republicans controlling that committee opposed any commander who didn't enthusiastically embrace their anti-slavery zealotry. The politically moderate Meade wasn't their type of general, doubly so because he had superseded Joe Hooker, who *was* their sort of man. Lee's escape after Gettysburg and the lack of a battle since presented these gentlemen with an opening. Jealous officers claiming that they had won the Pennsylvania fight instead of Meade encouraged the committee's interest. None of this had quite come to a head yet, but the winds were blowing unmistakably in that direction and the general knew it.[18]

*   *   *

Nonetheless, reputational threats mattered far less to Meade than the success and security of his army. Much to his vexation, however, a simmering strategic debate with his superiors complicated the AOP's operations. At times it seemed that President

---

17 *OR* 29, pt. 1, 106; Meade, *Life and Letters*, vol. 2, 138-41.

18 While convalescing in Washington from a Gettysburg wound, II Corps division commander Brig. Gen. John Gibbon defended Meade from criticism in October 1863. He felt Meade was attacked because he "was not quite so outspoken in what certain parties chose to denominate as loyalty, or did not indorse as fully as they did, what they considered the 'true policy' of the war." Gibbon thought the assaults on Meade politically inspired, but his defense failed. Meade's generalship reminded many of McClellan, who Lincoln had fired after Antietam and who had drifted into political opposition to the administration by 1863. The comparison opened Meade to charges of incompetence or "disloyalty." Gibbon's argument that all competent commanders followed the same military principles "irrespective of their. . . political opinions" won no converts to Meade's side. John Gibbon, *Personal Recollections of the Civil War* (New York, 1928), 206-20.

Lincoln and General-in-Chief Halleck were making more trouble for the army than Lee. The dispute between Meade and these men boiled down to a deceptively simple question: Should the Army of the Potomac use the O&A Railroad as its axis of advance? The administration insisted that it should; Meade had argued since August that it should not. His reasoning, patiently and thoroughly explained to Halleck and Lincoln, was hard to discount.

The single-track O&A ran southwest between Alexandria on the Potomac and Gordonsville in Orange County, Virginia. A Federal army marching down this nearly 100-mile long stretch of iron moved against no vital objective while simultaneously sidling away from Richmond—the Confederacy's capital and Lee's primary supply base. The farther Union forces moved astride the O&A, the longer grew Meade's line of communication. Since the entire railroad ran through enemy territory the Yankees had to station soldiers along its full length to prevent Rebel guerrillas from disrupting the army's flow of supplies.[19]

The commitment of thousands of troops to this task seriously weakened the AOP's combat power and would weaken it more as Meade marched south. That was especially problematic at a time when the North faced serious manpower woes. In 1863 a severe decline in recruiting had forced Congress to pass a conscription law whose July implementation resulted in severe rioting in New York City and other places. To quell these disturbances Lincoln had temporarily detached dozens of regiments from Meade's army to cow protestors and allow the draft's continuance. That early-August initiative had cost Meade a potential chance to push Lee's Gettysburg-battered army away from both the Rappahannock and Rapidan without a fight.

Besides this lost opportunity, difficulties surrounding the draft highlighted for Meade the dwindling pool of Union reserves—a problem he remained unconvinced conscription could solve. Even if he found a way to overcome the enemy's strong defenses behind the Rapidan (no sure thing), a possibly chronic shortage of replacements intensified his concerns about further offensives relying on the O&A for supplies.

Since operations along that line threatened few points the enemy must protect, Lee could simply retire before any Union thrust, drawing Meade deeper into Virginia and forcing him to detach more men to defend the railroad. Once the Rebels reached advantageous ground they'd turn to fight, probably from an entrenched position that the detachment-weakened Yankees could conquer only with disastrously high

---

19 At Gordonsville the O&A connected to the Virginia Central Railroad, which stretched west to the Shenandoah Valley and east to Hanover Junction where it joined the Richmond, Fredericksburg & Potomac RR whose tracks led north to the Rappahannock and south to Richmond.

casualties, if at all. No single battle could destroy Lee's army, Meade predicted, and if defeated it would merely back up to another strong position, shortening its supply line as it did so.

Any victory won under those circumstances would prove fruitless. Pursuit meant detailing additional manpower to secure lengthening communications, thus rendering the Federals weaker still for the next engagement. Even if it pushed Lee into Richmond's fortifications, the Union army lacked enough strength to besiege the city and the casualties incurred in achieving that feat could prove irreplaceable. At some point combat losses might render Lee's army stronger than Meade's own, allowing the enemy to assume the offensive against an enfeebled foe whose overextended supply line was vulnerable to cutting. The consequences might mean losing a battle, the army and the war.

Therefore, Meade saw little gain in continuing down the O&A. Better, he thought, to abandon the railroad and transfer the army's base to Aquia Landing on the Potomac River just 15 miles north of Fredericksburg. This would give him a safe waterborne line of communication, freeing up thousands of troops for combat duty while compelling Lee to abandon the Rapidan without a struggle, thus letting the AOP avoid assailing the Rebels' riverine defenses.[20]

Despite accepting much of Meade's logic, Lincoln and Halleck vetoed a change of base to Fredericksburg. They didn't like the idea of returning the army to the scene of its worst disaster and, more importantly, both men saw any such move as merely transferring difficulties from one spot to another. They felt certain Meade would find the Rebels waiting for him in a strong position no matter where he went. As the administration figured things Lee, not Richmond, was the AOP's objective. Meade's job was to fight the Rebels wherever they were with the goal of their destruction. That task would surely prove no easier at Fredericksburg than near Culpeper Court House.

The administration bridled whenever Meade reiterated the difficulties of operating along the O&A or attempting to fight his way over the Rappahannock and Rapidan. Recalling Maj. Gen. George B. McClellan's seemingly endless pretexts for failing to fight in 1862, Lincoln and Halleck sensed familiar excuse-making in Meade's arguments. Observing that he seriously outnumbered his opponent and enjoyed vastly more resources, they wanted their general to undertake aggressive action—to behave like Lee, who with fewer supplies and far fewer troops was always eager to attack regardless of odds.

---

20 Aquia Landing lay at the point where Aquia Creek emptied into the Potomac River from its southern shore. The Richmond, Fredericksburg & Potomac Railroad connected the steamboat landing with points south starting in 1846.

However, both men shrank from compelling Meade to act. Amid the July/August draft riot emergency and the September Chickamauga crisis, Meade's superiors sent conflicting messages. On one hand they told him that he shouldn't do anything rash or provoke a battle because they couldn't reinforce his command and on the other hand they urged him to harry Lee, slice off a part of his army or move forward and let circumstances dictate whether to undertake an offensive campaign.

That was too imprecise for Meade. If the administration wouldn't sanction his Fredericksburg shift and insisted that he advance along a route he didn't like, Meade wanted specific instructions and unambiguous approval for any operation undertaken. But when he asked for these things, he got unhelpful responses instead.

The president made lawyerly and intellectually astute observations about the nature of Meade's dilemma and occasionally vague suggestions about doing something coupled with the caveat that he didn't know enough "particulars" to give any positive instructions. Halleck maintained it wasn't his job to tell generals when or how to fight, arguing they must decide those questions for themselves and were unlikely to win victory if their superiors had to order them into battle. Beyond stressing that Lee's army was Meade's target, Halleck contented himself with quoting military axioms and pressuring the AOP to act. Whenever Meade's temper exploded in response, the general-in-chief offered pseudo-apologies and maintained that he was just passing on the Government's "wishes."[21]

Understandably this infuriated Meade. In letters home he bemoaned the administration's failure to grant the guidance or strategic flexibility he had a right to expect. It looked to him as if Halleck and Lincoln were mainly interested in keeping their fingerprints off any defeat the army might suffer. "They undoubtedly would be glad if I should attack and prove successful," he wrote his wife, adding, "They wish me to assume the responsibility so that in case of disaster, I may be made the scapegoat." The general wouldn't wear that mantle. He would happily assume sole accountability for the outcome of his own strategy. But he wouldn't do so while his superiors unfairly insisted that he act while simultaneously tying his hands, issuing no clear orders, and setting him up for blame if things went badly.[22]

*   *   *

All of this was a heavy cross to bear and Lee's October offensive had increased the burden significantly. Now the Union army was returning to the exact spot it occupied

---

21 *OR* 29, pt. 2, 354.

22 Meade to Margaret, Sept. 19, 1863, Meade papers, HSP.

at the end of the Gettysburg campaign almost three months ago. The enemy once more inhabited Culpeper County and held the Rappahannock line. Whatever little gains the AOP had won during the last 90 days were gone and Meade faced the same military quandaries that confronted him in August and September. The strategic debate with Halleck and Lincoln remained unresolved, its issues precisely what they had been.

Although the cumulative strain was enormous, Meade revealed its effects only to those closest to him. On October 26 he told Col. Lyman "I do wish the administration would get mad with me and relieve me; I am sure I keep telling them, if they don't feel satisfied. . . to relieve me." The next day the general sat down to write Margaretta, his spouse of 21 years who he invariably called Margaret. Atypically he hadn't corresponded with her for several days and he opened his letter by explaining that he was "so anxious and worried" by his "responsibilities" that he was "not in a fit condition to write" and therefore had not "written as often" as he "otherwise would have done."

Reassuring Margaret that his health remained decent, he confessed that he wasn't in "very good spirits owing to my anxiety." Washington was "very anxious" for a battle, which he was willing to fight so long as he could get "anything like an equality of chances." But he knew his foe too well to expect an easy opening and felt apprehensive that Lee might again "maneuver so as to take me at a disadvantage."

Meade's concern was hardly unfounded. On October 24, a northward lunge by Rebel infantry had embroiled elements of Brigadier General John Buford's 1st Cavalry Division in a day-long skirmish not far from Rappahannock Station. Suspecting another Confederate offensive underway, Meade sent infantry to join the action. Before Union foot soldiers arrived, however, the enemy pulled back; his entire purpose apparently fulfilled when Rebel engineers carried off five miles of O&A track not destroyed during Lee's recent withdrawal.

Far more worrisome were scouting reports about the existence of a heavily entrenched Confederate bridgehead on the north bank of the Rappahannock. At this distance it was hard to tell whether the enemy intended the position for defense or a launching pad for aggressive action. Either way, Meade remained in a watchful state lest his opponent once again do the unexpected.

With the administration breathing down his neck and Confederates active in his front, Meade couldn't help feeling uneasy. Despite his "every confidence in the valor and steadiness" of his troops, the anticipation of a Rebel attack was almost unbearable. Like many soldiers waiting for battle, he would welcome combat if for no other reason than to relieve "the uncertainty now attending" enemy movements.[23]

23 Previous paragraphs Ibid., Oct, 27, 1863, Meade Papers, HSP.

Whether Lee would oblige remained uncertain. But if the Virginian didn't pick a fight soon, conditions would compel Meade to attempt getting at a dangerous foe on the other side of a defended river. Regardless of who moved first, campaigning hadn't ended for 1863. Meade and Lee remained locked in their chess match while another bout of blood and horror stood on the horizon.

CHAPTER 2

"The Enemy Will Make One More Effort"

Confident Rebels—Robert E. Lee—Strategic Frustration—Riverine
Complexities—Options Blue and Gray—A Clever Defense

THE Army of Northern Virginia waited patiently along the Rappahannock for its Yankee counterpart to return within striking distance. Regardless of Lee's failure to destroy some part of Meade's command during the recent campaign, Confederate morale remained high. The shock of last summer's defeats had worn off months ago. The Federals' inability to capitalize on July's victories, the swift recovery of the ANV from Pennsylvania's rigors, and the stunning success at Chickamauga had all contributed to an upswing of Southern optimism. So too did Meade's October refusal to stand and fight. Rebel soldiers viewed his 46-mile flight to Centreville as proof their army remained "dauntless in spirit, powerful & to be feared."[1]

Beyond doubt Robert E. Lee's considerable talents were the cornerstone of this self-assurance. The Virginian's reputation as the South's greatest combat leader remained undisputed despite Gettysburg, and this status had quickly hushed sharp criticisms of him and the Pennsylvania campaign. Lee and his army stood now as "the mainstay & prop of the country's cause," according to one gray cavalryman, and Confederate Vice President Alexander H. Stephens publicly declared Lee's "military genius" the underpinning of ultimate Southern independence. The troops agreed, sharing with their commander a mutual pride and trust born of frequent victory. One Georgia solider expressed a pervading sentiment when he declared himself "ready for

---

1 Micajah Woods papers, UVA.

anything that may turn up, either to move forward or backward, run or fight, or anything Robert E. Lee tells me to do."[2]

The general's résumé was impressive. Son of a Revolutionary War hero, he graduated from West Point in 1829 ranked second in his class and without a single demerit. Two years later Lee entered into the most illustrious of Virginia families by wedding Mary Custis, the great granddaughter of Martha Washington, wife of the American Revolution's greatest leader and the nation's first president. Commissioned into the elite corps of engineers, Lee saved St. Louis from ruin by designing and building dams that prevented the Mississippi from diverting away from the city's shore. His daring reconnaissance missions in the Mexican War enabled Maj. Gen. Winfield Scott's successful campaign against Mexico City and earned Lee a colonel's brevet. After the conflict he served as commandant of West Point, then gained promotion to the permanent rank of lieutenant colonel along with an assignment to Texas with the 2nd US Cavalry.

Upon the death of his father-in-law Lee inherited Arlington plantation and while on extended leave to sort out the estate's chaotic finances, he led a contingent of US Marines that quashed abolitionist John Brown's October 1859 attack on Harper's Ferry. Ordered back to Washington when the secession crisis erupted, Lee declined an exploratory offer to command the US Army. Unable to reconcile his sense of duty with revulsion at the idea of invading the South, he resigned his commission. When Virginia seceded, Lee took charge of the Old Dominion's military forces and expertly marshalled them into service. Once the state joined the Confederacy, President Jefferson Davis made him a full general in the Rebel army.

Lee's reputation suffered during the conflict's first year. He insisted on building coastal fortifications when Southerners sneered at earthworks as an unmanly way to wage war. And his failure to redeem a hopeless military situation in Virginia's western mountains prompted calls for dismissal. Disregarding such sentiments, Davis made Lee his chief military advisor and when Gen. Joseph E. Johnston fell badly wounded at Seven Pines in May 1862, he put Lee in charge of Richmond's defenses. Renaming his new command the Army of Northern Virginia, Lee spent a month preparing an offensive campaign that drove the Federals away from the capital in a week-long sequence of battles. Shifting operations northward over the next year he won a series of stunning victories that derailed the careers of four Union generals and buoyed the entire Confederate cause.

---

2   Micajah Woods papers, UVA; *Richmond Examiner*, August 13, 1863; *Illustrated London News*, August 15, 1863; Mills Lane, *Dear Mother, Don't Grieve About Me, If I Get Killed, I'll Only Be Dead: Letters from Georgia Soldiers in the Civil War*, (Savannah, GA, 1977), 249-50.

Gen. Robert E. Lee
Library of Congress

Nonetheless, the strain of command was taking its toll on the 56-year old Virginian. He had suffered several bouts of ill-health, loosely diagnosed as "rheumatism," since the spring of 1863 and was noticeably ageing. Getting a close look at Lee that fall, Lieutenant Benjamin Justice recorded that the general's pre-war black hair was now transitioning "from grey to snowy," and he wore it combed over to hide his "almost utterly bald" scalp. Lee's "slightly aquiline" nose and gray beard accented a face "massive in its proportions" sitting atop a "full and fat" neck. The lieutenant thought Lee looked "burly and beefy" almost to the point of being "fat," and he noted that "coarse, bristly, black hair" grew out of each ear.

Despite this vaguely unflattering description, Lee presented a far more impressive picture than his separate features suggested. The general dressed simply, usually in a "very plain" gray frock coat with three stars of the "plainest order" on each collar as an indication of rank. Lt. Justice sensed "something animal" in Lee's physique but had to confess that the Virginian's manner and movements were the "very impersonation of dignity and manly power." The overall effect inspired such awe that Justice claimed it made "one feel better" just to look at him. 3

*　　*　　*

3　Benjamin W. Justice to Wife, Nov. 22, 1863, Fredericksburg-Spotsylvania National Military Park. Justice was commissary officer for the 47th NC infantry. Some historians suspect that Lee's "rheumatism" represented early signs of the fatal heart disease he died from in 1870. Prudence dictates viewing medical diagnoses from spotty 150-year old anecdotal reports with caution. The important fact is Lee's fading health and its impact on his operations.

Lee's well-earned fame obscured the fact that his impressive battlefield victories had merely maintained a stalemate in the war's eastern theater. Although hardly an inconsiderable achievement, especially in light of possible disastrous alternatives, it frustrated the general mightily. Well aware that the South contended against a foe armed with immeasurably greater manpower and resources, Lee always aimed at the enemy army's total destruction. Much to his regret, every time he defeated the Federals they escaped annihilation to fight another day. On the two occasions Lee invaded the North in search of potential war-winning triumph, ill luck and mistakes thwarted his goal.

The general hoped a rapid succession of defeats might undermine the North's willingness to continue the war. But he recognized that Union progress in the west often counterbalanced the Army of Northern Virginia's accomplishments. He thus continued to seek a decisive battle that would land the knockout punch. Even Gettysburg hadn't lessened his aggressiveness. Within weeks of the campaign's conclusion Lee was advocating a resumption of the offensive. Logistical problems along with the pressing need to revitalize his army forestalled that effort in August. But when Yankee columns threatened Knoxville and Chattanooga the next month, Lee secured Davis' permission to strike at Meade.

Once again, however, events derailed his plans. After Federal troops captured both cities in early September, the president directed Lee to transfer almost an entire corps under his most able subordinate, Lt. Gen. James Longstreet, to the Western Theater. But when the enemy countered by shifting two corps from the Virginia to Tennessee a few weeks later, Lee saw his chance and seized it. Initially the campaign went well. Major General James Ewell Brown (Jeb) Stuart's cavalry corps befuddled Meade as to the whereabouts of Lee's swiftly moving infantry, which was sweeping around the Union right flank. Before the Rebels could slam into Culpeper County, however, the Yankees withdrew north of the Rappahannock and out of reach.[4]

Denied his target, Lee swung west again, bloodying a Federal cavalry brigade as his troops rolled across the river beyond Meade's flank. The enemy responded with another retreat and the Rebels pursued, the two armies engaging in a footrace toward Manassas Junction; the Yankees followed a straighter and better route while Lee's men traveled a more difficult, circuitous path. Although most of Meade's army escaped, Lieutenant General Ambrose Powell Hill's Third Corps caught up with the Union rearguard at Bristoe Station. Engrossed with the chase, Hill behaved like the division commander he had once been rather then the corps commander he now was. Without

---

4 Two of Longstreet's brigades reinforced Confederate forces defending Charleston, SC.

a thorough understanding of the ground or situation he attacked too quickly with too little force and suffered a bloody repulse.

Following their rearguard victory, the Yankees took up a position behind Bull Run and the extensive earthworks surrounding Centreville. As heavy rain drenched both armies, Lee pondered his next move. After four months of dueling with Meade the Confederate leader felt familiar with his opponent. Recent events had validated his initial assessment that the Pennsylvanian would make no blunders while hastening to take advantage of any Rebel errors. In fact, Meade had made several missteps at the campaign's start, but he had recovered quickly enough from each of them to evade Lee's effort to force a battle and maul some part of the Federal army.[5]

Nonetheless, the campaign had revealed Meade's healthy sensitivity for his flanks and a predisposition toward caution. Whether those traits were flaws or assets, from Lee's vantage point they meant two things: trying to goad Meade into a fight was difficult but maneuvering him into retreat was relatively easy. With this in mind, Lee contemplated outflanking the AOP by marching into the Loudoun Valley—a move his opponent expected and one he admitted would compel his withdrawal into Washington's defenses. Although driving Meade into those fortifications would render him impervious to attack, it would at least push his army north of the Potomac. Despite a deep desire to shove the Yankees out of Virginia, Lee decided against making the move.

Forcing Meade into Maryland and keeping him there meant wintering the ANV in the Old Dominion's northernmost reaches. However appealing that might be from a strategic perspective, it was logistically untenable. Two years of war had so desolated northern Virginia that it was impossible for Lee's army to find food or fodder in the region. Moreover, thousands of Rebel soldiers were barefoot and virtually all of them lacked blankets, overcoats, or warm clothing. Reflecting on these factors and believing it virtually impossible for Richmond to keep the army supplied so far north, Lee concluded that his offensive had run its course. Ordering a withdrawal to the Rappahannock he directed his troops to thoroughly wreck the O&A as they pulled back, thereby crippling Meade's ability to follow rapidly.

The campaign's results disappointed Lee, who admitted that despite inflicting "some punishment upon the enemy" his army had "failed to manage as well as" it might. Operating for the first time without either Longstreet or Lt. Gen. Thomas J. "Stonewall" Jackson at his side, Lee had felt their absence "dreadfully." Save for Bristoe Station, his principle subordinates—Lt. Gens. A. P. Hill commanding the Third Corps and Richard S. Ewell, commanding the Second—had performed

5   George Cary Eggleston, *A Rebel's Recollections*, (New York, 1905), 145-46; Freeman, *R. E. Lee*, vol. 3, 64.

Lt. Gen. Ambrose Powell Hill
Library of Congress

well-enough, but that didn't erase Gettysburg-generated concerns that Lee may have promoted both men beyond their true capabilities.[6]

*   *   *

The auburn-haired Hill was just shy of his 38th birthday and in many ways the architype of Southern generalship: bearded, dashingly handsome, brave, touchy about his honor and argumentative when he felt slighted. A hard marcher and aggressive fighter better suited to offensive than defensive action, Hill was predisposed toward impatience and consequently impulsive on occasion, but a man whose timely attacks had saved the army on several battlefields.

Unfortunately, Hill had grown progressively less robust as the war went on, largely due to frequent urinary tract infections stemming from gonorrhea contracted while a West Point cadet. Bouts with yellow fever and typhoid during the Mexican War plus wounds he suffered at Chancellorsville further weakened the general's already compromised constitution. Hill had been ill at Gettysburg, and although he played a minor role there, many people criticized him for bringing on that fight against Lee's orders. Those critiques proved mild compared to the vitriol aimed at him after Bristoe Station. Castigated as an incompetent bungler by the press and a large part of the army, he had drawn a blistering personal rebuke from Lee for his handling of the action. Mindful of Hill's oft-demonstrated combat talents, however, the army's leader treated Bristoe as an unfortunate error and hoped the young general might learn from his mistakes there. Whatever the future held, Hill had yet to make his mark as a corps

6   James Longstreet, *From Manassas to Appomattox*, (Secaucus, NJ, 1984), note, 469-70.

Lt. Gen. Richard S. Ewell
Library of Congress

commander and after six months in that role some were starting to wonder if he ever would.[7]

Others were saying the same thing about Dick Ewell, perhaps with more justification. The courageous 46-year had been an outstanding division commander noted for his battlefield ability and habit of leading from the front. A tall, slender man, Ewell's restless eyes peered out from an unforgettable face graced by what one reporter called "extremely sharp features." His completely bald dome stood in stark contrast to jet black hair flowing from the side of his head into long sideburns that merged together in a bushy mustache sitting atop an equally robust goatee. Although gentlemanly, the Virginian was remarkably profane, at least until the August 1862 battle of Groveton where a Yankee bullet smashed his left knee, necessitating the leg's amputation above the shattered joint.[8]

Ewell's life took an extraordinary turn during the long convalescence that followed. He found religion, stopped cursing, got fitted for an artificial leg, and married a recently widowed former love—a match that made him a suddenly wealthy man. Promoted to lieutenant general and given command of the Second Corps after Jackson's death, Ewell handled his troops well during the Pennsylvania campaign, but fell short of expectations at Gettysburg where an opaque and difficult tactical situation compounded by discretionary orders rendered him indecisive. Although that was disappointing, Ewell was hardly the only Southern general who faltered on that field.

7   Tagg, *Generals of Gettysburg*, 301; James I. Robertson, Jr. *A. P. Hill*, (NY, NY, 1987), 186-89; Hunt, *Meade and Lee at Bristoe Station*, 375-77.

8   A Confederate, *The Grayjackets And How They Lived, Found and Died for Dixie* (Richmond, VA, 1867), 330. The best biography of Ewell is Donald CF. Pfanz, *Richard S. Ewell: A Soldier's Life* (Chapel Hill, NC, 1998).

Maj. Gen. Jubal Early
Library of Congress

Since then Lee had seen no glaring cause for complaint despite ample reasons for concern.

Lieutenant Colonel Sandie Pendleton had enthusiastically greeted Ewell's ascension to Jackson's old command. By early November, however, the spirited Second Corps chief of staff had soured on his new boss. Writing down what many observers were thinking, he told his mother that Ewell was "quick in military perception" and a "splendid executive officer" but "too irresolute for so large and independent a command as he has." The general, simply put, wasn't the man he'd been while serving under Stonewall. Speculating on why, Pendleton charged that Ewell was "worn out" by recurring infections caused by his ill-fitting prosthetic leg and distracted by his "unattractive spouse" who more often than not resided at corps HQ and upon whom he doted "foolishly" like a distracted newlywed.[9]

Col. Thomas H. Carter, who commanded a Second Corps artillery battalion, fretted more about Ewell's increasing reliance on the counsel of his admittedly talented division commanders, Maj. Gens. Robert Rodes, Edward "Alleghany" Johnson, and Jubal A. Early. The perceptive gunner complained that nowadays Ewell never did anything "except on the advice of Early or Rodes." And to many it did seem as if Early was assuming an increasingly prominent role at corps HQ—accompanying his superior to high command conferences and taking charge when Ewell's health necessitated sick leave.[10]

A study in contrasts, Jubal Anderson Early was intelligent but often opinionated and stubborn; articulate but lacking the knack of public speaking; a successful pre-war

9 William G. Bean, *Stonewall's Man: Sandie Pendleton*, (Chapel Hill, NC, 1959), 149-51. Pendleton was the Second Corps chief of staff.

10 Graham T. Dozier, ed., *A Gunner in Lee's Army: The Wartime Letters of Thomas Henry Carter* (Chapel Hill, NC, 2014), 205; Peter Hariston diary, Oct. 6, 1863, Southern Historical Collection/University of North Carolina (hereafter SHC/UNC).

lawyer and prosecutor but indifferent businessman; the son of a well-off family but a progeny owning hardly any property; ambitious for distinction but willing to flaunt society's conventions; a man so hurt by his first love's marrying someone else that he became a confirmed bachelor despite maintaining a public decades-long affair with a woman who bore him four children.[11]

Graduating from West Point in 1837, Early had participated in the Second Seminole War without seeing combat. Resigning his commission in 1838 to become a lawyer, he returned to uniform as a major of Virginia volunteers upon the outbreak of the Mexican War, during which he made a good record but once again saw no action. As a delegate to Virginia's secession convention he twice voted against leaving the Union, but promptly embraced the Confederate cause after Lincoln's post-Fort Sumter call for volunteers to put down the "rebellion."

Subsequently, Early had acquired a stellar reputation. As a brigade commander he helped win the battle of First Manassas and was later wounded at Williamsburg in May 1862. Returning to duty before fully recuperating, he had fought at Malvern Hill and in every major ANV action since. His counterattack at Sharpsburg helped save the army's left flank and earned him command of a division. When George Meade's Union brigades briefly broke A. P. Hill's line at Fredericksburg in December 1862, Early's soldiers plugged the hole and drove back the enemy. The native Virginian received promotion to major general a month later.[12]

Although only 46, Early struck many people as being 10–15 years older. Arthritis brought on by a Mexican War fever caused him to stoop, diminishing his slender 6-foot frame. A balding pate and unkempt graying beard lessened the otherwise striking impact of his piercing black eyes and dark hair, reinforcing the impression that he had aged prematurely. In this regard Early's personality wasn't helpful. Most people found him abrasive, overbearing, derisive, willful and sometimes sharply critical of all his superiors except Robert E. Lee.

Early's caustic persona didn't alienate everyone, however. Pendleton, for example, thought him "far superior" to Ewell as "a commander, more energetic. . . a good disciplinarian" and "more agreeable as an associate." Early's troops bridled at his exacting discipline—which occasionally verged on vindictive and sometimes made him seem a heartless martinet—but they did recognize his combat leadership, referring to him with some pride as "Old Jubal." Ewell and Lee were equally impressed. The

11 The best biography of Early is Charles C. Osborne's *Jubal: The Life and Times of General Jubal A. Early* (Chapel Hill, NC, 1992).

12 Osborne, *Jubal*, 63-70, 76-81, 121-39.

former thought Early a "very able and very brave" officer while Lee somewhat affectionately referred to him as "my bad old man."[13]

*　　*　　*

However promising Jubal Early's résumé, he remained a division commander, while Hill and Ewell, regardless of their merits, had so far proven poor substitutes for Longstreet and Jackson. Lee especially lamented the former's absence over the last six weeks. Without his corps it had proven impossible to fix Meade in place and oblige him to give battle on Confederate terms. Such an eventuality might have evened the score for Gettysburg and mangled all or part of the Yankee army. Instead Meade had slipped through Confederate fingers, though barely, and Longstreet's divisions remained in Tennessee.

That was especially galling since the Army of Tennessee (AOT), for whatever reason, hadn't capitalized on its great Chickamauga victory. Far worse, even as the siege of Chattanooga began, that army's generals had gone to war against each other. Bragg blamed his failure to destroy the Federals on a disobedient cadre of corps and division commanders, who in turn accused him of incompetence and bungling the chance for decisive victory. Long simmering animosity among these men stoked emotions until a dozen generals—Longstreet among them—petitioned Davis to remove Bragg from command. The president rushed to Tennessee hoping to sort out the mess, leaving Richmond only three days before Lee launched his October offensive. The commander-in-chief remained there as the month drew toward its close. His prolonged stay bode ill for a satisfactory conclusion of the western army's drama.[14]

Lee was hardly ignorant of the AOT's dysfunction. A letter from Lt. Gen. Leonidas Polk begging him to take charge in the west reached ANV headquarters just as the Bristoe offensive began. The Virginian had no more interest in that idea now than in early September when he had resisted a similar suggestion by Davis. Belatedly responding to Polk, Lee claimed poor health to politely sidestep the general's proposal. Still, the situation remained worrisome. No matter how much he trusted Davis' ability

---

13 Bean, *Stonewall's Man*, 151; Osborne, *Jubal*, 100; Robert Stiles, *Four Years Under Marse Robert* (New York, 1910), 189.

14 Historians have written a great deal about the crisis engulfing Bragg and his generals after Chickamauga. For a succinct overview of Davis' role see William C. Davis, *Jefferson Davis: The Man and His Hour, A Biography*, (New York, 1992), 518-22. A more recent and fine analysis of the affair is in Earl J. Hess, *Braxton Bragg: The Most Hated Man of the Confederacy* (Chapel Hill, NC, 2016), 169-97.

to resolve Bragg's "difficulties" or the latter's ability to retake Chattanooga, Lee couldn't help but ponder the hidden meaning in the western army's current crisis.[15]

The president's bold decision to transfer Longstreet's corps had misfired, at least for the moment. Although the maneuver had engendered success at Chickamauga, Bragg's command turmoil had reduced that triumph to the sort of fruitless victory both Lee and Longstreet had denigrated when the First Corps left the ANV. The bickering and lack of results in Tennessee had cost Lee a chance to fight Meade on even terms. His "earnest prayer" that everything would yet work out for the best aside, Lee might well have recalled his mid-September warning to Davis that Longstreet's troops "had gone where they will do no good" instead of staying in Virginia where they were "much needed" and, as he sighed in an October 26 letter to Longstreet, where they would have been "invaluable" in the late contest against Meade.[16]

*   *   *

Regardless of what might have been, Lee manfully faced his current reality. Upon reaching the Rappahannock on October 19, he found himself back where he had ended the Gettysburg campaign. The O&A's destruction would slow Union progress toward the river, and if the Federals were timid it might induce them to leave well-enough alone and go into winter quarters around Warrenton. But Lee doubted it.

On October 23, just four days after the Army of Northern Virginia returned to Culpeper County, Rebel scouts reported Yankee infantry on the move with its advanced elements at Catlett's Station. The enemy was assembling timber and cross-ties near Bristoe Station for repairing the bridges and railroad track Confederate troops had wrecked. Clearly Meade was up to something, although Lee couldn't yet "ascertain" his "future movements."[17]

Few things grated on the Virginian more than foregoing the initiative. Predicting that Meade would "come on again" and aching to strike first, Lee told his wife that if he could "only get some shoes and clothes for the men," he would save his foe "the trouble." Regrettably those necessities weren't forthcoming in needed quantities. Left

---

15 Clifford Dowdey & Louis H. Manarin, *The Wartime Papers of R. E. Lee*, (New York, 1961), 614.

16 OR 29, pt. 2, 720-21; OR 52, pt. 2, 549-50; Dowdy, *Wartime Papers*, 614; Longstreet, *From Manassas to Appomattox*, 437n., 469-70.

17 OR 29, pt. 2, 800.

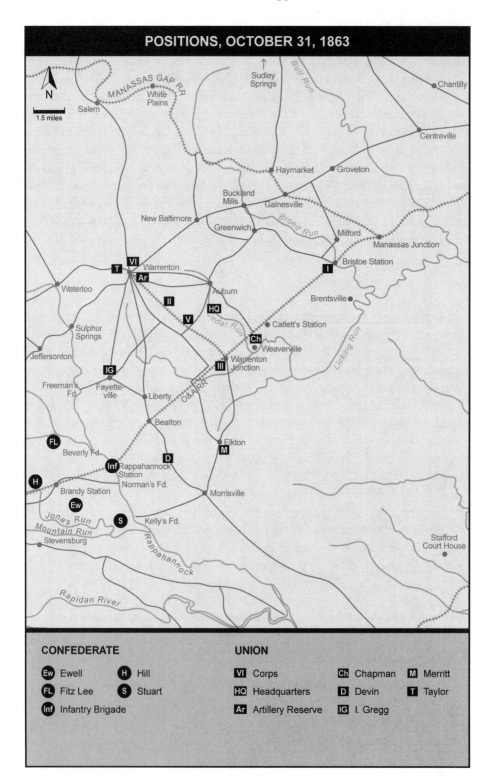

POSITIONS, OCTOBER 31, 1863

CONFEDERATE

Ew Ewell
FL Fitz Lee
Inf Infantry Brigade

H Hill
S Stuart

UNION

VI Corps
HQ Headquarters
Ar Artillery Reserve

Ch Chapman
D Devin
IG I. Gregg

M Merritt
T Taylor

with no alternative but to wait, he busied himself with plotting the enemy's discomfiture once he appeared.[18]

However much current circumstances compelled a defensive stand, they didn't dictate its location. That was up to Lee, who could select a position behind either the Rappahannock or the Rapidan. He knew the geographic pros and cons of each line intimately, of course, but recent history and his own combative instincts dominated the general's thinking as he contemplated which to take up.

The army currently occupied Culpeper County, a 383-square mile expanse of mostly open, gently rolling terrain mid-way between Washington and Richmond. The southeasterly course of the Rappahannock constituted the county's northern and eastern boundary, while the straighter line of the Rapidan marked its southern border. These two rivers formed a giant sideways 'V' whose maw opened toward Madison County and a chain of ridges steadily marching upward to the Blue Ridge Mountains and Shenandoah Valley. At Culpeper's southeastern apex the Rapidan flowed into the Rappahannock which then ran downstream 20 miles to shot-torn Fredericksburg before flowing on into Chesapeake Bay.

The Orange & Alexandria Railroad entered Culpeper from the northeast, running southwest until it reached Culpeper Court House where it turned south to eventually cross the Rapidan and connect with the Virginia Central Railroad at Gordonsville. The O&A once spanned the Rappahannock via a 500-foot long bridge at Rappahannock Station, but retreating Union troops burned the structure on October 13. Confederate engineers replaced it with a pontoon bridge 300 yards upstream six days later.[19]

The pretty little town of Culpeper Court House resided south of the Rappahannock exactly in the middle of its namesake county. Roads radiated from the city in all directions, many of them leading to fords on the Rappahannock or Rapidan. Adjacent to Culpeper neither of these rivers was navigable or broad, although each could quickly swell to significant size after even a modest storm. Every one of these crossing points presented a potential avenue of attack or retreat and a natural funnel for an army using it.[20]

---

18 Ibid., pt. 1, 610, pt. 2, 794, 800; Robert E. Lee, Jr., *Recollections and Letters of General Robert E. Lee* (New York, 1904), 111.

19 *OR* 29, pt. 1, 625. I have derived the distance between the pontoon bridge and the railway bridge from a map attached to Lee's report on the Battle of Rappahannock Station and Kelly's Ford as well as an examination of satellite imagery at www.googlearth.com. Rappahannock Station's citizens changed the locale's name to Remington in 1890. https://www.remingtonva.com/history accessed 2/1/20

20 Fredericksburg marked the head of navigation on the Rappahannock. The Rapidan's name originated from its habit of rapidly rising following a storm. Daniel E. Sutherland, "Culpepper County During the Civil War," Encyclopedia Virginia, Accessed April 17, 2018.

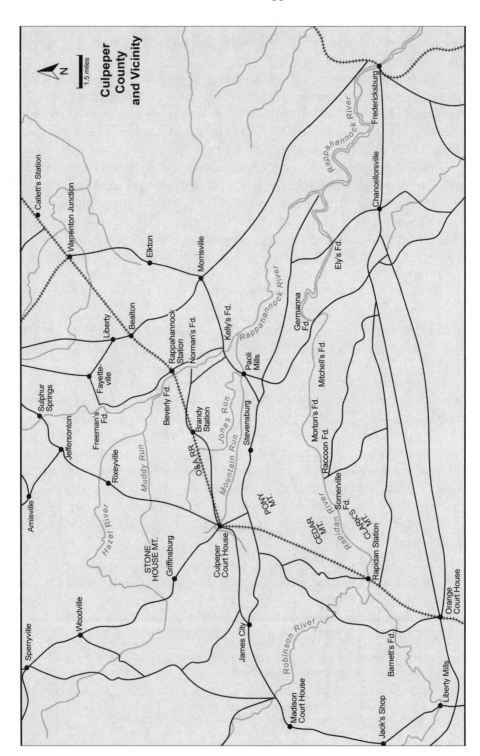

This August 1862 Timothy O'Sullivan photo looks west 200 yards toward the O&A Bridge near Rappahannock Station. Runaway Slaves and Union soldiers stand in the foreground at a "cow ford" adjacent to where Tin Pot Run empties into the river. *Library of Congress*

Within the last 15 months Lee had shielded behind both rivers to launch strategic offensives: the Rappahannock protecting the start of the Gettysburg campaign, and the Rapidan those of Second Manassas and Bristoe Station. But as a defensive position Culpeper County evinced serious topographical defects. Not only did its terrain provide few anchors for a battle line; the ground north of the Rappahannock and south of the Rapidan generally stood higher than that between the two rivers. Anyone attacking into the area could concentrate invading columns out of sight and then strike across the fords with little warning. The county's relatively narrow width—just 23 miles separated the Rappahannock from the Rapidan if one traveled down the O&A—meant a defending army defeated inside the 'V' risked being driven against a river where the fords became choke points and possible death traps.

At first glance the Rapidan appeared easier to hold. Higher ground along its south bank gave defenders an enormous advantage. Two good roads, the Orange Plank Road and the Orange Turnpike, ran parallel to one another below the waterway, making east-west movement relatively quick and easy. The infamous Wilderness—a dense, jungle-like mass of tangled second growth timber and home to Lee's great Chancellorsville victory—anchored the eastern end of the Rapidan front. Clark's Mountain, jutting up suddenly from the surrounding countryside below the river, provided an excellent post for signalmen to wig-wag messages or spy on enemy troops north of the stream. And should Meade reoccupy Culpeper he would make himself vulnerable to an October-style flanking movement.

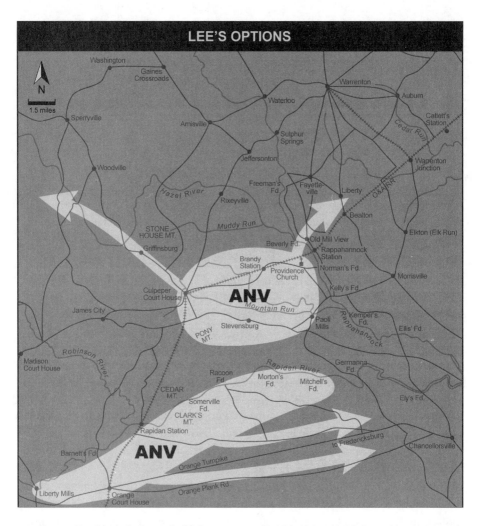

But a Rapidan defense held its own perils. Blocking a Union thrust through Culpeper or Madison counties against the Virginia Central Railroad would require Lee to center his army on Orange Court House. Even after spreading regiments along the Rapidan for 25 miles, he would have to leave the river's easternmost fords open to capture, with only cavalry patrols on hand to sound the alarm. Should the Federals strike there, even the quickest Confederate reaction couldn't stop them from getting over the river. Once below the Rapidan, Meade could drive south to get between Lee and Richmond or turn west to maul the Rebel army before it concentrated to meet him.[21]

---

21 The Virginia Central was a critical Confederate supply artery connecting Richmond to the agricultural bounty of the Shenandoah Valley.

The best Confederate response to either threat was a rapid eastward march to attack the enemy at the earliest possible moment. Any delay or mischance could prove fatal. If the Federals got too far south before Lee hit them, his army would have to make a desperate dash into Spotsylvania County to stay between the Yankees and Richmond. If, on the other hand, the bluecoats swerved west, they stood a good chance of assailing Lee's right before his left flank units reached the scene, giving the Northerners a glittering opportunity to destroy the ANV in detail.

Neither of these reactive scenarios appealed to Lee, who upon reflection found numerous reasons to maintain his current position on the Rappahannock. At Culpeper Court House he was poised for a spring offensive into the Shenandoah or Loudoun valleys or an encore of his October sweep around Meade's right. Holding the upper river provided another 23 miles of cushion between the Federals and the Virginia Central. It also kept the enemy farther from Richmond and put Lee on the flank of any Union advance into Madison County. More critically, with his army based around the courthouse Lee held interior lines and could rush troops rapidly to any point Meade might threaten. Should a Yankee offensive somehow compel a withdrawal from Culpeper, his army could retreat behind the Rapidan. These benefits didn't come without risk, however and Lee understood that the Rappahannock was defensible only if he negated the topographical advantage it gave his enemy.

Although the Yankees might lunge across the river's western reaches on the Confederate left, Lee judged this their least likely move. Marching that way would separate Meade from the O&A, necessitating a reliance on slow-moving wagons to haul his army's supplies. The Virginia Central Railroad, whose closest track lay 60 miles beyond Warrenton, presented the sole strategic target in that direction. From Culpeper Court House Lee could intercept any Union column well before it got there or force its retreat by cutting its supply line. The same held true if Meade tried to strike into the Culpeper 'V' from Madison County.

Lee knew his right presented the greater danger. The two armies were now situated almost the same as a year ago, with the Federals near Warrenton and the Confederates around Culpeper Court House. In November 1862 Burnside, then commanding the AOP, had opened the Fredericksburg campaign by seizing the Rappahannock fords and using part of his army to fix Lee in Culpeper while the remainder, concealed by the high ground along the river's northern bank, marched rapidly toward Fredericksburg.

Lee had suspected the maneuver, but an inability to verify it delayed his reaction. If the pontoon bridges Burnside needed to cross the Rappahannock had arrived at Fredericksburg as planned, the Yankees would have seized the town before the Rebels got there, forcing the ANV to fall back on the North Anna River before making a stand. Lee recalled these events all too well and realized that keeping his troops in Culpeper County risked a repeat Federal performance.[22]

He therefore devised a daring and innovative plan to thwart such a stratagem: maintain a fortified position on the river's north bank centered on the Rappahannock Station pontoon bridge. If the Federals sidled toward Fredericksburg, Lee could attack out of the bridgehead to assail their rear or cut Meade's supply line by assuming a strong post athwart the O&A. With an enemy army between them and Washington, the Yankees would have no choice but to turn back and assail Lee on his chosen ground where an engagement promised to wreck some, and perhaps all, of the AOP. Lee felt certain Meade wouldn't run that risk. His opponent had operated carefully since Gettysburg and had handled his troops skillfully if not boldly. He wouldn't ignore a Rebel bridgehead on the Rappahannock's north bank.

If Meade advanced, either on his own volition or under Washington's prodding, Lee expected an attempt to gain control of the Rappahannock as his foe's opening gambit. Any competent general would outflank rather than frontally assault a fortified position like Rappahannock Station. And Lee could easily imagine how an obviously competent Meade might assail the Rappahannock line. The Yankees would deploy a heavy screening force in front of the Rebel bridgehead. Though these troops might attempt an assault, their primary job would be preventing the Confederates from launching an attack there. The rest of the Union army would march downstream, probably to Kelly's Ford where high north bank hills frowned down on the crossing and nearby Kellysville. Although Rebel troops had dug extensive earthworks behind the river, any soldiers occupying them could only delay, not repulse a determined attack. If the Yankees wanted to cross the Rappahannock at Kelly's Ford no one wearing gray could stop them.[23]

Lee perceived that this fact worked to his advantage, however. If Meade stationed a strong force to watch Rappahannock Station (as he inevitably would) and sent the rest of his army to Kelly's Ford, he would divide his command. Separated by six miles and a river, the isolated portions of the Union army couldn't support one another. Whatever bluecoats crossed at Kellysville would enter a lion's den, the Confederates letting them march inland only as far as necessary to spring their trap. While holding some portion

---

22 For a good discussion of the opening phases of the Fredericksburg Campaign see Francis Augustín O'Reilly, *The Fredericksburg Campaign: Winter War on the Rappahannock*, (Baton Rouge, LA, 2003), 25-34.

23 Archie P. McDonald, ed., *Make Me A Map of the Valley: The Civil War Journal of Stonewall Jackson's Topographer*, (Dallas, TX 1973), 179. While serving on Ewell's staff as chief topographical engineer, Hotchkiss noted in his journal that Lee and Ewell spent the morning of Oct. 20 examining Kelly's Ford.

of Meade's troops in check with minimal force courtesy of Rappahannock Station's earthworks, Lee could hurl the bulk of his own command against whatever chunk of the AOP crossed Kelly's Ford and destroy it. If Meade gambled and left only a small force at Rappahannock Station, Lee could dispatch a large contingent over the pontoon bridge to assail the enemy's rear, severing his communications with Washington.

This plan wasn't foolproof. It relied on Meade dividing his force and Rappahannock Station's fortified defenders holding in check whatever Federals they confronted. If the enemy somehow got over the river in both places, Lee would face the prospect of fighting a defensive battle inside the Culpeper 'V' with all its attendant disadvantages and dangers. Still, his foe had behaved so prudently since Gettysburg that Lee felt fairly confident his scheme would work. At worst Meade might recognize the Rebel trap and avoid it by going into winter quarters. At best, the Yankees would blunder into the snare and give the Army of Northern Virginia an auspicious chance to inflict a potentially war-altering blow.

*   *   *

Though Lee had chosen his strategy and prepared appropriately, the future course of events lay in Union hands. Meade's intentions were the only unknown. Indeed, no one on either side seemed certain of his next move. Naturally speculation abounded and above the Potomac its tone wasn't kind to the general or his superiors. On the first day of November, *Harper's Weekly* "once more" bemoaned "the weary report that the campaign in Virginia is at an end." The newspaper found this inexcusable. Comparing the AOP to that army's western counterparts, it wondered whether the Old Dominion's mud was truly that "much more difficult to navigate than the swamps of the Mississippi, through which Grant and Banks marched their armies to victory."[24]

While conceding that the high command alone could properly adjudge the advisability of giving "Lee battle where he is," the paper underscored its own strategic impulse. Referencing the transfer of Longstreet's corps to Georgia and the Chickamauga disaster, *Harper's* proclaimed that "one does not need to be much of a solider to see that if Lee sends any considerable portion of his army to reinforce Bragg . . . it will be possible for Meade to attack him to advantage . . . mud or no mud, and that he ought on no account fail to do so."[25]

24 *Harper's Weekly*, November 7, 1863.

25 Ibid.

Numerous Yankee soldiers concurred and chafed at the continued Virginia "standstill." Thomas Carpenter, an ordnance clerk at army headquarters, gave voice to many comrades when he groused that the time had come to get on with "fighting the South into perfect submission even if that involves on their part perfect annihilation." While Northerners worried that their eastern army might hibernate until spring, Southerners thought otherwise. The year's fighting hadn't ended, proclaimed the *Richmond Examiner*, warning its readers that "there are many and strong indications that the enemy will make one more effort . . . before the cold weather and the reign of mud sets in." Time would soon tell which side's prognosticators were right.[26]

---

26 Thomas Carpenter to Mary, Nov. 3, 1863, Thomas Carpenter papers, MHS; *Richmond Examiner*, November 3, 1863.

CHAPTER 3

"My Plan Is Disapproved"

Coming Events—Union Options—Fredericksburg Proposal—Washington's
Refusal—Meade's Dismay—Alternate Plan—Mounted Pageantry

NOVEMBER 1, 1863 arrived pregnant with dread and anticipation. Affairs in Tennessee remained tense. During the final weeks of October, Grant had opened a supply line into besieged Chattanooga. Everyone expected him to launch a major attack soon. Even as Yankee strength grew around the city, Jefferson Davis sought to quell the internecine war among the AOT's high command by retaining Bragg and reassigning other officers. In the aftermath of that far from satisfactory solution, Davis and Bragg began discussing the possibility of sending Longstreet's divisions to recapture Knoxville.

Nearly 1,100 miles to the southwest, Union troops under Maj. Gen. Nathaniel Banks were 24 hours away from an amphibious invasion of Texas. Washington wanted them to seal off the Rio Grande, stop Rebel cotton from skirting the blockade via Mexico and warn French forces occupying that unhappy country to keep out of the American conflict. Whether Banks' movement would intimidate or provoke France remained uncertain.

In Gettysburg, Pennsylvania workers were struggling to finish a new cemetery populated with the bodies of Union boys killed there just four months earlier. Preparations for a special dedication ceremony on November 19 were well underway. The committee planning this occasion had enlisted famous orator Edward Everett to deliver a keynote address, postponing the event to accommodate his schedule. On November 2, the group's chairman invited President Lincoln to attend and make a few appropriate remarks.

That same day Meade informed Halleck that work crews had restored the O&A as far south as Warrenton Junction. Trains were unloading not far from the front, and the army had enough supplies on hand to renew its advance. The Rebels had massed along the Rappahannock some 19 miles distant and appeared disposed to "dispute the passage of the river." As Meade saw things, he had three offensive options: attempt to turn Lee's left flank with a move through Madison County, drive straight down the O&A and assail the enemy's river defenses, or sidestep the Rebels entirely with a quick dash to Fredericksburg accompanied by a change of base to Aquia Landing, which was downstream from Washington on the south bank of the Potomac.

Meade rejected a thrust into Madison County since it would dangerously lengthen the army's supply line as it drew away from the railroad. An attack on Lee's Rappahannock line looked equally unappealing. Scouts reported strong enemy fortifications along the river, and it seemed doubtful the Union army could assault them "with any probability of success." Should it drive the secessionists back, they would merely retreat behind the Rapidan. And if Meade followed, he would occupy the same position inside the Culpeper 'V' that Lee had so easily outflanked in October. Moreover, a continued reliance on the O&A for supplies perpetuated the deployment of thousands of men as railroad guards and the consequent loss of combat power to the army.

A movement against Fredericksburg, on the other hand, had much to recommend it. Changing the army's base to Aquia Landing would give Meade a waterborne line of communication and thereby free up thousands of men otherwise wasted defending railroad track. Furthermore, just-received intelligence indicated an absence of enemy troops in the town's fortifications. If the Federals acted swiftly, they could occupy those works before Lee knew what was happening, leaving him no choice but to hurry rearward in hope of interposing between the Federals and Richmond. After abandoning their Culpeper/Rapidan line without a fight, the Confederates would either have to attack the AOP while it stood on high ground or retire to a defensive line farther south. Either way, Meade told Halleck, "my object will be accomplished," and he therefore considered the Fredericksburg alternative his best available option.[1]

---

1   OR 29, pt. 2, 409; Peter G. Tsouras, *Major General George H. Sharpe and the Creation of American Military Intelligence in the Civil War* (Philadelphia, PA, 2018), 1-5, 157-59, 163, 182. This intelligence arrived at AOP HQ on November 1 courtesy of Col. George H. Sharpe, a 35-year old New Yorker whom Hooker had tapped to create an intelligence service in early 1863. Under the auspices of the AOP's provost marshal, Sharpe and his team created a bureau of military information (BMI) that not only gathered information using its own spies (euphemistically called scouts), but also received and analyzed the data collected from cavalry patrols, picket posts, Southern newspapers, captured mail, deserters, contrabands, and POWs. Anticipating 20th century military intelligence organizations by some 40 years, Sharpe and his men had rendered excellent service to Hooker and proven most helpful to Meade during the Gettysburg campaign. Despite this, the new army commander had altered the BMI's function by assuming its analytical role onto himself and diverting much of its information stream to army headquarters. Nonetheless, Sharpe's spy network remained useful as evidenced by its production of the November 1 intelligence gem. Grant would resurrect the BMI's specialized role upon becoming General-in-Chief in 1864.

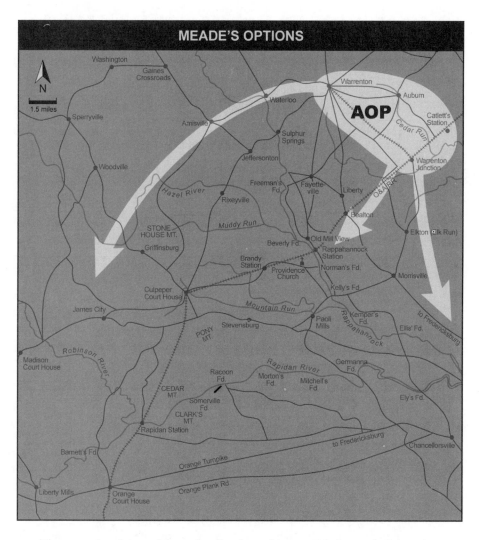

The general anticipated that talk of battle-seeking would please administration ears and help sell his program. Although he probably doubted Lee's willingness to fight on disadvantageous terms, Meade remained confident his operation would bloodlessly overcome two strong Rebel lines, simplify the army's supply problems, ease its manpower concerns and place his command in a far better jump-off position for 1864's spring campaign.

Of course this same reasoning had applied in August when Lincoln and Halleck had rejected this very plan, seeing in it the same maneuver that led Burnside to disastrous defeat the previous December. While conceding that "celerity" and secrecy were necessary to avoid a similar outcome, Meade nonetheless expected consent this time around. The general's confidence grew largely from his earlier prescience about operating along the O&A. Three months ago, when the army returned to Warrenton after Gettysburg, Meade had cautioned Washington that Lee could outflank any Union position on the Rapidan or upper Rappahannock. The administration disregarded those warnings and in October the Rebels had done exactly as Meade predicted. The resulting threat to the army's supply line had forced a retreat almost to the capital's gates.

With that evidence in hand, Meade felt sure Lincoln and Halleck would see logic in shifting the army's base. Fully anticipating their approval, he ordered his engineers to assemble pontoon trains for a Fredericksburg crossing of the Rappahannock. Then Meade matter-of-factly telegraphed Halleck that the army was about to launch itself southeastward, asking only for prompt notice if the administration disapproved the scheme.[2]

Enthused at the prospect of stealing a march on Lee but still worried the enemy might beat him to the punch, Meade busied himself on November 3 with visits to various headquarters. He spent some time with II Corps commander Maj. Gen. Gouverneur K. Warren and "in company with him took in a view of the country." Union troops observing this activity could not say what it meant, but some wistfully hoped Meade was selecting "a good location for winter camps."[3]

The general had something much different in mind of course, but his hopes, as well as those of his soldiers, were destined for disappointment. At noon army headquarters received Halleck's telegram vetoing Meade's campaign. Neither the general-in-chief nor Mr. Lincoln saw any reason for the "proposed change of base." The president doubted the maneuver would "produce any favorable result." Halleck "fully concurred" in that appraisal and chided Meade for suggesting it in light of the high command's views "heretofore communicated on this subject." The army could undertake "any tactical movement" Meade desired, but "an entire change of base under existing circumstances," Halleck would "neither advise nor approve."[4]

The next day a crestfallen Meade dutifully acknowledged these instructions and halted his Fredericksburg preparations. Despite Washington's rejection of his plan, Meade recognized that the administration still expected him to do something. Although Lincoln and Halleck offered no clue as to what that something should be, the general suspected that their patience with him was nearing its end.[5]

---

2   OR 29, pt. 2, 407.

3   Thomas Carpenter letters, Missouri Historical Society (MHS); Sparks, *Inside Lincoln's Army*, 303.

4   OR 29, pt. 2, 412.

5   Lyman, *Meade's Army*, 61; ibid., 415.

The feeling was mutual. Later that night Meade unburdened himself to Margaret, the tone of his letter becoming increasingly angry as he wrote. There was "no doubt," he admitted, that his "failure to engage Lee" in October had "created great disappointment" in the administration. The general "fully shared" that sentiment and although he had "seen and heard of no indications of absolute dissatisfaction" from the government, he worried it might exist "without its being manifested."

Whatever their feelings, Lincoln and Halleck were no more helpful now than before. The latter's constant insistence that the army "had better fight" was particularly irksome, since the general-in-chief couldn't "explain how" it could do so to advantage. For three months he and the president had goaded and prodded, clearly wanting action but refusing to issue direct orders or give clear guidance. Left alone to shoulder the responsibility of finding a way forward, Meade had finally "indicated" what he "thought feasible and practicable," only to have Washington reject the idea out of hand.

"My plan is DISAPPROVED," he exclaimed to Margaret, fuming at bosses who insisted he fight but denied him freedom of maneuver. The newspapers had no conception of this, of course, and their assertions that Meade refused combat grated on the general, who saw his reputation suffer and felt powerless to defend it. He could silence the naysayers with a victory, but administration intransigence denied his army its best chance for success. "Under these circumstances," the general moaned, "justice to me and the true interest of the country justify . . . selecting someone else to command."[6]

Regardless of these frustrations George Meade soldiered on. Bound by an implacable sense of duty and determined to do his best within the limitations Washington imposed, he endeavored to devise a campaign that wouldn't give Lee "all the advantage of defense and position." Fearful that he had exasperated the president, Meade wired Halleck assurances that he was "most earnestly anxious to bring matters to a termination."[7]

This was no hollow promise. Having carefully considered his three offensive options before selecting the Fredericksburg scheme, Meade shifted quickly to his second choice — an assault on Lee's Rappahannock line. Within hours of receiving Halleck's directive forbidding a change of base, Meade was "anxiously endeavoring" to imagine "some movement" that would produce a fight. Although he hadn't arrived "at

---

6   Previous paragraphs based on George Meade, *Life and Letters of George Gordon Meade*. 2 vols. (New York, NY, 1913), Vol. 2, 155. Capitalization in original.

7   *OR* 29, pt. 2, 415.

any satisfactory conclusion" to this riddle by late evening on November 4, he remained determined to find an answer soon.

Whatever he decided to do, Washington's mandate that the army continue relying on the O&A for supplies made protecting the railroad a vital concern. Meade flinched at every menace to the line, real or imagined. On November 3, after receiving intelligence that a Rebel cavalry brigade had crossed the Rappahannock at Fredericksburg with orders to "destroy the railroad," Meade dispatched Brig. Gen. Judson Kilpatrick's entire 3rd Cavalry Division to deal with the threat.

The Union troopers left Catlett's Station the next morning, but after spending an entire day in the saddle they encountered nothing more than a scattering of gray pickets who withdrew to Fredericksburg after a brief skirmish. Taking shelter in the city the Southerners traded fire with Kilpatrick's men until nightfall, when the Federals broke contact. After bivouacking for the evening the division returned to Catlett's Station, its troopers and horses worn out for no good reason.[8]

Confederate guerrillas operating near the O&A presented a more creditable hazard. Colonel John S. Mosby's partisan ranger battalion was particularly bothersome, snatching up unwary wagons, animals, and men daily. Such depredations made movement by anything less than a platoon outside Union camps highly risky and responding to such attacks kept Federal cavalry in constant motion. Nothing Northern commanders tried stymied these raiders, but at least their harassment hadn't yet threatened the railroad.

Mosby could set aside marauding at any moment, however, and concentrate on breaking the O&A. This possibility worried Meade greatly. If the raiders struck opportunely they could disrupt the army's supply line at a critical moment, derailing its upcoming offensive in the process. To blunt such a threat, on November 5 Maj. Gen. Andrew A. Humphreys—the army's capable, brusque, and aggressive chief of staff—ordered Maj. Gen. John Newton to send one of his I Corps infantry divisions to replace III Corps troops guarding the railroad. Detailed and specific instructions required Newton to station one brigade at Bristoe Station, another around the army's Warrenton Junction supply depot and a third along the track between Cedar and Kettle

---

8 Ibid., 413, 802; *New York Herald*, November 6, 1863. Union intelligence hadn't been completely wrong. Confederates had crossed the Rappahannock near Fredericksburg but on a mission to salvage railroad track around Aquia Creek. Lee had declined Richmond's request to send cavalry to protect the effort, saying he couldn't spare the troopers and arguing that speedy work would provide the expedition's best protection.

Runs. Detachments would guard every culvert or bridge while frequent patrols monitored the line between Manassas and Warrenton.[9]

Having looked to his rear, Meade considered his next move. Kilpatrick's recent foray to Fredericksburg wasn't without benefits as it had apparently drawn some enemy infantry in that direction. Spies just returned from behind Confederate lines reported the Rebels preparing for a movement. That might suggest an enemy offensive or that Lee intended sending significant forces below the Rapidan, to Fredericksburg, or even Tennessee. Either way, a sudden Union assault on the Rappahannock line might catch the enemy off balance. Meade knew these conditions could change quickly. If he wanted to strike, he had better strike soon.[10]

* * *

While the Yankee commander pondered options and fretted about the O&A's safety, pageantry stirred south of the Rappahannock. A month ago Robert E. Lee had reviewed his two infantry corps. Now it was the cavalry's turn and a collection of dignitaries, including Virginia governor John Letcher, came up from Richmond for the occasion. Many ladies were present, their charms adding a chivalrous aura to the affair.

No one loved pomp and circumstance more than Jeb Stuart and his horsemen were sure to put on quite a performance. General Lee felt fortunate to take part. Severe back pain had plagued him throughout the previous week and he had feared missing Stuart's show. Happily, he awakened on November 5 feeling much better. After mounting the ever-reliable Traveler, Lee rode with his staff to the Botts' Farm not far from Brandy Station. The rival cavalry forces had contested this ground many times in the last six months, and it had witnessed several reviews as well. Now it would host another.

The day was bright and cheerful, the temperature a pleasant 74 degrees. Appearing "in all his glory," Stuart, along with Letcher and Lee, galloped along the serried formations of mounted men. It was magnificent spectacle, the sun glinting off 6,000 drawn sabers and the polished tubes of an entire artillery battalion as bullet-pierced battle flags folded and flapped in the autumn breeze.[11]

---

9 Ibid., 417. Newton detailed his 3rd division, led by Brig. Gen. John R. Kenly to guard the railroad.

10 Ibid., 415, 417. Meade's intelligence was incorrect. Lee had sent no infantry toward Fredericksburg.

11 Krick, *Civil War Weather in Virginia* (Tuscaloosa, AL, 2007), 112 (the temperature readings in Krick's book were taken at Georgetown); Austin Dobbins, ed., *Grandfather's Journal* (Dayton,

After riding the length of each brigade, the three leaders moved to a prominent knoll from which they watched the gray regiments trot past. This awe-inspiring display of martial power dazzled onlookers and even impressed Rebel infantrymen who stopped by to take in the scene. The day concluded dramatically with a mock charge, the entire Cavalry Corps dashing forward "with sabers drawn and yelling like demons." Sadly, one trooper died, and several others were injured when their horses fell during the theatrical assault, somewhat marring the demonstration. But the overall effect provided everything Stuart could have wished: a lovely example of a storybook-kind of war that no longer existed. As gleeful civilians headed home flush with renewed admiration for Southern valor, Rebel soldiers returned to camp life's unglamorous realities and the "never-ending job" of digging entrenchments.[12]

Although Meade's army lay just 20 or so miles away, no Confederate seemed overly concerned with its activities. Not even Kilpatrick's day-long thrust toward Fredericksburg raised any alarm. Lee could do nothing until Federal infantry moved, and his future course depended on events. Many men dared hope the campaign season had ended, and numerous regiments started building winter quarters. The army's superstitious warned against complacency, however, and backed up their caution by pointing out that a campaign had followed every grand review in 1863. Why, they asked, should anyone suppose things would be different now?[13]

*   *   *

Thanks to Federal spies George Meade learned of Stuart's pageant shortly after it happened. Although Confederate dispositions hadn't altered significantly over the last several days, the Union general felt uneasy. On November 6, Rebel infantry crossed the Rappahannock at Kelly's Ford, pushing back vedettes from Brig. Gen. Wesley Merritt's Reserve Brigade. What first looked like trouble quieted down once it became clear the enemy merely wished to establish a picket line north of the river. Although minor, the

OH, 1988), 167; Walbrook D. Swank, ed., *Sabres, Saddles and Spurs: Lieutenant Colonel William R. Carter, CSA.* (Shippensburg, PA, 1998), 99; McDonald, *Make Me A Map*, 181.

12 Dobbins, *Grandfather's Journal*, 167; Swank, *Sabres, Saddles and Spurs*, 99.

13 Lee, *Recollections and Letters*, 115. The First Battle of Brandy Station and the invasion of Pennsylvania had followed a review of Stuart's troopers in June 1863, and infantry reviews in September foreshadowed Meade's thrust to the Rapidan followed by Lee's counterthrust to Bull Run.

incident touched a sensitive nerve because within 24 hours the Yankee army intended to hurl six infantry divisions over the river at this exact spot.[14]

Following Halleck's rejection of the Fredericksburg move, Meade spent a full day wrestling with how to breach the Rappahannock front. The fortified Rebel bridgehead north of the river loomed large in his thinking. Grasping its import Meade well-understood his enemy's defensive plan but saw no way to avoid playing Lee's game.

This was quite discouraging, especially since Meade felt certain his predicament stemmed, at least partly, from the administration's displeasure over his conduct of the last campaign and possibly all the way back to Gettysburg's aftermath. That supposition amplified the subtle but palpable pressure on the army to attack, even if it meant launching an operation of doubtful viability. Without recourse, however, the general prepared to throw his troops across the Rappahannock the following morning, November 6, only to have threatening weather advise a postponement.

While waiting for nature to decide its course, Meade took time to answer a letter from Maj. Gen. Winfield S. Hancock, who was anxious to rejoin his II Corps despite not having fully recovered from a Gettysburg wound. After discouraging his friend from resuming the rigors of field service too soon, Meade briefly described the army's October campaign and how he'd conducted it. "God knows," he told Hancock, "no one was more disappointed" than he that a battle hadn't resulted. Nonetheless, Meade realized that neither military logic nor his own distress at failing to fight Lee mattered to the administration. Although "they are very polite and civil to me in Washington," Meade continued, there seemed little doubt that his relief was inevitable and he therefore kept his "saber packed." Supposing that the president might choose Hancock as the AOP's next chief, Meade warned his old comrade that the job was far from pleasant and thanks to the administration's conduct, far from desirable.[15]

Venting to a friendly ear distracted Meade briefly as he kept a baleful eye skyward. Happily, the anticipated storm failed to materialize and with Virginia's roads still firm and dry the general retained the conditions he needed to go ahead. That evening army headquarters issued orders for a simultaneous November 7 assault on Rappahannock Station and Kelly's Ford.[16]

These instructions divided the army in two. Major General John Sedgwick had charge of the 26,000-man strong right wing, consisting of his own VI Corps and Maj.

14 OR 29, pt. 2, 423-24.

15 Meade to Winfield Scott Hancock, Nov. 6, 1863, Winfield Scott Hancock Papers, Duke University, Durham, NC.

16 Ibid.

Gen. George Sykes' V Corps. Their target was Rappahannock Station. Major General William H. French commanded the 29,000-man left wing. He would assail Kelly's Ford with his own III Corps and Warren's II Corps. If needed French could call on Newton's I Corps which, minus its division guarding the O&A, would mass at Morrisville and stand ready to move on Kelly's Ford.[17]

Meade's thorough directives left little to chance. Two pontoon trains would accompany each wing and the engineers were to keep their bridges available for immediate use. Heavy guns detailed from Brig. Gen. Henry J. Hunt's Reserve Artillery would support the attacking infantry: Battery M, 1st Connecticut Heavy Artillery and its quartet of 4.5-inch siege rifles would go with French, while Battery B, 1st Connecticut, and the 5th New York Independent Battery (both equipped with six 20-pounder Parrot rifles) marched with Sedgwick.[18]

Major General Alfred Pleasonton would mass his cavalry corps along the river, Buford's division assembling on the Sedgwick's right and Kilpatrick's division on French's left. Once Union infantry vaulted the stream, Buford would cross the Rappahannock at Sulphur Springs and move south to force a passage of the Hazel River and take Rixeyville before advancing on Culpeper Court House. Kilpatrick's division would seize Ellis' and Kemper's fords, cross the river on French's left and cooperate with his infantry as needed. Brig. Gen. David M. Gregg's 2nd Cavalry Division drew the job of protecting the army's trains and Hunt's artillery, both of which would park around Bealton and Morrisville. Gregg's assignment included securing the roads between Rappahannock Station and Kelly's Ford. This was a potentially vital task, for if Sedgwick couldn't destroy the bridgehead, he would need to shift troops rapidly eastward to reinforce French.[19]

Army headquarters specified that every foot soldier carry the standard allotment of 40 rounds. Only ambulances and vehicles hauling medical stores, ordnance supplies, or entrenching tools would accompany the troops. None save the hospital wagons should cross the Rappahannock until directed. All other trains would remain behind, those of the right wing concentrated at Bealton and those of the left wing at Morrisville. Meade expected these measures to hasten his march and facilitate tactical surprise. They would also disencumber the army if conditions necessitated a speedy retreat over the river.[20]

---

17 *OR* 29, pt. 2, 425. Sedgwick was the AOP's ranking corps commander and French was next in seniority.

18 Ibid; *New York Herald*, November 6, 1863. Meade assigned wing commanders based on seniority.

19 *OR* 29 pt. 2, 425; *OR* 29, pt. 1, 573-74, 608-609.

20 *OR* 29 pt. 2, 426.

A remarkable degree of secrecy cloaked Meade's plans. Not a word of the movement leaked out of headquarters, and the usually hyperactive rumor mill remained silent, perhaps because leadership had concocted the entire scheme in less than 48 hours. Col. Lyman, Meade's close confidant and aide, didn't suspect "an attack on hand" until late in the day of November 6 and then only after seeing the general "busy with maps and officers." He could merely guess that the army's target was "Kelly's Ford or thereabouts."[21]

Sedgwick and French learned the full details of their mission sometime that evening when headquarters issued meticulous instructions to the wing commanders, both of whom received copies of one another's orders. Their respective columns were directed to move at first light on November 7 and "effect a crossing" of the Rappahannock. This task would not be easy, Meade warned. Lee's army remained massed around Brandy Station, Culpeper Court House, and Stevensburg. Southern earthworks covered Kelly's Ford and Rappahannock Station, and the enemy would certainly contest all attempts to force the river. The odds of a powerful Rebel counterattack and major battle were high.

Consequently, it was essential that the Federals hit swiftly and decisively. Meade told French to attack "vigorously" and use his entire force if necessary. However, stealth and surprise were as important as power. French should conceal his march and make assault preparations as clandestinely as possible. Once Union guns secured "a lodgment on the heights overlooking" Kelly's Ford, the left wing's infantry should seize the crossing, advance over the river and move toward Brandy Station where it would link up with Sedgwick or strike Rappahannock Station's rear if the Rebels still held that place.

Sedgwick's instructions were similarly straightforward. He was to arrive at the enemy bridgehead before dark, attack "at once," drive the Confederates out of their fortifications "if practicable" and "commence operations" against their south bank defenses. Should the right wing succeed in overwhelming those positions Meade wanted Sedgwick to advance on Brandy Station. The AOP's commander shared in detail what he knew of Rappahannock Station's earthworks and made clear he remained uncertain whether they were vulnerable to assault. It was important, therefore, that Sedgwick keep in mind the "contingency" of hurrying most of his troops to Kelly's Ford and French.

Having issued these orders, Meade had committed his army to action. At 7 p.m. he wired his intentions to Halleck, sharing with him the latest intelligence and expressing belief in "a favorable result." But even as his staff prepared to relocate the army's command post to Morrisville next morning, Meade couldn't stop worrying. He knew he was taking a huge risk and walking right into the enemy's trap. But his only other option was to forego an offensive until spring, which was quite unthinkable. If Sedgwick and French performed well, if luck rode with the army, and if he surprised Lee, the plan should work. But every time Meade thought through the probabilities, those fortifications at Rappahannock Station conjured repulse and disruption.

Unable to sleep, he penned a midnight question to Sedgwick. If it proved impossible to overcome the enemy bridgehead's earthworks, did the VI Corps commander think he could "hold the fords in the vicinity of Rappahannock Station with two of your divisions and all your artillery?" Meade went on to explain the reason for his query: "If the column from Kelly's Ford advances and engages in battle, I desire to make it as strong as possible, as it will, undoubtedly, have to meet the main rebel army." Meade wanted Sedgewick's response "at once." (The dread Meade couldn't shake was that half his command would have to fight virtually all the Rebel army—just as Robert E. Lee intended. No record of Sedgwick's answer survives. One must assume that it was reassuring, although unlikely to have calmed the commanding general's nerves.)[22]

Sometime during the evening Meade sought to alleviate his tension by writing Margaret. Confessing that he found himself "in a most embarrassing position," he confided that tomorrow the army would attempt to fight its way across the Rappahannock. Although he hoped for the best, "previous experience in such operations" didn't leave him "over sanguine of success." Should the result "prove unfavorable" he fully expected Washington to hold him "responsible for the consequences" despite its having tied his hands by vetoing the Fredericksburg operation. That decision, he complained, rendered an attack against Lee's fortifications "the only practicable movement" available. If it failed, he had no idea what other course the army might pursue.

Meade was certain the press would crucify him for any defeat, even one built upon strategy he opposed. The public journals had certainly earned the general's jaundiced view of them. Editors had assailed him for one thing or another ever since his July failure to attack the Rebels at Williamsport. False accusations that he had disobeyed Halleck's order to fight rather than fall back peppered recent criticisms of the army's October withdrawal. Even now, Meade sighed, Philadelphia papers were claiming the

---

22 Previous paragraphs based upon OR 29, pt. 2, 424-25, 427-29, 326, 328, 380. No contemporary evidence indicates Meade's estimation of Rebel strength, although on October 15 he had told Halleck that Lee had 80,000 men. Halleck refuted this claim that same day citing intelligence from Richmond putting Lee's strength at 55,000. In the weeks leading up to Nov. 7, Meade received several rumors of Longstreet's return to Virginia.

administration had "peremptorily ordered" him "to advance on Lee with the penalty of supercedence [sic] if I do not obey." Halleck had issued "no such orders," the general ruefully observed, but it hardly mattered since "truthfulness is not to be expected nowadays from the press."

On October 27 Meade had admitted being "so anxious and worried" he found it difficult to author a letter home. Since then his anxiety hadn't abated. "I am in such a mental condition that I am not fit to write," he reiterated to Margaret, "indeed I try to avoid writing as much as possible." His stress seemed unrelenting. Army command was exacting an enormous toll on the general, and although he had believed he possessed a "pretty fair idea" of what that job entailed when he assumed the post, Meade now confessed that the "realities" had gone so "far beyond [his] wildest expectations" he "bitterly" regretted not "absolutely and firmly" declining the job back in June.

That point was moot, however. He had taken command "from a sense of duty and in obedience to an order," and as a good soldier he intended to continue discharging his responsibilities "in the same spirit." Although Meade would do his best, he had little hope of satisfying Lincoln or Halleck. Virtually predicting his ultimate dismissal, he told Margaret he was "prepared to submit with the same cheerfulness to the order relieving me" as he had to the one placing him in command.

Such circumstances left Meade feeling terribly alone and longing for the comforts of home and family more than usual. Thankful for his wife's sympathetic and knowing ear, he closed by telling her: "I am sure you will always stand by me and if I can only survive the storm and be once more restored to you I shall be quite indifferent to the mode of restoration and be perfectly willing to forego all honors and rewards. God bless you dearest. Don't believe for a moment I ever cease to think of you and to love you with my whole heart and soul."[23]

Whatever solace the general took from writing his beloved probably proved ephemeral. The army would march in a few hours. Only tomorrow could reveal whether he had set in motion a brilliant success or another Union disaster.

23 Previous paragraphs based on Meade to Margaret, Nov. 7, 1863 in George Gordon Meade papers, HSP.

CHAPTER 4

"Through Fire and Smoke, Mid the Shrieks of Wounded Men"

Union Advance—Kellysville—Rebel Defenses—Opening Shots—Surprised
Reaction—Ill-Fated Reinforcements—River Assault—Into Lee's Trap

As the Army of the Potomac's leaders worked and worried through the night of November 6, their troops bedded down "happy in the thought" that the campaign season had ended. There was a "general conviction" that headquarters would order everyone into winter quarters within a few days. This pleasant delusion evaporated when drummers began beating reveille at 4:30 a.m. The troops stumbled out of their tents "amazed, disappointed, drowsy," and certain, as one of them put it, that life "for the time being [was] a failure." Rather than send his regiments into a comfortable seasonable encampment, George Meade was launching them toward the Rebels.[1]

Despite their unexpected awakening, the army's veterans reacted to surprise marching orders with professional nonchalance. Hours before daylight their camps were "all astir, brilliant with fires, and bristling with preparation." Dawn broke clear and blustery as the Yankee columns began "streaming toward Dixie." Col. Lyman thought everyone looked "hearty" despite 36-degree temperatures and clouds of wind-driven dust. But even soldierly cheer couldn't hide the army's route, which pointed to the Rappahannock yet again. Some commands were heading toward their twelfth crossing of the river. One wit observed that they "had started so many times in

---

1 J. L. Smith, *History of the Corn Exchange Regiment, 118th Pennsylvania Volunteers: Antietam to Appomattox* (Philadelphia, PA, 1888), 336; Robert G. Carter, *Four Brothers in Blue* (Austin, TX, 1978), 361.

that direction and come back again like whipped puppies, the thing was getting to be a trifle monotonous."[2]

Although movement orders hadn't reached brigade level until almost midnight, the columns lurched into motion on schedule, French's III Corps exiting Warrenton Junction and Bealton Station about 7 a.m., Warren's II Corps leaving Warrenton Junction around the same time, and Newton's I Corps departing for Morrisville a bit later. Sedgwick's VI Corps began its 13-mile hike from Warrenton to Rappahannock Station at sunrise (6:52 a.m.), as did Sykes' V Corps, which moved from Three Mile Station.[3]

Tramping across well-known terrain wasn't without its revelations and the dramatic changes wrought by October's campaign shocked many men. Old landmarks had "entirely disappeared" under the skilled hands of Rebel demolition crews. Bealton Station, for example, was a "wreck of its former self," its buildings burned, telegraph poles chopped down, and railroad track destroyed. Similar scenes greeted the army everywhere it touched the O&A.[4]

It seemed highly probable that the name Kellysville would join the list of destroyed places before sunset. Located next to Kelly's Ford that town was the initial target of Meade's left wing and destined to see the day's first fighting. John Kelly had established the village in 1725, bequeathing his name to both the settlement and its nearby ford. Thanks to his business acumen and that of his descendants, Kellysville grew into Culpeper County's largest manufacturing center, boasting in 1860 a post office, general store, shoemaker, blacksmith, wheelwright, cooper shop, sawmill, clothing factory, and gristmill.

The town's antebellum prosperity faded quickly when Union forces swept into the area in mid-1862. Before their arrival, the clothing factory had shipped its looms to safety in Lynchburg. The imposing three-story brick gristmill still operated but at greatly reduced capacity, its manpower drained away by the army and its clients' fields ruined by the war. Now a shadow of its former self, Kellysville was about to become a battlefield.

---

2   Carter, *Four Brothers in Blue*, 361; Warren Goss, *Recollections of a Private* (New York, NY, 1890), 242; O. W. Norton, *Army Letters 1861-1865* (Chicago, IL, 1903), 188; Smith, *Corn Exchange Regiment*, 336. George Aggassiz, R., ed., *Meade's Headquarters 1863-1865: Letters of Colonel Theodore Lyman* (Boston, MA, 1922), 42; Krick, *Civil War Weather*, 112; Ruth L Silliker, *The Rebel Yell & the Yankee Hurrah: The Civil War Journal of a Maine Volunteer* (Camden, ME, 1985), 127.

3   OR 29, pt. 1, 561-62, 565; Carter, *Four Brothers in Blue*, 361; Bradley M. Gottfried, *Stopping Pickett: The History of the Philadelphia Brigade* (Shippensburg, PA, 1999), 185. Sunrise on Nov. 7 was 6:52 a.m. Krick, *Civil War Weather*, 112.

4   Carter, *Four Brothers in Blue*, 361.

A bit of command disarray plagued the Confederate units defending this area. The 322-man strong 2nd North Carolina guarded the Kelly's Ford sector. Its 32-year old commander, Col. William R. Cox, enjoyed an enviable reputation made at Chancellorsville, where despite five wounds he refused to leave the field until the fighting ended. Having missed Gettysburg due to his injuries Cox had returned to the army only recently. His regiment belonged to Brig. Gen. Stephen D. Ramseur's brigade which was part of Maj. Gen. Robert Rodes' division from Ewell's corps. Ramseur, however, had taken leave to get married, placing Cox in command of the brigade and Lt. Col. William Stallings in charge of the Tar Heel regiment.[5]

The 2nd North Carolina's zone of responsibility stretched from Wheatley's Ford, one mile north of Kellysville, to Mountain Run a mile and a half south of there. Cox had placed one company at each of these points and another at Stevens Ford, half a mile below Kelly's. The regiment's remaining seven companies, numbering some 225 men, manned earthworks protecting Kelly's Ford. On November 6, Stallings had deployed an advanced picket line on the Rappahannock's opposite shore as a trip wire in case enemies came looking for trouble.[6]

Kelly's Ford's well-designed fortifications were stout enough to fend off minor probes and harassment. But they could never withstand a heavy attack. High hills on the river's north side stared down on the crossing and its namesake town as if they were fish in a barrel. Any Yankee cannon placed thereon could command the ford, the village, and everything beyond it.

Behind Kellysville lay a broad, slightly broken plain, bisected by several fences and devoid of cover except for an unoccupied, partially completed two-gun redoubt. This 700-yard wide expanse of open ground rose steadily to a wooded hill which hosted the camps of Lt. Col. William W. Sillers' 30th North Carolina Infantry, numbering 500 men, and Capt. John Massie's Fluvanna Artillery. These units could assist the 2nd North Carolina if needed, but none of them were supposed to defend the ford against a heavy assault. Rather their job was to delay an attacker long enough for Rodes' division, camped a mile and a half west of the river, to prepare for action. In the event of an

---

5   Gary W. Gallagher, *Stephen Dodson Ramseur: Lee's Gallant General* (Chapel Hill, NC, 1985), 84-87; Darrell L. Collins, *Major General Robert E. Rodes of the Army of Northern Virginia: A Biography* (New York, NY, 2008), 322-23. National Archives, Complied Service Records, Col. William Cox. Also at www.fold3.com. Cox, wounded 11 times during the war, survived to serve three terms in the US House of Representatives. He died in 1919, one of the last surviving Confederate generals.

6   OR *Supplement* V, Pt. 1, 609-10; OR 29, pt. 1, 631. Stallings and Rodes say 2nd NC had 322 men in 10 companies, which averages to 32 men per company, and although undoubtedly not every company was this size, I've used it as an acceptable measure to deduce approximately how many men were at Kelly's Ford.

Robert Sneden, a cartographer on Gen. French's staff, made this post-war painting of Kellysville from a wartime sketch. The grist mill is too tall, having only three stories as opposed to the five depicted here. The earthwork occupied by Massie's battery is visible at left, as is the long slope across which the 30th North Carolina moved to reinforce the 2nd North Carolina. Rebel earthworks are apparent along the river bank. Lt. Aschmann's detachment attacked just above where the tall tree leans out toward the river. *Virginia Museum of History and Culture, Richmond, VA.*

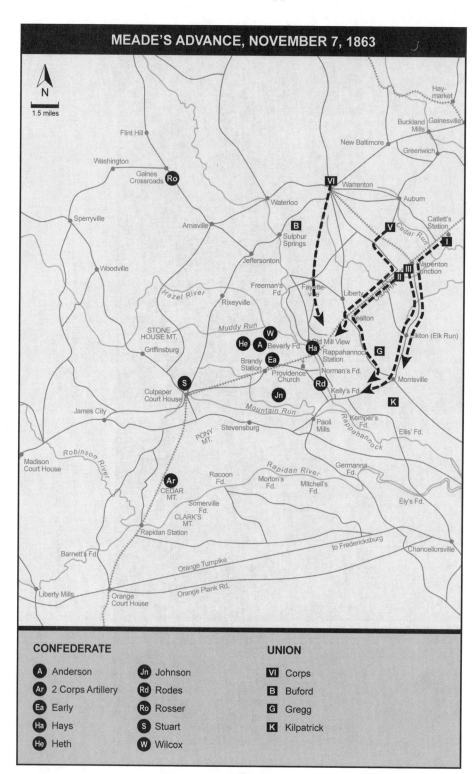

MEADE'S ADVANCE, NOVEMBER 7, 1863

N
1.5 miles

CONFEDERATE

- **A** Anderson
- **Ar** 2 Corps Artillery
- **Ea** Early
- **Ha** Hays
- **He** Heth
- **Jn** Johnson
- **Rd** Rodes
- **Ro** Rosser
- **S** Stuart
- **W** Wilcox

UNION

- **VI** Corps
- **B** Buford
- **G** Gregg
- **K** Kilpatrick

attack the duration of Rebel resistance would depend a great deal on the size of whatever enemy force assailed them.[7]

* * *

Throughout the forenoon of November 7, the 1,500 or so Confederates near Kellysville had no inkling that 29,000 Federals were trekking steadily in their direction. The Federal III Corps, temporarily under Maj. Gen. David Birney while French commanded the Left Wing, led the way, with Col. Regis de Trobriand's 3rd Brigade of Brig. Gen. John Hobart Ward's 1st Division heading the column. The 2nd US Sharpshooters provided an advance guard, while its sister regiment, the 1st US Sharpshooters, functioned as flankers. Warren's II Corps traipsed along behind Birney's men. By midday the temperature had risen into the low 60s and except for the wind, marching conditions were excellent.[8]

French's vanguard reached Mount Holly Church about a mile from Kelly's Ford around 1 p.m. A convenient ridge between the church and river screened the Federals from observation as their leading elements paused to make final preparations. Taking care to exercise the stealth Meade insisted upon, field officers prohibited drum or bugle calls and even lunchtime cook fires. Birney deployed his sharpshooter regiments as skirmishers and waited for an order to advance.[9]

The Federals' approach didn't go unnoticed. When the leading edge of French's column hove into view, Rebel sentries sent back word that the enemy was stirring. Troubled by this news, Lt. Col. Stallings rode across the river to see what was up. Reaching the scene before the main Yankee column arrived, he could see nothing more than its foremost scouts: a handful of Union cavalry and a small body of foot soldiers.

Meade's requirement that French conceal his movements now paid off. Although Stallings remained on the scene for some time, neither he nor his men detected the arrival of nearly half the Union army. Eventually concluding that he was looking at

---

7   OR *Supplement*, 609-10, OR 29, pt. 1, 631. Massie had six 12-pounder Napoleon cannon.

8   Charles Stevens, *Berdan's United States Sharpshooters in the Army of the Potomac* (St. Paul, MN, 1892), 366; Lyman, *Meade's Army*, 62; Krick, *Civil War Weather*, 112. Meade's creation of temporary wings produced a series of command changes on November 7. Ward stepped into division command when Birney took French's place at the head of the III Corps. De Trobriand assumed command of the 3rd Brigade when Ward took control of the division.

9   Heinz Meier, ed., *Memoirs of a Swiss Officer in the American Civil War* (Frankfurt, Germany, 1972), 129; John D. Billings, *The History of the Tenth Massachusetts Battery of Light Artillery in the War of the Rebellion, 1862-1865.* (Boston, MA, 1881), 112.

nothing more than a reconnaissance party, the colonel rode back to Kellysville feeling no need to advise his superiors of potential danger.

Such misapprehension suited William French just fine. The 48-year old general's portly physique, red faced complexion, and habit of blinking rapidly whenever speaking hardly suggested a dashing character. Though camp rumor labeled him a drunkard, no one ever offered up evidence proving the accusation. However, his unpopularity with III Corps veterans was unquestionable. They resented his appointment as their chief after Maj. Gen. Dan Sickles lost a leg at Gettysburg. These men thought one of their own division commanders ought to have gotten the job. Finding French a poor substitute for the rakish Sickles, most were disinclined to give their new leader much of a chance.[10]

In many ways this attitude was unfair to French. After graduating from West Point with an artillery corps commission in 1837 he earned two brevets for gallantry in Mexico, served in the Seminole War and co-authored an artillery manual with Henry Hunt and William F. Barry. French's actions during the secession crisis had marked him as a man to watch. When Texas left the Union in February 1861, he was a major stationed at Fort Duncan near Eagle Pass on the Rio Grande. Rather than surrender his command to secessionists he marched three batteries 350 miles to the Gulf of Mexico before managing to find a ship and sail them to safety at Key West, Florida.

Given an infantry brigade in September 1861, French's solid performance with the II Corps throughout the Seven Days battles earned him command of a division which he led at Antietam, Fredericksburg, and Chancellorsville. Promoted to major general in November 1862, the Baltimore native could rightly boast of having participated in the AOP's most desperate fights, including charging the sunken road at Antietam, assaulting the stone wall below Marye's Heights at Fredericksburg, and trying to blunt the Rebel onslaught at Chancellorsville. Put in charge of Harper's Ferry during the Gettysburg campaign, French had missed that action only to gain III Corps command when his division-strength garrison joined Meade during the post-battle pursuit of Lee. French's status as the AOP's third highest ranking major general led to his current assignment as a wing commander.

Although many men saw his July performance at Manassas Gap as unnecessarily cautious, since then he had done an acceptable job. If French's talent for independent command or ability to navigate uncertain tactical circumstances remained

---

10 Lowe, *Meade's Army*, 29; Silliker, *The Rebel Yell & Yankee Hurrah,,* 112; James C. Biddle to wife, August, 13, 1863, James C. Biddle Papers, HSP.

Maj. Gen. William French
Library of Congress

questionable, few doubted his capacity to oversee the kind of straight forward fighting he faced at Kelly's Ford.[11]

* * *

Satisfied by 1:30 p.m. that his subordinates had everything in order, French gave Birney the word to go ahead. A line of Federal skirmishers rose up from cover and started climbing the ridge between them and the Rappahannock. Cresting its summit, they walked out onto an open plain sloping down toward the river. An instant later Confederates opened fire from the cover of tall weeds and underbrush, their concealment so perfect the oncoming Yankees hadn't apprehended danger until bullets began "whistling" through their ranks.[12]

The outbreak of shooting rendered stealth unnecessary; any hope of tactical surprise having become moot. Freed from strictures of circumspection the sharpshooters broke into a double-quick and rushed their enemy's thin line. Having already raised the alarm Stalling's pickets gave way, rushing "pell-mell" toward the river with Federal marksmen in hasty pursuit.[13]

After splashing across Kelly's Ford the Rebel sentries sought safety inside their nearby earthworks, where they discovered surprisingly few comrades. Even while watching his men retreat, Stallings remained unclear as to the scale of threat he faced.

11 French's major general's commission made him the third ranking member of the AOP. Sedgwick received his major general's commission on July 4, 1862. Meade, Sykes and French all had a commission date of Nov. 29, 1862. Meade's brigadier general's commission (August.31, 1861) predated French and Sykes, both of who became brigadiers on September 1, 1862. French assumed command of the III Corps on July 7, 1863.

12 Stevens, *Berdan's Sharpshooters*, 367.

13 Ibid. Double-quick is a slow steady jog.

That uncertainty abated minutes later when Capt. Henry Sleeper's 10th Massachusetts Battery and Yankee infantry appeared on high ground southeast of Kellysville. It dissolved completely when more Federals materialized to the northeast along a Rappahannock tributary called Marsh Creek.

As Union cannon began swinging into position, Stallings sent couriers dashing off to alert Col. Cox, the 30th North Carolina, and Massie's artillery. Mindful of orders to hold the ford "if possible" and in defiance of the dreadful tactical circumstances imperiling his command, Stallings deployed his seven available companies to defend the crossing, Companies B, F, and K hurrying into the riverfront fortifications while the remainder took cover on some small hills just behind the earthworks. Here the North Carolinians waited to confront whatever was coming at them.[14]

* * *

That wait was short. On the other side of the Rappahannock Sleeper's six 3-inch Ordnance Rifles had already unlimbered and prepared for action. Spying a handful of horsemen galloping across the field behind Kellysville and suspecting they were Rebel officers Sleeper ordered his guns to commence firing. Their initial salvo did little more than hurry the distant riders along, but its echo accompanied the appearance of a heavy Federal skirmish line moving swiftly downhill toward the river. Unleashing a hot fire from the security of their trenches, Stalling's infantrymen forced the advancing bluecoats to take cover by ducking behind trees and rocks or scurrying into nearby ditches. Gaining this protection, the Yankees returned fire with their breech-loading Sharps rifles and soon it was "blaze away on both sides in good earnest," as one Northerner put it.[15]

Despite momentarily obstructing Meade's left wing, the Rebels were in a wretched spot. Their lightly-held position was anything but impregnable, and the crossing point untenable against serious attack. Northern cannon atop the heights overlooking Kelly's Ford enfiladed the Rebel earthworks and swept the ground in their rear. Attempting to retreat meant running a gauntlet of deadly artillery fire, as did any effort to reinforce the ford. No matter how gallantly Kellysville's defenders resisted, the only real obstacle opposing a Union advance was the Rappahannock itself.[16]

14 OR Supplement V, Pt. 1, 609-10, 611-12; OR 29, pt. 1, 631; Meier, *Memoirs of a Swiss Officer*, 129; Stevens, *Berdan's Sharpshooters*, 367; Walter Clark, ed. *Histories of the Several Regiments and Battalions from North Carolina in the Great War 1861-1865*. 5 Vols. (Goldsboro, NC, 1901), Vol. I, 171.

15 Billings, *Tenth Massachusetts Battery*, 113; OR Supplement V, Pt. 1, 609-10.

16 OR 29, pt. 1, 631.

Officers of the 10th Massachusetts Battery. Left to right: Capt. Samuel A. McClellan, Capt. J. Henry Sleeper (leaning against tree) and Capt. O'Neil W. Robinson. Harper's Weekly Special Correspondent Alfred R. Waud, standing on right, sketched Sleeper's Battery in action at Kelly's Ford. *Library of Congress*

Understanding this, Robert E. Lee had always intended no more than a delaying action at the ford for the purpose of buying his army time to deploy on more favorable ground a few miles inland. In fact, Lee *wanted* Meade to cross part of his force here and proposed giving him much grief for the effort. The potential success of that strategy required Lt. Col. Stallings to maintain his vulnerable post until the last possible moment before attempting to escape a virtually inescapable trap.

Determined to do what he could, Stallings advanced a skirmish line with orders to push Union infantry away from the river. Within seconds Sleeper's cannon and Yankee riflemen beat back that effort. Retreating into their trenches, the North Carolinians could only keep shooting at the opposite shore where, for the moment, Federal sharpshooters seemed content to stay.[17]

17 OR *Supplement* V, pt. 1, 610; Billings, *Tenth Massachusetts Battery*, 113.

US Artillery Firing on Kelly's Ford, drawn by Harper's Weekly Special Correspondent Alfred Waud. The dominating position of the Federal batteries is readily apparent. *Library of Congress*

Unfortunately for the Confederates, Union officers were hurrying to take advantage of the Rappahannock's topographical favors, and their tenuous stalemate was already unraveling. Captain George Randolph, commanding the III Corps' artillery brigade, ordered Capt. Franklin Pratt's Battery M, 1st Connecticut to take its six 4.5-inch siege guns into line on the left of Sleeper's guns. Pratt's long-range guns, like Sleeper's 3-inchers, could hit Kellysville easily and blast anything moving over the fields beyond town. Once his pieces were in position, Stalling's men were all but doomed.[18]

That doom wouldn't descend until Federal sharpshooters got over the river, however, and just now vicious enemy fire pinned down the blue marksmen. Chaffing to help the infantry, Randolph ordered Lt. John Bucklyn's Battery E, 1st Rhode Island Light Artillery to deploy within canister range of the ford. Galloping forward through a

---

18 OR 29, pt. 1, 566. The 4.5-inch siege guns were often mistakenly referred to as Rodman Siege guns.

swarm of enemy bullets, the New Englanders raced their six 12-pounder smoothbore Napoleons to a slight rise within 300 yards of the river. Unlimbering behind the sharpshooters, the battery swiftly went into action.[19]

The effect of this close-range cannon fire forced the entrenched Rebels to keep their heads down and drove the four companies outside the trenches to seek cover in Kellysville. Once there, a goodly number of men occupied the three-story brick gristmill and started sniping at Yankee cannoneers. Gen. Birney ordered Pratt's siege guns to silence these Rebel sharpshooters, and obliging Connecticut artillerists happily turned their guns against Kellysville. The battery's first shot struck the mill between a pair of second story windows, passing entirely through the building and into the woods beyond before exploding. The next few rounds did better work, one shell bursting against a corner of the mill and another crashing through its roof, sending a shower of brick dust and fragments into the air.[20]

19 Ibid, 568.

20 *OR* 29, pt. 1, 574.

*   *   *

The sound of Union artillery ripping apart Kellysville sent shock waves through the Army of Northern Virginia. Up until that moment everything had been "going on very quietly" in the various Rebel camps spread out in a great semi-circle north, east, and west of Culpeper Court House. Major General Richard H. Anderson's division had held a review that morning and as the sun passed its zenith innumerable details of men scattered across the landscape foraging animals, felling trees, collecting firewood, and hauling timber for winter quarters.

No one anticipated trouble until the bark of distant cannon broke the early afternoon calm. Although the swelling rumble announced that a "very heavy artillery duel" raged somewhere, most Southerners assumed it was one of their own batteries "taking a little practice" against Yankee pickets and thought no more about it. But once the cannonade grew too heavy and sustained for a minor skirmish, men shared puzzled looks and posed speculative questions to comrades who offered nothing but unsatisfactory answers. Only when couriers dashed into camp carrying abrupt orders to prepare for movement did everyone realize an actual crisis at hand. The Confederate cantonments instantly fell into confusion as regiments raced to assemble and quartermasters received instructions to pack up—an especially arduous task since equipment and stores lay strewn far and wide in anticipation of winter quarters.[21]

Ramseur's brigade, as unready for battle as any other Rebel outfit that afternoon, was closest to the action, its camps lying just beyond sight of the Rappahannock. The 4th North Carolina's chaplain was preaching a Saturday sermon and beginning his benediction when French's guns opened on the ford. Gray clad parishioners looked toward the river, "very much" surprised by an unexpected barrage which grew "heavier by the minute."

Enemy projectiles overshooting Kellysville suddenly came "sparkling and hissing thro' the air in every direction, exploding above and around" the camp while "scattering fragments uncomfortably near on all sides." Within minutes the "thick and fast" rattle of small arms blended into the boom of cannon, followed almost instantly by the heart-stopping notes of drummers beating the long roll. As men leapt to their feet in a scramble for weapons and accouterments, Stalling's courier reached Col. Cox carrying the now-redundant report that Yankees were attacking Kelly's Ford.

Cox forwarded this dispatch to Gen. Rodes before mounting his horse and racing toward the river. Behind him the 4th North Carolina formed column and rushed to the

21 Ibid.; Sarah Bahnson Chapman, ed., *Bright and Gloomy Days: The Civil War Correspondence of Captain Charles Frederic Bahnson, a Moravian Confederate* (Knoxville, TN, 2003), 87-90.

summit of its hilltop encampment. Before long both Cox and the Carolinians could see "the whole mischief," and a most unwelcome sight it was. The hills opposite Kellysville were lined with cannon and "glittering full of bayonets," while Yankee infantry already occupied the bottomland close alongside the river.[22]

Rodes, who had ridden forward after reading Cox's message, saw the same sight. Although glimpsing only a portion of the blue horde threatening Kelly's Ford the general immediately dispatched aides carrying orders placing the rest of his division under arms. As these riders flew westward, the appearance of more enemy infantry confirmed that this was no mere reconnaissance but a major push.

Rodes knew Lee had anticipated such an enemy movement and that it was his job to delay the Federals long enough for Johnson's division to reach the field. If these two commands could contain the enemy, the rest of the army would have a chance to come up and launch a devastating attack that might hurl the Federals into the river and destroy them. But unless Rodes and his fellow division commander had time to deploy their men that tantalizing opportunity would vanish. Ramseur's soldiers must purchase that interval with their lives if necessary.[23]

The cost of delaying the Union onslaught quickly grew painfully high. As Col. Cox came onto the field a shell fragment bruised his right shoulder and badly lacerated his face, knocking him out of action and forcing him next day into a Richmond hospital. With Cox down, command and control of Ramseur's brigade evaporated. Either word of Cox's wounding didn't reach the next senior colonel or it arrived too late to do any good. The resulting leadership vacuum soon allowed the price of looming disaster at Kellysville to rise most unnecessarily.

*   *   *

In the absence of orders or oversight, Lt. Col. Sillers brought his 30th North Carolina out of the trees sheltering its camp, advancing the regiment's battle line 100 yards down the long slope leading toward Kelly's Ford before halting it in front of the empty artillery redoubt. Leaving his troops there, the colonel rode a short distance toward the river, supposedly to find Stallings (who outranked him) and ask for instructions. Before reaching the front, however, Sillers apparently saw enough to

---

22 Previous paragraphs based on E. B. Munson, ed., *Confederate Correspondent: The Civil War Reports of Jacob Nathaniel Raymer, Fourth North Carolina* (Jefferson, NC, 2009), 102.

23 *OR* 29, pt. 1, 632.

decide what to do. Wheeling his horse around he dashed back to his men, ordered them to fix bayonets and hurry toward the Rappahannock.[24]

Although doubtless motivated by a desire to aid his fellow North Carolinians at the ford, Sillers should have resisted the impulse. A single regiment couldn't help Stallings, whose position was already hopeless, as even a casual glance at the Yankee batteries bucking and roaring along the hills made clear.

Heedless of those guns, Sillers ordered his command to the double-quick, hoping to speed it across the open quarter-mile wide field between him and the village. That proved impossible. Broken, uneven ground slowed the advance and strained the regiment's alignment. Already discombobulated from jogging over poor terrain, the Tar Heels encountered a fence running obliquely across their path. Hitting the wooden barrier *en echelon*, their line broke like a wave slicing across a rocky shore, some companies struggling to climb over the obstruction before others even reached it.[25]

The obstacle broke up Sillers' formation so completely his regiment lost all cohesion. Spotting the North Carolinians, Yankee gunners took them under a devastating fire as did Union infantry shooting across river. "Scattered and broken," the Rebels could only run for the protection of Kellysville where they might rally.

Before the 30th got there, misfortune struck again; its center encountered another fence, this one a stout affair surrounding a home on the outskirts of town. With Federal shells bursting all about, men bulled their way through this latest impediment or dashed around it. Now devoid of any organization whatsoever, Sillers' soldiers mostly sprinted for shelter behind buildings or went tumbling into cellars for protection. Some men having no stomach for shellfire or additional risk turned back towards the woods. The majority, however, found cover in the town's structures and began firing on the enemy.[26]

As Sillers' men reached Kellysville, Captain Massie's battery of six 12-pounder Napoleons galloped into the fray, swiftly traversing the open ground toward the two-gun earthwork 100 yards in front of its wooded camp. Hurriedly unlimbering, the Confederate artillerists engaged Sleeper's battery, which was busy hammering the 30th

---

24 *OR Supplement* V, pt. 1, 612; Billings, *Tenth Massachusetts Battery*, 113. An 1859 graduate of Harvard's Scientific School and an experienced officer, the 25-year old Sillers had worked his way up from 1st lieutenant to major before being wounded at Malvern Hill in July 1862. Promoted to lieutenant colonel on September 3, 1863 he cared deeply for his soldiers' welfare and many of his men viewed him as something of a father figure.

25 Ibid.

26 *OR* 29, pt. 1, 632, 568; *OR Supplement* V, Pt. 1, 612; Michael Taylor, ed., *To Drive the Enemy from Southern Soil: The Letters of Col. Francis Marion Parker and the History of the 30th Regiment North Carolina Troops.* (Dayton, OH, 1988), 303.

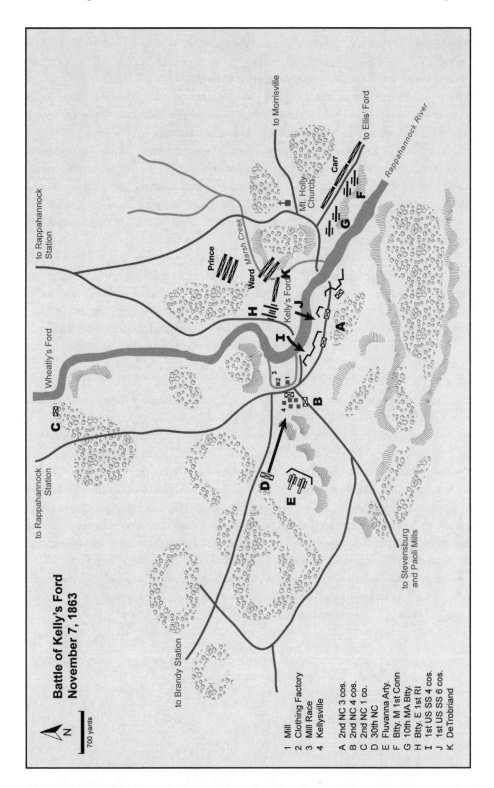

Battle of Kelly's Ford
November 7, 1863

N

700 yards

1   Mill
2   Clothing Factory
3   Mill Race
4   Kellysville

A   2nd NC 3 cos.
B   2nd NC 4 cos.
C   2nd NC 1 co.
D   30th NC
E   Fluvanna Arty.
F   Btty. M 1st Conn
G   10th MA Btty.
H   Btty. E 1st RI
I   1st US SS 4 cos.
J   1st US SS 6 cos.
K   DeTrobriand

to Rappahannock Station
to Rappahannock Station
to Morrisville
to Ellis' Ford
Rappahannock River
Carr
Mt. Holly Church
Prince
Ward   Marsh Creek
Kelly's Ford
Wheatly's Ford
to Brandy Station
to Stevensburg and Paoli Mills

North Carolina and Kellysville. Totally absorbed in that task the Massachusetts gunners didn't notice Massie until hearing an unexpected but familiar crack from beyond the town. Federal cannoneers shifted their gaze in time to see a white "puff of smoke and catch sight of a black speck rising against the sky." That dot was a Rebel shell and transfixed Union artillerymen watched it grow relentlessly bigger until it struck the ground just in front of their guns and ricocheted over their heads.[27]

The Confederates had the range from the first shot, no doubt having calculated the trajectory from their earthwork to the hill many weeks ago. A second projectile screeched over the Federals and a third crashed into a fallen tree just behind the Massachusetts battery. The enemy's angle of fire gave Sleeper's New Englanders the rare and unsavory opportunity of watching virtually every round leave its tube and fly rapidly in their direction.

Nonplused by this experience, the veteran Northern gunners forgot about Sillers' forlorn regiment and turned their attention toward Massie's cannon. During the dramatic duel that followed, one Federal shell exploded directly between two Rebel guns; seconds later a Southern solid shot reciprocated and tore into the ground between a pair of Yankee limbers. Another Confederate shell bounced off the earth, fracturing an ammunition chest and slicing through a bundle of clothing strapped to its exterior before coming oddly to rest, without exploding, between a pair of spare boots.[28]

Despite such good shooting, the Fluvanna Artillery speedily found itself in serious trouble. The Federals had a superior position and rifled guns to take on Massie's smoothbores, only two of which found protection in the partially completed redoubt. Already overmatched by Sleeper's battery, the Rebels quickly drew the attention of Pratt and Bucklyn, who each turned their fieldpieces against the Virginians. Facing a concentrated bombardment from 16 Yankee cannons, Massie tried shifting his battery to another position hoping to better answer the Union fire. As his men limbered their pieces, shells from Pratt's siege artillery began exploding nearby as if to highlight the Southerner's precarious position. Out-ranged and out-gunned, Massie recognized that continuing the fight would destroy his battery. And though it had fired only 10–12 rounds per gun, the captain ordered his command back into the woods from which it had sallied a short time ago. The price of its brief foray: one man mortally wounded, another severely hurt, seven slightly injured and three horses killed.[29]

---

27 OR 29, pt. 1, 572, 568-69; Billings, *Tenth Massachusetts Battery*, 114.

28 Billings, *Tenth Massachusetts Battery*, 115-16.

29 OR 29, pt. 1, 574, 636.

The Fluvanna artillery's fate foretold that of the Rebel infantry. Observing the 30th North Carolina's disorganized mass sheltering among Kellysville buildings, Stallings told Sillers to withdraw his men to their starting point. They were contributing little but casualties to the ford's defense and were of no use in their current condition. Having unsuccessfully tried to reform his troops several times already, Sillers accepted his superior's logic and ordered a retreat.[30]

Withdrawing across the shell-swept field behind Kellysville required no small amount of desperate courage. Nonetheless, two-thirds of the 30th North Carolina headed for the woods, although admittedly making the dash in "considerable confusion." The remaining third of the regiment—some 180 men—recoiled from the challenge, refusing to budge despite officers' pleas and Union shells battering Kellysville to pieces. For some time, Lt. Col. Sillers endeavored to "get all [his] men out" but finally gave up the task as hopeless and made his own way back to the woods, regretfully leaving Stallings' regiment to its fate.[31]

*   *   *

As Union artillerists chased away Massie's guns and wrecked Sillers' reinforcement attempt, Maj. Gen. Birney pondered the evolving situation. Federal cannon had isolated the ford and pinned down its defenders. But shellfire alone wouldn't drive the enemy from his works. Only infantry could do that, and the time seemed ripe to strike. Trotting over to his lead brigade, Birney found Col. de Trobriand and ordered him to take Kelly's Ford. The highly competent Frenchman-turned-New Yorker had seven regiments under his command just now—his own five and the attached 20th Indiana and 2nd US Sharpshooters. All these units lay massed behind a "roll in the ground" near the river, save the two sharpshooter units already engaged near the ford.[32]

De Trobriand tapped Lt. Col. Casper Trepp's 1st US Sharpshooters to lead the attack, not only because this unit was closest to the enemy but also because its 33-year-old Swiss-born leader was one of the army's most experienced soldiers. Before

30 OR *Supplement* V, Pt. 1, 610, 612.

31 Ibid., 612; *OR* 29, pt. 1, 630-31. Although Brig. Gen. Ward commanded the 1st Division while Birney led the III Corps, Birney seems to have bypassed him during the Kelly's Ford fight and issued orders directly to brigade commanders.

32 Regis de Trobriand, *Four Years With the Army of the Potomac* (Boston, MA, 1889), 548; George Lewis, *Battery E, First Rhode Island Light Artillery 1861-1865* (Providence, RI, 1892), 237. Birney had temporary command of the III Corps while French led the left wing, but at Kelly's Ford it appears he ran his own division and only assumed a larger role once the Federals got over the river.

immigrating to the United States he had served as a drill master in Gen. Giuseppe Garibaldi's Italian nationalist army and fought in the Crimean War as a British infantry captain and engineer. In 1861 he helped Hiram Berdan recruit and train the sharpshooter regiments, and many people credited Trepp as the real brains behind those organizations. A veteran of most of the army's battles, the colonel knew his business and if anyone could successfully shepherd a daring charge across a heavily defended river it was him. Once Trepp breached the ford, the rest of de Trobriand's brigade would surge over the Rappahannock and exploit the breakthrough.[33]

Recognizing his assignment as an invitation to slaughter, Trepp had no intention of dashing headlong into Rebel musketry. Instead he would send Lt. Rudolf Aschmann with companies B, C, G, and I to cross the river a few hundred yards north of the ford. Trepp guessed (perhaps hoped is a better word) that enemy defenses there were minimal and far less deadly than those at the ford itself. Aschmann's job was to get over the river quickly and outflank the primary Rebel fortifications. If the attack succeeded, his men could disrupt the Confederate line and materially facilitate the main assault.[34]

It was a good plan—if it worked—and as Trepp's marksmen nerved themselves for the effort Aschmann hurried his four companies into position. This didn't take long, although the delay seemed interminable to expectant sharpshooters crouching in assault positions. Once in place, the lieutenant waited for Federal artillery to shift fire back onto the ford and as soon as it did, he ordered a charge.

Jumping up from cover and racing down to the waterline, Companies C and I plunged into the river, while companies B and G poured a rapid fire into the opposite bank. Momentarily taken aback by the Rappahannock's cold, waist-deep water and swift current, Aschmann's men soon discovered that they hadn't surprised the Confederates at all. As the Yankees struggled through the water a North Carolina sharpshooter detachment rose up from concealed rifle pits along the riverbank to deliver a "galling fire" into the attackers.[35]

The blast shot down 10 men in midstream, but the Southerners had taken a tactical gamble with their action, counting on one fearsome volley to sow enough devastation in enemy ranks to buy time for reloading and delivering a second murderous fusillade. The gamble failed. During the vital 20 or so seconds it took the Southerners to reload, Aschmann's men closed on the riverbank and got below the Southerners' line of sight. Now forced to stand fully erect to shoot, the Rebels couldn't aim without exposing

33 "Officers of Berdan's Sharpshooter Regiments," http://berdansharpshooter.org/officers.htm, accessed 3-17-19; de Trobriand, *Four Years*, 548.

34 Meier, *Memoirs of a Swiss Officer*, 129; Lewis, *Battery E*, 237.

35 Meier, *Memoirs of a Swiss Officer*, 129.

themselves to the deadly fire of companies B and G. Most of the Carolinians understandably declined to take that chance, and the attackers gained the river's southern bank without further loss.[36]

The soaked Federal marksmen huddled against the muddy bank for a few minutes, gasping for air. But once his men caught their breath, Lt. Aschmann ordered a charge on the Rebel trenches. Assailed from the front and pinned down by accurate musketry from across the river, the outnumbered defenders began surrendering.

Sadly, capitulation in the heat of battle isn't always a safe bet. Men spun up on surging adrenalin sometimes reacted instinctively to hostile uniforms rather than recognize a surrender attempt. One such Federal fired his weapon into a rifle pit filled with helpless Rebels waving their hats in submission. The round tore "through one man's head and into another's shoulder, killing both." Luckily, this lamentable incident didn't ignite a massacre, and the shooting stopped long enough for the remaining Confederates to give up.[37]

With Companies C and I in control of the opposite bank, Aschmann's remaining troops crossed the river. Pausing only long enough to secure his prisoners, the lieutenant led his little command downstream to strike the left flank of Kelly's Ford. Seeing this movement Gen. Birney ordered Col. Trepp to launch a frontal attack across the river with his remaining six companies. Rather unexpectedly, however, the elite Northern marksmen wouldn't budge. Veterans to a man, they suspected Rebels hiding in thick underbrush along the enemy shore were waiting to deliver a lethal fire the moment Union troops started forward. Hardly anxious to take foolish risks, the battle wise sharpshooters "very naturally hesitated to advance."[38]

*   *   *

David Birney disapproved such prudence. Trailed by orderlies, the 38-year old general had spent most of the firefight displaying the cool disregard for danger that enlisted men expected and officers believed fortified soldier courage. While waiting for the ordered assault to begin, he gathered his staff near Bucklyn's battery where it could observe the coming charge.

Indifferent to the pounding they were taking, Rebel snipers inside Kelly's Mill had kept the Rhode Island gunners under a steady fire since they first unlimbered. Now the graycoats began plunking Minié bullets into the ground close to Birney's entourage,

---

36 Ibid.

37 Stevens, *Berdan's Sharpshooters*, 369.

38 Lewis, *Battery E*, 239.

Maj. Gen. David Birney
Library of Congress

giving it attention that the Alabama-born, Northern-raised general didn't appreciate. His father, James B. Birney, had converted from slave holder to radical abolitionist well before the war, twice run for the presidency on the Liberty Party ticket, and bequeathed to his son an anti-slavery zeal. After graduating from Phillips Academy in Massachusetts, David Birney built a successful law practice, and had started studying military science as the sectional crisis worsened. He became a lieutenant colonel soon after the conflict began and in February 1862 gained a brigadier's star.

Although political influence gifted Birney his initial rank, he displayed a talent for command which earned him a division and promotion to major general in September 1862. Lyman described the Pennsylvanian as a "pale, Puritanical figure, with a demeanor of unmovable coldness," a "spare" body, "thin face, light-blue eye and sandy hair." Deep-set pupils, a straight nose, drooping mustache and prominent chin beard conferred on Birney a stern, warrior-like visage. Though respecting and appreciating his battlefield skill, Birney's troops found their general a chilly character. Private John Haley said he looked like "a graven image," who "could act as a bust for his own tomb being utterly destitute of color" and "as expressionless as Dutch cheese."[39]

Today, however, bedeviled by Rebel sharpshooters, his statuesque persona came alive. Furious at the continuing harassment of Bucklyn's gunners and his own exposure, Birney decided enough was enough. The time had come to end this business. Having ordered an assault, but with no attack seemingly forthcoming, he galloped forward to find out why. Locating Trepp, the highly "irritated" general used "superlatives" not found in "the military tactics or the church catechism" to "very forcibly" demand an immediate charge. This furious verbal assault did the trick, and seconds later 120 or so sharpshooters leapt from cover and rushed the river.[40]

---

39 Ezra J. Warner, *Generals in Blue: The Lives of the Union Commanders* (Baton Rouge, LA, 1964), 34; Haley, *Rebel Yell and Yankee Hurrah*, 39; Bill Hyde, *The Union Generals Speak: The Meade Hearings on the Battle of Gettysburg* (Baton Rouge, LA, 2003), 146-48.

40 The strength of the 1st USSS is uncertain. Between them the 1st and 2nd USSS took 450 men into battle at Gettysburg where they lost 89 members to all causes. By November 1863 the

Dashing into the water they met a furious fire. Rebel rounds not thudding into men raised small geysers as the Yankees half-ran, half-waded through the swirling current. Although it seemed longer to men struggling through water, they reached the far shore swiftly. Thundering up the riverbank the sharpshooters hurled themselves onto the Rebel parapets, initiating a vicious close quarters struggle.

At that same instant Lt. Aschmann's four companies struck the Confederate left, getting to within ten feet of the enemy rifle pits before the Southerners unleashed a point-blank volley that flew just a hair too high and thus scored few hits. Once again taking advantage of their enemy's need to reload the Yankees rushed the entrenchments. Luckily for the Federals so many graycoats had crowded into these works they couldn't work their ramrods and cartridge boxes efficiently. That difficulty allowed Aschmann's sharpshooters to swiftly gain the trench's edge unhurt. Pointing breechloaders down at a crowded mass of 80 Rebels holding half-loaded muskets, the Federals demanded surrender.

Recognizing their hopeless position most of the Confederates dropped their weapons. One North Carolina sergeant refused to quit, however, and demanded his comrades pick up their muskets and "drive the Yankees back!" Northerner soldiers promptly killed him, although admitting afterwards they admired his "gritty" performance.

The struggle for the remaining rifle pits was, if anything, more violent than the first. Despite the futility of their circumstances Stallings' men fought on, selling their lives dearly. The equally determined Federals drove home their assault, finally taking the enemy trenches "through fire and smoke, mid groans and shrieks of wounded men, some bayoneted; others blown through by opposing rifles."[41]

Once the earthworks fell, the Northerners turned toward Kellysville. Realizing he couldn't hold the town with the ford lost, Stallings ordered a retreat. After darting through a hail of enemy artillery fire, he and most of the 2nd North Carolina's survivors reached safety. In sharp contrast, 140 men from the 30th North Carolina refused to withdraw and clung to shelter in Kellysville where they capitulated as soon as Union troops entered the town.[42]

Federal guns finally fell silent as the tail-most of Stalling's fugitives disappeared into the woods. The entire fight had consumed just two hours and Birney's final assault a mere 30 minutes. For the soldiers engaged, it had seemed a lifetime.

With Kelly's Ford won, the rest of de Trobriand's brigade moved rapidly to consolidate its success. French ordered a pontoon train forward, and Federal engineers

---

1st USSS probably numbered about 200 soldiers and the 2nd USSS (which had only 8 companies) around 150. Stevens, *Berdan's Sharpshooters*, 367-373; OR 27, pt. 1, 514-519.

41 Previous paragraphs based on Stevens, *Berdan's Sharpshooters*, 369.

42 *OR* 29, pt. 1, 633, Stevens, *Berdan's Sharpshooters*, 369-71.

The 1st United States Sharpshooters storm across Kelly's Ford. Alfred Waud. *Library of Congress*

were soon launching boats and laying planks. By 3 p.m. Birney's entire division was on the Rappahannock's southern shore. Three hours later the engineers finished their first bridge and began work on another.[43]

The Federals had suffered 42 casualties, including seven dead, one of them a victim of friendly artillery fire, in the brief battle. French reported taking 300 prisoners and burying 40 enemy corpses. Apparently, his troops didn't go out of their way to comb the battlefield for others. Days later, members of the III Corps' staff discovered at least 3 or 4 additional Confederate bodies.[44]

Rodes reported at least 5 dead, 59 wounded and 295 missing in Ramseur's brigade. Massie's artillery listed 9 men wounded, one fatally. Rebel fatalities totaled at least 45. Just how many of the missing had been killed or wounded was uncertain.[45]

---

43 OR 29, pt. 2, 431.

44 OR 29, pt. 1, 569, 633; Charles F. Bryan, Jr. & Nelson D. Lankford, *Eye of the Storm* (New York, 2000), 138.

45 OR 29, pt. 1, 617, 630-33; 636; Taylor, *Drive the Enemy From Southern Soil*, 305; "30th NC," www.civilwardata.com/active/hdsquery.dll?RegimentCasualty?140&C&1&41&20, Mar. 17,

But if casualty lists remained murky, not so the damage suffered by Kellysville. Projectiles had shot away half the gristmill's chimney, riddled its roof, and put a 20-foot crack into the building's upper exterior. Several homes showed heavy damage while the abandoned clothing factory was "shattered very much." Over the following days Union troops would dismantle the town's fences for firewood, empty the mill of flour, and confiscate every hog, chicken, or cow in sight.[46]

*   *   *

Kellysville's misery was incidental to larger events. Aided by Yankee artillery, French's men had neatly executed Meade's opening stratagem, but the campaign's next steps remained in doubt. Robert E. Lee had foreseen this Federal move weeks ago, and

---

2019; *New York Herald*, Nov. 11, 1863, lists the seriously wounded CS prisoners sent to Washington hospitals. Postwar analysis shows that the 30th NC suffered 187 casualties: 10 killed/mortally wounded, 10 injured, and 156 prisoners (146 uninjured). One recent conscript deserted. Deducting these numbers from Rodes' total gives a 2nd North Carolina loss of 166 men. Seven of these reached a hospital; the Federals killed at least 43, leaving a total of 116 captives, 2 of whom were mortally and another 9 seriously wounded.

46 Bryan, *Eye of the Storm*, 139.

although its actual timing caught his army unawares, the general's pre-planned response was already underway. Even as Union engineers laid their bridges, Rodes was hastening into a blocking position, Johnson's division was hurrying to reinforce him, and the five artillery battalions in Ewell's corps were preparing to depart their Cedar Mountain camps south of Culpeper Court House and head to Stevensburg.[47]

Despite their losses, Ramseur's regiments were busily bluffing along the hills west of Kellysville, moving to the edge of the woods sheltering their camps as if to counterattack, drawing fire from Sleeper or Pratt, then fading back into the trees. Behind this ruse Rodes deployed his brigades. Uncertain whether the enemy would strike toward Brandy Station or Stevensburg, he posted units to cover both possibilities. Anchoring his left flank on the Rappahannock, Rodes drew a line running from Wheatley's Ford to just south of the Stevensburg road, stationing Brig. Gen. Junius Daniel's North Carolina brigade on the division's right flank.[48]

Rodes hoped to counterattack before the Yankee bridgehead solidified. By the time his men were in place, however, the number of Federals massed in their front precluded any successful assault. Deciding to delay offensive action until the momentarily expected arrival of Johnson's division, already ordered into the field by Ewell, Rodes confined himself to keeping a close eye on enemy movements. As he anticipated, the Yankees ignored Stevensburg and began pressing toward Brandy Station in an evident attempt to threaten Rappahannock Station from the rear. Parrying this move by hurrying Daniel's brigade from his right to his left, Rodes made "every arrangement. . .to give the enemy a warm reception."[49]

As the sun touched the western horizon desultory artillery fire continued all along the front. Eventually the rival skirmishers drew close enough to engage, their muzzle flashes stabbing at one another in the developing twilight. This sparring did little harm except when a stray bullet found its mark. Lt. Col. Sillers of the 30th North Carolina was among ten Confederates who fell that evening, the much-admired officer suffering a mortal wound when a bullet pierced both his lungs.[50]

Johnson's division arrived on the field shortly after dark. Quickly forming on Rodes' right, it extended the Rebel line all the way to Mountain Run. Although the day

---

47 Dozier, *A Gunner in Lee's Army*, 216; William H. Runge, ed., *Four Years in the Confederate Artillery: The Diary of Private Henry Robinson Berkeley* (Richmond, VA, 1991), 60. Cedar Mountain was the site of the August 9, 1862 battle between Stonewall Jackson and Nathaniel Banks.

48 OR 29, pt. 1, 632, Stevens, *Berdan's Sharpshooters*, 372-73.

49 Ibid.

50 OR 29, pt. 1, 633; OR Supplement V, Pt. 1, 613; Taylor, *Drive the Enemy From Southern Soil*, 304; Gary F. Williams to Dr. Holmes, Nov. 11, 1863, Sillers-Homes Family Correspondence, Manuscripts of the American Civil War, University of Notre Dame.

had seen some tense hours, the ANV finally had a continuous line facing French. The unfortunate affair at Kelly's Ford aside, nothing other than some low-lying terrain near an indefensible river crossing had fallen into enemy hands.[51]

At 5:10 p.m. French amplified his earlier dispatch to Meade: Birney's troops were probing the enemy's line behind an earthwork in some woods cutting across the road to Brandy Station. Brigadier General Joseph Carr's 3rd Division was crossing the newly laid pontoon bridge, but nightfall precluded doing much more than preparing to push ahead in the morning. Still, the left wing's commander sounded confident. Unaware of Sedgwick's circumstances at Rappahannock Station, he assured Meade there was ample room to deploy the VI and V corps west of Kelly's Ford should Meade shift them in that direction. French promised to "force the fighting as early tomorrow as the troops can see" though he warned that the coming contest would prove a "bushwhacking affair" until he broke into open ground around the O&A.[52]

The Confederates were also confident. Lee's plan remained intact. So long as he held in check the Yankees who had appeared before Rappahannock Station that afternoon, Meade's army remained divided and opportunity beckoned. Tomorrow the ANV would either throw the bulk of its strength against French or go storming out of their north bank bridgehead to cut its enemy's line of communication.[53]

As darkness embraced Virginia's landscape it looked like everything would turn out all right. The Rebels had stumbled slightly at Kelly's Ford, but it was highly probable they would more than make up for it tomorrow. The first major battle between Meade and Lee since Gettysburg appeared only hours away.

51 *OR* 29, pt. 1, 633.

52 Ibid., 209; Frank L. Byrne and Andrew T. Weaver, *Haskell of Gettysburg: His Life and Civil War Papers* (Madison, WI, 1970), 230. By nightfall, two III Corps divisions were over the river. Its remaining division under Henry Prince crossed after dark.

53 *OR* 29, pt. 1, 612.

"A Glorious Pageant of Real War"

Meade Anxious—John Sedgwick—Rappahannock Station—Alarm Sounded—Cautious
Gambit—Union Advance—Missed Chance—Closing on the Bridgehead—Skirmishers'
Duel—Bombardment—Reinforcements—Lee's Calculation—Early's Concern

GEORGE Meade remained at headquarters long enough on the morning of November 7 to ensure his army got moving without a hitch. Finally satisfied, he headed for Warrenton Junction. Reaching there about 9:30 a.m., he paused for some time to receive progress reports. Once reassured all was going well, the general moved south, following the wrecked railroad's path until he reached a "smoke stained chimney" which represented all that remained of Bealton Station. Finding Warren standing beside his horse watching the II Corps march past, Meade stopped to share the view. Since the station's skeleton sat atop a hill, the generals could see a long way and in every direction. Troops, batteries and wagons swarmed over the countryside. An impressed Lyman thought the display of "muskets glittering in the sun" above the "great, black" infantry columns made a "fine sight."

Still riding high from his Bristoe Station performance three weeks ago, Warren bubbled with enthusiasm. Seemingly never in want of confidence and anxious to burnish his reputation, the recently-minted corps commander looked forward to a fight. Although the most junior of the army's major generals, he spoke as though he oversaw the left wing rather than French. Climbing into the saddle he turned to Lyman before riding off after his troops and boldly announced "as soon as I get there I shall bring on a general action right off."

Meade left Bealton Station not long after his eager subordinate. Traveling east towards Morrisville he turned south a little short of the village and headed toward a farm pre-selected for his command post. As he cantered along in the warming sunshine the sound of light skirmish fire welled-up from the vicinity of Rappahannock Station. By 1:30 p.m., when the general was halfway to his destination, he could see battle smoke coiling into the air near Mount Holly Church, some two and a half miles away. A few moments later the echo of cannon drifted in from Kelly's Ford.[1]

These telltale signs were encouraging, indicating that Sedgwick and French had reached their targets and promptly engaged the enemy. More definitive news arrived around 4 p.m. when Meade received an hour old dispatch from French confirming his capture of Kelly's Ford. The III Corps already had a division over the Rappahannock and more units wading across. Engineers were bringing up their pontoon train and would have a bridge down soon. Hopefully French could push farther inland before nightfall and get most of his men south of the stream by early dawn on November 8.[2]

These gratifying developments were hardly unexpected. The geographic realities near Kellysville had always ensured a successful assault there. Nonetheless, French's initial triumph was merely the first step in a far more dangerous game, placing half the Union army within reach of a counterattack by Lee's entire force. If the Rebels struck while the AOP remained divided, the outnumbered corps at Kelly's Ford would fight with their backs to a river only a few miles away. Meade found it easy to imagine disaster in such a scenario.

Uniting the army was his sole means of avoiding such a battle, and there were only two ways to do that. Sedgwick could either bludgeon his way over the river at Rappahannock Station or contain its bridgehead with minimal force while transferring most of his troops to French. Since the latter course would take considerable time and risk Lee's storming out of his fortifications to try severing the army's O&A supply line, Meade much preferred the first option. Regardless, he couldn't afford a long wait before deciding what to do. He wanted to give Sedgwick sufficient time to take his objective, but if that effort stalled, Meade needed to order most of the right wing toward Kelly's Ford sooner rather the later.

. To his consternation, however, by late afternoon he had heard nothing from Sedgwick. Beyond the rumble of distant artillery fire, which could mean anything, Meade knew nothing about affairs at Rappahannock Station. Understandably anxious, he felt a pressing need for information. French's report exacerbated uncertainty. Now that half the army was walking knowingly into Lee's suspected trap, Meade's sense of urgency grew with each passing minute. Acutely conscious that any delay in

---

1 Previous paragraphs based on Lowe, *Meade's Army*, 62; Aggassiz, *Meade's Headquarters*, 42-43. Meade had his HQ 3 miles from Warrenton Junction (modern day Calverton, VA) and a half mile north of the Warrenton Branch RR. It took him 30 minutes to ride to Warrenton Junction that morning. Meade established headquarters on the Carter farm. Soldier letters and diaries sometimes called Morrisville Morristown.

2 *OR* 29, pt. 2, 430.

Maj. Gen. John Sedgwick
Library of Congress

concentrating his command might prove catastrophic, he instructed Maj. Gen. Humphreys to inquire after Sedgwick's status.

In a 4 p.m. dispatch, the army's chief of staff relayed news of French's progress and then got right to the point. "The indications are that the battle will be fought within a mile of Kelly's Ford," he told Sedgwick. Meade wanted to "know the condition of things in your front." Headquarters also needed information on the number and disposition of Confederate forces at Rappahannock Station. If the right wing's commander wasn't "confident of being able to cross" the river soon, he should stand ready to reinforce Kelly's Ford after dark. As the courier carrying this urgent message galloped away, Meade and Humphreys could only hope Sedgwick had things well in hand and that they would hear from him shortly.[3]

* * *

The great grandson of a Revolutionary War general and still a bachelor at 50, John Sedgwick was honest, likable, and witty. Col. Lyman described him as a "stout, sturdy man, with a bright kindly eye and a face full of intelligence." Lieutenant Frank Haskell noted his "florid complexion. . . curly short chestnut hair," and close-cut beard with "a little gray in it." Addicted to playing "endless games of solitaire," he could be stern in action. Nonetheless his men loved him, calling him "Uncle John" in appreciation of his courage, lack of pretension and attention to their well-being.[4]

---

3   Ibid. Meade suggested Sedgwick consider crossing at Norman's Ford if he couldn't take Rappahannock Station. However, that ford was well-defended by Confederate earthworks.

4   Lyman, *Meade's Army*, 47; Larry Tagg, *The Generals of Gettysburg: The Leaders of America's Greatest Battle* (Campbell, CA, 1998), 103. Sedgwick graduated 24th out of 50 in a West Point class that included Joe Hooker and Confederate generals Braxton Bragg, Jubal Early and John Pemberton.

Born in Cornwall, Connecticut, during the War of 1812, Sedgwick obtained an appointment to West Point in 1833. Following graduation, he served in virtually every major army operation before 1860: combating Seminoles in Florida, moving the Cherokee west of the Mississippi, battling Cheyenne, Kiowa, and Comanche on the frontier, fighting under Winfield Scott in Mexico, enduring the Mormon Expedition, and helping tamp down sectional conflict in Kansas. Through it all he earned a reputation for steadfastness and won three promotions along the way.

A colonel and assistant inspector general when the Civil War broke out, Sedgwick missed First Bull Run due to illness, but gained a general's star in August 1861 prior to leading a brigade and ultimately a division in the 1862 Peninsula Campaign. He saw action at Yorktown and Seven Pines before, like Meade, suffering two wounds at Glendale. Those injuries kept him out of Second Bull Run but didn't deter his promotion to major general on July 4.

The September 1862 fight at Antietam nearly cost Sedgwick his life after II Corps commander Maj. Gen. Edwin V. Sumner committed the Connecticut native's division to action so ineptly it lost half its men in 15 minutes. Sedgwick took three bullets in short order, one fracturing his wrist, another piercing a leg and a third ripping into his shoulder and knocking him unconscious. He escaped capture only because stretcher bearers carried him from the field. Although a three-month hospital stay spared Sedgwick participation in the Fredericksburg debacle, leadership turmoil following that defeat opened the door for his appointment as VI Corps commander in February 1863.

This assignment surprised those who doubted his worthiness for enlarged responsibilities. Given Sedgwick's utterly pedestrian record provost marshal Marsena Patrick feared the recently healed general wasn't "good enough" for his new position. Such concerns appeared vindicated in May 1863, when Hooker divided his army during the Chancellorsville campaign and put a large part of it under Sedgwick's command, much as Meade was doing now.[5]

Taking most of his troops to turn Lee's left flank, Hooker directed Sedgwick to use 40,000 men in the VI and I Corps to fix Rebel attention on Fredericksburg. Despite a cautious performance, the recently promoted commander managed to hold the enemy's attention for two days. At that point, however, Confederate leaders called his bluff and moved the entire ANV save Jubal Early's division to face Hooker.

After Lee used Stonewall Jackson's corps to crush Hooker's right flank, 'Fighting Joe' called on Sedgwick to save the day by attacking Lee's rear. Although garbled, contradictory orders and communications breakdowns complicated his efforts, Sedgwick eventually pushed the badly outnumbered Rebels off Marye's Heights. His

5 Tagg, *Generals of Gettysburg*, 104. David S. Sparks, ed. *Inside Lincoln's Army: The Diary of Marsena Rudolph Patrick, Provost Marshall General, Army of the Potomac* (New York, 1964), 238.

subsequent advance proved so slow, however, that Lee had time to shift troops from Hooker's to Sedgwick's front where a Confederate counterattack at Salem Church drove the VI Corps back against the Rappahannock. Only hard fighting, bad terrain, and Southern command difficulties allowed the Federals to escape across the river.[6]

In Chancellorsville's wake Hooker tried shifting blame for defeat onto his subordinates, including Sedgwick. It didn't work, largely because VI Corps troops had successfully stormed the same Rebel fortifications that had resisted the entire Union army last December. Although that triumph masked Sedgwick's lackluster showing in the aftermath of his assault, nothing he had done since had really redeemed his disappointing performance. The VI Corps reached Gettysburg last, and beyond detaching brigades to assist other commands, it had played little part in the battle.[7]

Nonetheless, after the July death of Maj. Gen. John F. Reynolds and Maj. Gen. Hancock's wounding, many considered Sedgwick the army's best surviving corps commander. Meade clearly liked him, appreciating both his military skill and professional support. When someone suggested making Sedgwick army commander after Chancellorsville, he had proclaimed that Meade ought to have the job and announced his willingness to serve under him even though his own major general's commission pre-dated the Pennsylvanian's by almost 5 months. When Lincoln finally assigned Meade the post, Sedgwick was the first to congratulate him.

Although the VI Corps was well-drilled, highly disciplined, and reliable, its leader hadn't exactly earned his reputation as a superior combat commander. Brigadier General Horatio G. Wright, who led its 1st division, thought his boss "a good soldier, but not a great soldier." And while Hooker bore chief responsibility for the Chancellorsville defeat, his critique of Sedgwick had some merit. The general had indeed moved far too cautiously, thus missing opportunities to quickly overwhelm topographically strong but weakly held positions. He would face a similar challenge on November 7 and react in a similar way.[8]

*   *   *

Loosely speaking, Sedgwick's target was Rappahannock Station, a relatively new locale not even in existence until O&A work crews built a bridge over the

6 For an excellent examination of Sedgwick's operations see Chris Mackowski and Kristopher D. White, *Chancellorsville's Forgotten Front: The Battles of Second Fredericksburg and Salem Church, May 3, 1863* (El Dorado, CA, 2013). Hooker ordered the I Corps to the Chancellorsville front before Sedgwick's assault on Maryes' Heights.

7 Mackowski & White, *Chancellorsville's Forgotten Front*, 320.

8 William B. Styple, *Generals in Bronze* (Kearny, NJ, 2005), 210.

Rappahannock River in 1851. The small village of Bowenville had sprung up aside and immediately west of the railway depot before the war, but Federal troops burned most of its buildings in July 1862 and the Confederates destroyed what was left in October 1863. A road paralleling the river passed close by Rappahannock Station, connecting Freeman's Ford to the northwest and Kelly's Ford to the southeast. Known as the Riverside or Freeman's Ford Road, it ran about a half mile north of the stream and roughly 200 yards beyond the fortified ridge outlining Lee's bridgehead. Slightly sunken from decades of use and erosion, this route intersected with another road leading down to the river and which passed through the Confederate perimeter's midsection.[9]

Rappahannock Station resided in farm country, with only a few communities breaking up the lush landscape. The closest was a hamlet called Old Mill View, a tiny place, located about a half mile west of Bowenville. It sat at the junction of two roads, one leading to Freeman's Ford and the other veering northwest to Lawson's Ford and a small burg called Foxville. A thoroughfare stretching south from Warrenton via Fayetteville met the Lawson's Ford road a few miles northwest of Old Mill View, and it was along this route that the AOP's VI Corps was marching to assail Lee's bridgehead. The impending confrontation would mark the war's third clash of arms near the railroad bridge.[10]

*   *   *

Rappahannock Station endured its first bout of combat on March 28, 1862 when Federal forces under Brig. Gen. Oliver Otis Howard probed toward Culpeper Court House after Gen. Joseph E. Johnston withdrew his army from Manassas Junction into central Virginia. Confederate cavalry led by Jeb Stuart and Southern infantry under Richard Ewell, both brigadiers, fought a delaying action against the Yankees as they pushed down the O&A toward the railroad bridge.

In a scene worthy of Hollywood, Union artillery shells burst above the landscape as Ewell's rearguard leapt aboard a waiting train and black smoke coiled skyward from burning buildings. Once the troop-laden locomotive started racing for the river, south bank Confederate artillery opened fire on pursuing bluecoats who were only a half mile

9 Bowenville got its name from a prominent local family who owned much of the farmland around Rappahannock Station.

10 Old Mill View was called Mill View until 1850 by which time most of its merchants had relocated closer to Lawson's Ford, taking the town name with them. For a summary of Rappahannock Station's history and the military campaigns around it see http://thenewoanda.weebly.com/blog/rappahannock-station,accessed 6/28/2020.

distant when the boxcars rattled over the bridge. Seconds later, a thunderous explosion rent the air as Rebel engineers blew up one of the span's stone pylons, collapsing part of the structure and starting a fire that sent the entire edifice crashing into the water. Although skirmishing continued until nightfall, Howard decided against pressing matters and pulled his troops back to Warrenton Junction next day.[11]

The war next visited Rappahannock Station in July 1862, when Maj. Gen. John Pope invaded Culpeper County with his newly formed Army of Virginia. In the wake of this advance Federal laborers rebuilt the O&A bridge, completing their task on August 8, just one day before the battle of Cedar Mountain. That contest threw Union forces into reverse and spawned two weeks of maneuvering between Lee and Pope which ignited a sharp fight around the railroad bridge on August 23. After that battle Federal troops burned the just-rebuilt structure and every nearby building whose timber might aid in its reconstruction.[12]

The combatants returned to the upper Rappahannock in October, 1862 following the battle of Sharpsburg. This time Confederate engineers rebuilt the railroad bridge, but their handiwork led as short a life as its Yankee predecessor. Union soldiers captured and burned the span in November during the opening stages of Maj. Gen. Ambrose Burnside's Fredericksburg campaign. The bridge lay in ruins until early August 1863 when Federal engineers reconstructed it for George Meade, only to burn it again on October 13 when the AOP began its northward retreat during the Bristoe Station campaign.[13]

Nineteen months of military ebb and flow across Fauquier County had left Rappahannock Station's environs denuded of crops, livestock, and people. Between them the rival armies had torched or dismantled almost every building in the area and confiscated anything edible within reach. Unable to survive amid such desolation, most civilians had fled for safer points, their once bountiful fields marred by clusters of landscape scarring earthen fortifications, each a monument to some past campaign.

The Confederates constructed the sector's first breastworks in March 1862, building entrenchments on both sides of the Rappahannock to protect the railroad

---

11 OR 12, pt. 1, 412-17; Randolph McKim, *A Soldier's Recollections: Leaves from the Diary of a Young Confederate* (New York, 1910), 75-77; Daniel E. Sutherland, *Seasons of War: The Ordeal of a Confederate Community, 1861-1865* (New York, 1995), 100-101. Howard had four infantry regiments and a battery of artillery. Stuart and Ewell both commanded a brigade supported by the Confederate Baltimore Artillery. It is uncertain whether Union shells, retreating Confederates, or a combination of the two set the buildings on fire.

12 OR 12, pt. 3, 530.

13 Ibid. 21, 765; For an excellent overview of the war in Culpeper County and along the upper Rappahannock, see Clark B. Hall, "Upper Rappahannock River Front: The Dare Mark Line," Brandy Station Historical Foundation (Middleburg, VA, 2011).

bridge and several fords located to its east and west. That July, Pope's Yankees re-engineered some of these works to face south. Lee's men reversed those efforts in October, altering the emplacements to again look north. When Meade's troops reoccupied the area in August 1863, they reconstructed the fieldworks to defend against attack once more from the south. After the ANV retook control of the upper Rappahannock in October, Rebel laborers remodeled the works to face north and expanded those near the railway stop to create a continuous perimeter around Lee's bridgehead. The AOP's generals were familiar with the fortifications south of the river but were far less certain about whatever works the enemy had created north of the stream or how many Confederates occupied them.[14]

*   *   *

Whatever Union commanders knew or didn't know about Rebel dispositions along the Rappahannock, they were intimately familiar with their route to the river, having crossed and re-crossed it near the railway bridge three times during the October campaign. Sedgwick brought Sykes' V Corps down along the railroad from Three Mile Station, while the VI Corps—under Brig. Gen. Horatio Wright while Sedgwick led the wing—moved from Warrenton toward Old Mill View on a parallel path seven miles to the west.

Federal commanders set a brisk pace, and one soldier recalled that rest stops "were few and far between and only for five minutes" duration when they came. Screened by flankers and advanced guards, the columns "sped over fifteen miles of road in a very few hours," kicking up considerable dust clouds as they moved south.[15]

The lead elements of each corps arrived within a mile and a half of Rappahannock Station around noon. Reaching assembly areas marked out by Sedgwick, the V Corps began going into line east of the O&A, while the VI Corps did the same west of it, each deploying behind a line of skirmishers. Unlike at Kelly's Ford, Confederates noted the main Federal columns' approach. Rebel vedettes sitting their horses "with the coolest

---

14 For a map of earthworks in the area before Nov. 1863. see George B. Davis, Leslie J. Perry & Joseph W. Kirkley, *The Official Military Atlas of the Civil War* (Washington, DC, 1891), plate 105, and Earl B. McElfresh, *Maps and Mapmakers of the Civil War* (New York, 1999), 133.

15 "To the Front and Fight" *Providence Evening Press* (RI) Nov. 14, 1863. Sykes' route lay just west of the railroad on a road running through Germantown. At what point the V Corps crossed over the tracks is unknown.

Bartlett's Column of Divisions

□ = 1 Company

Bartlett's Column of Divisions

Hayes
- 118th PA
- 18th MA
- 22nd MA
- 1st MI

Switzer
- 4th MI
- 62nd PA
- 9th MA
- 32nd MA

Chamberlain
- 83rd PA
- 16th MI
- 44th NY
- 20th MA

impudence" watched from mere "pistol shot" distance as the arriving Yankees arrayed for battle.[16]

Wright placed Brig. Gen. Albion P. Howe's two-brigade 2nd Division on the VI Corps right. The three brigades in Brig. Gen. Henry D. Terry's 3rd Division occupied its center and Wright's own three-brigade 1st Division, today under Brig. Gen. David A. Russell, took post on the left. Each division formed a double line—meaning that two regiment-wide lines of battle were stacked one behind the other.[17]

Sykes arranged his V Corps in column of divisions which put each brigade into two-regiment wide battle lines arrayed one behind the other, with each regiment in a double column of companies. Brig Gens. Romeyn B. Ayres' 2nd Division and Brig. Gen. Samuel W. Crawford's 3rd Division constituted the main line, while Brig. Gen. Joseph J. Bartlett's 1st Division supported the skirmishers. Colonel Joseph Hayes 1st Brigade held the right of Bartlett's line, while Col. Jacob B. Sweitzer's 2nd Brigade, and Col. Joshua L. Chamberlain's 3rd Brigade occupied its center and left respectively. Sykes assigned Brig. Gen. Kenner Garrard to take command of the 933 pickets thrown out across the Federal front.[18]

The terrain separating each corps from the Rappahannock offered unique yet similar challenges. Wright's VI Corps, standing about a mile and a half from the river, faced mostly open ground that rose gradually over 880 yards to a pair of "low hills"—about 60 feet high—running parallel to the Union battle line. Beyond these

---

16 OR 29, pt. 1, 576-77, 584. George T. Stevens, *Three Years in the Sixth Corps* (Albany, NY, 1866), 284-84. The VI Corps' 1st Div. led the march, followed by the corps artillery and its two other divisions.

17 OR 29, pt.1, 584-85. It is possible the VI Corps also formed its regiments in column of divisions, but Wright's report uses the vague phrase "double line" and I have stuck with a minimal interpretation of that phrase absent other evidence.

18 Ibid., 577-82. Both Hayes and Chamberlain were temporarily commanding brigades on Nov. 7. Garrard led 363 men from the 1st Div., 363 from the 2nd, and 207 from the 3rd.

This August 1862 photograph by Timothy O'Sullivan looks north across the O&A Bridge. Union troops burned the mill on the left in 1862, but its stone foundation walls remained standing and repair crews eventually built two water tanks atop the ruin. The flat terrain east of the railroad is visible. Note also the steep northern bank down which the 6th Louisiana would retreat on the evening of November 7, 1863. *Library of Congress*

Rappahannock Station in August 1862. The Confederates burned these buildings in October 1863. Note the open nature of the terrain east (left) of the railroad. *Library of Congress*

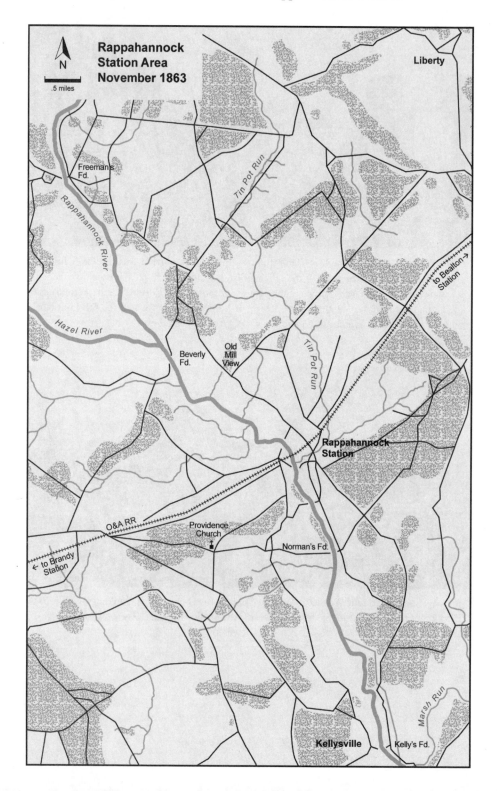

heights the terrain followed a gentle downward slope for another half-mile to the foot of a low ridge or bluff topped by Rebel fortifications.[19]

East of the railroad Sykes' V Corps stood at the base of a broad wooded ridge beyond which lay a 350-yard wide plain stretching all the way to the Rappahannock. The O&A bordered this flatland to the west while to its east sat another wide and heavily forested ridge, this one 100 feet high, paralleling the railroad and extending southward toward the river. Confederate artillery emplacements south of the waterway had an unobstructed view of this open ground, which seemed a made-to-order killing zone for Rebel guns.

West of the railroad a narrow stream called Tin Pot Run flowed along the northern base of those hills farthest from the Union position. The creek coursed eastward in a straight line until passing under a shattered O&A trestle, after which it curved gently southward toward the Rappahannock, emptying into the river 160 yards or so below the destroyed bridge. Although the brook's course carried it across the entire VI Corps front, its path east of the railroad impeded only the V Corps' right flank. In neither instance did it present more than a minor obstacle to Sedgwick's command.

The destroyed O&A bisected the two sets of heights facing the Federals, its path running more-or-less straight until terminating at the burnt railway bridge. For the most part the railroad rested on an embankment built across low or swampy ground. In places it was high enough to shield maneuvering troops from enfilade fire coming from the opposite side of the line. Although Confederates had removed the rails and burnt Rappahannock Station's buildings in October, the easily seen railroad bed formed a handy boundary between the V and VI corps.

*   *   *

As the various Federal regiments and brigades took up position, officers ordered their men to stack arms and break ranks. Since no one had mentioned a possible fight, everyone assumed they were on a routine march. Having eaten nothing since dawn, hungry soldiers immediately built little fires and started boiling coffee.[20]

19 Ibid., 585; Stevens, *Three Years*, 284; John S. Wilson, "Captain Fish and the 121st New York Volunteers at Rappahannock Station, Virginia" *Military Collector & Historian: Journal of the Company of Military Historians*, Vol. 48, no. 3 (Washington, DC, Fall 1996), 116. Federal sources vary on the distance between the VI Corps starting position and the river, some claiming it was a mile and half, others a mile and a quarter. An excellent interactive online map that presents the topography of Rappahannock Station clearly is at https://en-us.topographic-map.com/maps/s0np/Fauquier-County/ (accessed 2/21/2020).

20 Daniel G. MacNamara, *History of the Ninth Regiment Massachusetts Volunteer Infantry* (Boston, MA, 1899), 349; J. Gregory Acken, ed., *Inside the Army of the Potomac: The Civil War Experience of*

The generals, of course, knew what was up and reacted dramatically to numerous smoke columns wafting into the air. Alert to subtle signs of pending trouble, enlisted men quickly spotted activity among their commanders. Within minutes, staff officers came rushing up with orders to extinguish all cooking fires lest they give away the Federal position. As disappointed troops doused nascent flames, one Pennsylvanian groused that if "a fire could not be built at high noon there must be somebody pretty close whose purposes were unfriendly."[21]

Pondering this logic, a V Corps sergeant decided to find out how near the enemy might be. Climbing the ridge between his regiment and the Rappahannock, he soon had his answer. Hastening back to his company the man excitedly told comrades that he'd seen a large enemy force entrenched on the other side of the hill. At that same instant, a column of ambulances rumbled up to the front. With a blood chilling shudder, Federal infantrymen realized that "these forerunners of suffering" meant "a fight was imminent."[22]

Although a logical conclusion, battle, in fact, wasn't certain. Scarcely inclined to rush blindly at enemy earthworks, Sedgwick had demonstrated his methodical approach to dealing with fortifications at Fredericksburg. Meade's orders stressing the strength of Rappahannock Station's defenses and doubts about their susceptibility to assault reinforced his disposition for similar prudence on November 7. The general would take his time.

*   *   *

Southern troops occupying the undermanned Confederate bulwark north of the Rappahannock were ill-prepared to fend off a serious attack. Ewell's corps defended this area, and two of its three divisions, led by Major Generals Edward "Alleghany" Johnson and Jubal Early, were camped between Brandy Station and Culpeper Court House. Both men were hard-fighting, highly competent veteran officers, and Ewell had arranged for them to rotate responsibility for defending the bridgehead. A fresh brigade, alternately detailed from Early or Johnson, would occupy the position each week. On November 6, two of the ANV's most famous units had exchanged places

---

Captain Francis Adams Donaldson (Mechanicsburg, PA, 1998), 384; Stevens *Corn Exchange Regiment*, 337; "The Sixth Maine's Superb Gallantry at Rappahannock Station," *National Tribune*, July 28, 1887.

21 Stevens, *Corn Exchange Regiment*, 337.

22 Ibid.

Left: Col. Davidson Penn. *Valentine Museum.* *Right:* Brig. Gen. Harry Hays. *Library of Congress*

inside the post, the Stonewall Brigade from Johnson's division marching out and the Louisiana Tigers of Early's division marching in.[23]

The five regiments in this brigade enjoyed a well-deserved reputation as crack troops. Their Tennessee-born commander, 43-year old Brig. Gen. Harry T. Hays, was equally distinguished. As colonel of the 7th Louisiana Infantry he had gained notoriety as a hard drinker and harder fighter at First Manassas and during the Valley Campaign. Wounded at Port Republic in May 1862, he returned to duty after a brief convalescence, was promoted to brigadier, and subsequently participated in all the army's major actions. At Gettysburg his troops briefly overran Cemetery Hill in a July 2 dusk attack that failed only for want of proper support. Competent and aggressive, Hays personified just the sort of officer needed in an exposed post. But he had court-martial duty on November 7, and his senior colonel, Davidson B. Penn of the 7th Louisiana, commanded the bridgehead.[24]

23 Rodes' division took part in that rotation in late October but escaped the duty when it moved closer to Kelly's Ford.

24 Warner, *Generals in Gray*, 130. The 5th, 6th, 7th, 8th and 9th LA infantry regiments comprised the Louisiana Tigers. Orphaned at an early age, Harry and his brother Jack grew up with a Mississippi uncle. In 1836 Jack "Coffee" Hays went to Texas and won military fame defending the new republic. A few years later Harry left for Baltimore to study at St Mary's College. He relocated to New Orleans after graduation, opened a law office and, following a

Fortunately for the Confederates, 27-year old Penn was an outstanding leader. After graduating from the Virginia Military Institute in 1856, he had briefly studied law before moving to New Orleans and starting a cotton press business. When war broke out, he raised a company that became part of 7th Louisiana, then under Harry Hays' command. Penn worked his way up through the ranks and in July 1862 became the regiment's colonel after Hays' promotion. Both men had learned the business of soldiering under Stonewall Jackson. Hays couldn't have left his brigade in better hands.[25]

Penn had about 900 infantrymen in five regiments of varying strength; the smallest of which fielded just 125 men while the largest mustered only a hundred or so more. Penn had routinely deployed his command for surveillance rather than defense on November 7. His three most advanced units were posted a quarter mile in front of Rappahannock Station atop high ground on either side of the O&A: Col. William Monaghan's 6th Louisiana held a wooded ridge east of the tracks, while Capt. Antoine L. Gusman's 8th, and Lt. Col. Thomas M. Terry's 7th Louisiana regiments occupied a mostly barren pair of elevations west of them. The 5th Louisiana, under Capt. John G. Angell, picketed the river's south bank; its outpost spread out in a trench stretching from the railroad one and a half miles to Norman's Ford. The Louisiana Guard Artillery occupied the bridgehead's fortifications alongside Lt. Col. William R. Peck's 9th Louisiana.[26]

A line of mounted vedettes stood watch about a mile in front of the most distant infantry regiments and around 10:30 a.m. they reported seeing enemy troops marching eastward. Within the next half hour Rebel scouts sent back word of another infantry column advancing in the same direction. Concerned by the cavalry's sightings, Penn and the brigade's assistant adjutant general, Capt. William J. Seymour, rode out to look things over for themselves.[27]

Mexican War stint with the 5th LA Cavalry, became active in politics before being elected colonel of the 7th LA after secession.

25 OR 29, pt. 1, 626-627; Terry Jones, ed., *The Civil War Memoirs of Captain William J. Seymour: Reminiscences of a Louisiana Tiger* (Baton Rouge, LA, 1991), 90; Bobby L. Roberts, *Portraits of Conflict: A Photographic History of Louisiana in the Civil War* (Fayetteville, AR, 1998), 71.

26 OR 29, pt. 1, 626-627, 629; *Lamoille News Dealer* (Hyde Park, VT) Dec. 23, 1863. Terry led the 7th LA at the extreme left of the Rebel line while Penn directed the brigade. Once Harry Hays arrived, Penn reverted to command of the 7th LA. Hays' official report says that he had 800–900 men on Nov. 7. No official tallies report regimental strength, but we can gauge accurate data from the number of prisoners taken when the bridgehead fell. The 5th LA surrendered 123, the 7th LA 180.

27 OR 29, pt. 1, 626-627, 629; Jones, Civil War Memoirs of Captain Seymour, 91. The vedettes had spotted part of French's wing.

After verifying his men's observations, Penn alerted Early via an 11:45 a.m. dispatch that large bodies of Union troops were moving toward Kelly's Ford. Early's division headquarters lay nearly six miles to the south, and Penn realized it would take considerable time for his message to arrive. In the interim he stayed on the outpost line to monitor the situation. Thus he was on hand thirty minutes later when the vanguard of two Yankee corps suddenly appeared on the horizon, each heading straight for Rappahannock Station. After watching the enemy formations join hands and begin going into line, an alarmed Penn sent Early a second message, dated 1:15 p.m., warning of growing Federal strength near the bridgehead and noting that light skirmishing had already started.[28]

Penn's first report took almost two hours to reach Early. Instantly grasping its startling import, he ordered signalmen to wig wag Penn's alert to Lee's and Ewell's respective headquarters and say he was riding immediately to the front. Before leaving, Early ordered his division's other three brigades to march for Rappahannock Station. Galloping north, the general was painfully aware that the Yankees had caught his units flatfooted. Significant numbers of men from every regiment were scattered throughout the countryside gathering building materials for winter quarters. Getting those soldiers back into ranks would consume a lot of time. Until then his brigades would face a looming threat without their full strength.[29]

On his way to the river, Early met the rider carrying Penn's second dispatch warning of Federals approaching the bridgehead. He also learned that Ewell was away from corps headquarters and probably hadn't received the signal flag message about Union movement toward Kelly's Ford. Early forwarded Penn's latest message to army HQ and sent an aide to find Ewell and convey all current information. Having passed along everything he knew Early resumed his ride, only to encounter Gen. Lee a few moments later.[30]

28 OR 29, pt. 1, 626-27. Seymour's *Civil War Memoirs*, 90, locates Early's HQ in a belt of woods a mile and a half south of Brandy Station and four miles north of Culpeper Court House.

29 OR 29, pt. 1, 619; Jubal A. Early, *Lieutenant General Jubal Anderson Early, C.S.A. Autobiographical Sketch and Narrative of the War Between the States* (New York, NY, 1994), 309.

30 McDonald, *Make Me A Map*, 179. Ewell's corps HQ was two miles southwest of Kelly's Ford in Dr. Joseph Pembroke Thom's house. Thom had served as a 2nd Lt. in the 11th US Infantry during the Mexican War before going to medical school and becoming a US Navy assistant surgeon from 1853–57. Thom captained Company C, 1st VA Infantry Battalion at the start of the war. A serious hand wound at Kernstown (March 1862) ended his field service, and he transferred to the quartermaster department in Richmond in June, 1862, and was eventually promoted to major. www.Geni.com/people/Maj-CSA-Joseph-Thom/6000000029717939827 Accessed 9/1/19.

This October 13, 1863 Edwin Forbes' drawing of the AOP's Bristoe Station Campaign retreat reveals a great amount of detail relevant to November 1863. The Confederates laid their pontoon bridge (foreground) in the same place. The small redoubt (before reconstruction) is visible on the hilltop to the left. Graham and Dance placed their batteries on the hill to the right. The distance between the railroad and pontoon bridges is very clear as are the Rappahannock's steep banks and its width behind the Rebel earthworks. Note the five pontoon boats spanning the stream. *Library of Congress*

Like Ewell, the army commander hadn't been at his headquarters to receive the earlier signal flag message. Nevertheless, he already knew a great deal about the situation. After learning of enemy activity at Kelly's Ford, Lee suspected Meade was at last endeavoring to breach the river. Since that undoubtedly meant menacing Rappahannock Station as well as Kellysville, he had hurried toward the bridgehead and wasn't surprised when Early said it too was threatened. Although Meade had moved unexpectedly, he *was* moving as anticipated. What happened next, depended principally on events north of the river and, together with Early, Lee continued toward the Rappahannock.[31]

---

31 Early, *Autobiographical Sketch and Narrative*, 309; Douglas Southall Freeman, *R. E. Lee*, 4 vols. (New York, NY, 1935), Vol. 3, 190. Lee's HQ stood near Brandy Station and closer to the river than did Early's. The two generals most likely met north of there when Early caught up with

While the two generals hurried forward, John Sedgwick was busily consolidating his strength. Unsure of Confederate numbers or dispositions, he declined starting a fight until his entire force was up and deployed for action. The couple of hours required for the last V and VI corps units to reach the field and go into line afforded the off-balance Rebels a crucial respite. Col. Penn used that time to bring all but one company of the 5th Louisiana north of the river and withdraw the 6th, 7th and 8th Louisiana into the fortifications surrounding the bridgehead. Only a skirmish line remained behind to give warning of an enemy advance.

Lee and Early reached the Rappahannock a little before 3:00 p.m. and quickly parted company as the latter rode across the stream to confer with Penn. As the division commander hastened north, Lee trotted to the top of a heavily fortified hill located just west of the railroad. From here he could look down on the pontoon bridge as well as appraise Penn's fortifications and see a good bit of the territory to their front.[32]

Lee, who was already riding toward the bridgehead. See Taylor to Bettie, Nov. 7, 1863, in R. Lockwood Tower, ed., *Lee's Adjutant: The Wartime Letters of Colonel Walter Herron Taylor, 1862-1865* (Columbia, SC, 1995), 82.

32 Freeman, *R.E. Lee*, Vol. 3, 190.

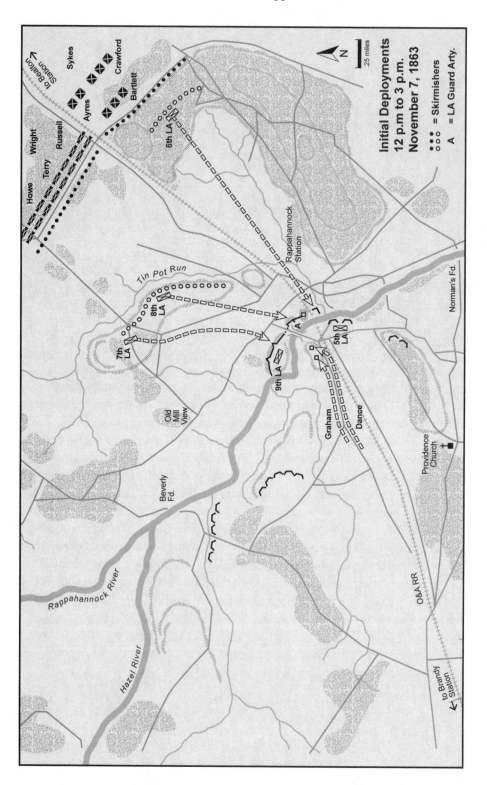

Initial Deployments
12 p.m to 3 p.m.
November 7, 1863

••• = Skirmishers
○○○ = Skirmishers
A = LA Guard Arty.

As Lee surveyed the situation Capt. Archibald Graham's Rockbridge Artillery galloped onto the scene. Surprised by the call to action like every other Rebel unit this afternoon, the battery arrived at the river without its full complement of cannoneers, a portion of whom were gathering firewood miles away when the summons to limber up arrived. Shrugging off that handicap, Graham had taken to the road as quickly as teamsters could hitch up their guns. His four fieldpieces were the first reinforcements to reach Rappahannock Station.[33]

Rather than send these cannons into earthworks east and west of the bridgehead where they could establish crossfire on the ground directly in front of the position, Lee directed them into an emplacement on the same hilltop from which he was observing the field. As the Rockbridge gunners deployed, Capt. Willis Dance's Powhatan Artillery arrived. Lee had it unlimber in an entrenchment built on a knoll of the same hill—closer to, but still west of, the ruined bridge. From these works Graham and Dance could fire on several ridges beyond the Rebel line and into most, but not all, approaches to it. More importantly, from their new posts the two batteries could pummel the bridgehead's fortified crest to cover Penn's brigade if circumstances required it to abandon the river's north bank.[34]

*   *   *

As the Confederate high command scrambled to strengthen Rappahannock Station's defenses, Federal regiments finished preparing to advance. Sedgwick designed a cautious opening strategy. Personally riding to Sykes and Wright he explained his plan. Both men would advance their skirmish lines and one division simultaneously, leaving the rest of their units in reserve. The V Corps task was to establish skirmishers along the north bank of the Rappahannock east of the railroad and screen Rebel fortifications on that side of the O&A. Wright's skirmishers had a similar objective west of the railroad, but the principal VI Corps job was to seize two hills overlooking the enemy position, establish batteries on those heights, and then

---

33 Edward Moore, *The Story of a Cannoneer Under Stonewall Jackson* (New York, NY, 1907), 206.

34 OR 29, pt. 1, 634, 627; At the start of the Gettysburg Campaign Lt. Washington Roebling, a prewar civil engineer on the staff of AOP chief engineer Brig. Gen. Warren, wrote a detailed analysis of the fords, hills and military features along the river near Rappahannock Station. This work contains invaluable information. Titled *Map Memoir (map & commentary) June 12, 1863 Reports on Riflepits and Earthworks thrown up at Rapphk. St. and Beverly Ford*, it is located in the Manuscripts and Special Collections division of the New York State Library, Albany. Readers can also find a copy of this three-page document in Earl B. McElfresh, *Maps and Mapmakers of the Civil War* (New York, 1999), 133. Roebling would supervise the building of the Brooklyn Bridge between 1868 and 1883.

Top Left: Brig. Gen. Joseph Bartlett. *Library of Congress* *Top Right:* Maj. Gen. George Sykes. *Library of Congress* *Left:* Capt. Dendy Sharwood. *Philadelphia Civil War Museum and Library*

attempt shelling the Southerners out of their bridgehead. The movement would begin once each corps reported itself ready to advance.[35]

At 41-years of age George Sykes was Regular Army to his core. After graduating from West Point in 1842 he had fought Indians in the Southwest, Seminoles in Florida and Soldados in Mexico. Jutting away from his chin like a locomotive's prow, the general's full beard suggested a combative nature, while his thin frame and "red, pinched, rough looking skin," bespoke someone who had spent a life soldiering. Leading mostly regular troops through the first half of the war, he had advanced from regimental to brigade and division command before inheriting the V Corps when Meade took charge of the army. Although capable of charm and kindness, the gentlemanly Sykes struck some people as cold and stolid. His

35 *OR* 29, pt. 1, 577; 585.

proclivity for stern discipline and total devotion to duty gave him the "air of one who is weary and a little ill-natured," Lt. Frank Haskell once said.[36]

At West Point the future general had earned the nickname "Tardy George" due to his punctilious adherence to regulations. He was anything but slow his afternoon, however. After receiving his orders, Sykes directed Brig. Gen. Garrard to reorganize his pickets as skirmishers and prepare to occupy the Rappahannock's north bank as far east as Norman's Ford, while at the same time getting close enough to the enemy right flank to pin its defenders inside their fortifications.

After receiving Sedgwick's instructions Sykes rode to Brig. Gen. Bartlett, who had transferred from the VI Corps just last night to replace an ailing Brig. Gen. Charles Griffin at the head of the V Corps 1st Division. Sykes told the 29-year old New Yorker to move his newly inherited outfit in support Garrard's skirmishers. Since the VI Corps would advance concurrently west of the railroad, the corps commander stressed that Bartlett's men must not slip across the tracks and interfere with Wright's troops.[37]

To emphasize this edict and ensure everyone understood it, Sykes rode over to the 118th Pennsylvania, which stood next to the O&A on the division's right flank. Pulling up in front of the unit, he called out for its commanding officer. Captain Dendy Sharwood, a 46-year old English immigrant, stepped forward. Sykes fixed him with a hard stare and in a voice loud enough for everyone to hear gravely intoned that the VI Corps was about to undertake "some specially delicate duty." Under no circumstances, he continued, were the Pennsylvanians to extend their line beyond the railroad separating Bartlett's and Russell's divisions. The general's manner clearly indicated that Sharwood would suffer personally if his men failed to follow this order. The captain solemnly accepted this responsibility and promised the 118th would do as directed.[38]

While Sykes issued his orders, Horatio Wright gave the job of seizing Sedgwick's targeted ridge to Albion Howe's 2nd Division. To bolster that effort, the ersatz corps commander detached Brig. Gen. Alexander Shaler's 1st Brigade from Terry's 3rd Division and sent it to reinforce Howe. With two of Shaler's five regiments absent on special duty, he had on hand only the 67th New York, 82nd Pennsylvania, and 122nd New York. Uncertain of whether Wright knew this, Terry detailed the 7th and 10th

36 Tagg, *Generals of Gettysburg*, 81-82; Warner, *General in Blue*, 492-93; Byrne & Weaver, *Haskell of Gettysburg*, 133.

37 OR 29, pt. 1, 578, 579; Smith, *Corn Exchange Regiment*, 335-36; A. E. Mather to Brother, Nov. 11, 1863, Mather Letters, Dartmouth College, Hanover, NH.

38 Acken, *Inside the Army of the Potomac*, 386; Stevens, *Corn Exchange Regiment*, 338-39. Sharwood died of typhoid fever on Nov. 21, 1863—just two weeks after the battle of Rappahannock Station.

Massachusetts from Brig. Gen. Henry L. Eutis' 2nd Brigade to fill out Shaler's command.[39]

The VI Corps skirmish line—consisting of companies drawn from the 2nd Vermont on the right, the 43rd and 121st New York in the middle, and the 6th Maine on the left closest to the railroad—would precede Howe. Its mission was to clear the high ground in front of the Rebel entrenchments and pave the way for its occupation by the 2nd Division and Union artillery.[40]

Although dangerous duty, skirmishing offered men a freedom of movement no regular battle line allowed. Spread out five paces apart and allowed to seek cover whenever possible, skirmishers enjoyed a somewhat dubious sense of governing the chances they took. For many soldiers that compensated for greater exposure to enemy sharpshooters. Certainly, the skirmish line was the place to earn a reputation if a man were so inclined. Capt. John D. Fish eagerly sought just such an opportunity. A cascade of recent personnel actions had installed him as second in command of the 121st New York and consequently he found himself leading a 53-man skirmish line charged with covering the 2nd Brigade's front.[41]

This put him directly under Col. Emory Upton's control and after deploying his troops he rode over to the colonel for final instructions. Those turned out to be brief and blunt. Fish would begin his advance when Howe's skirmishers moved off on his right. He would then proceed with the rest of the line to drive off enemy troops holding the ridge blocking access to the river. The captain was "free to use his own judgment in carrying out the mission," Upton continued, but he was to "remember one thing" and

---

39 OR 29, pt. 1, 585, 605, 606. Shaler's missing regiments were the 23rd PA and 65 NY. Eustis had only a single regiment (the 2nd RI) after the detachment.

40 Ibid., 585; https://dmna.ny.gov/historic/reghist/civil/infantry/43rdInf/43rdInfCWN3.pdf, accessed 2/21/2020.

41 Fish's somewhat ironic route to enlarged responsibilities—he had been twice passed him over for promotion—began with Brig. Gen. Bartlett's temporary V Corps assignment which resulted in Col. Upton stepping away from the 121st to command the 2nd Brigade of Russell's division. This arrangement should have left Lt. Col. Egbert W. Olcott in charge of the regiment, but he had taken sick leave 24 hours earlier after injuring his knee in a horse fall. With Olcott gone, Maj. Andrew E. Mather assumed command of the regiment and Fish, as senior captain, received a temporary field officer's assignment. Perhaps overly proud of his new post, the ambitious 29-year old had donned his full dress uniform on the morning of November 7, mounted a borrowed horse and set off with his regiment toward Rappahannock Station. Wilson, "Captain Fish," *Military Collector*, Vol. 48, no. 3, 116; A. E. Mather to Brother, Nov. 11, 1863, Mather Letters, Dartmouth College.

that was to get the 2nd Brigade's skirmishers on the high ground no later than the units to his left and right.[42]

* * *

Somewhere close to 3 p.m.—Federal accounts differ as to the precise time—Wright and Sykes completed their arrangements and reported themselves ready to move. Sedgwick had used up half the afternoon preparing for his advance and, like an exacting director, he had insisted that everything was just as he wanted it before the production began. Indeed, the result of all this time and effort was something akin to a staged pageant. For a long moment the battlefield resembled a theatrical spectacle with each actor and thousands of extras in place, everyone awaiting the command "action!"

Mother Nature provided a stunning backdrop to the scene: the bright autumn sun "flung a mellow glow over the landscape" while a breeze strong enough to float unfurled regimental colors caressed the countryside. West of the O&A Northern skirmishers resting inside the safety of a large wood sweated out the order to advance. Just 100 yards ahead they could spy a light screen of Rebel cavalry. No one doubted that enemy infantry lay somewhere behind those gray horsemen. East of the railroad Union and Confederate skirmishers "knelt or lay at their posts" waiting for something to happen, yet wondering, after two hours of sitting still, whether anything would. Tall grass hid all but the men's heads or musket barrels, and although a mere 500 yards separated the opposing troops, no shots were being fired by either side.[43]

Sedgwick's order to go ahead shattered this deceptive quiet. Upon command the V Corps skirmishers stood up, delivered a volley, and surged forward even as the 6th Louisiana's outpost line opened fire in reply. Musketry proved unnecessary on the other side of the tracks as Confederate vedettes whirled about and made for the rear as soon as Wright's infantry emerged from its sheltering timber.[44]

Walking out into the warm sunlight VI Corps skirmishers found themselves on "a smooth" treeless field offering neither obstacle nor concealment to their advance. The 7th and 8th Louisiana veterans watched and waited patiently as the approaching Yankees drew nearer. Mounted officers were visible behind the thin wall of blue

42 OR 29, pt. 1, 587-88; Stevens, *Three Years*, 284-85, Wilson, "Captain Fish," *Military Collector*, Vol. 48, no. 3, 116.

43 Acken, *Inside the Army of the Potomac*, 386-87; Stevens, *Corn Exchange Regiment*, 338-39; A. E. Mather to Brother, Nov. 11, 1863, Mather Letters, Dartmouth College. I have been unable to identify the small Confederate cavalry detachment present at Rappahannock Station.

44 Stevens, *Three Years*, 285; Oliver Wilcox Norton, *Army Letters, 1861-1865* (Chicago, Il, 1903), 189.

uniforms, which was coming on "steadily in perfect line and in perfect stillness," its men under orders not to fire until fired upon. Wright's troops braced for a volley as they passed inside musket range, but nothing happened. Seventeen-year old corporal Clinton Beckwith found the enemy's silence more unnerving than the sound of his guns, later recalling that "an age" seemed to pass before the action began. Riding along behind his command Capt. Fish likewise puzzled over the lack of Rebel resistance.

From their hilltop perch Hays' officers waited with remarkable coolness for the Northerners to come within "pistol shot range" before giving the order to open fire. One heartbeat later the crack of a single rifle punctured the still air followed immediately by the angry crash of a volley erupting from the ridge. Looking down, John Fish saw his horse's mane flip upward as bullets zipped past the animal's neck and other projectiles whistled around his own head. Shouting an order to double quick, the captain heard his own troops commence shooting as they ran toward the enemy. Fortunately for the Yankees, Penn's Louisianans had aimed their initial volley too high and casualties were minimal.

Unable to break Federal momentum and keenly aware of the massive force behind Wright's skirmishers, the Southerners hurriedly departed the ridge and began falling back toward the river. A minute or two later Union soldiers swept up onto the abandoned crest where they found at least one mortally wounded Reb and caught their first glimpse of Confederate earthworks along the Rappahannock. The quarter-mile deep open plain between the ugly earthen scar outlining Lee's bridgehead and Wright's just captured ridge bristled with Louisiana skirmishers. A few wounded Rebels were "limping away" to the rear, but the rest of Penn's Tigers withdrew grudgingly and by the book—skirmishers operating in pairs, leapfrogging backward, one man firing, the other reloading behind him. The slow, steady process ensured loaded weapons were always closest to the enemy and that the entire line never turned its back to the foe.[45]

Advancing down the crest, Federal skirmishers employed the same tactic but in reverse, constantly pressuring the Rebels and pushing them relentlessly rearwards toward their entrenchments. Having crested the ridge, however, the Yankees now faced the fury of Southern artillery stationed on both sides of the river where it could easily wreak havoc upon the captured heights and the nearly 900 yards separating them from the Confederate breastworks. Almost from the instant Union skirmishers became visible a dozen Rebel fieldpieces started pouring shellfire into the advancing bluecoats. Though noisy, this barrage did little more than "annoy" the enemy. There

---

45 Previous paragraphs based on Wilson, "Captain Fish," *Military Collector*, Vol. 48, No. 2 & 3, 116; Isaac O. Best, *History of the 121st New York State Infantry* (Chicago, IL, 1921), 100, 101; "To the Front and Fight!" *Providence* [RI] *Evening Press*, Nov. 14, 1863; A. E. Mather to Brother, Nov. 11, 1863, Mather Letters, Dartmouth College.

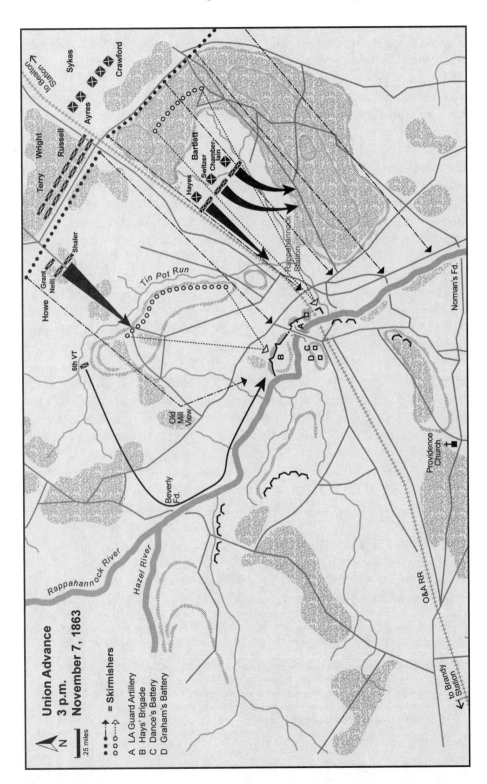

Union Advance
3 p.m.
November 7, 1863

N

.25 miles

●●●● = Skirmishers

○○○ ↗
•••• ↗

A   LA Guard Artillery
B   Hays' Brigade
C   Dance's Battery
D   Graham's Battery

Rappahannock River

Hazel River

Beverly Fd.

Old Mill View

5th VT

Tin Pot Run

Howe   Grant   Neill

Shaler

Terry   Wright   Russell

to Bealton
Station

Sykes
Crawford
Ayres

Bartlett

Switzer
Chamberlain

Hayes

Rappahannock Station

B
A
D C

Providence Church

Norman's Fd.

O&A RR

to Brandy Station

were too few Southern guns on hand to smother the approaching Yankee skirmish lines, which were hard-to-hit marks in any case, and the available batteries had to split their attention between Federal troops on either side of the O&A, further reducing effectiveness. Confederate artillery west of the railroad suffered the additional handicap of finding no easy targets, largely because Brig. Gen. Howe was careful to keep most of his troops beyond the reach of Rebel gunners.[46]

The 45-year old Maine native had graduated from the US Military Academy in 1841, ranked eighth in his class and with a commission in the artillery corps. After earning a brevet for gallantry in Mexico, Howe had gone on to a mix of rough frontier duty and more pleasant eastern posts, including an instructorship at West Point. Still a captain in 1859, he led the artillery detachment supporting then Lt. Col. Robert E. Lee's suppression of John Brown's Harper's Ferry raid. Howe spent the first half of the Civil War as an artilleryman, participating in George McClellan's 1861 West Virginia campaign and leading an AOP artillery brigade until promoted to brigadier and transferring to the infantry in June 1862. Despite little combat experience, he received command of the VI Corps 2nd Division in November 1862. Although Howe had seen only slight action at Fredericksburg and none at Gettysburg, he had performed exceptionally well in the Chancellorsville campaign.[47]

His knowledge of artillery tactics would greatly benefit his troops today. Assigned by Sedgwick to occupy the ridge overlooking Rappahannock Station, Howe waited long enough for the skirmishers to get several hundred yards ahead of his line before ordering the advance. The division moved forward with Shaler's brigade on the left and Neill's on the right—each formed in two lines and with the attached regiments from Eustis' brigade constituting Shaler's second line—while Col. Lewis A. Grant's Vermont brigade marched behind Neill in a column of regiments. As Howe's division trailed along behind the VI Corps skirmishers, he detached Maj. Charles P. Dudley's 5th Vermont from Grant's brigade and sent it toward the Rappahannock at a right

---

46 Best, *121st New York*, 101; Wilson, "Captain Fish," *Military Collector*, Vol. 48, No. 3, 116.

47 Warner, *Generals in Blue*, 239-40; Tagg, *Generals of Gettysburg*, 111-12; Hyde, *The Union Generals Speak: The Meade Hearings on the Battle of Gettysburg*, 79-98. Howe would lose his division and be reassigned to an artillery depot command in Washington during the AOP's March 1864 reorganization into three corps. Shortly afterwards he denigrated Meade's handling of the Gettysburg campaign in testimony before the Joint Committee on the Conduct of the War. While serving in the capital Howe ingratiated himself well enough with Radical Republicans to receive a brevet promotion to major general in 1865 and assignment to the honor guard that stood watch over Lincoln's corpse as well as a spot on the commission that tried John Wilkes Booth's gaggle of conspirators. Howe remained in the regular army after the war and retired as an artillery colonel in 1882. He died in 1897.

angle from the rest of the division with orders to secure Beverly Ford, then wheel left and drive down the riverbank toward the enemy earthworks.

As Dudley moved off, Howe's formation climbed the gradual slope of the ridge Wright wanted to seize. Gaining the crest "without check and with but little loss" the 2nd Division briefly became visible to Southern gunners. But enemy artillerymen managed to hurl only a few ineffective shells at Howe's men before the old gunner placed them on the ridge's reverse slope and out of the direct line of fire.

Elsewhere Union skirmishers were busily driving the Rebels into their breastworks. Dudley's 5th Vermont reached Beverly Ford without meeting opposition, swung left as ordered, and began a rapid advance down the riverbank, its progress hardly slowed when it ran into Rebel skirmishers who gave way with relative ease. It briefly appeared the aggressive Vermonters might overrun the Confederate left flank and crumple the bridgehead all by themselves. To Dudley's disappointment, however, the enemy properly manned his line before the Federals could exploit their opportunity. Although the 5th Vermont drove Confederate skirmishers back into their works, Union progress ground to a halt roughly 140 yards in front of the enemy fortifications. Howe shifted Neill's brigade into position behind Dudley's skirmishers and anchored both units' right flank on the Rappahannock.[48]

Along Russell's front things were much the same. Pursuing the Rebels down the southern slope of their abandoned ridge, skirmishers from the 121st New York and 6th Maine twice halted to maintain contact with the 43rd New York and 2nd Vermont on their right—both of which needed to execute a series of half left wheels as they advanced in order to bring their front parallel to the Confederates. Shells continued bursting overhead as the Yankees moved forward. These caused some damage but not as much as Southern rifles. Once the Louisiana skirmishers scurried into their breastworks, they left a clear field for Rebel sharpshooters whose fire became "very warm" very quickly.[49]

Union casualties began mounting. Captain Fish's New Yorkers had already lost four men severely wounded before the Federal advance went to ground in a sunken section of the Freeman's Ford Road and a nearby ditch, each some 200 yards from the enemy line. That was well within killing range of the canister rounds enemy artillerymen were mixing in among their shells and about as far as skirmishers could push things without actually assaulting the earthworks. From their new-found cover, the Yankees "commenced a sharpshooting duel" with the Confederates; "firing on every head" they saw "rise above the parapets." The Rebels responded in kind,

48 Previous paragraphs based on OR 29, pt. 1, 602-04, 606.

49 Wilson, "Captain Fish," *Military Collector*, Vol. 48, No. 3, 116.

shooting at any blue uniform exposing itself to view. Although no one on either side knew it, they had just begun a two-hour long contest.[50]

*   *   *

Sykes' advance east of the railroad was equally dramatic. It took Bartlett's division 20 minutes to get up and over the wooded crest confronting it, each brigade still formed in double column. Since the eastern end of the ridge ran parallel to the railroad, Sweitzer's and Chamberlain's brigades (the division's center and left, respectively) moved adjacent to a sheltering forest. Hayes' brigade on the right was closer to Rebel cannon and more exposed. As it emerged from the trees and onto the plain Rebel gunners greeted the division with a spattering of shells. In response Bartlett halted his troops and ordered each brigade to deploy its left and right regiments, throwing them 200 paces ahead of the main body before resuming their advance.[51]

For those who had a chance to see it, this movement was a memorable sight. The division-wide formation was visible from end to end, flags snapping in the wind above orderly blue ranks marching with parade ground precision as shell-bursts dotted the sky. At least one Yankee infantryman thought the scene "a glorious pageant of real war."[52]

Visions of martial grandeur swiftly disappeared when "a puff of smoke" blossomed against the dark wall of a Rebel redoubt. Seconds later a projectile struck the ground 20 yards in front of the 118th Pennsylvania, ricocheted over the regiment and detonated in its rear. More shells followed in quick succession, each one bursting in "uncomfortable proximity" to the advancing Northern line. Explosions threw mud and gravel into the faces of wincing and dodging Union soldiers who somehow managed to maintain their formation if not always their cadence. Although the munitions inflicted little harm, the "reckless way" they "hurtled, whistled and flew" about readily reminded Bartlett's veterans of "bitter experiences" on "other fields."[53]

---

50 OR 29, pt. 1, 635. The Louisiana Guard Artillery's four guns fired nearly 400 rounds (78 canister) during the engagement.

51 Ibid., 579; John J. Hennessy, ed., *Fighting with the Eighteenth Massachusetts: The Civil War Memoir of Thomas H. Mann* (Baton Rouge, LA, 2000), 211-13. In 2020 the ground over which Bartlett advanced remained agricultural, and its expanse can be seen readily if one drives east across the railroad tracks in Remington, VA on County Road T651. This road crosses over Tin Pot Run on a small bridge. A satellite image of the area is at https://earth.google.com/web/@38.52902094,-77.80563481,79.67757979a,1908.29593633d,35y,332.8541802h,0t,0r

52 Stevens, *Corn Exchange Regiment*, 338-39; Acken, *Inside the Army of the Potomac*, 387.

53 Stevens, *Corn Exchange Regiment*, 339-340; Hennessy, *Fighting with the Eighteenth*, 211.

Those memories became more acute when 1st Lt. Robert L. Moore's Louisiana Guard Artillery found the range. Stationed inside redoubts anchoring the east end of the Rebel line, its two 10-pounder Parrott guns and two 3-inch Ordnance Rifles were well-situated to hurt Sykes' troops.[54]

Hayes' brigade took the brunt of Moore's fire, his densely massed 1st Michigan and 18th Massachusetts proved especially vulnerable to enemy shells. Private Thomas H. Mann watched as Confederate shot "plowed some bad gaps" through the Eighteenth's ranks, knocking down several men at a time. Enduring such punishment required more discipline and fortitude than some of the Bay State regiment's recently absorbed 200 draftees or substitutes could muster. Several of them "dropped from the ranks in a dead faint and as white as real corpses," Mann remembered. The majority, however, grimly closed ranks and kept coming.[55]

So did the 22nd Massachusetts and 118th Pennsylvania, although in the Pennsylvanians' case with greater difficulty. Deployed in line of battle they made a more difficult target for enemy gunners. Nonetheless, the regiment escaped neither Rebel attention nor causalities. Zeroing in on the unit's colors, Moore's cannoneers along with Graham's and Dance's batteries began scoring numerous near misses.[56]

Adjusting their aim, Southern artillerists soon hit home, and a shell ripped away the foot of an unfortunate solider in Company K. As blood spurted from his mangled limb, enemy rounds sliced through the air around the regiment's left flank. Reacting instinctively, men on that side of the line veered right to escape these deadly missiles. The resulting press of bodies began pressuring the 118th's color guard, whose flag bearers tried to resist the growing compression and keep marching straight ahead. Before long, however, the unremitting weight of humanity from the left jammed together both the color guard and the companies to its right. With arms pinned against their sides and bodies turned almost sideways, soldiers tried to hold their place in ranks. The resulting crunch of men became so severe the compacted regiment unwittingly

---

54 OR 29, pt. 1, 607 gives the armament of Moore's battery. Capt. Charles A. Green, commander of the Louisiana Guard Artillery, was absent on November 7, 1863 and Moore led the battery, which belonged to Lt. Col. H. P. Jones Artillery BN.

55 Hennessy, *Fighting with the Eighteenth*, 199, 211-13. The 18th MA received 200 draftees and substitutes on Sept. 9, 1863. Mann said most draftees made good soldiers, while many substitutes did not. He had some compassion for those who couldn't stomach combat, noting that "All the courage of 'Frederick the Great' will not make a man face the music whose nerves serve him such a trick."

56 The height of the Confederate fortifications and the uneven ground in Bartlett's path caused enemy shot to strike at an angle and bounce upwards before exploding or bouncing again. The Pennsylvanians' right flank adjacent to the railroad embankment was relatively safe from Rebel fire.

bore a gravely wounded corporal several yards before its formation could "yield sufficiently to let him drop out."[57]

Eventually the pressure exerted by hundreds of men pushing right was too insistent to deny. Despite Sykes' warning, the center and right of the 118th Pennsylvania had to give way or fall out of line completely. A few men sank back, but most finally sidled to the right, crowding ever closer to the railroad tracks and the VI Corps zone of advance.

A mortified Capt. Sharwood cried out, "again and again: The guide is left! The guide is left!" (which meant the regiment's left flank should move straight ahead, and the rest of the command conform to its course.) Unwilling to walk sheep-like into Rebel fire everyone on the regiment's left nonetheless continued angling right thereby pushing the entire 118th over the line Sykes had forbidden it to cross. With "earnest gestures" Sharwood reiterated the proper axis of advance, but it was useless. Tired of the captain's ceaseless admonition that the "guide is left" one Yankee hollered back, "No he isn't; he's being pushed right, along with the rest of us."

That witty retort came just as the distracted regiment unexpectedly encountered a 5-foot deep ditch concealed in waist-high grass. Tumbling blindly into the depression, the troops floundered in "knee-deep . . . green and slimy water." Disgusted by their unwanted dunking, men began clawing their way out of the shallow gulley in an impulsive effort to escape the stagnant water. Officers yelled at everyone to keep going, while cursing file closers manhandled the less surefooted forward. With the greatest alacrity they could muster, the bedraggled Pennsylvanians struggled up onto the gulley's other side, grabbing the hands, arms, or extended muskets of comrades already on solid ground.[58]

As Sharwood's men regained their footing, the right flank of Garrard's skirmish line arrived within easy range of the enemy entrenchments, halted and began sharpshooting at Rebel gunners. A few moments later, his left flank units took control of 800 yards of riverbank and the north side of Norman's Ford.

General Sykes watched all of this with intense interest. Riding forward just behind his skirmishers he had coolly taken up an observation post on a small hill west of the railroad which afforded an excellent view of Rappahannock Station's fortifications.

---

57 Hennessy, *Fighting with the Eighteenth*, 211-13; Acken, *Inside the Army of the Potomac*, 388-89.

58 Stevens, *Corn Exchange Regiment*, 340; Acken, *Inside the Army of the Potomac*, 388-89. A quick glance at a satellite image of the area clearly shows the almost straight line of the ditch Sharwood's men stumbled into. It appears manmade and was probably dug during railroad construction to either provide soil for building the O&A embankment or drain water away from it and into Tin Pot Run. On Nov. 7 it was full of stagnant water that had failed to enter the creek after the heavy rain storm of October 19. The satellite image can be found at https://tinyurl.com/yxej6v64, accessed Aug 18, 2020.

Once Garrard's men reached their objectives, all the corps commander had left to do was position his 1st Division where it could best support the skirmishers and, if ordered, attack the redoubts. Tin Pot Run, which coursed along the northern base of Sykes' little hillock only 500 yards from the Rebel redoubts, seemed a perfect stopping place, "too near" the enemy's guns for "effective shell work, but not near enough for canister."[59]

Once Bartlett's division neared that landmark, Sykes sent his assistant adjutant general, Capt. Walter S. Davis, to halt its advance. The timing of these orders worked out nicely for the 118th Pennsylvania, whose unauthorized crossing of the railroad brought it to a stop behind the welcome protection of Sykes' hilltop.[60]

Before the corps commander could appraise anyone else of his decision, Brig. Gen. Hayes watched the 118th not only cross the railroad in violation of instructions but grind to a halt without his orders. Riding over to find out what the Pennsylvanians thought they were doing, he learned from Sharwood and Davis that Sykes had suspended the advance and wanted every unit to find cover. Hayes immediately ordered the 18th Massachusetts and 1st Michigan against the shelter of the railroad embankment, and the 22nd Massachusetts into the forested ridge to its left.

He then sent Bartlett word of what he'd done and why. Upon receiving this report, Bartlett stopped the rest of his division, sending Sweitzer's and Chamberlain's brigades onto the wooded ridge to their left, where both laid down for cover. Bartlett ordered Chamberlain to move the 83rd Pennsylvania and 44th New York forward 600 yards to the farthest point of the ridge. Although this brought them within musket shot of the Rebels, it better posted the regiments to support Garrard's skirmishers along the riverbank. Chamberlain wisely kept the rest of his brigade 400 yards farther back and out of the Confederate artillery's sight.[61]

---

59 Hennessy, *Fighting with the Eighteenth*, 211-12; Acken, *Inside the Army of the Potomac*, 386. Barren in 1863, this hill is now heavily wooded and sits at the northern terminus of County Road T656 in Remington, VA (Rappahannock Station's name today). Tin Pot Run flows on the north side of the hill. https://tinyurl.com/yxej6v64, accessed 18Aug 2020.

60 *OR* 29, pt. 1, 580-81. After the battle Sykes asked Sharwood why he allowed his regiment to cross the railroad. The captain replied that "Jesus Christ himself" couldn't have kept the men from veering right. Sykes laughed and said that if such a distinguished character couldn't prevent the 118th from violating orders, a corps commander certainly could not. Sykes declined to punish Sharwood. Acken, *Inside the Army of the Potomac*, 391.

61 *OR* 29, pt. 1, 581-82. Hennessey, *Fighting with the Eighteenth*, 212; Edwin C. Bennett, *Musket and Sword, or The Camp, March and Firing Line in the Army of the Potomac* (Boston, MA, 1900), 166. The 18th MA and 1st MI right-faced and double-quicked to the railroad embankment. The 22nd about-faced, wheeled right, and marched into the woods on the ridge paralleling the O&A.

*   *   *

By 3:30 p.m. a semicircle of Union troops paralleled the Confederate bridgehead at an average distance of between 200–500 yards. Virtually all the Rebel skirmishers had retired inside their works. On the Federal left, Garrard controlled a long stretch of Rappahannock shoreline and screened Norman's Ford, while on the right Dudley's 5th Vermont occupied Beverly Ford and had already swung downstream to confront Penn's western flank. Having sealed off the enemy position, Horatio Wright told Col. Charles H. Tompkins, commanding the VI Corps artillery brigade, to deploy guns atop Howe's just captured ridge. The 29-year old officer promptly directed Capt. Richard Waterman's Battery C, 1st Rhode Island Artillery, and Lt. Leonard Martin's Battery F, 5th US Artillery onto the high ground, placing the two units on either side of a road leading to the bridgehead.[62]

At 3:45 p.m. Waterman's and Martin's twelve 10-pounder Parrott guns opened fire on the Confederate redoubts at a range of 1,300 yards. Moore, Dance, and Graham responded with counterbattery fire. Facing an equal number of enemy cannon, Tompkins brought forward Capt. Elijah Taft's 5th New York Battery, on loan from the army's artillery reserve. Positioning its six 20-pounder Parrotts a half-mile from the river, the colonel told Taft to subdue the Rebel fieldpieces south of the Rappahannock while Martin and Waterman suppressed those inside the bridgehead.[63]

The ensuing "spirited" artillery duel wasn't particularly destructive. The rival batteries, positioned on ground of equal height (75-90 feet) and shooting at long range, didn't inflict much damage. A Rebel shell broke the wheel of an unlucky Rhode Island piece, severely wounding one Federal in the neck and another in the hand. Beyond this, the Confederates barely drew blood. Despite mortally wounding a gunner in Graham's battery, the Yankees managed no better, but they did establish an effective harassing fire on the pontoon bridge.[64]

*   *   *

---

62 OR 29, pt. 1, 607. Waterman's battery deployed west of the road; Martin's guns took position east of it.

63 Ibid., 588. Confederate batteries generally had four guns; Union batteries generally had six.

64 OR 29, pt. 1, 621, 628 & pt. 2, 130-31; OR *Supplement* V, Pt. 1, 615; Moore, *Cannoneer Under Stonewall Jackson*, 206; Early, *Autobiographical Sketch*, 310. Robert S. Bell of Winchester, VA, Dance's Battery, had "a large piece" of Union shell "pass through his body." During the hour it took him to die, those comrades who could leave their posts came to say goodbye (see Moore, 206).

Though only vaguely obvious at the time, Sedgwick's decision to halt his infantry and try shelling the Rebels out of their fortifications cost him a grand opportunity. Colonel Penn's situation had grown increasingly desperate as Yankee skirmishers pushed nearer his earthworks. To block the 5th Vermont from slipping along the riverbank into his rear, he had shifted the 7th and 5th Louisiana to his western flank, even as the V Corps advance compelled him to keep the 8th and 9th Louisiana around the redoubts and the 6th Louisiana in a detached earthwork east of the railroad. These necessary deployments left the Rebel center defended by nothing more than a thin picket screen.[65]

Fortunately for the Louisianans, Sedgwick didn't spot their weakness; otherwise he might have used his numerical superiority and forward momentum to swamp the bridgehead, rather than merely displace its skirmishers. If the idea of such a bold rush occurred to him, Sedgwick probably discounted it given Rappahannock Station's reputed strength and cautions about possible counterstrokes from its bastions. Choosing to forego an immediate infantry assault despite having expertly brought his troops into attack position, the general put Tompkins' artillery to work in the dubious hope it might drive Penn into retreat. Hardly an indefensible decision in the face of an entrenched foe of unknown strength, the time required to implement it immensely aided a Confederate army taken off guard by Meade's advance.

*   *   *

Robert E. Lee eyed his opponent's advance with increasing disquiet. Jubal Early had recrossed the Rappahannock with news of Penn's perilous circumstances just before Tompkins' bombardment began. Endeavoring to aid the Louisianans with the few resources at hand, Lee directed Capt. Dance to shift a fieldpiece east of the railroad where it could more readily hit Sykes' infantry. Garrard's blue skirmishers took control of the riverbank opposite Dance's designated position before the Confederate artillerymen could even move, however, and Lee countermanded his order lest Federal sharpshooters kill the captain's horses and immobilize his gun.[66]

As four o'clock neared it looked increasingly likely that Sedgwick would overwhelm the bridgehead and either destroy Penn's regiments or force them into a desperate withdrawal across the pontoons. This gloomy aspect of affairs took a surprising turn when Sedgwick's infantry unexpectedly skidded to a halt. Minutes later Dame Fortune's smile broadened for the Rebels as the first of Early's reinforcing

65 Hariston Diary, Nov. 7, 1863, SHC/UNC.

66 OR 29, pt. 1, 612-13, 620-21.

columns hove into view and Brig. Gen. Hays (who had abandoned his court martial duties) galloped up to resume command from Penn.

The reinforcements belonged to Brig. Gen. Robert Hoke's North Carolina brigade, minus its commander and the 21st North Carolina, both gone home to round up deserters. In Hoke's absence 32-year old Col. Archibald C. Godwin, a six-and-a-half-foot tall Virginian, led the unit's three remaining regiments—the 6th, 57th and 54th North Carolina. Relieved to see his first unit reach the Rappahannock, Early hurriedly intercepted Godwin and directed him to strengthen the bridgehead as quickly as possible.[67]

Brigadier General John B. Gordon's command arrived shortly after Godwin moved off. Early dispatched its six Georgia regiments to occupy Jamison's Hill—a fortified rise of ground controlling the road to Norman's ford east of the O&A. Soon thereafter Brig. Gen. John Pegram's five Virginia regiments came onto the field. Early sent the 31st Virginia to confront Garrard's skirmishers but kept the rest of Pegram's brigade as a reserve, posted about a mile behind the hills hosting Dance's and Graham's artillery.[68]

* * *

Union commanders alert for possible counterattack, immediately noticed the appearance of Rebel reinforcements. Wright promptly ordered Russell and Terry to bring their divisions up alongside Howe. Following the same route taken by the 2nd Division an hour ago, the two units crossed a mile of ground exposed to intermittent Confederate shelling. Fortunately for the advancing Federals this bombardment wasn't directed at them but resulted from Southern gunners overshooting Tompkins' batteries. Shielded from direct observation by Howe's intervening ridge, Wright's 1st and 3rd divisions suffered little harm as they assumed position near the northern base of the two hills overlooking Rappahannock Station's defenses.[69]

Having mustered the VI Corps on a single line, the Federal right wing was well-posted to meet an attack. But Meade expected much more from Sedgwick than

---

67 Hoke's brigade received Early's summons to the front at 2:15 p.m. At the age of 19 Godwin moved to California where he became a wealthy miner and rancher before coming within one vote of winning the Democratic nomination for the state's governor in 1860. Early thought highly of him and pressed hard for his exchange (in summer 1864) after his capture the previous November. Promoted to Brig. Gen. in August 1864 Godwin was killed by artillery fire at the 3rd Battle of Winchester on Sept. 19, 1864. Hoke and his regiment returned to NC on Lee's orders in Sept. 1863. Paul Branch, "Godwin, Archibald Campbell, 1831-19 Sept. 1864," https://www.ncpedia.org/biography/godwin-archibald-campbell, accessed Jan. 10, 2020.

68 *OR* 29, pt. 1, 613, 621; Early *Autobiography*, 310-11.

69 *OR* 29, pt. 1, 585.

containing Lee's bridgehead. Acutely aware of this, Sedgwick and Wright rode out alone to within a quarter mile of the Rebel lines to get a better look at their objective. Unhappily, the works looked every bit as strong as Meade had warned. With their caution reinforced, the two officers rode back to the ridge and rejoined their staffs.

Still hopeful of avoiding a costly infantry assault, Sedgwick decided to strengthen his bombardment and sent word for V Corps artillery to enter the battle. At 4:30 p.m. six 3-inch Ordnance Rifles from Capt. Charles Phillips' Battery E, 5th Massachusetts Light Artillery, along with six 10-pounder Parrott guns in Lt. Benjamin F. Rittenhouse's Battery D, 5th US Artillery, trundled up to the firing line. Unlimbering in front of Sweitzer's brigade lying prone on the wooded ridge east of the O&A, they added their tubes to the 18 pieces already blistering Confederate defenses.[70]

The Federal bombardment's increasing intensity, plus Union skirmishers' long range musketry, made the Rebel pontoon bridge a hazardous place. Captain Seymour of Hays' staff testified that whenever he carried a message across the span Yankee projectiles "whistled" around his head "in a manner. . . not musical in the least." After running this hazardous gauntlet several times, Seymour's luck finally gave out when a shell splinter struck his horse, ending its messaging career. In the face of Sedgwick's escalating barrage Hays pulled the last of his skirmishers behind the entrenchments. Seymour, like the rest of the brigadier's troops, found himself pinned down inside the bridgehead impatiently waiting for dark to end the shooting.[71]

A concerned but unalarmed Lee witnessed all of this. He had ordered A. P. Hill to send Maj. Gen. Richard H. Anderson's division forward and assign it to block any Union thrust over Beverly Ford. The rest of Hill's Corps was preparing for action and standing by to head toward Kelly's Ford or Rappahannock Station as events warranted. Those steps and the concentration of Early's brigades seemed to have stabilized the current situation.[72]

Neither Lee nor Early were taking anything for granted, however, and they carefully monitored the flow of events. The two generals were sitting their horses near Graham's position when Hoke's brigade, obeying Early's order to reinforce Hays, came swinging up the road toward the pontoon bridge. Apparently, the division

70 Ibid., 583; John S. Kidder to Wife, Nov. 8, 1863 in James M. Greiner, *Subdued by the Sword: A Line Officer in the 121st New York Volunteers* (Albany, NY, 2003), 93; Jones, *Lee's Tigers*, 182-83; Mark Boatner, III, *The Civil War Dictionary* (New York, NY, 1959), 820-21.

71 Terry Jones, *Lee's Tigers: The Louisiana Infantry in the Army of Northern Virginia* (Baton Rouge, LA, 1987) 182-83.

72 Albert L. Peel diary, Nov. 7, 1863. Peel, adjutant of the 19th Mississippi in Posey's brigade, says that Anderson's division received movement orders at 5 p.m. and "came near Brandy Ford" where it halted. http://freepages.rootsweb.com/~peel/family/peelnov.html

commander hadn't informed Lee of this decision, and he was somewhat surprised to see the North Carolinians start across the bridge.[73]

The general felt a twinge of concern as he watched Godwin's 900 veterans double quick over the bobbing pontoons; each man ignoring bursting shells as though they were distant peels of thunder. Uncertain of Meade's intentions, Lee hadn't decided whether to throw the bulk of his own strength north of the river or concentrate it near Kelly's Ford. Determined to maintain optimum flexibility, Lee wondered aloud whether Early wasn't sending too many men into the fortifications. Knowing the odds facing Hays, Early said he felt it necessary to reinforce the bridgehead but would order Godwin back if desired. After slight consideration, Lee told Early that since the brigade was already crossing it might as well go on.[74]

Upon entering the fortifications, Godwin's men quickly plugged the dangerous void in Hays' center. Colonel Kenneth M. Murchinson's 54th North Carolina, took post on the brigade's left next to the 5th Louisiana. Colonel Robert F. Webb's 6th North Carolina went into line beside them, while Lt. Col. Hamilton Jones, Jr.'s 57th North Carolina assumed position on the brigade's right, connecting with the 8th Louisiana near the road leading to the pontoon bridge. Around 2,100 Confederate infantrymen now manned the bridgehead alongside Moore's 78 gunners and four cannons.[75]

If anyone could hold Rappahannock Station these battle-hardened, well-disciplined troops and their excellent officers could. Certain of that, Lee remained disinclined to commit additional force north of the river. With Godwin's regiments in place, the general inquired if Hays needed more help. Early referred the query to Penn

---

73 Freeman, *R. E. Lee*, Vol. 3, 190, 19n.; *OR* 29, pt. 1, 621.

74 *OR.* 29, pt. 1, 612-13, 620-21, 629; Early, *Autobiographical Sketch*, 310-11; J. G. DeRoulhac Hamilton, ed., *The Diary of Bartlett Yancey Malone* (Chapel Hill, NC, 1919), 43. Exactly when Lee alerted Hill and ordered Anderson forward is vague. In his report Lee says that he acted "upon receiving information" about the large Union force in front of Rappahannock Station. That probably occurred after Early returned from meeting with Penn, but it might have taken place when Early and Lee first met and the former relayed the import of Penn's earlier dispatches.

75 Early, *Autobiographical Sketch*, 311; *OR* Vol. 29, pt. 1, 625, 628-629, 630. There are no clear returns for Hays' and Hoke's brigades before the Battle of Rappahannock Station. The former reported he had 800–900 men on November 7, 1863, of which 702 became casualties. Colonel Tate of Hoke's Brigade reported his casualties as 928. Early says Moore's Battery lost 42 killed, wounded, or missing. The combined casualty figures totaled 1,630 men. Early states that 450 infantry and 28 artillerymen escaped from the bridgehead. This yields a total of 2,080 infantry occupying the bridgehead on November 7, 1863.

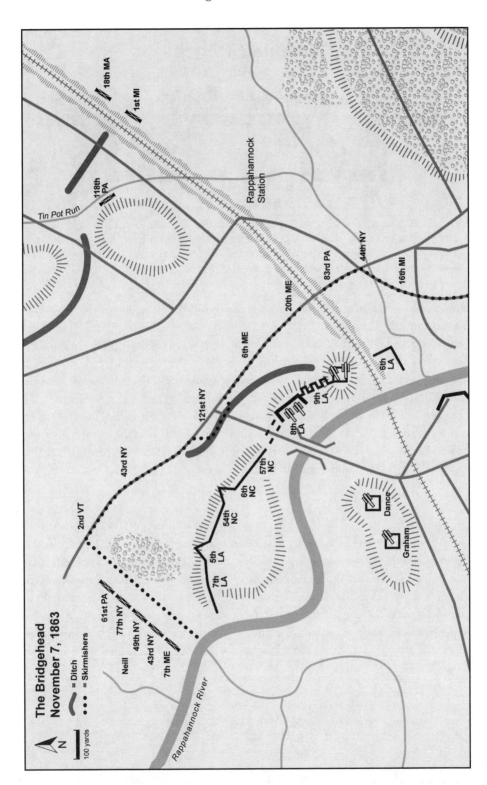

The Bridgehead
November 7, 1863

= Ditch
••• = Skirmishers

N
100 yards

18th MA
1st MI
118th PA
Tin Pot Run
Rappahannock Station
83rd PA
44th NY
16th MI
20th ME
6th ME
6th LA
9th LA
8th LA
121st NY
57th NC
6th NC
43rd NY
54th NC
5th LA
Dance
Graham
2nd VT
7th LA
61st PA
77th NY
49th NY
43rd NY
7th ME
Neill
Rappahannock River

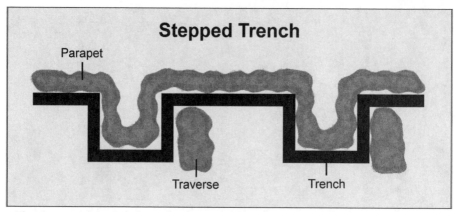

This diagram of the Rebel trenches between the two redoubts derives from a sketch Col. Theodore Lyman drew in his journal just after the battle. *Chris Hunt Source: David Lowe, ed., Meade's Army: The Private Notebooks of Lt. Col. Theodore Lyman (Kent, OH, 2007), 65.*

who replied none were required as he "could hold the position against the whole Yankee army."[76]

No doubt finding the colonel's confident declaration reassuring, Lee weighed the question of troop strength inside the bridgehead. He wanted to hold the enclave with minimal force, but he also wanted it kept secure from attack. The Yankee host arrayed against Hays and Godwin was enormous, but poor odds had never awed Robert E. Lee. He had been compelled to run huge risks from the moment he had taken command, most, but not all, of which had worked to his benefit. In each instance, however, the general had calculated the probabilities carefully before making his gamble. Here on the Rappahannock he did so again.

*   *   *

Although the enemy fielded a vast numerical superiority, Lee reasoned that the Federals couldn't attack along a greater front than his own troops presented. That meant one-to-one odds at the point of contact and in those conditions Rappahannock Station's earthworks should provide a decisive advantage. Roughly semicircular, these entrenchments followed the contour of high ground overlooking a gentle curve in the Rappahannock, whose watercourse anchored both ends of the line. A breastwork ran across flat ground east of the railroad for approximately 145 yards until it met Tin Pot

---

76 OR 29, pt. 1, 612, 621; Martin McMahon, "From Gettysburg to the Coming of Grant." *Battles and Leaders of the Civil War* (New York, NY, 1956), Volume 4, 87.

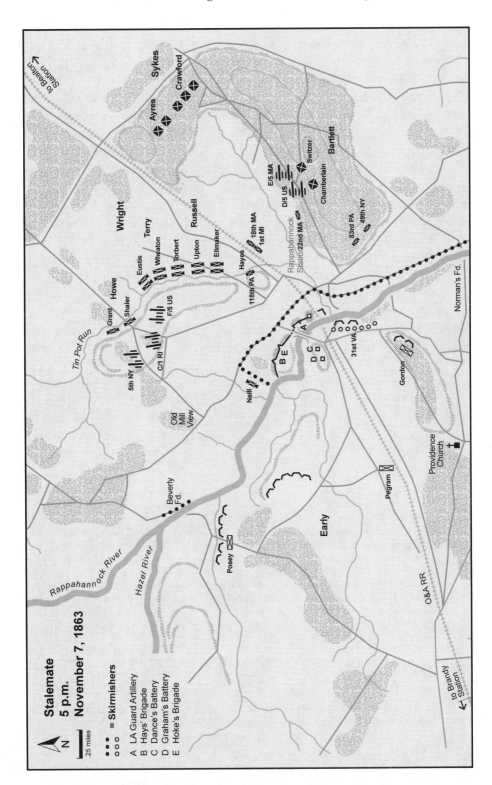

Stalemate
5 p.m.
November 7, 1863

N

.25 miles

••• = Skirmishers

A LA Guard Artillery
B Hays' Brigade
C Dance's Battery
D Graham's Battery
E Hoke's Brigade

Run where the creek turned south to flow into the river. The eastern flank of the trench bent back in the same direction using the stream as a small defensive moat.[77]

Two redoubts—one small and fully enclosed, the other large and open-backed, strengthened the fortifications west of the railway. The smaller one was built atop a steep 75-foot high hill close to the O&A, and its counterpart on an 80-foot elevation in the perimeter's right center next to a road leading downhill to the pontoon bridge. Each position had four embrasures cut into its parapet to accommodate cannon.[78]

About 360 yards of trench line dug in a "stepped" pattern separated the forts. This style of trench had traverses located every 15 or 20 yards. These provided protection from oblique artillery fire and prevented an enemy from enfilading the entire line should he get into the work. The design also divided defenders into penny packets of 10 or 20 men holding the trench sections between each traverse. Such a deployment complicated the officers' job allowing them to see only small parts of their commands unless they chose to expose themselves by climbing out of the trench.[79]

From the larger redoubt westward lay a half-mile of rifle pits dug in a broad zig-zag pattern that one Yankee said gave the Confederate line a "serrated" appearance. The resulting angles created salients protruding from the main line in places where the terrain jutted northward a bit. Troops manning these rifle pits during an assault could deliver enfilade fire into attackers threatening certain portions of the bridgehead's perimeter. The trenches in this sector lacked both traverses and the stepped design's complexity. They were simple ditches with excavated earth thrown in front of them to form a low parapet. A large patch of tall trees projected northward at the point where the line curved south. From these woods the trenches ran downhill until they touched

---

77 *OR* 29, pt. 1, 619. Early in describing the position for his official report starts on the Confederate right flank and verbally works his way to the left. In speaking of the position east of the railroad he writes: "of a rifle trench on the right, circling round to the river." Combat artist Edwin Forbes, who was present at the Battle of Rappahannock Station, made a detailed drawing of the Federal assault from his vantage point east of the O&A. This drawing clearly shows a breastwork east of the railroad, including its sharp bend conforming to Tin Pot Run. Several traverses are visible extending back from the parapet, as are the heads of a few defenders while Union skirmishers are visible in the foreground moving on the work. The drawing is included in this book, but readers can also access it at https://www. loc.gov/pictures/item/2004661444/ and zoom in to explore this drawing in great detail. Accounts of the 6th Louisiana's retreat over the river near the bridge pylons only make sense if the regiment occupied this part of the line.

78 *OR* 29, pt. 1, 619; Washington Roebling, *Map Memoir (map & commentary) June 12, 1863 Reports on Riflepits and Earthworks thrown up at Rapphk. St. and Beverly Ford,* New York State Library, Albany, NY.

79 Lowe, *Meade's Army,* 65. Lyman drew a sketch of the trenches in his journal, reproduced here, and wrote that the Rebel "pits were constructed with traverses and carefully laid out."

the Rappahannock just east of a little creek called Hubbard Run, which emptied into the river along its south bank.

A dam built in the 1840s just above the burnt bridge posed a latent threat to the defenders. Constructed by the Rappahannock River Canal Company to create a large pond for docking barges, it rendered the waterway directly behind the earthworks too deep for fording. All traffic going into or out of the position had to use the single pontoon bridge over the river.[80]

Lee thought these works "slight," the west flank rifle trenches being newly dug while Rebel engineers had recently converted the trench east of the railroad and the two redoubts from Yankee-built works looking south to forts looking north. Gaps existed in the entrenchment where the road running up from the river passed through the center of the fortifications just west of the large redoubt. That bastion was partially shielded by a drainage ditch 50 yards or so to its front. Except for this mild impediment and the smaller redoubt's steep hillside, nothing other than open terrain rising gently toward the earthworks fronted the bridgehead. Such ground offered little hindrance to an enemy attack. Moreover, no obstructing abatis protected the bridgehead's perimeter, perhaps because it would have complicated using the position as a springboard for offensive action.[81]

In Lee's opinion lack of these features didn't preclude successful resistance. The enemy would have to cross nearly 500 hundred yards of empty space to strike the fortifications. Southern cannon and riflemen could savage him every step of the way and break up any probable assault. Having "paid frequent visits to the works," Ewell concurred with his commander's assessment. Noting that "much labor had been

---

80 Previous paragraphs based on OR 29, pt. 1, 615; Wilson, "Captain Fish," *Military Collector*, Vol. 48 No. 3, 119; Adam Clark Baum, Map of the Battle of Rappahannock Station, Nov. 1863 (manuscript number GLC06013.03) Gilder Lehrman Institute of American History, NY; Lowe, *Meade's Army*, 65; M.A. Thesis, Donald Callaham, *The Rappahannock Canal*, The American University, 1967; VA Dept. of Transportation, *State Highway Commission Plan and Profile of Proposed State Highway, Fauquier and Culpeper Counties from 0.02 Mi. N. of S.C.L. of Remington to 0.667 Mi. South*, Sheets 1-5, October 24, 1927; J. T. Toler, "One of Fauquier's Historic Treasures: Rappahannock River Canal, 1816-60," *News and Notes form the Fauquier Historical Society*, 1994, Vol. 16, #2, 1, 3-5. Descriptions of a river assumed the observer was always looking downstream. "Above" meant upstream, or west, while "below" meant downstream, or east. When period documents mention the left or right bank, the left bank means the north shore and the right bank the southern shore.

81 Although Early explicitly states the entire perimeter lacked a defensive ditch, multiple Federal accounts speak of encountering some sort of ditch during their attack on the large redoubt. This battlefield feature might have been dug to provide earth for constructing the nearby O&A embankment, but it was probably a naturally occurring drainage ditch.

bestowed" upon the fortifications, he shared Lee's belief that the defensive emplacements were quite sufficient.[82]

Jubal Early wasn't so sanguine. He thought the earthworks "very inadequate" and later claimed he hadn't been shy about saying so to engineers supervising their construction or renovation. Not only was the lack of abatis and defensive ditches a grievous oversight, the sloping walls of the redoubts and low trench parapets, in his opinion, offered no meaningful challenge to an attacker determined to scale them. Further, Early adjudged that in some spots work crews had sited rifle pits for maximum protection rather than effective shooting, placing trenches so far rearward that their occupants couldn't fire on an assailant until he was dangerously close. Moore's cannon labored under similar disabilities, their redoubts' narrow embrasures offering limited traverse and constricted fields of fire.

Early also considered the bridgehead's lack of depth a serious defect. Should the enemy breach its right or center at any point he might quickly cut off the garrison from its pontoon bridge. Losing access to that span would be tantamount to losing every unit in the position. Early had advocated building a second bridge near the enclave's western flank as an alternate means of escape or succor, but no one had acted on his suggestion.[83]

Whether these imperfections were fatal or inconsequential mattered only if the enemy attempted an assault. With daylight steadily fading away that seemed increasingly unlikely, but not impossible. At Gettysburg Hays' and Hoke's brigades had launched a twilight charge that nearly won the battle by briefly capturing Cemetery Hill. Knowing better than most the possibilities of such a move, the Louisiana Tigers and their Tar Heel comrades remained vigilant. The Confederate high command, however, appeared to relax.[84]

From their vantage point Early and Lee could see muzzle flashes blink along the bridgehead's perimeter but thanks to a stiff south wind couldn't hear the firing. They also dimly perceived movement by Yankee infantry, but discounted it as nothing more

---

82 *OR* 29, pt. 1, 588, 611-12, 618.

83 Ibid., 619. Pontoon bridges were valuable and rare assets. This one was fairly short, just 5 boats long, and according to a Nov. 10, 1863 newspaper report in the *Republican·Standard*, the Rebels had captured the boats during the 1862 Peninsula Campaign.

84 Bradley M. Gottfried, *Brigades of Gettysburg: The Union and Confederates Brigades at the Battle of Gettysburg* (Cambridge, MA, 2002), 496-506. Since Hoke was still recovering from a Chancellorsville wound, Col. Isaac E. Avery had commanded the brigade at Gettysburg. He suffered a mortal wound during the unit's July 2 night attack on Cemetery Hill at which point Godwin assumed command. The 54th North Carolina did not fight at Gettysburg, having been detached to guard the substantial number of prisoners taken at the June 1863 Battle of Second Winchester.

than a demonstration. Neither general apprehended a serious threat, each convinced that Meade's army lacked "enterprise enough to attempt any serious attack after dark."[85]

Certain that nightfall was ending the day's fighting and observing Graham's and Dance's guns "producing little or no effect" on the enemy, Lee had the batteries cease fire. After directing Anderson to take all but one of his brigades back to camp and Early to keep his division ready for action but send no more troops across the river, Lee started toward his headquarters to sift through intelligence reports and make plans for tomorrow.[86]

Riding away he had no idea of what was happening north of the river. Without realizing it, Lee and Early had witnessed the virtual destruction of their bridgehead and the two brigades defending it. Indeed, at the same moment Lee ordered his artillery to cease fire, three Confederate regiments were on the verge of surrender, and the Federals were consolidating their possession of almost the entire line of Rebel earthworks. The sleepless night Lee and his soldiers already anticipated hardly resembled the one they were about to experience or the coming dawn's unforeseen dangers.

85 OR 29, pt. 1, 625.

86 Ibid., 612-13, 621; Albert L. Peel diary, Nov. 7, 1863, http://freepages.rootsweb.com/~peel/family/peelnov.html, accessed Mar. 1, 2020.

Chapter 6

"A Terrible and Indescribable Struggle"

Aggressive Instincts—Russell's Plan—Ellmaker's Assault—Into the Works—Desperate
Fighting—Upton's Advance—Union Guile—Confederate Disaster

WHATEVER Robert E. Lee and Jubal Early thought, John
Sedgwick wasn't certain the fight at
Rappahannock Station was ending. But he did know time was running out. The V and
VI corps had been in the presence of Rebels since noon and actively engaged since 3
o'clock. It was now nearly 5 p.m. The sun would set within 15 minutes and before
another hour expired the obscurity of a virtually moonless night would envelop the
landscape.[1]

Federal batteries were still blasting away at the enemy redoubts and their
fieldpieces south of the river, all of which continued shooting. Yankee skirmishers
drove one Rebel gun crew near the railroad away from its piece, but that was the extent
of Union success after an hour-long effort to silence Confederate artillery.[2]

Northern leaders watching their "handsomely executed" bombardment
concluded it was making "little impression" on the Rebels and unlikely to drive them
from their works. That would require an infantry assault, and neither Sedgwick nor
Wright evinced eagerness to hurl one against such a "formidable" position. Whatever

1 Sunset on Nov. 7, 1863 was 5:08 p.m. Krick, *Civil War Weather*, 112. Moon phase on that
date was a waning crescent https://www.moongiant.com/calendar/November/1863/,
accessed May 10, 2019.

2 *OR* 29, pt. 1, 578. V Corps skirmishers silenced one gun in the redoubt next to the railroad,
putting it out of action at roughly 4:15 p.m. and keeping it so until the fort was overrun. The
Union assault on the bridgehead was well underway when Lee ordered Dance and Graham to
cease fire.

Top Left: Brig. Gen. Albion Howe. *Top Right:* Maj. Gen. Horatio Wright. *Left:* Brig. Gen. David Russell. *All Library of Congress*

flaws marred the Southern fortifications remained invisible to Yankees eyes. From their vantage point, those "extensive and carefully constructed" earthworks looked like a death trap, and the terrain over which any attack must travel appeared "well calculated to check the impetuosity of a charge."[3]

Nonetheless, both generals felt the weight of Meade's expectations. Although Sedgwick had received no communication confirming the fact—Humphrey's 4 p.m. dispatch not yet having arrived—it was highly likely French had already captured Kelly's Ford and crossed the river. Thoroughly understanding Meade's strategy, the right wing's commander knew it was vital to unite the army as quickly as possible, lest Lee throw his whole weight against French's fraction of the AOP.

3   Ibid., 585, 575, 587, 608, 613, 621; Peter Wilson Hairston papers and Diary, SHC/UNC; Martin T. McMahon, "From Gettysburg to the Coming of Grant," *B&L,* vol. 4, 86.

Howe and Russell knew it too. Six months ago, during the Chancellorsville campaign these men had successfully stormed Marye's Heights at Fredericksburg. Schooled by that experience they lacked an instinctive belief in the impregnability of earthworks. Having sensed Rebel weakness from the moment their skirmishers neared the river, they were primed and eager to attack.

Brigadier General Howe had lobbied for permission to assail the Rebel left soon after seizing the high ground overlooking the Rappahannock. Though admiring his subordinate's zeal, Wright demurred, pointing out that Confederate south bank artillery could obliterate such an advance in a hail of canister fire. That admonition was premature, however, since enemy cannon weren't deployed west of Rappahannock Station when Wright vetoed Howe's request, which at any rate came before Union artillery got its chance to carry the day.[4]

When Brig. Gen. Russell obtained a view of the battlefield more than an hour later circumstances had changed. A West Pointer (Class of 1845) and veteran of 15 years regular army service which included combat in Mexico and fighting Indians in the Pacific Northwest, Russell had begun the war as colonel of the 7th Massachusetts before earning a brigadier's star in November 1862. Now 41 years old, the New Yorker enjoyed a solid reputation as a brave and skillful officer with a penchant for reconnoitering on the skirmish line—a habit that was about to pay huge dividends.[5]

With his boss temporarily leading the VI Corps, Russell had charge of Wright's 1st Division, which had advanced nearly to Tin Pot Run when Early's reinforcements began appearing on the field. Russell's skirmish line, consisting of five companies from the 6th Maine and Capt. Fish's reinforced company from the 121st New York, had taken position along the Freeman's Ford Road and a ditch some 200 yards from the Rebel redoubts.[6]

Despite shouldering enlarged responsibilities, Russell indulged his inclinations and rode well forward to survey the field and deduce enemy dispositions. The landscape between his division's main body and the Confederates hardly facilitated an easy approach. Beyond the low ridge shielding his brigades, the ground sloped down slightly until reaching a steep-sided 4- to 6-yard wide, 5-foot deep ditch half full of mud and water. This obstacle gave way to a weedy tree-stump covered field which in turn led to a

4 OR 29, pt. 1, 586; Wright to Anderson, Oct. 18, 1898 in *Proceedings at the Annual Meeting of the Association of Fifth Wisconsin Volunteer Infantry* (Milwaukee, WI, 1901), 36-37; James S. Anderson, "The Battle of Rappahannock Station" *Proceedings. . . Fifth WIS*, 30; https://babel.hathitrust. org/ cgi/pt?id=mdp.39015078124883;view=1up;seq=1 accessed 6/21/19.

5 Tagg, *Generals of Gettysburg*, 110; Warner, *Generals in Blue*, 416.

6 OR 29, pt. 1, 588; "Rappahannock" *National Tribune*, Jan. 22, 1885. The skirmishers were: 121st NY, Company D and 24 men from Company B; 6th ME, companies A, D, C, F and I.

level plain of packed dirt used by the area's current and former occupants as a drill field. That space ended at a slightly sunken section of the Freeman's Ford Road occupied by the division skirmishers.[7]

The first of two redoubts securing the enemy's right flank loomed a mere 200 yards from this depression. A 4-yard wide, 5-foot deep dry ditch roughly 150 yards in front of the skirmish line yawned between the sunken road and the nearest fort. This modest chasm bordered the gently sloping 50-foot rise leading to the closest Rebel bastion, a re-engineered open-backed lunette mounting two guns; 360 yards of eastward trench connected this fort to its smaller companion—a fully enclosed redoubt with two fieldpieces—standing on a steep hilltop alongside the railroad. A somewhat semicircular, half-mile long zigzag trench line punctuated by an occasional salient stretched westward from the larger redoubt before gradually curving south to touch the Rappahannock.[8]

In all this Russell saw opportunity rather than threat. Suspecting the Rebel works weakly held and confident in the "well-known character" of his men, most of whom had helped carry far more forbidding entrenchments six months earlier, the temporary division commander sought permission to attack. Forwarding this request through Capt. Henry R. Dalton, stationed nearby as a corps liaison officer, Russell waited expectantly for a reply as the sun's burnt orange orb finally dipped below the horizon.[9]

Whether Russell sent a detailed plan to Wright is unknown. Neither general mentioned the nature of the proposal in their after-action reports, although Wright's post-battle account strongly suggests Russell offered a thorough briefing. Either way, it was Wright's decision to make. The temporary VI Corps commander's light blue eyes, athletic build, and curly hair made him look younger than his 43 years. Although he had ranked second in the West Point class of 1841, his battlefield capacity remained uncertain. Wright's pre-war career had included teaching at his alma mater and a ten-year stint building forts and improving harbors in Florida. Missing the Mexican War had denied him any opportunity for distinction before 1860, which found him a

---

7 OR 29, pt. 1, 588; Anderson, "Rappahannock Station" *Proceedings. . . Fifth WIS*, 30. This is not the same ditch that had discomfited the 118th PA. The origin of this obstacle is unclear and only a few first-person accounts mention it. The obstacle might have been a natural feature, or a long-ago excavation associated with the O&A or the defunct Rappahannock Canal. No evidence yet uncovered answers questions surrounding it. Homes built in the late 20th and (despite pleas and efforts to preserve the battlefield) the early 21st century cover the entire route of the Federal advance during the battle as well as most of the CS defensive works.

8 OR 29, pt. 1, 588, 619-20; Anderson, "Rappahannock Station" *Proceedings. . . Fifth WIS*, 30. Union Observers differed on which of the two redoubts was the larger. Some Federals perceived the two positions and their connecting trench as a single fort.

9 OR 29, pt. 1, 588. Dalton was Brig. Gen. Wright's Assistant Adjutant General.

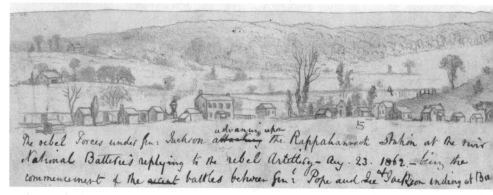

The rebel Forces under fire: Jackson advancing upon the Rappahannock Station at the river National Batteries replying to the rebel Artillery — Aug. 23. 1862 — being the commencement of the recent battles between Gen: Pope and Lee Jackson ending at Bu—

Edwin Forbes' drawing of the August 1862 fight at Rappahannock Station reveals many details about the terrain on which the November 1863 battle was fought. The image looks south from the ridge crest Russell's troops crossed during their advance. The village of Bowenville is on the left with the smokestack of a southward facing locomotive pulling a line of boxcars visible just behind the two-story house and marking the line of the O&A. The ridge in the center, here occupied by Union troops, hosted Confederate fortifications in 1863, with the small redoubt taking the place of the two dwellings (leftmost number 6), which retreating Federal troops

deskbound assistant to the army's chief engineer and still a captain after 19 years of service.

In April 1861, while taking part in a daring expedition to destroy the Norfolk Navy Yard, Wright fell into Confederate hands and spent a month in Rebel custody. After gaining his freedom he drew a series of staff assignments before serving briefly as a district commander in western Kentucky. The only test of Wright's combat leadership thus far had come in June 1862 when he led a division during the battle of Secessionville, South Carolina. Because he hadn't joined the AOP until after Chancellorsville, and his command had been in reserve at Gettysburg, the youthful looking general had yet to see action in the Virginia theater.[10]

Perhaps that lack of battlefield experience weighed on Wright's mind as he wrestled with Russell's proposal. Consenting might produce a brilliant victory. On the other hand, it could generate a horrible slaughter and since that looked more likely than not, he shrank from authorizing an attack on such a daunting position, initially considering any such effort utterly "hopeless." Upon reflection, however, Wright changed his mind.[11]

---

10 Styple, *General in Bronze*, 208; Tagg, *Generals of Gettysburg*, 106. Congress rejected Wright's initial appointment as a major general.

11 *OR* 29, pt. 1, 585-86.

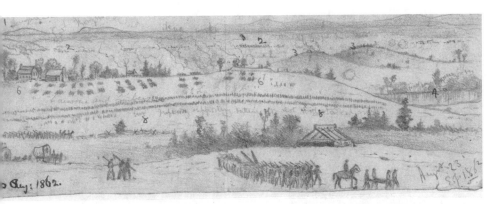

burned along with Bowenville not long after Forbes captured this scene. The number 4 marks the course of the river while the two number 3s indicate the position held by south bank Rebel artillery on November 7, 1863. The number 8 corresponds with the route of Freeman's Ford Road, from which the 6th Maine launched its attack. The gentle slope of the ridge is obvious, although it was longer than what Forbes shows here and he neglected to draw the finger of woods extending northward from the Rebel left. *Library of Congress*

Besides the manifest inability of Federal artillery to drive away the Rebels, several factors supported launching an attack in the handful of minutes remaining before nightfall. The presence of Sykes' corps to the east and Howe's division to the west should fix Rebel troops in place and prevent them from easily shifting strength to meet a specific threat. Union artillery ought to keep the enemy's head down, while the converging trajectory of its fire created a triangular zone directly in front of the larger redoubt through which Russell's division could advance. Confederate guns on the south bank couldn't shoot directly into this sector because their own north bank fortifications blocked it from view, leaving assault troops to face fire only from their immediate front.

The clock also favored a charge. Enough twilight graced the sky to facilitate an attack. But dusk would settle by the time Union soldiers reached their objective, rendering enemy artillerists beyond the Rappahannock inert from an inability to distinguish friend from foe. Under these circumstances Russell stood a good chance of getting inside the fort. And if support troops reinforced him in time, gathering darkness might assist them in achieving a breakthrough and overrunning the entire bridgehead.

Buoyed by these mental calculations, Wright sent Dalton back to Russell with authorization for an attack. As the captain rode off, the general dispatched an aide to Col. Tompkins with orders to continue a brisk bombardment. Another courier hurried to Sykes requesting that his gunners do the same.[12]

---

12 Ibid., 585-86. In his official report Wright doesn't mention informing Sedgwick of Russell's impending attack or involving him in any decision making, although the pair had together

Top Left: Col. Thomas Allen, 5th Wisconsin Infantry. *Wisconsin Veteran's Museum.* *Top Right:* Col. Benjamin Harris, 6th Maine Infantry. *Bangor Public Library.* *Right:* Maj. Walter Morrill, 20th Maine Infantry. *Library of Congress*

*   *   *

Wright's approval invigorated Russell who quickly rode to his leading unit, which, either by happenstance or design, was his own 3rd Brigade, commanded in his stead by Col. Peter Ellmaker, a 50-year old pre-war notary public and militia officer who usually led the 119th Pennsylvania. With time pressing, Russell had Ellmaker summon together the brigade's regimental commanders so he could explain their roles in his plan.[13]

---

inspected the field earlier in the afternoon. Wright's official report clearly states he took the decision alone. Sedgwick's acting AAG, Col. Martin McMahon, gave a different account of how the decision to attack was made. For a full discussion of this matter see Appendix Two.

13 Richard F. Miller, ed., *States at War*, 6 Vols. (Hanover, PA, 2014) vol. 3, 363.

Lieutenant Colonel Benjamin F. Harris's 6th Maine would spearhead the attack. Five of that regiment's 10 companies were already out as skirmishers, their line stationed in a sunken road near the base of the ridge leading up to the earthworks just 200 yards away. While the artillery kept up a hot fire, Harris would lead his regiment's five reserve companies to the skirmish line and merge them with the troops already there. Russell knew Confederates would spot this movement but expected them to interpret it as nothing more than the routine relief of one body of skirmishers by another and pay it scant attention.[14]

Once fully assembled, the 6th Maine would launch an immediate charge. Colonel Thomas S. Allen's 5th Wisconsin would follow as a second wave, while Ellmaker's other two regiments, the 49th and 119th Pennsylvania, advanced as a third. Each regiment would form a column of divisions to concentrate its strength, giving it a two company-wide front with the divisions arrayed one behind the other. The 5th and 119th would have five lines while the 49th Pennsylvania, with just 4 companies, would have two. Thus formed, they resembled human battering rams and their weight of numbers imposed on a narrow front should overwhelm any defense, providing the enemy didn't slaughter the attackers before they reached their target.[15]

Ideally Harris would get to the Rebel redoubt swiftly and keep its defenders busy until the 6th Maine's sister regiments came up and broke through. Russell's other brigades would join the fight as needed. If everything worked properly the attackers would catch the enemy off guard, seize his forts, take the bridge, and then capture or destroy Early's whole garrison.[16]

Russell was too good a soldier to believe everything would go smoothly. No plan ever did, and in an attempt this daring a lot could go wrong. The Rebels might counterattack and hurl back the attackers. Union reserves might not get into action fast enough. Enemy cannon might blast apart any Federal column nearing the pontoons. But failure was guaranteed if the 6th Maine failed to reach the Confederate line.

To realize its goal the regiment had to cross the 200 yards between its skirmishers and the enemy fortifications as quickly as possible. Any pause, hesitation, or delay

---

14 OR 29 pt. 1, 595; "The Sixth Maine's Superb Gallantry at Rappahannock Station," *National Tribune*, July 28, 1885.

15 "The Sixth Maine at Rappahannock," *National Tribune*, April 12, 1888. The regiments were in "close column of division on the center division." "Close column" means that the divisions did not maintain wheeling distance but stood right behind one another. "On the center division" means that the four left flank companies formed behind the two center companies, i.e. those on either side of the color guard in line of battle, while the four right flank companies formed in front.

16 OR 29, pt. 1, 588; Peter Michie, *The Life and Letters of Emory Upton* (New York, NY, 1885), 82.

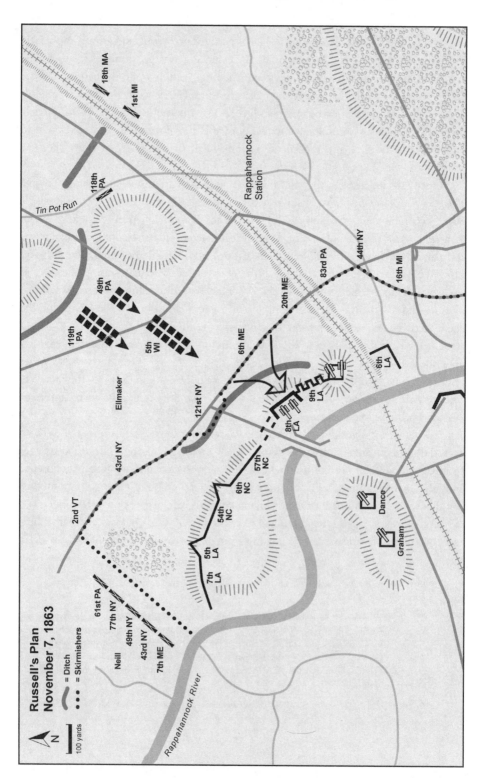

Russell's Plan
November 7, 1863

= Ditch
= Skirmishers

N
100 yards

Tin Pot Run

18th MA
1st MI
118th PA

Rappahannock Station

44th NY
16th MI
83rd PA
20th ME

49th PA
119th PA
5th WI
6th ME
6th LA
9th LA
8th LA

Ellmaker

121st NY

43rd NY

57th NC
6th NC
54th NC
5th LA
7th LA

Dance

Graham

2nd VT

61st PA
77th NY
49th NY
43rd ME
Neill

Rappahannock River

allowing the Confederates time to deliver multiple close-range volleys could spell disaster. Russell knew that once fired upon men tended to stop and return fire. More importantly, he knew that getting a halted line moving again was almost impossible.

If the Sixth made that mistake its charge was doomed. Determined to avoid such a fate, Russell ordered Harris's soldiers to remove the percussion caps from their muskets, rendering the weapons incapable of firing until recapped. Col. Allen, commanding the 5th Wisconsin, got the same order. Unable to discharge their rifles, the troops would have to drive home their assault with the bayonet or break and run away.[17]

Inevitably, some men's nerves would falter in such circumstances, and although Russell believed most of his veterans would stand the test, he tried to bolster their courage. Riding along the Sixth's reserve line he assured pensive soldiers that the enemy held his works with nothing more than a "strong skirmish line." Stopping at the regiment's center and noting that its banners remained furled inside their oilcloth covers, Russell told Color Sergeant John A. Gray, "Take off the case and unroll your flag, sergeant; we want you to put it on that fort."[18]

*   *   *

Having offered what inspiration he could, Russell ordered his plan into motion. The 6th Maine's reserve companies moved to the hilltop overlooking the Rappahannock, paused to deploy as skirmishers and then swept down the hill toward the sunken road, molested only by an occasional shell. Formed into a column of divisions, the 5th Wisconsin advanced 100 yards behind the New Englanders. But as the regiment neared Tin Pot Run an "ominous growl" rose from its ranks and the men slowed to a "half stop." When a concerned officer asked what was wrong, everyone within ear shot answered: "We're not loaded. You're taking us in with empty guns." One of Russell's aides riding behind the formation tartly replied "Forward! Your orders are to depend entirely upon the bayonet!"

The veterans greeted this retort with a "hoarse murmur" and outright disobedience, loading their muskets as they continued forward in utter disregard of the aide's instructions. As the rattle of ramrods increased, Col. Allen, riding ahead of his

---

17 OR 29, pt. 1, 599; Charles A. Clark, *Campaigning with Sixth Maine* (Des Moines, 1897), 46; "The Sixth Maine's Superb Gallantry at Rappahannock Station," *National Tribune*, July 28, 1887.

18 "The 6th Maine at Rappahannock Station," *National Tribune*, June 14, 1888; "The Sixth Maine's Superb Gallantry at Rappahannock Station," *National Tribune*, July 28, 1887. Gray, a native of Eastport, ME, was the first man over the stone wall below Marye's Heights at Fredericksburg in May, 1863. Then, like now, he carried one of the Sixth's flags.

regiment, finally caught wind of what was happening. Turning about he ordered his men to halt and load at will, urging them to be quick since the 6th Maine was steadily drawing farther away and closer to the enemy.

Desperate to reiterate Russell's intent, the insistent aide shouted at the troops to leave their muskets uncapped and rely solely on the bayonet. The only response was the sound of cocking hammers as men seated percussion caps onto the nipples of their weapons. Corporal James S. Anderson overheard someone mutter: "That fellow must think we're a pack of greenhorns."[19]

Loaded and capped, the 5th Wisconsin resumed its march, splashing across Tin Pot Run and starting up the hill separating it from a view of the Rebel entrenchments. The brief pause had been costly, however, and the distance between the 6th Maine and 5th Wisconsin now stretched to more than 200 yards. Col. Allen's regiment would need an additional five minutes to reach the enemy line. That interval condemned the New Englanders to a longer than anticipated bout of close combat without support. Hopefully, those 300 seconds hadn't already sentenced the assault to failure.

*   *   *

Unaware of the commotion behind it, the 6th Maine's reserve companies had moved unhurriedly toward the sunken road in skirmish formation. As expected, the Rebels spied the movement, "but supposing it simply a relief, paid but little attention." Upon reaching his destination, Lt. Col. Harris merged the two halves of his regiment together and quickly relayed the attack plan to those companies on the original skirmish line, simultaneously instructing them to uncap their muskets. The 32-year old former lumberjack then passed along word to fix bayonets. Once the clatter of sockets sliding onto barrels and locking rings clicking into place died out, Harris shouted the order to advance. Springing out of their sunken road the Northerners moved toward the Rebel works, each man marching at a steady quick-step and carrying his musket at trail arms.[20]

Although Russell's plan envisioned a solo attack by the 6th Maine, the regiment unexpectedly found itself accompanied by skirmishers on its flanks. Seeing the rest of

---

19 Previous paragraphs based on Anderson, "Rappahannock Station" *Proceedings. . . Fifth WIS*, 31-32.

20 Michie, *Letters of Emory Upton*, 83; OR 29 pt. 1, 597, 601; "The Sixth Maine's Superb Gallantry," *National Tribune*, July 28, 1887; Jane E. Schultz, ed., *This Birth Place of Souls: The Civil War Diary of Harriet Eaton* (Oxford, NY, 2011), 262. "Trail arms" was a standard arms position for rapid movement: the soldier carried the musket in his right hand at the balance of the piece halfway up the barrel and with his right arm fully extended. This gave the weapon a 45-degree angle at his side and made running fairly easy even with a fixed bayonet.

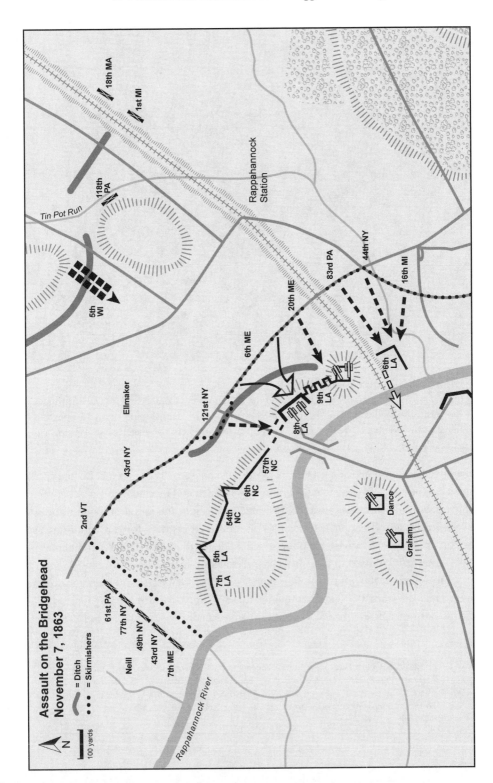

Assault on the Bridgehead
November 7, 1863

= Ditch
= Skirmishers

N

100 yards

18th MA

1st MI

118th PA

Tin Pot Run

5th WI

Rappahannock Station

20th ME

83rd PA

44th NY

16th MI

6th ME

9th LA

6th LA

8th LA

121st NY

Ellmaker

57th NC

43rd NY

6th NC

54th NC

Dance

Graham

2nd VT

5th LA

7th LA

61st PA

77th NY

49th NY

43rd NY

7th ME

Neill

Rappahannock River

Edwin Forbes, an artist/correspondent for Frank Leslie's Illustrated Newspaper, accompanied the V Corps on November 7 and sketched the assault on the Confederate bridgehead from a spot east of the railroad. This detail from his work shows V Corps skirmishers attacking the Rebel earthwork east of the tracks. The viewer can easily discern the small redoubt (1) atop the

the 6th Maine coming forward Capt. Fish had asked one of its officers if he had come out as a relief. Discovering what was about to happen and recalling Upton's caution to stay up with the foremost advance, Fish decided to join the assault, though it looked like a "reckless and daring" proposition, and ordered his men forward alongside the Sixth. Most of the New Yorkers obeyed and made for the Confederate entrenchments, but "some few" refused to take the risk and stayed in their ditch.[21]

Deployed on the left of the 6th Maine, the 20th Maine's skirmishers attacked as well. Detailed from Bartlett's command, these 75 men formed part of Garrard's V Corps skirmish line and had advanced in front of their division earlier that afternoon.

21 Edwin B. Quiner Scrapbook: Correspondences of the Wisconsin Volunteers. Vol. 8, 337, Wisconsin Historical Society, Madison, Wis.; "Rappahannock," *National Tribune,* Jan. 22, 1885; Wilson, "Captain Fish," *Military Collector* Vol. 48, No. 3, pg. 116-17; Best, *121st New York,* 101. To Fish's disgust the officer commanding the 121st New York's skirmish reserve failed to follow the advance.

dominating height beyond railroad embankment. The contour of the eastern earthwork is readily visible, as are the river (2), the stone pylons of the burnt bridge and the dam just upstream (3), as well as the fortifications south of the river (4) manned by Dance's and Graham's batteries and from which Lee and Early monitored events. *Library of Congress*

Led by Capt. Walter G. Morrill they had moved in a straight line, their right flank resting on the O&A until its bed made a slight jog to the east, at which point 50 of Morrill's troops found themselves west of the railroad. When Garrard called a halt, the 20th Maine's contingent stood next to and on the same side of the tracks as the 6th Maine's skirmishers.

While Union gunners tried to evict the Confederates from their fortifications, Morrill had wandered over to visit friends in the Sixth and was thus on hand when Harris brought up his reserve and laid out the assault plan. Maj. George Fuller noticed Morrill eavesdropping on the briefing and asked him if he would like to join the charge. More than willing, the captain ran back to his troops crying out: "Boys, the 6th Maine is on our right; let's go in with them!" Certain that their home state brethren ought not attack alone, the 20th Maine's skirmishers west of the railroad scrambled forward alongside Harris's command.[22]

22 Frank Moore, ed. *The Rebellion Record: A Diary of American Events*, 12 vols. (New York, NY, 1895), Vol 8, 163. Morrill had served as an NCO under Fuller earlier in the war. His actions at Rappahannock Station earned him the Medal of Honor.

On the other side of the O&A, the Twentieth's remaining skirmishers saw Morrill's advance. Assuming it resulted from orders which hadn't reached them, these 25 men moved forward as well. This in turn triggered an advance by the 83rd Pennsylvania's skirmishers and those of the 44th New York and 16th Michigan, all of whom assumed the same and moved against the Rebel earthwork east of the railroad.[23]

* * *

It was 5:15 p.m. The sky grew steadily darker as Federal soldiers trotted toward the Confederates. Russell's hope that twilight might conceal his movement evaporated when the 6th Maine let lose a spontaneous, almost primeval scream. The tumult, audible despite a noise dampening south wind, released a near unbearable tension welling up in the charging troops. One Rebel thought the "wild yelling" sounded as if "the whole Army of the Potomac" was launching an attack.

Nonetheless, waiting Southerners met the Sixth's cheer with a "murderous" volley that erupted like a "sheet of flame" from the breastworks and gouged huge holes in Union ranks. In the middle of this maelstrom 1st Lt. Charles A. Clark, the 6th Maine's 23-year old adjutant, estimated that this first scythe-like blast struck down nearly a third of the regiment's 321 men. With all hope of surprise gone, Harris ordered his soldiers to double quick—a slow jog that would maintain their formation and with it the advantage of mass upon hitting the enemy line. But his troops had other ideas and broke into an all-out run, their orderly line dissolving completely as they tried to cover ground as quickly as possible.

Although everyone charged at full tilt, the battle unfolded as if in slow motion. Lieutenant Clark felt like he was "marching against a blind, inscrutable force, which defied all efforts to reach it or grapple with it." As the Yankees struggled forward a second volley slammed into their ranks. Sergeant Gray and two other members of the color guard toppled with fatal wounds, another three fell injured. Throwing down his rifle, 22-year old Cpl. Reuben N. Maker of Company F, picked up the flag and ran toward the works Gray would never reach.[24]

Another withering fusillade tore into the 6th Maine, leaving a swath of devastation almost "impossible to describe." Close range muzzle blasts from hundreds of muskets

---

23 John J. Pullen, *The Twentieth Maine: A Volunteer Regiment in the Civil War* (Dayton, OH, 1984), 163; Oliver W. Norton, *Army Letters 1861-1865* (Chicago, IL, 1903), 189; Eugene A. Nash, *A History of the Forty-fourth Regiment New York Volunteer Infantry in the Civil War 1861-1865* (Chicago, IL, 1911), 172.

24 OR 29, pt. 1, 588; Clark, *Campaigning with 6th Maine*, 46, 48; *National Tribune*, April 19, 1894.

super-heated the air, leaving Union troops gasping for oxygen and adjutant Clark feeling as if every breath were scalding his throat and lungs.[25]

Confederate fire felled men "with fearful rapidity," yet somehow enough blue uniforms survived to scramble into and out of the dry ditch laying some 50 yards before the redoubt. As Yankees began laboring up the gentle slope Rebel resistance increased to a fever pitch. So too did the desperation of the attackers, who appeared "seized with the wildest transports of rage and frenzy." A slug slammed into Lt. Col. Harris, shattering his left thigh and knocking him back into the ditch. Other officers fell in quick succession. Major Fuller assumed command but could do nothing more than advance alongside the ever-shrinking number of men who inexplicably remained unhurt.[26]

After racing across 200 yards of bullet-swept terrain, Russell's first wave finally struck the Confederate defenses; or least part of it did. From inside the works, Capt. Seymour saw "hundreds" of Northerners go down before they had "ascended halfway up" the rampart. Many of those were dead or bleeding. Some slipped and fell while dozens more simply hit the dirt in search of cover, either too exhausted or too stunned by what they had just experienced to keep going.

Small groups of brave men jumped into the fort, entering it "attenuated and scattered" according to Lt. Clark, "a handful here and there," only to encounter "swarms of the enemy." Although most Confederates had taken a few steps backwards as Union troops surged onto the earthworks, the defenders recovered within seconds and threw themselves at the invaders. This counterthrust forced the smattering of Federals inside the work "to leap back over the trenches," where most of the regiment had gone to ground.[27]

*   *   *

The 121st New York's skirmishers had better luck, at least initially. Captain Fish with fewer than 50 men struck the Rebel works just west of the large redoubt where the road leading to the pontoon bridge crossed through the fortifications. Unable to build a solid wall at this point, Rebel engineers had left two gaps in the line through which traffic could travel. To defend these intervals they had also constructed a pair of small

25 Clark, *Campaigning with 6th Maine*, 46.

26 OR 29, pt. 1, 599, 588; Clark, *Campaigning with 6th Maine*, 46; Anderson, *5th Wisconsin Proceedings*, 32; Acken, *Inside the Army of the Potomac*, 390. Harris would lose his left leg to amputation.

27 Matthews, "The Sixth Maine's Superb Gallantry," *National Tribune*, July 28, 1887; Clark, *Campaigning with 6th Maine*, 47.

outworks as barriers some yards in front of the openings. Vehicles or troop columns passing in or out of the bridgehead had to zigzag through these staggered mounds of dirt. Although designed to allow men in the rearmost positions to fire between the forward posts, this was unquestionably the most vulnerable sector of the enemy line.[28]

The New Yorkers faced no ditch or other obstruction as they began running up the gradual 100-yard slope leading toward this part of the bridgehead. Confederate troops behind the disconnected works delivered a volley that killed one man, hit a sergeant in the arm and "dangerously wounded" Capt. Marcus R. Casler of Company B while a spent round knocked Capt. Fish to the ground breathless. Recovering his wind after a moment and realizing he wasn't bleeding Fish jumped up to hurry after his men, who were now 30 or 40 yards ahead of him.

Catching them just as they reached the entrenchments, Fish leapt over one of the smaller breastworks and instantly found himself face to face with a Rebel who "leveled his piece" at the officer's breast. Fortunately for the captain he held a cocked revolver and was able to get off the first shot, killing his enemy instantly with a bullet through the forehead. As the dead man slumped to the side Fish realized the rifle pits were full of Southerners outnumbering his small command three or four to one.

Doing the only thing possible Fish boldly shouted a demand for surrender which his men echoed while pointing bayoneted muskets at graycoats packed into their rifle pits. To the captain's amazement these Rebels, most holding empty or half-loaded rifles and all stunned by the sudden and unexpected dusk assault, threw down their weapons and raised their hands. Seizing on his remarkable good fortune Fish detailed a few men to hustle 127 prisoners to the rear.

His delight with this easy success soon soured, however. With less than 40 men left, the captain quickly found his position inside the bridgehead untenable. To his right stretched at least a half mile of entrenchments filled with hundreds of Rebels. The closest of these pivoted to face Fish and came charging in on the isolated New Yorkers who were forced back against the west face of the large redoubt, which itself had been cleared of Union troops.[29]

---

28 Adam Clark Baum, "Map of the Battle of Rappahannock Station," Nov. 1863, Gilder Lehrman Institute of American History, NY. A native of Otsego, NY, Baum was the 31-year old assistant surgeon for the 50th NY Engineers. He drew a map of the bridgehead shortly after the battle that clearly shows the staggered entrenchments as the road cut through the Rebel position. It also depicted the shape of the two forts and the salients in the Confederate line. The map corresponds with testimony from Capt. Fish and others in the 121st NY who claimed two lines of enemy breastworks.

29 Previous paragraphs based on Best, *121st New York*, 101; Wilson, "Captain Fish," *Military Collector* Vol 48, No. 3, 117. Elements of the 8th LA held this part of the Confederate line; the counterattacking force came from the 57th NC.

Capt. Ruel Furlong, Company D, 6th Maine Infantry. *Bangor Public Library*

For an instant Russell's assault was a failure. Having defeated the 6th Maine's initial effort, Harry Hays claimed that most of Harris's "shattered and disorganized" command "laid down" for cover against the fort's sloping wall and "cried out that they surrendered." However, more stalwart souls speedily supplanted men pleading for quarter. With some less fleet-footed New Englanders reaching the parapet, officers and others again shouted "Forward!" In response willing men scrambled upwards and over the mounded dirt into the redoubt.[30]

Hays' Southerners again yielded a few steps before countercharging. Those Federals not expelled from the position a second time fought desperately with their backs against its walls. Among these was Capt. Reuel W. Furlong of Company D, a tall, powerfully built man affectionately known as "the big captain." The 27-year old native of Milltown, Maine, had emptied his revolver and lost his sword during the Sixth's first foray into the redoubt. Now he found himself furiously swinging a clubbed musket to fend off a mob of ferocious Louisianans. Lieutenant Henry H. Waite tried fighting his way to Furlong's assistance only to receive a mortal wound before reaching him. Minutes later the captain succumbed to overwhelming odds, his body dropping to the ground beside several Rebel corpses produced by his final blows.[31]

Not every man in blue craved a martyr's death, however. Trapped and surrounded, some threw down their arms before crying out their capitulation. Others scrambled

30 OR 29, pt. 1, 628; Jones, *Civil War Memoirs*, 93; Matthews, "The Sixth Maine's Superb Gallantry," *National Tribune*, July 28, 1887; Clark, *Campaigning with 6th Maine*, 47; Moore, ed., "A Rebel Narrative," *Rebellion Record*, Vol. 8, 165.

31 Clark, *Campaigning with 6th Maine*, 49; Matthews, "The Sixth Maine's Superb Gallantry," *National Tribune*, July 28, 1887; "Reuel Williams Furlong" https://www.findagrave.com/memorial/82058966/reuel-williams-furlong accessed July 15, 2020. Waite died in a hospital on November 15, 1863.

Edwin Forbes sketched the assault on Rappahannock Station from a position east of the railroad. It is difficult to place the exact moment Forbes captures, but in all likelihood, it depicts events about 10 minutes after the attack started. The 6th Maine (note flag) is attacking the large redoubt, while the 20th Maine's skirmishers charge the trench connecting it to the

back over the parapet as the Confederates regained the entrenchment for a second time, only to lose it again when the 5th Wisconsin belatedly joined the battle.[32]

* * *

Col. Allen's regiment, delayed by its pause to load, had hurried forward as fast as it could behind the 6th Maine. Still wearing knapsacks, the Mid-Westerners marched at the quick step until crossing the ridge and the wet ditch near its base separating them

32 OR 29, pt. 1, 628; Jones, *Civil War Memoirs*, 93; McMahon, "From Gettysburg to the Coming of Grant." *B&L*, Vol. 4, 86-87.

small redoubt and the 5th Wisconsin's column of divisions (dense mass of Union troops) reaches the foot of the ridge. In the foreground V Corps skirmishers charge the 6th Louisiana's trench east of the O&A *Library of Congress*

from the battlefield. Emerging from that soggy obstacle, the 5th Wisconsin heard the "crackle and roar" of musketry echoing from the Rebel fortifications. Even in the waning light they glimpsed the battered Sixth "clinging" to the enemy parapets. "Little groups of twos or threes" stood at the "very edge of the works," their bodies silhouetted against the dimming skyline, some fighting and more "casting anxious glances" rearward "to see if help was coming."[33]

The sight of Union men "falling thick and fast" along the battle line elicited from the Wisconsinites "a terrible shout" of "rage. . . vengeance [and] encouragement" all at once. With or without orders—which never became clear—men threw off their knapsacks and began moving at the double quick toward the fight. Leaking winded or

33 Anderson, *5th Wisconsin Proceedings*, 32.

irresolute stragglers, the regiment maintained its column of divisions despite "a torrent of spherical case" fired into it by Rebel guns. The 57th and 6th North Carolina delivered an enfilade fire into this dense mass, but the Yankees ignored their losses, coming on with such "great impetuosity" that at least one defender felt certain their courage sprang from the "free use of whiskey." Out of breath and wrapped in a "terrible significant silence" Allen's troops crossed a quarter mile of deadly ground before finally reaching the dry ditch. As the panting regiment began clambering across this final barrier, a 6th Maine lieutenant atop the breastwork shouted, "For God's sake, 5th Wisconsin, hurry up!"[34]

The mid-westerners needed no further encouragement. Struggling up the slope toward the fort, their right flank companies aimed for the redoubt while the left wing veered east to assault the trench line between the Rebel forts. A "storm of bullets" blistered the attackers. Colonel Allen suffered a devastating wound to his left hand just as he neared the parapet. Major Horace M. Wheeler fell shot in the back near the ditch. Twenty-two-year-old Capt. Horace Walker took a bullet through his brain only a few steps from the earthwork. First Lieutenant James Ordway made it a little farther, reaching the redoubt before collapsing with a fatal wound while brazenly demanding the enemy inside surrender. Heedless of the losses Lt. Col. Theodore B. Catlin led the regiment "pell-mell" into the fortifications, ending the 6th Maine's 10-minute long stand-alone duel and instigating an even more "terrible and indescribable" hand-to-hand struggle.[35]

The fighting was pitiless and intensely personal. Men shot one another at such close range powder burns singed uniforms. Others fenced with bayonets and when they found that weapon too cumbersome used their muskets as clubs. A Wisconsin private snapped off the butt of his rifle hitting one Rebel hard enough to "shatter" his skull "to fragments" in a gruesome spray of blood and brains. The "handsome curly-haired" Federal died an instant later when a bullet ripped through his head.[36]

It was virtually dark now, leaving Union artillerymen unable to see and silencing their guns. But along the Confederate right flank, muzzle flashes punctuated the

---

34 Ibid.; Jones, *Civil War Memoirs of Seymour*, 93. Spherical case shot was a round shell filled with lead balls and a bursting charge. A timed fuse inserted into the projectile, ignited by discharge from the gun, detonated the shell and sprayed the lethal balls over a wide area.

35 OR 29, pt. 1, 598; Anderson, *5th Wisconsin Proceedings*, 33; Moore, ed. "Boston Journal Account," *Rebellion Record*, Vol. 8, 164; H. E. Matthews, "The 6th Maine," *National Tribune*, March 15, 1888. Allen recovered and continued in service through the end of the war. Wheeler died on November 19, 1863.

36 Anderson, *5th Wisconsin Proceedings*, 33. Anderson says this soldier's name was Jeff Davis. However, no such name appears on the regimental roster nor does it show a member of the regiment with that surname killed in action during the war.

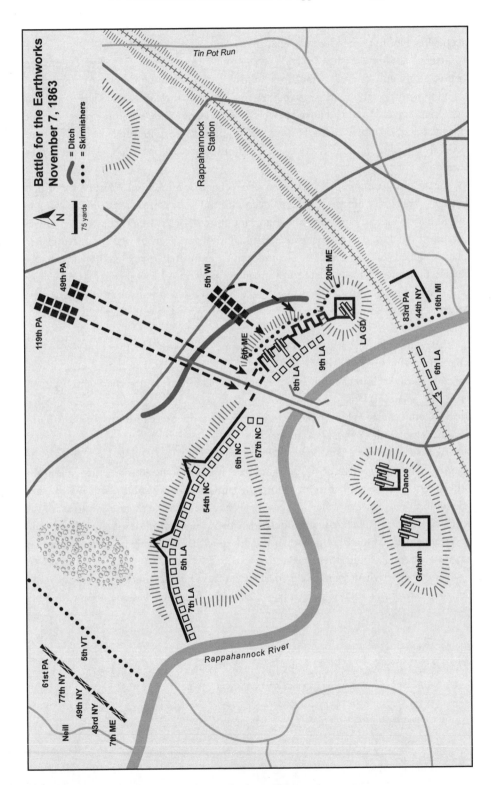

Battle for the Earthworks
November 7, 1863

= Ditch
= Skirmishers

N

75 yards

Tin Pot Run

Rappahannock Station

119th PA

49th PA

5th WI

6th ME

8th LA

9th LA

20th ME

LA Gd

83rd PA

44th NY

16th MI

6th LA

54th NC

6th NC

57th NC

5th LA

7th LA

Rappahannock River

Dance

Graham

61st PA

77th NY

49th NY

43rd NY

7th ME

5th VT

Neill

deepening gloom as men tore at each other with barbaric savagery. The air "filled with a medley of shouts, shrieks and groans, calls to surrender, yells of defiance, imprecations and curses" which rose above the unrelenting "crash of musketry." Fighting with ferocity worthy of their nom de guerre, the Louisiana Tigers "clubbed their muskets and used them freely over Yankee heads" and "when the work was too close for that, dropped their guns and [began] pummeling with their fists." Desperate Federals forgoing the time needed to reload, threw stones or hurled bayonets at their foes.[37]

Seized by primitive instinct, men shed civilized inhibitions. Beset by multiple enemies, Lt. Clark plunged his sword deep into the body of one assailant. Rushing to the adjutant's aid, an intensely pious sergeant known for praying earnestly every night regardless of place or circumstance, morphed into a murderous brute. An astonished Clark watched the "gigantic" non-com let out "an infuriated yell" and wade into the Rebels. Spewing the most "fierce and appalling" profanity, he slashed with his bayonet before clubbing his musket in a successful effort to rescue the beleaguered lieutenant. Mortified by his own behavior, the soldier later begged Clark to forget his heroically blasphemous conduct.[38]

Sergeant Otis Roberts felt no such compulsion as he led five other men in a sanguinary attack on the 8th Louisiana's color guard. The ensuing contest proved extraordinarily vicious as rivals in butternut and blue thrust and parried with bayonets until the Federals killed, captured, or drove off the defenders, leaving their blood-spattered flag in Union hands. Rather than produce a call for obscurity, Roberts' conduct earned him a medal of honor.[39]

The struggle for Lt. Moore's artillery raged with equal violence. Confederate gunners had stood to their posts, pouring a deadly fire into the attackers throughout the 6th's Maine's seesaw effort to break into the larger redoubt. With the 5th Wisconsin's added numbers, however, the Yankees finally amassed sufficient strength to assail the fort's fieldpieces. Rebel artillerists defended their guns with "desperate bravery and determination," continuing to load and fire despite the increasing proximity of enemy troops clustering around them.

One Southern lieutenant declined to retreat from his surrounded piece: attaching a line to the weapon's friction primer he was about to fire when a Maine officer shouted,

---

37　Ibid.

38　OR 29 pt. 1, 598; Anderson, *5th Wisconsin Proceedings*, 32; Clark, *Campaigning with 6th Maine*, 47; McMahon, "From Gettysburg to the Coming of Grant." *B&L*, Vol. 4, 86-87.

39　OR. 29, pt. 1, 600; Martin Graham and George Skoch, *Mine Run: A Campaign of Lost Opportunities. October 21, 1863–May 1, 1864* (Lynchburg, VA, 1987), 23; Jones, *Lee's Tigers*, 183.

"Drop that lanyard!" The lieutenant refused and Federal infantry shot him dead before he could discharge his gun. A few yards away the fort's other cannon managed to get off a last canister round. The charge blasted "to atoms" those Yankees in its path but the gun had hardly finished recoiling before infuriated Northerners swarmed over the piece, bayoneting two of its crew at their stations.[40]

Capturing the cannon hardly assured victory. Near the pontoon bridge Gen. Hays was busily assembling elements of the 8th and 9th Louisiana for a counterattack. Seeing this, Sgt. Joe Goodwin of the 5th Wisconsin collected a few men and pivoted the stricken artillery lieutenant's still-loaded cannon to face the accumulating Rebels. After getting off a round he was attempting to wheel the gun back into position for another shot when a bullet entered his heart, instantly killing the dark haired 20-year old.[41]

Goodwin's fate seemed to underline the Federal's precarious position. Lt. Col. Jones' 57th North Carolina had reoriented itself to shoot at the Federals from the west, while elements of the 9th Louisiana between the two redoubts were firing into 5th Wisconsin from the east. Already suffering under this "hot enfilading fire," Harris' and Allen's regiments now faced a violent frontal assault as Hays hurled the 8th Louisiana and parts of the 9th at the Yankees with such fury one Northerner said it felt "like a pack of hungry wolves were jumping at our throats."[42]

*   *   *

General Russell knew the moment of decision had arrived. Although mounted and an easy target, he had trotted forward just behind the 6th Maine during its advance and continued to hover not far from the firing line as the 5th Wisconsin threw itself into the mêlée. Despite suffering a bad wound to his foot, he refused to leave the field. Alarmed by the intensity of Rebel resistance, Russell realized his assault would fail unless reinforcements quickly reached the harried, exhausted men struggling in the redoubt.

---

40 OR 29, pt. 1, 595; M. McNamara, "Lt. Charlie Pierce's Daring Attempts to Escape from Johnson's Island" *SHSP*, 1880, vol. 8, 61-67; Clark, *Campaigning with the 6th Maine*, 47; Anderson, *5th Wisconsin Proceedings*, 33; Stevens, *Corn Exchange Regiment*, 343; Carter, *Four Brothers in Blue*, 363; Acken, *Inside the Army of the Potomac*, 390.

41 OR 29, pt. 1, 628; Anderson, *5th Wisconsin Proceedings*, 33; "Joseph Goodwin" https://www.findagrave.com/memorial/95205768/joseph-goodwin accessed 7/7/19.

42 Matthews, "The Sixth Maine's Superb Gallantry," *National Tribune*, July 28, 1887; Anderson, *5th Wisconsin Proceedings*, 34; Wilson, "Captain Fish," *Military Collector*, vol. 48, No. 3, 119. The sequence and timing of Confederate counterattacks is a bit confusing as the Federals facing them each had a different vantage point and obviously were trying to recall events taking place amidst a chaotic and fluid situation. The North Carolinians counterattacked at least twice and Hays' troops possibly three times.

Impatiently looking for the 49th and 119th Pennsylvania, which together made up the third assault wave, Russell dispatched first his own aide-de-camp and then Capt. Albert M. Tyler of Wright's staff to hurry the regiments up.[43]

The expected units, each arrayed in a two-company-wide column of divisions, had moved forward at the same instant as the 6th Maine and 5th Wisconsin; Lt. Col. Thomas M. Hulings' 49th Pennsylvania was on the left and the 119th Pennsylvania (under Lt. Col. Gideon Clark while Col. Ellmaker led the brigade), on the right. Starting 100 yards or so behind the second wave and briefly delayed by its pausing to load, the Pennsylvanians had advanced at quick time, sloshed across Tin Pot Run and then climbed to the hilltop overlooking the battlefield, where they finally caught sight of the wild fight some 500 hundred yards distant.

Burdened with knapsacks and carrying a bulky load of eight days' rations, Hulings' and Clark's men crossed the muddy ditch below the hill and then covered the ensuing quarter-mile as fast as they could. That trek took at most ten minutes, but for the troops trying to fend off Hays' counterattack, the wait seemed "interminable." Finally spotting the 49th and 119th draw near the sunken road, Russell spurred his horse rearward to urge haste. Coming up to the regiments he ordered them to double quick. Two minutes later, shouting that the Rebels were pushing their comrades back, the general issued the command to run.

Alive to the critical nature of the moment, the Pennsylvanians gave a yell and "dashed" toward the enemy breastworks. This final surge left behind many soldiers too fatigued or breathless to keep up with their units. Their ranks disordered by the sprint, both regiments struck the enemy line just west of the large redoubt, the men going to ground and gulping air on the outer edge of the small parapets guarding the road. Winded stragglers continued joining the line for some minutes after it took cover and several more minutes would elapse before the two units regained enough stamina for further exertion.[44]

43 *OR* 29, pt. 1, 589; H. E. Matthews, "The 6th Maine," *National Tribune*, March 15, 1888; Anderson, *5th Wisconsin Proceedings*, 34; McMahon, *B&L*, vol. 4, 88n. Russell represented his wound as slight, but it proved more serious than that, eventually requiring such a lengthy hospital stay it exceeded the 60-day period after which current regulations required the army to muster an officer out of service. It took the strenuous efforts of Meade, Sedgwick, and Wright to keep Russell in uniform. Eventually returning to the field, Russell continued compiling a fine record until his death at the Battle of Third Winchester (also called the Battle of Opequon) on Sept. 19, 1864.

44 Previous paragraphs from *OR* 29, pt. 1, 588, 601; Robert S. Westbrook, *History of the 49th Pennsylvania Volunteers* (Altoona, PA, 1898), 168; Anderson, *5th Wisconsin Proceedings*, 34; Matthews, "The 6th Maine," *National Tribune*, March 15, 1888.

Nonetheless, the opportune arrival of these reinforcements marked the battle's turning point. Although it seemed years to the men in it, the fight thus far had consumed a mere 15 minutes and within that brief period Yankee infantry had fatally wounded the Confederate fortifications.

*   *   *

As Ellmaker's brigade bled for the large redoubt, skirmishers from the 20th Maine had stormed the smaller fort which sat near the railroad atop such a steep hill that its gunners couldn't depress their cannon sufficiently to fire on their attackers. Benefiting from this topographical flaw in the enemy line, Capt. Morrill's troops managed to scale the elevation without taking serious casualties and then break into the position to silence its one remaining operational gun. This created a crisis for Col. Peck's 9th Louisiana. With some of its manpower already fighting around the large redoubt, the regiment's main body found itself assailed by V Corps skirmishers and the 5th Wisconsin's left wing, leaving it no choice but to abandon the rifle pits spanning the two redoubts. Forced out into the open, most of the Ninth drifted back toward the pontoon bridge.

Colonel Monaghan's 6th Louisiana was embroiled in just as dire a predicament. Its position east of the O&A isolated it from the rest of Hays' brigade while the railroad embankment kept it from seeing much of anything to the west. Already on edge after watching Bartlett's division sweep forward earlier in the afternoon and fully aware that two Union corps stood in their front, the Louisiana regiment's 172 men knew they couldn't hold their trench against a serious attack.

Monaghan realized that assault had begun when he heard a sudden onset of yelling and firing to his left. A minute later he saw 275 skirmishers from the 20th Maine, 83rd Pennsylvania, 44th New York, and 16th Michigan come swarming toward him. Certain his regiment faced annihilation if it didn't immediately evacuate its untenable position, the colonel ordered his men to move by their left flank, exit the earthworks along the embankment leading to the burnt railroad bridge, and attempt escape by fording the Rappahannock. Reaching the shoreline first, the Sixth's left flank companies scurried down the riverbank and sloshed their way to safety, some of the Louisianans tossing aside their rifles to facilitate escape, while Col. Monaghan swam his horse over the river. The regiment's right flank wasn't so lucky, and its companies were still wading through armpit deep water, when Federal skirmishers reached the shore and began pouring a "pitiless" fire into the fugitives. A survivor of the ensuing carnage recalled seeing ill-fated comrades sink beneath the frigid water "with a bubbling shriek," after being shot in the back, "losing thus whatever chance of life was left after the bullet had done its work."[45]

Even to battle hardened veterans this seemed no better than murder. Suddenly revulsed by what they were doing, Union troops ceased fire and yelled for the survivors to come back and surrender. Although some men kept going, nearly 100 helpless escapees reversed course in hope of saving their lives. But as the sodden Louisianans neared the north bank one of their officers stepped out from behind a bridge abutment, flourished his sword and demanded they renew their retreat. Obediently wheeling about, the Rebels "began splashing their way" back to the opposite shore only to have the Yankees open fire again. Caught under a "hail of bullets" 75 Southerners sought shelter behind the scorched stone pillars and cried out for quarter, which the Federals eventually granted.

No one ever recorded the identity or fate of the Rebel officer involved in this episode or an exact number of men gunned down in the river. But at least one Federal witness troubled by what he had seen labeled the incident "a terrible affair." Regardless, the action cost the regiment 90 men missing in action out of 172 engaged.[46]

Corporal Godfrey Gaisser, the 6th Louisiana's 21-year old color bearer, was among those captured. Upon reaching the Rappahannock he had pulled the regiment's flag from its staff, thrown the pole into the river and hidden the banner under his uniform. Grateful for having survived the shower of enemy bullets, Gaisser felt a surge of relief when his captors failed to search their prisoners before escorting them to the rear. Eventually confined in a Yankee prison camp, the resolute New Orleanian kept

---

45 Anderson, *5th Wisconsin Proceedings*, 34; Jones, *Lee's Tigers*, 185; "A Daring Lieutenant," *The Anderson Intelligencer*, April 22, 1880; Seymour, *Memoirs*, 93-94; unit records for Green's Louisiana Guard Battery at www.fold3.com, accessed July 21, 2019. Capt. Orpheus S. Woodward of the 83rd PA led the V Corps skirmishers who attacked east of the RR. The actions of the 6th LA at Rappahannock Station are obscure. Either Monaghan didn't file a report, or it was lost. I have constructed my account from available evidence. Since Monaghan escaped, and no one ever accused him of abandoning his regiment and such a large number of its members tried to evade capture in the same way at the same time, it seems logical that the colonel led his men to the bridge site in a mass escape attempt that allowed a good portion of the 6th LA to elude capture. Edwin Forbes drawing of the battle clearly illustrates the regiment's isolation and its logical line of retreat toward the bridge. Union accounts of capturing 2,000 muskets but only 1,600 prisoners indicate that many of the 6th LA's men might have thrown down their rifles, which would have fatally encumbered any attempt to wade the river.

46 OR 29, pt. 1, 629; OR *Supplement*, 24, 118; Anderson, *5th Wisconsin Proceedings*, 34; Jones, *Lee's Tigers*, 185.

his prize hidden through five months of captivity and returned it to service upon his release in a March 1864 prisoner exchange.[47]

*　　*　　*

Notwithstanding Gaisser's symbolic triumph, the bloody business near the destroyed bridge foreshadowed the fate of Early's entire garrison. The 20th Maine's capture of the smaller redoubt had ruinously pierced the Rebel line, while the arrival of Ellmaker's reinforcing regiments swung the fight for the larger redoubt in the Union's favor. Physically exhausted by repeated attempts to recapture their stronghold, the 8th and 9th Louisiana finally conceded possession of the fort. This allowed Federal infantry to take post overlooking the pontoon bridge and continue firing on the two Louisiana regiments' battered survivors, who were clustering near or falling back across the floating span.[48]

Most, but not all, of the Yankees were happy to see them go. Still caught up in the frenzy of battle, 6th Maine privates Robinson Kitching, Thomas W. Chick, and Lawrence O. Laughlin rashly pursued the fleeing Rebels toward the river. Discharging their muskets into a throng of disorganized Confederates, the New Englanders boldly demanded the Louisianans' surrender. Rattled by having lost the redoubt, crowded into something resembling a mob as they funneled toward the narrow pontoon bridge, and uncertain how many Federals they faced in the darkness, 178 Southerners raised their hands in submission.[49]

As the lucky trio of brave Northerners marched their captives to the rear, Corporal Henry B. Minnichan and 18 men from the 49th Pennsylvania appeared near the bridge with orders to deny its use to the enemy if possible. This small body of Federals both

---

47 *Charleston Mercury*, March 22, 1864. "Godfrey Gaisser" service record at www.fold3.com accessed 7-18-2019 accessed 7-18-2019. A March 1864 prisoner exchange released more than 600 men from Hays' brigade. Promoted to ensign shortly after returning to duty, Gaisser survived to surrender with the remnant of the 6th LA at Appomattox Court House on April 9, 1865.

48 Thomas W. Cutrer & T. Michael Parrish, eds., *Brothers in Gray: The Civil War Letters of the Pierson Family* (Baton Rouge, LA, 1997), 210-12. The movements of the 8th and 9th LA after being driven from the fort are vague. It was logical for them to fall back toward the bridge, and Federal troops nearly captured Hays near there. Cpt. Reuben A. Allen, commanding Co. C, 9th LA, wrote his father on Nov. 20, 1863 that of the 52 men in his company 20 were lost in the battle, but 32 escaped. Allen doesn't record how they evaded capture, but so large a body getting away would indicate a rapid means of egress, which could only have been the bridge.

49 *OR* 29, pt. 1, 600.

hastened and complicated the retreat of those 8th and 9th Louisiana survivors ill-disposed to risk death or capture north of the Rappahannock.[50]

Witnessing all of this, Lt. Col. Jones of the 57th North Carolina sent word to Lt. Col. Samuel Tate, commanding the 6th North Carolina on his left, that the Yankees had taken the bridgehead's largest bastion and driven a wedge between the position's eastern and western flanks. Col. Godwin, who received the same urgent message, knew his own troops and Hays' two regiments to his left were doomed if they didn't retake the lost ground and open a way to the bridge.[51]

Pulling the rest of the 57th and all the 6th North Carolina out of their rifle pits, Godwin refused his flank, bending it back at a right angle to form a line facing eastward between the trenches and the Rappahannock. As Fuller's battered 6th Maine attempted to advance out of the redoubt, the Tar Heels riddled it with a "very destructive. . . raking fire down the length" of its formation. Rounds that failed to strike home plunged into the right flank of the 119th Pennsylvania, which was still catching its breath near the gapped portion of the Rebel trenches. Surprised by this unexpected deluge many of the startled Pennsylvanians shot back, their rounds passing through the 6th Maine in search of enemy targets beyond.[52]

Friendly fire posed the least of the New Englanders' problems. Seconds later, the North Carolinians launched a fierce counterattack that fell like a body blow on the disorganized, exhausted Maine regiment and Capt. Fish's small cohort of New Yorkers. "Bullets flew like hail" as twilight's last glimmer vanished from the field, and the Tar Heels pushed the Federals back into the redoubt. As the 6th Maine, 5th Wisconsin, and Fish's New Yorkers frantically struggled to fend off yet another enemy thrust, an unidentified Union officer brashly walked along the parapets demanding the 49th and 119th Pennsylvania get up and take the trenches.[53]

Somewhat recovered from their final sprint to the earthworks, the two regiments obediently surged around the small fortifications guarding the road, uncoiling from their column of divisions as they did so. This sudden blue wave stalled the Rebel assault

50 Westbrook, *49th Pennsylvania*, 168. Cpl. Minnichan's detachment is most likely responsible for almost capturing Brig. Gen. Hays before his horse bolted and carried him to safety across the pontoon bridge.

51 *OR* 29, pt. 1, 630.

52 Ibid., 599; Clark, *N C Regts*, vol. 3, 417.

53 Corporal East, "The 6th Maine at Rappahannock," *National Tribune*, April 12, 1888; Wilson, "Captain Fish," *Military Collector*, vol. 48, No. 3, 117. As these two regiments surged up onto the earthworks their personnel suffered a considerable number of leg wounds that eventually required amputation, the result of close range gunshots while the Federals briefly stood exposed on high ground. See casualty analysis for each of these commands on www.civilwardata.com.

Top: Emory Upton as a brevet major general in later 1864. *Library of Congress. Bottom:* Col. Clark Edwards, 5th Maine Infantry. *Maine State Archives*

and relieved pressure on Maj. Fuller's hard-pressed line. Now it was the North Carolinians' turn to wilt in the face of enemy firepower as the Pennsylvanians delivered a fusillade into the stalled Tar Heels.[54]

Nonetheless, the issue hadn't been settled, and the battle remained stalemated. Godwin could call on nearby support from the 54th North Carolina as well as the 5th and 7th Louisiana. These relatively fresh units had remained lightly engaged along the bridgehead's western flank. By contrast more than half of Ellmaker's badly bloodied command stood at the limit of its endurance. Another Confederate counterattack might yet retrieve Southern fortunes, or at the least open an escape route to the pontoon bridge. Whichever side threw more troops into the struggle first would carry the field.[55]

*   *   *

No one understood this better than Russell, who, one Wisconsinite snidely remarked, "finally seemed to realize that he had led his brigade against large odds." If the general had misconstrued enemy strength, he swiftly recognized his error and the possible disaster it invited. Even as

54 *OR* 29, pt. 1, 599; Clark, *NC Regts*, vol. 1, 619.

55 *OR* 29, pt. 1, 599.

Ellmaker's third wave crested against the earthworks, Russell rapidly dispatched a succession of couriers to Col. Emory Upton, temporarily commanding the 2nd Brigade, ordering him to hurry forward two regiments and reinforce the fight in the earthworks.[56]

At 24-years of age Upton enjoyed a youthful, somewhat dashing appearance that belied his ambitious, opinionated nature. Assigned to the artillery after graduating from West Point in 1861, he had served as a staff officer and been wounded at First Bull Run before going on to command a battery in the Peninsula Campaign and an artillery brigade at Antietam. Transferring to the infantry in October 1862, Upton became colonel of the 121st New York and subsequently fought at Fredericksburg and Salem Church during the Chancellorsville campaign. Since then, like the rest of the VI Corps, he had seen no significant action. Other than sending out Fish's skirmishers, the colonel's role at Rappahannock Station so far had involved advancing his brigade to a point overlooking the river and witnessing the "well-nigh" successful Confederate efforts to drive Ellmaker from their fortifications.[57]

Naturally aggressive and eager to fight, Upton enthusiastically greeted every courier carrying Russell's order to move forward. At that moment the 2nd Brigade lay prone behind a little rise of ground, arrayed in a column of divisions; Major Andrew E. Mather's 121st New York and Col. Clark S. Edwards' 5th Maine respectively were on the left and right of the first line, while the 95th and 96th Pennsylvania regiments constituted the second line.[58]

Alert to Ellmaker's perilous situation, Upton swiftly rode to Mather and Edwards, telling them to stand up their troops and follow him to the Rebel redoubts, loading as they advanced. The two regiments promptly moved off, their soldiers tearing at paper cartridges, charging and ramming rounds then capping their pieces as they advanced. Once the muskets were loaded, Upton ordered his 568-man formation to

---

56 Ibid., 589, 592; Anderson, *5th Wisconsin Proceedings*, 34.

57 OR 29, pt. 1, 592; A. E. Mather to Brother, Nov. 11, 1863, Dartmouth College, NH. Watching the battle wasn't without its dangers. A group of 10 or 12 Federals, among them the 5th Maine's Maj. A. E. Mather and Lt. Col. Henry R. Millet, made the mistake of clustering too close together beside Union artillery which was under Confederate fire. Two shells exploding near the Yankee guns showered the spectators with fragments, causing "considerable confusion" while lightly wounding Millet and a soldier from the 96th PA.

58 Mather commanded the regiment because Upton had stepped up to lead the 2nd brigade and the 121st's lieutenant colonel was on sick leave.

double-quick, their destination invisible save for the flashes of Rebel musket fire along the bridgehead's perimeter.[59]

Despite darkening skies and faltering accuracy Confederate guns south of the river continued firing. Pushing forward, Upton's troops found the air full of "spiteful projectiles" whose burning fuses traced "bright red" arcs through the night sky.[60]

As Upton neared the bridgehead, Russell hurried over to meet him and described a greatly improved situation. Ellmaker now had a firm grip on the redoubt, Union troops were firing on the pontoon bridge, and the Rebels seemed badly confused. Nonetheless, the 54th North Carolina still delivered an enfilade fire from an angle in the earthworks along a little knoll in the left center of the Rebel line, and something like 1,200 Confederates remained in the western end of the bridgehead. Howe's division blocked any chance of these men escaping toward Beverly Ford, which meant their only path of retreat lay through Ellmaker's tattered brigade tentatively blocking access to the bridge.[61]

Anxious to preempt a Rebel breakout attempt, Russell knew he couldn't launch an attack until he stifled the enfilade fire flaying his 3rd Brigade. Upton's newly arrived command was the only unit available for the job and finding it fortuitously positioned to strike in the required direction, the general told the young New Yorker to forget about reinforcing the redoubts and instead take the offending angle.[62]

Exhilarated by his new assignment, Upton rode back to his troops and reoriented their line of advance slightly westward toward their new objective. Advancing to within roughly 275 yards of the enemy works, he ordered Mather and Edwards to deploy their regiments from division columns into line of battle. Once both units fanned out into

59 OR 29, pt. 1, 592, 594; James M. Greiner, Janet L. Coryell and James R. Smither, eds., *A Surgeon's Civil War: The Letters and Diary of Daniel M. Holt, M.D.* (Kent, OH, 1994), 155-156. The 121st NY had 233 men and 21 officers; the 5th ME 299 men, 15 officers. Charging a round means pouring the gunpowder down the barrel and placing the bullet into the muzzle so the soldier can ram it down onto the powder at the weapons' breech.

60 Frances W. Morse, *Personal Experiences in the War of the Rebellion: From December 1862 to July 1865.* (Albany, NY, 1866), 54. Lee had not yet ordered these guns to cease fire but would do so within minutes.

61 OR 29, pt. 1, 629-30; A. E. Mather to Brother, Nov. 11, 1863, Dartmouth College, NH; John Kidder to Wife, Nov. 8, 1863, in Greiner, *Subdued by the Sword*, 93-94; Best, *121st New York*, 103; Cleveland J. Campbell to Editor, *New York Tribune*, Nov. 20, 1863 in Wilson, "Captain Fish," *Military Collector*, vol. 48, No. 3, 120. Confederate strength remaining is derived from the number of prisoners taken from each regiment.

62 OR 29, pt. 1, 589; Michie, *Life and Letters*, 83-85.

Harper's Weekly correspondent Alfred Waud drew this sketch of Upton's attack after the battle. Since Waud was at Kelly's Ford on November 7 he didn't witness this scene, which bears little resemblance to the actual assault. However, Waud does provide a clear look at the

linear formation, Upton led them into a shallow ditch roughly 140 yards from the rifle pits and prepared for an attack.[63]

Rebel infantrymen dimly perceiving this movement kept up a steady fire, but in the darkness shot too high and scored no hits. Confederate artillery remained a menace, however, and shells continued screaming over the field. One projectile landed next to the 121st New York's 18-year old adjutant, 1st Lt. Francis W. Morse, who was standing beside his horse writing a dispatch when the round detonated in a blinding flash. Suddenly covered with blood, the stunned officer thought he had been hit, but turning around he realized that the welter of gore on his uniform came from a nearby orderly whom the explosion had "torn to pieces" severing "his shoulder . . . from his body." The horror of that moment would haunt Morse for the rest of his brief life—he died of disease, aged 35—but just now he hadn't time for anything other than amazement at

63 OR 29, pt. 1, 592; Cleveland J. Campbell to Editor, *New York Tribune*, Nov. 20, 1863, in Wilson, "Captain Fish," *Military Collector*, vol. 48, No. 3, 120. Maj. Mather referred to the ravine as a "ditch" and estimated it was 150 yards from the Rebel line.

salients in the Rebel earthworks and a good view of the terrain leading down to the pontoon bridge, which he depicts with the exact number of boats. The stone pillars of the railroad bridge and the two redoubts are visible in the background. *Library of Congress*

still being alive. Mercifully, duty offered an honorable escape from the hellish scene and mindful of his message, the lieutenant mounted his horse to deliver it himself.[64]

As Morse galloped rearward, enemy artillery fire suddenly ceased. Grateful for that reprieve, Upton glanced up at his target. Waving Rebel flags and numerous muzzle flashes tracing the Confederate line warned that any assault up that "gently rising knoll" was apt to prove "deadly work." Upton concluded that speed offered his only chance of getting into those fortifications without a massacre. Ordering the 121st New York and 5th Maine to drop their knapsacks and fix bayonets, he rode along the line exhorting the men with appeals to unit and state pride before issuing "the strictest orders not to fire" and telling them they must take their objective at the "point of the bayonet." In a final oratorical flourish, the colonel exclaimed: "Some of us will fall,

64 Morse, *Personal Experiences*, 54; A. E. Mather to Brother, Nov. 11, 1863, Dartmouth.

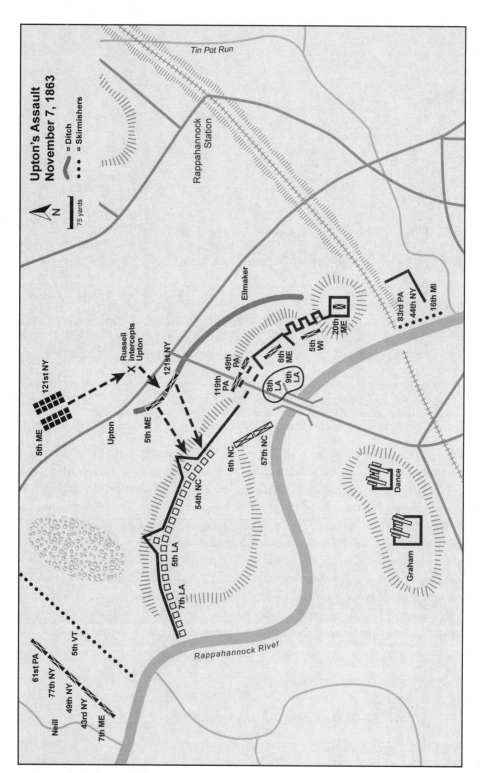

Upton's Assault
November 7, 1863

= Ditch
= Skirmishers

N

75 yards

Tin Pot Run

Rappahannock Station

Ellmaker

83rd PA
44th NY
16th MI

20th ME

5th WI
6th ME
49th PA

Russell
intercepts
Upton
X

121st NY

121st NY

5th ME

Upton

119th PA
49th PA

8th LA
9th LA

5th ME

6th NC

57th NC

54th NC

5th LA

7th LA

Dance

Graham

61st PA
77th NY
49th NY
43rd NY
7th ME

5th VT

Neill

Rappahannock River

those who do will go to Heaven. Those who remain will take the work. Forward 5th Maine and 121st New York!"[65]

Deftly clambering out of their sheltering depression the Federals advanced at quick time, climbing steadily upward through the dark ever closer to the enemy breastworks. Within 30 yards of the rifle pits Upton shouted the order to charge. A kaleidoscope of movement and violence followed. Union troops broke into a run as the Carolinians unleashed a "terrific volley" into the attackers. Four New Yorkers went down with fatal head wounds and more than a dozen others fell wounded, but the Yankees, beneficiaries of another volley aimed mostly too high, drove on heedless of their losses. Speeding across the intervening ground the assault's leading edge quickly flowed up onto the parapets.[66]

Luckily for the Federals they struck a sector held by only a few companies of the 54th North Carolina, which had extended its right wing to occupy part of the line earlier vacated by the 6th North Carolina. Once Upton's men mounted the parapet, they held a decisive positional advantage. The short distance between the defenders and the Federals towering over them prevented the former from taking proper aim. Those who managed to shoot, one Yankee recalled, were forced to fire "almost perpendicularly and did little execution."[67]

Before anyone in gray could reload or scramble rearward to more equal ground, the rest of Upton's men reinforced those already on the works. Here and there handfuls of determined secessionists met their foes with bayonets or rifle butts, and for an instant vicious fighting swirled around the 54th's flag. Then, to everyone's surprise, the struggle abruptly ceased as the Confederates began surrendering or fled to the rear.

---

65 OR 29, pt. 1, 630; Michie, *Life and Letters*, 84; Wilson, "Captain Fish," *Military Collector*, vol. 48, No. 3, 119; Greiner, *Subdued by the Sword*, 93; A. E. Mather to Brother, Nov. 11, 1863, Dartmouth.

66 OR 29, pt. 1, 592, 594; Moore, *Rebellion Record*, Vol. 8, 164; Michie, *Life and Letters*, 83; John M. Lovejoy, "Rappahannock," *National Tribune*, Dec. 25, 1884; Greiner, *A Surgeon's Civil War*, 155-56; Best, *121st New York*, 103; A. E. Mather to Brother, Nov. 11, 1863, Dartmouth. Quick time is average walking speed.

67 Cleveland J. Campbell to Editor, *New York Tribune*, Nov. 20, 1863 in Wilson, "Captain Fish," *Military Collector*, vol. 48, No. 3, 120; Best, *121st New York*, 103. I've based the strength of Confederate defenders at this point on Capt. Campbell's implicit contrast of Rebel troop density in the two sectors where Upton breached the works. In referencing Upton's second attack, Campbell says the Federals "for the second time went over the works. This time they were crowded with the enemy." This strongly implies that the trenches attacked first were less robustly manned than those that were struck second. Fewer defenders at the first breach would also explain the brief period of resistance and the ease of Union success.

Without firing a shot the Federals found themselves in possession of the 54th North Carolina's colors, dozens of prisoners, and a considerable length of trench.[68]

Relieved but perplexed by the fight's brevity, Col. Edwards surmised that the "sudden and unexpected," Federal assault had "paralyzed" the enemy and enfeebled his resistance. Upton inferred the same lesson. When subordinates reported "confusion" among the Rebels to their west, the colonel saw an opportunity to exploit his initial success. Explaining the situation to Russell in a quick note, Upton announced that he had taken his objective and was preparing to renew his attack.[69]

Not waiting for a reply, the self-assured colonel wrestled briefly with a tactical dilemma. The design of the Rebel trench system presented a real problem. Enemy troops beyond his right flank had taken post behind angles in the earthworks and stood ready to fire at anyone advancing in their direction. Any attack down the trench would require Federal troops to move single file like rats in a maze until the lead man suddenly confronted an enemy musket and got shot.

Discarding that idea, Upton also realized he couldn't simply move forward from his captured trench. That would leave too many Confederates in his rear and likely expose his men to a murderous crossfire. Unable to move straight ahead or go directly to his right, the colonel hit upon an unorthodox strategy. Detailing a portion of Col. Edward's command to hold the already taken works, he next directed Maj. Mather to take the 121st New York's left wing and seize the pontoon bridge. Then Upton pulled the rest of his command a short distance to the rear and reassembled it on the north side of the fortifications. Once the ranks were in tolerable order, he right-faced his troops into a column of fours, then ordered the formation to double quick across the enemy's front. Darkness and poorly located enemy rifle pits, which just here were dug too far on the reverse slope for effective shooting, shielded the Yankees from real danger as they moved parallel to the earthworks.

Finally reaching a point where the rear of his column was opposite enemy occupied trenches Upton shouted the order "by the left flank!" His still moving men faced left, undoubling their files to form a two-rank deep battle line just before the colonel yelled "Halt!" With his troops about to storm another line of entrenchments, Upton reminded everyone not to fire but rely on the bayonet. Then, in an impromptu piece of psychological warfare, he shouted "The first line will lie down when fired on, as there are three others to support them." Hoping this fiction would unsettle Rebel ears, he ordered the charge.

68 OR 29, pt. 1, 592, 594; Moore, *Rebellion Record*, vol. 8, 164; Michie, *Life and Letters*, 83; John M. Lovejoy, "Rappahannock," *National Tribune*, Dec. 25, 1884; Greiner, *A Surgeon's Civil War*, 155-56; Best, *121st New York*, 102.

69 OR 29, pt. 1, 592, 594. The 54th NC numbered approximately 308 men.

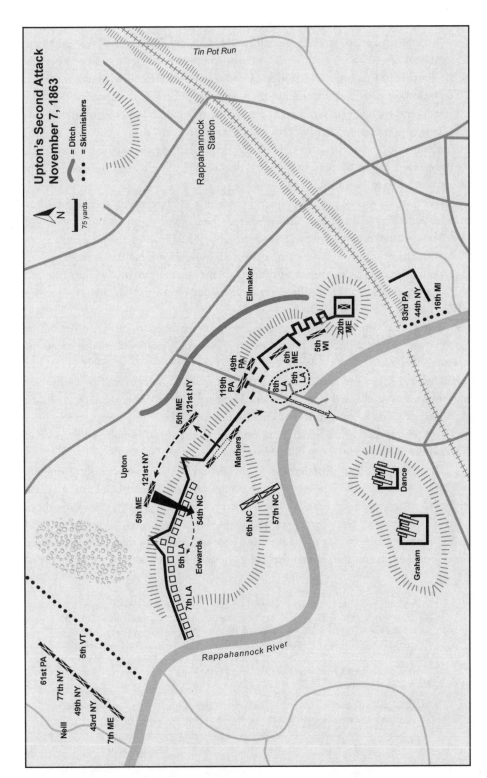

Upton's Second Attack
November 7, 1863

= Ditch
•••• = Skirmishers

N

75 yards

Tin Pot Run

Rappahannock Station

Ellmaker

83rd PA
44th NY
16th MI

20th ME

5th WI

6th ME
49th PA

119th PA

8th LA
9th LA

5th ME
121st NY

Mathers

Upton

121st NY

5th ME

54th NC

5th LA

Edwards

6th NC

57th NC

Dance

7th LA

Graham

Rappahannock River

Neill

61st PA
77th NY
49th NY
43rd NY
7th ME

5th VT

Upton's deception worked magnificently. Colonel Murchinson's 54th North Carolina holding this sector of trench had been in position less than an hour when the battle started. In that brief time it had learned (courtesy of Louisiana comrades) that 20,000 Yankees were in its front and then watched in dismay the speed with which seemingly endless waves of attackers had taken the rifle pits and forts to its right. By the time Upton perpetrated his ruse, recalled a Union officer, "it was quite dark and the enemy could not see the smallness of our numbers." In those circumstances the Rebels easily believed, as one of them later put it, "that all Hell was coming" and resistance to overwhelming numbers futile.[70]

The Carolinians were as ill-prepared physically as they were psychologically to resist assault. The Federals had already overrun part of the regiment and captured its flag. Many of those who managed to escape that debacle had darted toward the river. The troops nearest the lost works were confused, some abandoning the trenches to run away, others staying. Along most of the line men remained "crowded" into rifle pits whose parapet offered slight protection against attack but gave the enemy a decisive advantage once he surmounted them.

Worst of all, Murchinson and his officers had little chance to impose order before Upton's second assault fell on the regiment. When the Yankees clambered onto the parapet, the bulk of the 54th found itself facing the same dilemma that had overwhelmed the other part of the regiment. Unable to effectively fire at the blue uniforms looming above them, disheartened by a rapid series of blows that had broken their perimeter, and convinced that endless hordes of Federal reinforcements were about to swamp the entire bridgehead, most of the North Carolinians surrendered. Upton personally accepted Col. Murchinson's capitulation.[71]

The Fifty-Fourth's downfall doomed the 7th and 5th Louisiana still occupying rife pits facing west, with the 7th closest to the Rappahannock. Other than hearing a great deal of wind-muted shooting and yelling to their rear, these regiments knew little about what was happening elsewhere along the Confederate perimeter, although they did know an unfordable river lay to their left and a lot of Yankees to their front. Reassured that Gen. Hays hadn't summoned them elsewhere and understanding the necessity of

70 Previous paragraphs based on *OR* 29, pt. 1, 592, 594; Moore, *Rebellion Record*, vol. 8, 164; Michie, *Life and Letters*, 83-85; John M. Lovejoy, "Rappahannock," *National Tribune*, Dec. 25, 1884; Salvatore G. Cilella, Jr., *Upton's Regulars: The 121st New York Infantry in the Civil War* (Lawrence, KS 2008), 240-41; Morse, *Personal Experiences*, 54; Best, *121st New York*, 102; Cleveland J. Campbell to Editor, *New York Tribune*, Nov. 20, 1863 in Wilson, "Captain Fish," *Military Collector*, vol. 48, No. 3, 120; Greiner, *Subdued by the Sword*, 93. The 121st NY's left wing numbered around 100 men.

71 Michie, *Life and Letters*, 85; Best, *121st New York*, 103; Campbell to Editor, *New York Tribune*, Nov. 20, 1863 in Wilson, "Captain Fish," *Military Collector*, Vol. 48, No. 3, 120.

holding their own part of the line, they depended on sister regiments to protect their flank and rear. Such reliance proved unwarranted when the 54th North Carolina collapsed.[72]

As most of Upton's troops busied themselves with gathering and disarming prisoners, Col. Edwards led about a dozen 5th Maine men off into the darkness intending to snag any graycoats attempting escape. Running behind the rifle pits stretching off to their right and curving back toward the river this little band suddenly stumbled into the rear of the 5th Louisiana. Unexpectedly finding himself standing behind an enemy battle line, a shocked Edwards realized he'd gotten into serious trouble.

With death or capture imminent, the quick-thinking colonel decided to bluff and cheekily demanded to know the location of whoever commanded this sector of breastworks. "Here and who are you, Sir?" Capt. John Angell replied. Edwards identified himself and demanded the Louisianans' surrender. Taken aback, Angell stalled and requested for time to consult his officers. "Not a minute will I give you," Edwards responded. Menacingly swinging his arm toward Union troops herding captured North Carolinians over the parapets, he lied "Don't you see my columns advancing?" adding emphatically "Your forces on the right have all been captured and your retreat is cut off."

Peering through the darkness at an indistinct body of moving troops, Angell hesitated. Fearing his subterfuge was failing Edwards played his last card by shouting an order for the 5th Maine and 121st New York to advance. None of Upton's men could hear that command, of course, but Angell did. With his command facing the wrong way and fearful of seeing it slaughtered by an irresistible attack, the stunned captain agreed to surrender his 123-man strong regiment.[73]

The same fate befell the 7th Louisiana, which found itself caught in a hopeless situation once Angell capitulated. Although Lt. Col. Terry and a few others escaped by swimming the Rappahannock, 180 men, Col. Penn among them, laid down their arms without a fight. Shocked and mortified by their uncontested submission, some Louisiana officers threw away their swords to avoid the humiliation of handing them to the enemy. Lieutenant Charlie Pierce broke his weapon over a knee before passing the

72 Terry Jones, *Lee's Tigers Revisited: The Louisiana Infantry in the Army of Northern Virginia*. (Baton Rouge, LA, 2017), 253-54. The 5th LA numbered 123 and the 7th LA 180 men.

73 Previous paragraphs based on *OR* 29, pt. 1, 629; *Lamoille News Dealer* (Hyde Park, VT) Dec. 23, 1863.

bladeless hilt to a Federal officer and receiving some "rough treatment" from his captors in exchange.[74]

Pierce's experience aside, the Louisianans' bloodless acquiescence generated more civility than harshness. Some Union and Confederate troops shook hands as if they had just finished a ballgame rather than a battle. Most officers behaved with genteel politeness, including Col. Edwards who graciously allowed Capt. Angell to keep his sword. Such magnanimity allowed Pvt. Leon Bertin to conceal the 7th's regimental flag, which he had torn from its staff and hidden under his uniform before surrendering. Congenial Federals spurned searching their captives before ushering them rearward, thus enabling Bertin to burn his secreted banner in a late-night campfire, thereby ensuring it would never fall into Yankee hands.[75]

*   *   *

Just 40 minutes after the 6th Maine had charged out of its sunken road, Robert E. Lee's foothold north of the Rappahannock had disappeared. Union troops held the position's entire line of rifle pits as well as both its redoubts and all the Louisiana Guard's fieldpieces. Three full Southern regiments along with significant portions of another three had either surrendered or been driven demoralized across the river. Nevertheless, the Confederates could still redeem their situation. A prompt counterattack across the pontoon bridge made while south bank artillery disrupted Union forces inside the post's broken perimeter might yet carry the day. And although the odds against such an endeavor were long, a fast closing window of opportunity existed for such a strike.

Confusion ruled the Federal side of the battlefield. Large numbers of soldiers were wandering about, some in organized units, some as prisoners, and others separated from and searching for their regiments. In many instances Yankee victors mingled with

---

74 OR 29, pt. 1, 629; McNamara, *SHSP*, Vol. 8, 61-67; "A Daring Lieutenant," *The Anderson Intelligencer*, April 22, 1880.

75 OR 29, pt. 1, 592, 629; OR *Supplement* 24, 20; McNamara, *SHSP*, vol. 8, 61-67; "A Daring Lieutenant," *The Anderson Intelligencer*, April 22, 1880. The 5th LA surrendered 123 men, the 7th LA 180; Clark Edwards to Wife, Nov. 8, 1863, Clark Edwards Papers, Pearce Civil War Collection, Pearce Collections Museum, Navarro College, Corsicana, TX. These regiments suffered few killed or wounded. Since Edwards was the only US officer in the area, so many Confederate officers surrendered to him that at one point he had 17 swords. Casualty analysis for the 7th LA and 5th LA on www.civilwardata.com shows only Pvt. James Fitzgerald wounded in the 5th. Shot in the face, he lost his left eye. http://www.civilwardata.com/active/hdsquery.dll?SoldierHistory?C&561484, accessed July 22, 2019. Bertin asked Penn what to do with the 7th LA flag and the colonel suggested burning it.

Based on a prewar photograph, this drawing of Col. Archibald Godwin, 57th North Carolina Infantry, shows him wearing the rank of a brigadier general. Although appointed to that rank, Godwin's death at the September 19, 1864 Battle of Opequon prevented the Confederate Senate from confirming his promotion. *Library of Congress*

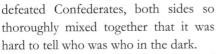

defeated Confederates, both sides so thoroughly mixed together that it was hard to tell who was who in the dark.

Although Cpl. Minnichan and his 18-man detail from the 49th Pennsylvania hovered near the northern end of the pontoon bridge, but they couldn't do much more than shoot at Rebel fugitives. Such a small force stood no chance of stopping or even slowing an assault from across the river. Virtually all other Union units in the area remained close to the captured earthworks and far from the pontoons.

Absorbed in disarming or assembling prisoners, Upton's men on the western flank were momentarily unprepared for further action. Ellmaker's troops in the center of the line were in bad shape, especially the exhausted 6th Maine and 5th Wisconsin, which had both lost many officers and taken significant casualties. Along the eastern end of the perimeter the Federals had only the 350 V Corps skirmishers who had taken part in the attack. No Union reinforcements had come forward to strengthen Russell's grip on the bridgehead and it would take time for Northern officers to pull together their commands and ready them for additional combat.

If the Rebels struck immediately, they might drive their disorganized enemy from his captured works and save what remained of Early's north bank garrison. But no attack came. In fact, an attack was impossible, largely because Confederates south of the Rappahannock didn't yet realize the Federals had attacked the bridgehead. Even if Early and Lee had understood what was going on, the resources for a rapid counterassault weren't available. Additional batteries of Rebel artillery remained far to the rear, and given the almost impenetrable darkness those guns on hand couldn't fire into the bridgehead for fear of hitting friendly troops. Aside from the 31st Virginia manning earthworks near the burnt railroad bridge, no Confederate infantry units were closer than a mile or two away. It would take 30–60 minutes for these to come up and by then chances of successful attack would have considerably diminished.

Even if the Confederates overcame all these difficulties, the arrival of Maj. Mather's wing of the 121st New York near the pontoon bridge likely snuffed out any hope of redeeming the already substantial disaster that had befallen Southern arms. Replacing Minnichan's small guard, the New Yorkers deployed on high ground overlooking the bridge. From here they could block further escape attempts over the span or a counterattack across it.[76]

That spelled real trouble for the 6th and 57th North Carolina which remained the last organized Confederate units still fighting north of the river. Pulled out of the rifle pits by Col. Godwin following Ellmaker's conquest of the large redoubt, they had tried several times to retake the fort. Though unsuccessful, their efforts had spared them entrapment in the trenches and, at least so far, wholesale destruction or capture. Nonetheless Godwin's holdouts were in a dangerous situation. Even with stragglers from other units rallying to their colors, the Tar Heels were outnumbered, surrounded on three sides with their backs to the Rappahannock's deep, cold water. It was just a matter of time before the enemy concentrated his forces to wipe out this last pocket of Rebel resistance.

Accepting the actual situation for what it was, Lt. Col. Tate, commanding the 6th North Carolina, hurried over to Godwin and urged him to cut a way through to the bridge and escape the trap fast closing around his troops. To Tate's dismay Godwin refused. Displaying more valor than logic the colonel said that without instructions to retire, he would try to "retake the position and hold it until. . . ordered back."[77]

Godwin's determination might have been admirable, but it was patently foolhardy. His pair of North Carolina regiments had started the battle with something like 620 men. Thus far they had suffered fewer than 34 casualties and if one counted the stragglers joining these units, Godwin had at least 600 men to attempt a breakout. If he advanced quickly the only obstacle standing between him and the pontoon bridge was Maj. Mather's 100 or so New Yorkers, whose sole source of nearby help was Ellmaker's exhausted and shot-up brigade. Against a determined attack by two or three times their number, these Yankees probably couldn't stop Godwin's men from reaching and crossing the bridge. However heavy the casualties incurred trying this, they would surely fall well short of total annihilation, which is what the North Carolinians faced by clinging to the Rappahannock's north shore.

But Godwin declined to even consider the option, thereby discarding the ANV's last chance of salvaging something from the unfolding disaster at the bridgehead. Rather than attack toward the pontoons, he stubbornly held his ground, foregoing any chance of escape until Upton eventually brought his men down from the

---

76 OR 29, pt. 1, 592, 594; Westbrook, *49th Pennsylvania*, 168.

77 Peter W. Hairston Diary Nov. 12, 1863, SHC/UNC; The 6th NC had roughly 323 men at the start of the battle; the 57th counted 296.

entrenchments to finish off the Rebel garrison. As Federal troops closed in, hundreds of trapped North Carolinians saw the futility of their predicament and began surrendering. The ever-shrinking number of those still resisting fell back onto the sloping ground leading sharply down to the river. Such poor terrain made maneuvering difficult while an almost impenetrable darkness undercut Godwin's efforts at keeping his men together or effectively directing their action.

Adverse to capture, some Rebels gave up the fight and attempted escape, among them Lt. Col. Tate who slipped back to the river bank and hid there with a few other men until he thought it safe to dash across the pontoon bridge. Not everyone trying to flee managed to do so, however. Having lost his horse Col. Jones of the 57th North Carolina leapt into the river just before Yankees reached him. Shocked by the frigid water temperature he cried out involuntarily "Oh! How cold it is!" A New York sergeant pointed his rifle at the stunned officer and shouted "Come back or I will make it hot for you!" Half frozen and unwilling to try out-swimming a bullet, Jones waded back to shore and captivity. Other men managed to make it over the river, although in all likelihood some drowned in the icy waters.[78]

Meanwhile, relentless Yankee pressure whittled away at Godwin's strength until only 60–70 men remained in the ranks. Even then he refused to quit. When a disembodied voice cried out that the colonel had ordered everyone to surrender, the Virginian shouted back demanding to know who was spreading such a lie and threatened to "blow his brains out." Avowing "to fight to the last moment," Godwin urged his fast-shrinking cadre to "stand by him." Fiery determination couldn't substitute for manpower, however, and within minutes Federal troops overpowered and captured the stalwart colonel and the last of his little band.[79]

With that the battle came to a desultory end. David Russell's daring assault—bravely executed, aggressively led, and expertly timed—had smashed the Rappahannock Station bridgehead and completely undermined Lee's scheme to lure the AOP into a lethal trap. Meade could now concentrate the AOP without much fear of an enemy offensive threatening its railroad supply line. Sedgwick and French had handed their chief a grand opportunity. If he moved swiftly on the morrow, Meade might catch the ANV inside the Culpeper V and wreck it once and for all.

78 A. E. Mather to Brother, Nov. 11, 1863, Dartmouth.

79 *OR* 29, pt. 1, 623-24.

CHAPTER 7

"Time Is Of the Utmost Importance"

Signs of Disaster—Bridge Burning—News Delayed—Late Night Orders

CONFEDERATE forces below the Rappahannock were slow to comprehend the bridgehead's fate, partly because a strong southerly wind prevented them from hearing the fighting and partly because deepening darkness cloaked what was happening above the river. Even though myriad muzzle flashes tracing the battle's course had been visible, most Rebel observers—Lee and Early included—had assumed it amounted to little more than intense skirmishing.[1]

The first hint of trouble appeared when a staff officer sent to arrange for provisioning the north bank garrison returned with rumors that Yankees had taken a section of earthworks. Although Jubal Early thought this highly unlikely, he couldn't help feeling uneasy. Unable to satisfactorily explain the earlier display of gunfire or its sudden cessation, the general dispatched Maj. John Daniel to find Harry Hays and "ascertain the state of things." Still concerned, Early directed Captains Dance and Graham to man their guns and John Pegram to bring his brigade up to the river.[2]

These movements had barely gotten underway when refugees bearing tales of disaster began reaching the Rappahannock's south bank. Initially some Rebels scoffed at stories of defeat, even those borne by "almost breathless. . . half-naked" and-soaked-to-the skin infantrymen staggering inland. An officer in the Rockbridge Artillery angrily accused one such escapee of cowardice when he stumbled into the

---

1 OR 29, pt. 1, 613, 621; Kirkpatrick diary, November 7, 1863, UT. The staff officer was Early's assistant adjutant general, Maj. Samuel Hale.

2 OR 29, pt. 1, 622; Early, *Autobiographical Sketch*, 313.

battery's bivouac. Within minutes, however, the arrival of additional fugitives altered perceptions.[3]

These refugees had gained freedom by running across the bridge or plunging into the Rappahannock and swimming to safety, both extremely dangerous undertakings. Swimmers risked drowning in the icy waters, while Yankee riflemen targeted anyone fleeing over the pontoons. One North Carolinian who chose flight over surrender testified that a "considerable number" of those attempting to sprint across the span "fell pierced with balls and tumbled headlong into the river."[4]

Having a horse dramatically increased a man's chances of flight and survival. The Louisiana brigade's mounted officers, along with several aides or couriers, succeeded in eluding both capture and enemy lead—some by swimming their animals across the river and others by galloping over the bridge. The latter course was especially hazardous for the horses (and their riders) since Federal bullets hit most of the beasts and struck some multiple times.[5]

Luckily for the Confederates, Brig. Gen. Hays successfully evaded capture, his daring escape occurring after encircling Yankees spooked his horse into an impromptu dash over the pontoons amid a storm of musketry. Major Daniel encountered the fortunate Louisianan just after he had reached safety and learned that the greater "part of his brigade was captured, the enemy in possession of the works, and Godwin cut off from the bridge."[6]

Rushing rearward to deliver this terrible news, Daniel didn't get far before meeting an anxious Jubal Early, who had ridden forward to inspect affairs himself. After absorbing the dismaying message, Early dispatched a courier to alert army headquarters and another to tell Pegram what had happened and to quicken his march. Squinting into the darkness, the general saw the last stabs of musketry accompanying Godwin's futile defense. The general would never forget his "mortification" at witnessing that "final struggle" or his sense of impotence at being unable to save those stranded troops.[7]

---

3   Moore, *Cannoneer Under Stonewall Jackson*, 207.

4   Clark, *NC Regts*, Vol. 1, 319-20.

5   McNamara, *SHSP*, Vol. 8, 61-67; Jones, *Lees' Tigers*, 183-85. The escapees included Col. William Monaghan and Maj. William H. Manning from the 6th LA, Col. Thomas Terry of the 7th LA, the 9th LA's Col. William Peck as well as Capt. Seymour and courier Charlie Stewart of the brigade staff. Lt. Col. Tate of the 6th NC also escaped capture.

6   *OR.* Vol. 29, pt. 1, 623; McNamara, *SHSP*, Vol. 8, 61-67; Jones, *Lee's Tigers*, 183-85. Exactly when Hays escaped is uncertain, but most likely that took place when the 121st NY's left wing neared the bridge.

7   *OR.* 29, pt. 1, 622.

* * *

If watching the Yankees snuff out Godwin's resistance mortified Early, the uncertainty following Godwin's defeat introduced a new, highly dangerous situation. From south bank hilltops Confederates could detect a great deal of milling about north of the river. Ellmaker's brigade was straining to manage the estimated 550 prisoners it had taken, and Upton's two regiments were still sending what looked like another 1,300 north of the earthworks. The action had left every Federal regiment disorganized to some degree. Dead, wounded, and dying lay everywhere, but especially around the large redoubt. Little knots of men had gathered beside suffering comrades and occasionally their plaintive calls for a chaplain or surgeon were audible. Innumerable soldiers blown loose from their commands by the fighting, were seeking their proper places, leaving the field looking like a newly kicked-over anthill.[8]

Highly conscious that Rebel artillery might open a devastating bombardment at any moment, the wounded Russell tried to bring order out of chaos as rapidly as possible. Summoning forward the two remaining regiments of Upton's brigade, he detailed Lt. Col. Edward Carroll's 95th Pennsylvania to move all the prisoners rearward and then sent William H. Lessig's 96th Pennsylvania to hold the north end of the pontoon bridge. This done, the general shifted the badly shot up 6th Maine into the redoubt nearest the railroad and directed Ellmaker to keep the rest of his men in the larger fort and its adjacent trenches. Upton's 5th Maine and 121st New York would occupy the rifle pits they had taken such a short while ago.[9]

This put most of Russell's men under cover, leaving only Lessig's troops truly exposed to enemy fire. However regrettable the Pennsylvanians' situation, the general felt he had no other choice. If Sedgwick wanted to launch an assault over the pontoon bridge tomorrow, someone had to prevent the Rebels from burning it tonight. Logic dictated giving that job to a fresh regiment rather than a spent one. The Ninety-Sixth would have to take its chances. If everything worked out, the enemy would keep his distance and no one else north of the Rappahannock would die before dawn.

* * *

8   The actual prisoner count was 1,600—a few hundred less than the combined total of Ellmaker's and Upton's initial reports.

9   OR 29, pt. 1, 593, 595, 596, 599, 601. The captured guns were turned over to Brig. Gen. Taylor's VI Corps reserve artillery.

A scant hundred yards away, Confederate commanders scrambled to manage a situation that had turned from promising to "extremely dangerous" almost instantaneously. Initially they could do little more than they had already done to block a Yankee thrust over the Rappahannock. Since midafternoon Gordon's brigade had guarded Norman's Ford, and just before nightfall Anderson's division from Hill's corps had come up to protect Beverly Ford, posting Posey's brigade—under Col. Harrison Harris's command since Bristoe Station—behind the crossing before returning to camp.[10]

While these dispositions secured Early's flanks, the bridgehead's loss left his center protected solely by Dance's and Graham's eight fieldpieces. Although well-sited to fire on the pontoons, these guns were doomed once enemy artillerists planted more batteries on high ground north of the river. The displacement or destruction of Rebel cannon would then allow Union infantry to swarm over the span and establish a south bank foothold into which Sedgwick could ultimately pour two entire corps.[11]

Brigadier General John Pegram's command was Early's only immediate means of forestalling such a calamity. After halting the brigade within a mile of the river earlier that afternoon, he had sent its 31st Virginia to man trenches below the Rappahannock east of the bridgehead and detailed the 13th, 49th, 52nd, and 58th Virginia regiments as a reserve. Left to idle away the final hours of daylight, Pegram's troops had watched distant flashes of soundless artillery fire before turning to cooking rations in expectation of an early reveille.

The arrival of messengers bearing urgent orders for a northward march fatally disrupted the brigade's camp routine. Assembling with commendable speed, the Virginians reached the river in just 30 minutes. Although shocked to learn that the bridgehead and its garrison had been captured, Pegram's men rapidly filed into the nearby rifle trenches surrounding Dance's and Graham's gun pits and girded themselves against a Yankee attempt to cross the river.[12]

---

10 OR, 29, pt. 1, 622; Albert L. Peel diary, Nov. 7, 1863, http://freepages.rootsweb.com/ ~peel/family/peelnov.html.Accessed May 5, 2019. Wounded at Bristoe Station, Posey died of his wounds on Nov. 13, 1863.

11 No one recorded what Hays' surviving troops did after crossing the river. Early doesn't mention them in reporting his defensive efforts after the bridgehead's fall. Understandably worn out and disorganized, the brigade was no longer militarily effective, and the general most likely directed Hays to rally his shattered command somewhere in the rear, possibly in its former camps, which would have been a natural destination for scattered troops.

12 Moore, *Cannoneer Under Stonewall Jackson*, 207; Douglas Carroll, *The Letters of F. Stanley Russell: The Movements of Company H Thirteenth Virginia Regiment* (Baltimore, MD, 1963), 36-37. Exactly when Pegram's men reached the river is uncertain. Moore says it was around 9 p.m., but 1st Lt. Sam Buck of the 13th VA indicates it was somewhat earlier.

No fortifications blocked the southern exit of the bridge, however, and Pegram ordered the 13th Virginia to plug that particular gap. Its leader, 25-year old Lt. Col. James B. Terrill—an 1858 VMI graduate and veteran of all the army's battles save Gettysburg—was an excellent choice for such a critical assignment. Audaciously leading his command forward until the sound of Yankee voices sounded clearly in the dark, Terrill instructed his men to entrench just 50 yards from the Rappahannock's lapping waters. With bayonets, tin cups, and any other handy implement, the Virginians quietly dug into the sandy soil, all of them acutely conscious of occupying the center of a bullseye.[13]

* * *

As long as the pontoon bridge remained in place the threat of an enemy assault remained likely. Hence, the span's destruction became Early's paramount concern. Riding over to Dance's battery, he asked for a volunteer to burn the floating thoroughfare. Private William H. Effinger "promptly" expressed a willingness to try. Although everyone expected a maelstrom of Yankee fire to confront the 23-year old's arson attempt, he managed to ignite some of the bridge planks and return to his gun without the Federals firing a single shot.[14]

Unfortunately for the Confederates, the earlier stiff wind had subsided and without its help Effinger's handiwork quickly evaporated. Lt. Jesse Porter of the 13th Virginia decided to try again. Boldly walking to the bridge as though there was no danger whatsoever, he managed to kindle "a slight blaze" which quickly illuminated the riverfront, forcing Porter to race for cover amid a hail of enemy musketry. To the Rebels' dismay, however, the bridge again refused to burn and by 9 p.m. Porter's

---

13 OR 29, pt. 2, 925-26; Samuel Buck, *With the Old Confeds: Actual Experiences of a Captain in the Line* (Baltimore, MD, 1925), 93. Terrill's brother, William R. Terrill (USMA 1853) remained loyal to the Union, earning the rank of brigadier general before his death at the Battle of Perryville, KY in Oct. 1862. James Terrill died at the Battle of Totopotomoy Creek (Bethesda Church) on May 30, 1864. The Confederate Congress posthumously approved his promotion to brigadier the next day.

14 Moore, *Cannoneer Under Stonewall Jackson*, 207-208. Wounded at Sharpsburg when a bursting shell burned his face, Pvt. William H. Effinger (Rockbridge Artillery) endured a three-month hospital stay before returning to duty. Recognizing Effinger's efforts at Rappahannock Station and his previous service, Gen. Lee transferred him to the 1st Regiment of Engineers on Dec. 9, 1863 and promoted him to 1st lieutenant. https://www.fold3.com/image/271/9003454 Accessed March 17, 2020.

nascent fire had sputtered out. To the frustration of everyone in gray, this particular set of pontoons seemed to enjoy a charmed existence.[15]

Early could see well enough in the darkness to discern that the bridge remained undamaged. Its continuing viability became more ominous when the distinctive sound of horse-drawn guns arose from the bridgehead shortly after Porter's flames ebbed away. The source of this unsettling noise was a detachment of artillerists from Battery F, 5th US, which Col. Thompson had sent to retrieve the quartet of captured Rebel guns lying silent inside the captured redoubts. Feeling their way in the darkness the Federals managed to withdraw all four cannons and one limber, but had to leave behind three other limbers and four caissons which sat too close to the Rappahannock for safe recovery.[16]

Unaware of what the Yankees were doing, Confederate leaders might have suspected that the sounds meant Sedgwick was deploying batteries to support a thrust across the pontoons. Although no evidence confirms Early noticed the rolling fieldpieces, this Union activity might help explain the three-hour gap that ensued between Porter's attempt on the bridge and a follow-up effort. The only other plausible explanation is that Early, loathe to risk more lives in another assault on the stubborn edifice, hoped wind or luck might resurrect some lingering spark and engulf the troublesome structure in flame. Either way, after vainly waiting several hours for good fortune or a Union bombardment, Early realized he had no choice but to instigate another foray against the bridge. Seeking out Pegram, the general asked if he knew an officer bold enough for such a desperate undertaking.

A newcomer to the ANV, the handsome 31-year old brigadier had transferred from Tennessee just a few weeks earlier to assume command of William "Extra Billy" Smith's old unit. Having had so little time with his troops, Pegram couldn't suggest anyone, but his assistant adjutant general, Capt. Robert N. Wilson, knew just the man: the brigade's youngest officer, 1st Lt. Samuel Buck, currently commanding the 13th Virginia's Company H. Early turned to his own AAG, Major Samuel Hale, and told him to go with Wilson, find Buck, and ask if he'd volunteer to finish off the bridge.[17]

15 Buck, *With the Old Confeds*, 93. 2nd Lt. Jesse J. Porter (Co. D, 13. VA).

16 *OR* 29, pt. 1, 607.

17 Smith was elected governor of Virginia prior to the Gettysburg campaign and left the ANV shortly after the battle. An 1854 graduate of West Point, Pegram had resigned his Federal commission when Virginia seceded. Casting his lot with the South he became the first former US Army officer captured in Rebel service when he controversially surrendered his regiment during the July 1861 battle of Rich Mountain. Exchanged after six months of captivity, the Virginian was promoted to colonel and undertook a brief assignment as the AOT's chief engineer before assuming a chief of staff posting in Gen. Edmund Kirby Smith's Army of East Tennessee. Appointed a cavalry brigadier in November 1862, he couldn't get along with key

Lt. Samuel Buck, Company H,
13th Virginia Infantry
Samuel Buck, With the Old Confeds:
Actual Experiences of a Captain in the Line
(Baltimore, MD, 1925), Front End Page

The two officers promptly located the 22-year old lieutenant standing behind his company, whereupon Hale relayed Early's "request" that Buck destroy "that bridge." The general wanted it understood that he wasn't issuing an order, but the lieutenant saw through that pretense and recognized receiving a command "in complimentary disguise." When Buck inquired just how to go about such a tricky job, Hale answered that he could choose his own methods. As the lieutenant processed that unhelpful answer, Jubal Early appeared to repeat his "request" by adding that Buck could have as many men as needed to get the job done.

Face to face with the general and offered unlimited resources, the young man could hardly decline this appeal. Buck quickly developed a brutally simple plan: he would gather volunteers, fight his way to the bridge, and under covering fire, lead a few hand-picked men onto the span and set it alight. Pegram's brigade and all nearby artillery would open at the same time in hopes of diverting Federal attention from Buck's desperate sortie.

Word of the lieutenant's proposal spread quickly through the 13th Virginia's ranks and stirred so little enthusiasm that when Buck called for volunteers, only a few men stepped forward. Initially he had better luck with the brigade's other regiments, where

subordinates and generally made a poor record, but not one sorry enough to forestall his gaining command of a division in Lt. Gen. Nathan Bedford Forrest's cavalry corps. Engaged to a Maryland belle living in Richmond, in the fall of 1863 Pegram asked for and received a transfer back to Virginia, delaying his return only long enough to play a small part in the battle of Chickamauga. The genteel Pegram fit in much better with his fellow West Point-trained Virginians than he had with western comrades and seems to have quickly earned Early's trust.

men supposed joining the lieutenant would carry them to a safer place and away from the bridge. Learning otherwise most of those volunteers changed their minds and quickly bowed out of the project, leaving Buck with just 12 men.[18]

These paltry numbers engendered a new plan. Now his modest party would leave their weapons behind and rely on protective fire from the brigade alone. After stripping off sword, pistol, frock coat, and boots, Buck led his little troop beyond friendly lines and quietly slipped down to the bridge without attracting enemy notice. Crawling up onto the pontoons he then slithered across the planks cutting any rope he could reach, all the while listening to every word spoken by Union troops standing just yards away on the Rappahannock's northern shore.

Eventually squirming back to his starting point, Buck and Pvt. Charles Seevers—a pre-war militia comrade—crawled down to the waterline and made their way to the first pontoon boat looking to discover some means of firing the bridge. Seeing no easy way, Buck told Seevers to go back and ask Pegram to have his troops gather any combustible material they could find and pass it bucket brigade style to the lieutenant's men lying prone between the river and the 13th Virginia's battle line. The general complied and as hay, straw, grass, and sticks traveled from hand to hand all the way to the bridge, Buck began stuffing it into every available crevice.

Satisfied he had enough kindling the lieutenant ordered his volunteers back to their regiments while he sat alone on a pontoon in the bitter cold and "awful stillness" watching Yankee pickets walking their beat in the dim starlight. Contemplating his probable death in the next few minutes, the young Virginian knew he would be an easy target once he struck a match. His only chance then would be to light a fire quickly and avoid getting shot long enough to jump into the river in hopes of drifting safely downstream without drowning. One severe problem with this plan was the unreliability of Confederate matches, which were notoriously difficult to ignite. Buck nonetheless was preparing to take his chances against stiff odds when he accidentally brushed against an ash-covered board and saw a "live coal" fall into the water.

Checking another charred plank and finding it too hid a smoldering ember courtesy of previous arson attempts, the lieutenant suddenly saw a chance to burn the bridge and escape with his life. Grasping the ashen lumber, he held it up to a pile of cloistered hay which started to smolder almost instantly. As white smoke coiled upward from his hidden fuel, Buck crawled from the bridge to the shore, jumped up,

---

18 Buck, *With the Old Confeds*, 93-95. In his postwar memoirs Buck listed 8 of the 12 men who accompanied him, unable to recall the other 4 names. He got some of his information wrong, however. Buck listed two men from the 49th VA: John I. Fristoe (James F. Fristoe of Company I) and S. Cooper (for whom there is no service record). The rest of Buck's known compatriots were from his own 13th VA: Charles W. Seevers (Co. H), Henry H. and Rawson M. Thompson (both Co. F), Reuben L. Cave (Co. A), Peter and Thomas Berlin (both Co. E).

and ran toward his regiment. Reaching cover, he turned toward the river and waited anxiously for a long minute before seeing a "sharp tongue of flame" leap up from the pontoons and began spreading across the span.

Within minutes the blaze was bright enough for Union and Rebel soldiers to see one another across the river. A few Southerners let loose some warning rounds to discourage any efforts at extinguishing the growing fire, which the enemy seemed disinclined to attempt. Returning to where he'd left Early and Pegram, Buck found the generals and Maj. Hale holding his belongs, which they happily returned. "Very little was said," the daring young Virginian latter recalled, "But great relief was felt." The lieutenant and brigadier clambered down into a ditch where they could monitor the fire's progress and were eventually gratified to see the southernmost pontoon's mooring lines burn through, allowing the unwieldy craft to drift down the Rappahannock like a flaming funeral pyre.[19]

Although Buck's labors destroyed only one of the bridge's five boats, he had damaged the span badly enough to deter any Federal dash over the river—at least for a while. Surely, however, the enemy would undertake a cross-river assault at dawn or shortly afterwards. Until Early received contrary orders his job was to halt any such venture at the water's edge. As his pocket watch ticked relentlessly toward daybreak, the odds against his division seemed to worsen by the minute.[20]

*   *   *

Concern over the future bedeviled George Meade as much as it did Jubal Early. Since reaching the Carter farm south of Morrisville around 2 p.m. the general and his staff had fitfully awaited news from the front. Word of French's seizure of Kelly's Ford and his lodgment on the river's south bank only increased their anxiety, especially since they hadn't heard anything from the right wing, upon whose progress Meade's entire program depended. Impatient for intelligence, Meade had Maj. Gen Humphreys send Sedgwick a 4 p.m. request for information. Thirty minutes later the sound of vigorous artillery fire welled up from the west only to stop abruptly an hour later—and still no word came from Rappahannock Station.[21]

Reliance on mounted couriers to transmit messages largely explains the spotty communications. Even moving at a steady trot, it took a good horse and rider 70 minutes to traverse the eight miles of dirt roads separating Meade's headquarters from

19 Previous paragraphs based on Buck, *With the Old Confeds*, 93-98.

20 *OR* 29, pt. 2, 624, 925-26.

21 Byrne & Weaver, *Haskell of Gettysburg*, 230.

Sedgwick's command post. That almost two-and-a half-hour gap between sending a dispatch and getting a reply consigned Meade to lengthy periods of worry and speculation. The resultant strain left the general on tenterhooks.[22]

When 6:30 p.m. passed and Humphreys still had no response to his 4 p.m. missive, Meade calculated enough time had expired for Sedgwick to have received and replied to that earlier request. Exasperated by his subordinate's silence, Meade had Humphrey's pen another message, this one pointedly telling Sedgwick that army headquarters was "anxiously awaiting" a reply to its previous inquiry. Assuming no news meant bad news, Humphreys also asked Sedgwick how many men and guns he would need to forestall a Confederate offensive out of the bridgehead.[23]

This message had hardly left the Carter farm when a dusty horseman arrived at Meade's command post with an untimed dispatch from Sedgwick saying that he had forced the enemy into his riverside fortifications but had "not taken the works" and didn't think he would before night. Though disappointing, this belated report at least provided some idea of Sedgwick's status. It may have done far more, however, since the courier also likely relayed verbal word of Russell's assault, which would have started around the time he left Rappahannock Station.[24]

That supposition is the only plausible explanation for the hour-and-a-half delay before Humphreys wrote Sedgwick again at 8 p.m. The chief of staff was still putting ink to paper when a messenger appeared to announce the VI Corps' capture of Lee's bridgehead along with four guns and numerous prisoners. Sedgwick capped off this

---

22 Ihave deduced the time necessary for a courier to ride between Army HQ and Rappahannock Station from a message Sedgwick sent to Humphreys at 7:40 p.m. (OR 29, pt. 2, 924) stating that the right wing commander had just received a dispatch Humphreys had sent at 6:30 p.m. The average horse can walk about 4 mph on dirt roads and trot between 8 and 12 mph. https://animals.mom.me/what-is-the-average-distance-a-horse-can-travel-in-a-day-3117039.html, Accessed Aug. 2, 2019. An army telegraph team accompanied Meade on Nov. 7, stringing wire from Warrenton Junction as it went, establishing telegraphic connections between the line leading to Washington and Meade's Carter Farm HQ, 3 miles from Kelly's Ford, by 5 p.m. Apparently no similar effort was undertaken to connect Sedgwick and Meade. In the same 7:40 p.m. dispatch mentioned above Sedgwick speaks of sending "two messengers" to Army HQ which indicates he had no telegraphic link with Meade. Luther A. Rose diary, Nov. 7, 1863, Luther A. Rose Papers, LC.

23 OR 29, pt. 2, 431. Humphreys' question on the strength needed to screen the bridgehead echoed Meade's midnight inquiry to Sedgwick regarding the same subject on the night of Nov. 6-7.

24 Ibid., 924.When Sedgwick's courier arrived is unknown. Certainly, it was after 6:30 p.m. If we assume that Humphreys' 4 p.m. dispatch reached Sedgwick between 5:10 and 5:20, and that he responded within 10 or 15 minutes, the courier would have arrived at Army HQ around 6:45 p.m.

unexpected communique by confidently asserting his ability to seize the south bank fortifications "in the morning."[25]

This encouraging news, Col. Lyman recorded, put everyone at headquarters "in good spirits." But it also left Meade desperately craving more details, and he had Humphreys fire off a message asking Sedgwick if he had taken the Rebel pontoon bridge and whether it was possible to throw down an additional span at Norman's Ford. Once this message was on its way, Meade took time to inform Halleck of the day's successes and pledge a continuation of the "advance and attack... tomorrow."[26]

Making plans to keep that promise required more information than Meade had at the moment, however, and much to his chagrin the flow of communication maintained its tepid pace. Although Sedgwick was sending in more frequent reports, they mainly amplified his list of prisoners and casualties. Although interesting, none of that gave Meade what he needed. Without allowing his 8:30 p.m. dispatch time to even reach Rappahannock Station, Meade had Humphreys write another letter at 9:30 p.m. reminding Sedgwick that Army HQ was still "anxiously waiting" a response to its previous questions and begging him to "answer at once, as time is of the utmost importance."[27]

The information Meade wanted finally started arriving at 10 p.m., an hour after his reception of Sedgwick's announcement that he had captured the Rebel pontoons and all enemy earthworks north of the river. Follow up messages expanded on the number of prisoners, reiterated Union possession of the bridge, confirmed that enemy soldiers still controlled the river's south bank and declared that Sedgwick had asked Col. Ira Spaulding's 50th New York Engineers to lay a bridge at Norman's Ford.[28]

Through these reports Meade realized that although the right wing had won an impressive triumph, it wasn't the victory he wanted. The general had hoped Sedgwick would get over the river and into position for an early morning linkup with French at Brandy Station. Instead Sedgwick's wing remained north of the Rappahannock, and although the III Corps had gotten two divisions across the stream by dusk, its remaining division wouldn't join them until well after dark. French's other units lingered on the opposite shore, Newton's I Corps at Morrisville and Warren's II Corps

---

25 Ibid., 432, 924.

26 Ibid., 429, 432; Lyman, *Meade's Army*, 63.

27 OR 29, pt. 2, 433, 924.

28 Ibid., 924-25.

massed near Kelly's Ford. Those troops would await daylight before passing the river, as would Buford's cavalry division at Sulphur Springs and Kilpatrick's at Ellis' Ford.[29]

Russell's destruction of the bridgehead had forestalled the likelihood of an enemy attack on the Meade's O&A lifeline, but Sedgwick's failure to capture the Rappahannock's south bank left open the possibility of such a thrust, however remote. More importantly, the continued presence of Confederates in riverside earthworks precluded an easy right wing advance to link up with French. Strategically, therefore, the bridgehead's capture did nothing to alter Meade's worst-case-scenario thinking beyond reducing the number of troops he had to leave around Rappahannock Station. The only sure way of uniting the army remained bringing most of Sedgwick's troops to Kelly's Ford speedily enough to prevent Lee from swamping French before the V and VI Corps reinforced him.

Meade's late night dispatches reflected that reality. At 10:15 p.m. he asked French how far forward he had pushed reconnaissance patrols and what they had revealed about the enemy's "force and position." The commanding general also stressed the importance of making sure the entire left wing came south of the Rappahannock as fast as possible, directing French to order Newton's I Corps to move from Morrisville to Kelly's Ford "at early daylight" if it wasn't already on the way. Finally, he assured French that Kilpatrick's cavalry would wade the Rappahannock via Ellis' Ford at daylight with instructions to protect his left flank.[30]

At 11:30 p.m. Meade ordered Sykes' V Corps to leave Rappahannock Station at 4 a.m. and march to Kelly's Ford, where it would cross the river in support of French. Sedgwick was to send a pair of VI Corps brigades with Sykes and station another brigade at Norman's Ford. Those elements of the VI Corps remaining near Russell's captured redoubts would launch a robust artillery barrage at daybreak. This feigned attack would divert Rebel strength away from French, it was hoped, and buy time for Sykes to reach the left wing. If Sedgwick saw a chance to turn his feint into a real assault, he should do so. Meanwhile French's troops would move to strike Rappahannock Station from the rear, and if necessary open a way for Sedgwick to get over the waterway.[31]

---

29 Byrne, *Haskell of Gettysburg*, 230; James A. David, ed., *"Bully for the Band!" The Civil War Letters and Diary of Four Brothers in the 10th Vermont Infantry Band* (Jefferson, NC, 2012), 99-100; Keifer to Eliza, Nov. 9, 1863, J. Warren Keifer papers, LC. Keifer says the entire III Corps had crossed the Rappahannock by 9 p.m. November 7. Herbert George of the 10th VT wrote home that the 3rd Division, III Corps crossed at 10 p.m. Newton had his 1st and 2nd divisions at Morrisville. His 3rd Division guarded the O&A.

30 OR 29, pt. 2, 433.

31 Ibid., 434.

These directives laid bare Meade's intentions for tomorrow. First, he would strengthen his left wing against an enemy attack and then unite his army, after which he would move south in search of a battle with the Confederates. If things worked out properly that contest might cripple the Army of Northern Virginia. At the least it would prove to harping editors and politicians that George Meade wasn't afraid to fight.

CHAPTER 8

"That Which Will Preserve. . . Lives"

Packing Up—Abandoned Quarters—Vehicular Chaos—Fortifying A New Line

EXACTLY when word of the disaster at Rappahannock Station reached Robert E. Lee is uncertain, but it was probably around 8 p.m.—the same time Meade learned of the bridgehead's fall. Federal leaders required three more hours of messaging before AOP headquarters understood the situation well enough to formalize a plan for November 8. Their Confederate counterparts needed almost no time: Lee realized immediately that the bastion's capture destroyed his entire defensive strategy by preventing him from dividing Meade's army and assailing it in detail. Now facing potential attacks against both flanks, Lee confronted the prospect of battle against heavy odds on unfavorable ground. Any defeat inside the Culpeper 'V' might trap his command against the Rapidan and lead to its substantial destruction.

Avoiding this meant falling back across the river into Orange County. The general directed ANV engineers to put down a pontoon bridge at Barnett's Ford near Liberty Mills, where the river was too deep for fording, then ordered a staged withdrawal that would send the army's supply trains behind the Rapidan and its combat units into a new battle line north of Culpeper Court House. Executing that directive wouldn't be easy. Expecting a prolonged stay near the Rappahannock, most Confederate regiments had completed or were still building winter quarters. Many had brought forward conveniences stored in rear area warehouses during the campaigning season. Moreover, the army had already started establishing ration dumps and quartermaster's depots throughout Culpeper County.[1]

---

1 I have been unable to find an order from ANV HQ directing the building of pontoon bridges. However, several of Hill's troops relate crossing the Rapidan on "hastily constructed"

The resource-challenged Rebels couldn't afford to abandon or destroy these precious commodities. Wagon trains would have to haul as much material as possible below the Rapidan before Lee's infantry withdrew behind the river. At best that was a day-long job and perhaps longer. But until teamsters completed this task, the army was compelled to risk battle on disadvantageous terms. Lee might avoid a general engagement if the Yankees acted with their customary caution. But if instead they displayed the same aggressiveness as on November 7, a fight was certain and the Virginian wasn't sure he could win it.[2]

*   *   *

Lee's decision to retreat surprised everyone except the troops around Rappahannock Station. Since mid-afternoon Confederate soldiers had anticipated imminent action and a pressing desire to protect partially completed winter cantonments merely amplified their combativeness. Rebel troops couldn't predict whether they would attack or defend, but they were certain of success and that their leaders would, as usual, dictate the course of events. That conviction dissolved around 9 p.m. when withdrawal orders began filtering down the chain of command.[3]

Instructions to evacuate the army's encampments startled quartermasters and teamsters alike. Early, Rodes and Johnson had marched their divisions to the front leaving tents standing, new cabins largely furnished, and baggage "strewed around everywhere." Rodes had wisely ordered his camps packed up as soon as he learned that Federals were attacking Kelly's Ford, and although this foresight afforded his men extra time, it couldn't surmount other difficulties. With most unit strength on the battle line, nothing but a relative handful of rear area personnel remained to gather, sort, and load a mountain of material. The shortage of transportation was worse than the shortage of manpower and Lee's army had far too few vehicles to haul off everything in the one trip conditions mandated. Moreover, since the infantry's movement to more

---

bridges "near Liberty Mills." Marching from Culpeper Court House to Liberty Mills required a roundabout journey through Madison County that would take more than 12 hours. Since Rebel accounts make clear that Hill's corps crossed the river at dawn on Nov. 9 they must have done so at Barnett's Ford (just east of Liberty Mills) which was connected to Culpeper by a direct road. Julius A. Lineback Diary, Nov. 7-8 (University of North Carolina, Chapel Hill (UNC-CH); Dobbins, *Grandfather's Journal*, 168.

2   *OR* 29, pt. 2, 609.

3   John Casler, *Four Years in the Stonewall Brigade* (Marietta, GA, 1951) 196.

defensible ground had to take place that night, the supply echelons were allowed only a few hours to accomplish their work.[4]

Those time constraints were especially galling for commands that had sent wagons to distant depots earlier in the day or whose transportation had bivouacked far from regimental camps. All those vehicles would have to return to their units before anyone could load anything. That hours-long journey drastically curtailed the already meager interval available for packing critical supplies. Some trains arrived so late loading had barely begun before wagon masters ordered their charges back onto the road.

Logisticians and regimental details packed as much as they could as fast as they could, but the job was simply too big, the amount of transport too small, and the allotted hours too few to save everything. Nonetheless, some quartermasters seemed determined to leave nothing behind. Time-conscious officers had to reiterate departure orders multiple times before reluctant teamsters begrudgingly pulled out of camp. Even then, numerous wagons headed for the Rapidan only half-full.

Despite leaving behind a great deal of furniture, tentage, personal items, and clothing, the Rebels managed to save most of their rations, munitions, and essential camp equipage. That success was attributable to the fortitude of Lee's rear echelon, which accomplished a minor miracle in shipping off as much as it did. Still, the hurried vehicular retreat quickly descended into chaos. One 4th North Carolina soldier admitted that the wagon columns "struck out pell-mell for the Rapidan" without inquiring "about anybody or anything" or even asking "questions about roads or fords." Inevitably the supply trains soon "scattered to the four winds," and got so thoroughly separated from their parent commands that they couldn't issue rations for two days, leaving the troops to go hungry for just as long.[5]

*   *   *

Once the vehicles got enough of a head start, Confederate units began pulling back toward a makeshift defensive line two miles in front of Culpeper Court House. Johnson's division withdrew around 10 p.m. Ewell's artillery left Stevensburg at midnight. Rodes' division abandoned its line at the same hour. Several outfits had the unsavory experience of hustling through their camps without being able to salvage personal belongings, extra clothing, or even blankets. Here and there the Rebels burned what they left behind. Elsewhere dispossessed soldiers rescued abandoned material via large scale larceny. Pausing to rest in Rodes' deserted winter quarters, the

---

4   OR 29, pt. 1, 631; Chapman, ed., *Bright and Gloomy Days*, 87-90.

5   Munson, *Confederate Correspondent*, 103.

Stonewall Brigade of Johnson's division "thoroughly plundered" forsaken cabins rather than consign their contents to enemy capture.[6]

While Ewell's corps backpedaled, Hill's regiments cooked rations and prepared for movement at a "moment's notice." Most men anticipated an advance toward the enemy, but when the corps artillery commenced rolling at midnight it headed south. A few hours later the infantry trekked in the same direction. Hill's troops puzzled over the meaning of this unexpected route until news from Rappahannock Station skipped through the ranks and explained their line of march all too well.[7]

ANV headquarters evacuated alongside Hill. After issuing his retreat orders, Lee had ridden out to the picket line seeking information. That move horrified his acting Assistant Adjutant General—Maj. Walter H. Taylor—who felt certain that being up with the outposts was "not exactly the place" for an army commander. As usual Lee disregarded his own safety to gain a clearer sense of the situation, a duty he may have felt more keenly after misconstruing enemy intentions a few hours ago.[8]

Upon returning to Brandy Station sometime after 9 p.m. Lee directed his staff to break camp, load the headquarters wagons, and dispatch them toward the Rapidan. Accompanied by his key aides, the general stayed behind to monitor the retreat's progress and issue any necessary final instructions. To pass the time comfortably, some officers built "immense" fires in recently built wood and mud chimneys, wrapped themselves in overcoats, and laid down to get a little sleep. Rest wasn't an option for the army commander and he gently teased Taylor for napping in such circumstances. When the general and his entourage finally rode south at midnight, departing aides committed their chimneys and accumulated firewood to the flames rather than leave them for enemy use.[9]

Early's division covered the army's withdrawal, maintaining its line south of Rappahannock Station until 3 a.m. when, leaving behind a picket screen and preceded by Dance's and Graham's batteries, it pulled back so stealthily that adjacent Federals

6   Park, *War Diary*, SHP, vol. 26, 18-26; Casler, *Four Years in the Stonewall Brigade*, 196; Chapman, *Bright and Gloomy Days*, 87-90; Dozier, *Gunner in Lee's Army*, 219.

7   Kirkpatrick diary, Nov. 7, 1863, UT; Thomas Bailey Diary, Nov. 7, 1863, Gettysburg National Military Park (GNMP); Julius A. Lineback Diary, Nov. 7-8 (University of North Carolina, Chapel Hill (UNC-CH); Francois Bienvenu Cire Memorandum Book, Nov. 7-8, United Daughters of the Confederacy Memorial Library, Richmond, VA (UDC); Clark, *NC Regts*, vol. 3, 248; Moore, *Cannoneer Under Stonewall Jackson*, 209-10.

8   Tower, *Lee's Adjutant*, 82.

9   Ibid, 86-87.

didn't notice its disappearance until well after dawn. By then Early's regiments were slipping into Lee's new battle line above Culpeper Court House.[10]

The Confederate position stretched from the Rixeyville Road northwest of town to Pony Mountain southeast of the village. The O&A bisected the Rebel front, with Hill's Corps deployed west of the railroad and Ewell's east of the tracks. Wilcox's division straddled the Rixeyville Road near Chestnut Fork Church and held the extreme left flank. Anderson's division went into line on Wilcox's right, its front running across the fields of Samuel Bradford's extensive farm. Heth's division, deployed as a column of brigades, occupied Hill's right filling the space between Anderson and the O&A.

Early's battered command, on the left of Ewell's corps, connected with Heth at the railroad and then fanned out southeastward until it met Rodes' division. The latter took post on Early's right, its line running through heavy woods and behind the steep, miry banks of Mountain Run where the creek briefly traveled north to south. Johnson's division held the far right flank of Lee's line, its troops arrayed along the eastern slope of Pony Mountain from whose crest Confederate signalmen could see almost all the way to the Rappahannock.[11]

As each regiment or battery moved into position, its personnel instantly began erecting breastworks. "Using tin cups, tin plates and bayonets" in lieu of the shovels and picks that had disappeared with the supply wagons, they threw up a line of "rude fortifications" with remarkable alacrity. Marveling at "how soon and how well the work was done," Dr. Harvey Black of Ewell's staff praised the troops for having learned "to do that which will preserve their lives."[12]

10 OR 29, pt. 1, 624; OR 29, pt. 2, 926. Early's report does not mention leaving behind a picket screen, although doing so in such situations was common military wisdom. On the morning of Nov. 8 Sedgwick reported enemy pickets along the river's south bank. I have concluded that when the Confederates withdrew they left men in place to create the illusion that they maintained their line.

11 Previous paragraphs based on Kirkpatrick diary, Nov. 7, 1863, UT; OR, 29, pt. 1, 637; Clark, NC Regts, vol. 2, 663; McMullen, A Surgeon with Stonewall Jackson, 68; Munson, Confederate Correspondent, 103; Swank, Sabres, Saddles and Spurs, 101; John Walters, Norfolk Blues: the Civil War diary of the Norfolk Light Artillery Blues (Shippensburg, PA, 1997), 99; Carter, Gunner in Lee's Army, 219; Carrie Esther Spencer & Bernard Samuels, A Civil Marriage in Virginia: Reminiscences and Letters (Boyce, VA, 1956), 201; Hairston Diary, Nov. 7, 1863, SHC/UNC. Heth's column of brigades put a dense mass of Rebel infantry in place to defend the open ground immediately west of the O&A, the most vulnerable sector of Lee's front.

12 Park, War Diary, SHP, vol. 26, 18-26; Kirkpatrick diary, Nov. 7, 1863, UT; Bailey Diary, GNMP; McVicar Diary, Nov. 7, 1863, Handley Regional Library, Steward Bell Jr. Archive, Winchester, VA (HRL); McMullen, A Surgeon with Stonewall Jackson, 68.

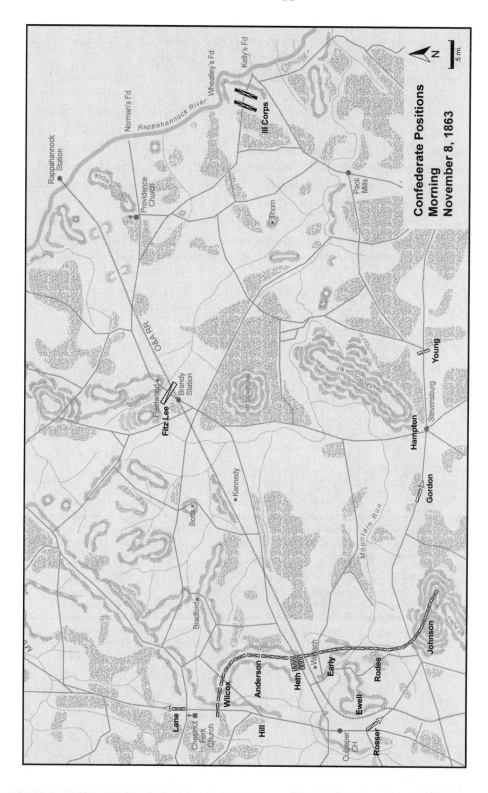

Confederate Positions
Morning
November 8, 1863

Indeed, Lee's veterans had come to understand the value of entrenchments from both tactical and personal perspectives. Their skillful fortifying mimicked that of mid-July when, backed against a flooded Potomac following Gettysburg, they had constructed a line of seemingly impregnable breastworks overnight. Now in a similar if far less dire predicament, Southern soldiers dug instinctively and often without needing orders.

Neither the diggers nor those admiring their rapidly rising earthworks realized they were witnessing a profound alteration of the war's very nature. The entrenchments in front of Culpeper not only resembled those built in July at Williamsport; they presaged even more elaborate works soon to appear south of the Rapidan along Mine Run. This sequence of troop-built field fortifications constituted the start of a tactical revolution which would become not only an inescapable battlefield reality the next spring, but such a dominant feature of the conflict that it threatened to determine the war's outcome in late 1864.

At the moment, however, all that mattered to Confederate soldiers was preparing for the arrival of an enemy supposedly in hot pursuit of Lee's army. Rebel morale remained high despite disturbing reports from Rappahannock Station and a withdrawal of several miles. Men anxious to settle accounts for Gettysburg and Bristoe Station eagerly awaited battle and a chance to slaughter Yankees charging newly erected breastworks. One Alabama officer noted in his diary that his supremely confident troops were more than "ready to welcome" Meade's "cohorts to hospitable graves." The only question was whether the enemy would offer the Rebels that chance.[13]

---

13 Park, *War Diary*, *SHSP*, Volume 26, 18-26.

CHAPTER 9

"A Show of Fight"

Cavalry Positioning—Lee's Vulnerabilities—Morning Intelligence—Uniting the AOP

NEITHER army's horsemen had been busy on November 7. As Sedgwick and French advanced on Rappahannock Station and Kelly's Ford, Brig. Gen. Buford's 1st Cavalry Division, reinforced by Brig. Gen. Wesley Merritt's Reserve Cavalry Brigade, concentrated at Sulphur Springs, 11 miles west of the burnt railroad bridge. At the same time, Kilpatrick's 3rd Cavalry Division rode to Kemper's and Ellis' fords on French's left and Brig. Gen. David Gregg's 2nd Cavalry Division gathered around Bealton Station to protect the army's rear.[1]

In contrast to this modest activity, Confederate cavalrymen not on picket were idle. After the November 5 grand review, Stuart's brigades had returned to their bivouacs and daily routine around Culpeper Court House. On the sixth, Brig. Gen. Thomas L. Rosser's brigade accompanied by a gun section from Capt. Roger P. Chew's battery shifted position to Gaines Crossroads, about 15 miles northwest of Culpeper. For them and the cavalry corps' remaining five brigades, November 7 passed quietly until midnight couriers arrived with instructions to break camp, send wagons rearward, and ride to the front.[2]

---

1 Robert J. Trout, *After Gettysburg: Cavalry Operations in the Eastern Theater July 14, 1863 to December 31, 1863* (Hamilton, MT, 2011), 290-91.

2 George M. Neese, *Three Years in the Confederate Horse Artillery* (New York, NY, 1911), 234. Camping close to Culpeper placed Stuart's brigades within easy distance of the O&A and the trains carrying grain for the army's horses. Lee's artillery bivouacked in the same vicinity for the same reason. The movement to Gaines Crossroads was a preliminary step to reinforcing

Maj. Gen. James E. B. Stuart
Library of Congress

Responding swiftly, Stuart's regiments trotted onto the roads well before dawn and kept moving throughout the remaining hours of darkness. Under orders to impede a Union advance down the O&A, Maj. Gen. Fitzhugh Lee directed his three brigades—led respectively by Col. John R. Chambliss, Jr., Brig. Gen. Lunsford L. Lomax and Brig. Gen. William C. Wickham—to take position near the old battlegrounds at Fleetwood Heights and Brandy Station. Stuart sent the bulk of Maj. Robert F. Beckham's horse artillery battalion to the same sector. By sunup, Fitz Lee's troopers, Chew's remaining section, and three batteries under Captains James Breathed, William M. McGregor and Marcellus N. Moorman were in place and ready for whatever came their way.[3]

Stuart deployed Maj. Gen. Wade Hampton's division to confront any Federal advance from the east. A Gettysburg wound had sidelined its talented commander for the last 16 weeks, during which time Stuart supervised the division personally. Still shouldering that responsibility, he sent two brigades under Brig. Gen. Pierce M. B. Young and Brig. Gen. James Gordon along with Capt. James F. Hart's battery toward Stevensburg, which lay along the most direct route between Kelly's Ford and Culpeper Court House. As these commands headed out, Rosser left the 10th Virginia Cavalry to watch the Rixeyville road and then led his brigade and Chew's first section south from

---

Confederate forces in the Valley in response to Union activity there, but the threat subsided before the reinforcements moved closer to the Blue Ridge.

3 Walbrook D. Swank, ed., *Sabres, Saddles and Spurs* (Shippensburg, PA, 1996), 99-101; Richard Henry Watkins to Mary, Nov. 11, 1863 (Richard Henry Watkins letters, Virginia Historical Society, Richmond, VA); Charles W. McVicar Diary, Nov. 6, 1863, HRL; Samuel Nunnelee Diary, Nov. 8, 1863, ACWM. Chambliss led W.H.F. "Rooney" Lee's brigade while Lee remained a prisoner of war.

Maj. Gen. Gouverneur K. Warren
Library of Congress

Gaines Crossroads to Culpeper. Reaching the courthouse about dawn on November 8, they turned east and hurried after the rest of Hampton's division.[4]

Stuart's cavalry had the critical task of slowing Meade's inevitable advance from the Rappahannock and preventing him from striking the main Rebel line before dusk. Failure wasn't an option, for once Meade got his entire force over the river, he could take advantage of superior numbers to attack or turn Lee's flanks, both of which offered alluring opportunities to Federal commanders.

Although the heights of Pony Mountain somewhat anchored the Rebel right, only a few miles separated its summit from the Rapidan. An aggressive enemy thrust south of the elevation might interpose Union troops between Lee and the river. Should that happen Meade would compel the Southerners to conduct a desperate fighting withdrawal across the stream or an equally desperate retreat into Madison County—a move that would put the Federals between Lee and Richmond. A blow against the Rebel left didn't pose as great a strategic threat, but it presented a grimmer tactical danger. Bereft of commanding terrain of any kind, this end of the Confederate line was "in the air" and susceptible to a flanking movement. Successful Yankee attacks here might crumple Lee's entire position, forcing his army back against the Rapidan and exposing it to destruction.

In short, if Meade defeated the ANV anywhere in front of Culpeper Court House he might get a chance at the war-winning blow he had failed to inflict in July or October. Although Lee's battle wise soldiers were confident of beating back a frontal attack, they understood their army's vulnerability. Many of them correctly surmised

---

4 Neese, *Three years*, 234; Samuel Nunnelee Diary, Nov. 8, 1863, ACWM.

that their commander's purpose wasn't to invite battle but rather make "a show of fight" and buy time for his trains to escape.[5]

* * *

Whether Confederate cavalry and a "show of fight" could keep the Yankees at bay depended a great deal on how George Meade managed his affairs on November 8. The general and his staff awoke before dawn fully anticipating combat. No one knew whether the Rebels or the AOP would be the day's aggressor, but everyone expected a fight not long after sunrise. Eager to witness his first large-scale action, Col. Lyman quietly ate breakfast, all the while keeping an ear cocked for any sounds that would "announce the opening of [a] great battle."[6]

No matter who attacked, uniting the Union army remained Meade's paramount concern. Per his orders its various components were already moving to achieve that concentration. Sykes' V Corps and two VI Corps brigades had left Rappahannock Station for Kelly's Ford at 4 a.m. Newton's I Corps exited its bivouac around Morrisville at the same time for the same destination. A few miles farther south Warren's II Corps began crossing Kelly's Ford pontoon bridges soon after daylight.[7]

As these units approached, Gen. Birney prepared the III Corps for an assault against the high ground in its front. His mission was to cut through to Rappahannock Station and displace whatever Confederates still faced Sedgwick. The first step in that plan required shoving Robert Rodes aside, a task Birney assigned to Brig. Gen. Carr's 3rd Division which would make the corps' main effort while Brig. Gens. John Hobart Ward's 1st Division and Henry Prince's 2nd Division advanced on Carr's left and right respectively. As soon as Warren got the II Corps into place on Birney's southern flank, the assault would begin.[8]

At 4 a.m. Carr dispatched Col. William H. Ball with a pair of Ohio regiments to reconnoiter ahead and report enemy dispositions. To their surprise, the midwesterners

5   Kirkpatrick diary, November 7, 1863, UT.

6   Lyman to wife, Nov. 9, 1863, *Meade's Headquarters*, 44-46.

7   OR 29, pt. 2, 439. Acken, *Inside the Army of the Potomac*, 393; Robert Goldthwaite Carter, *Four Brothers in Blue: Or Sunshine and Shadows of the War of the Rebellion: A Story of the Great Civil War from Bull Run to Appomattox* (Austin, TX. 1979), 363; Allan Nevins, ed., *A Diary of Battle: The Personal Journals of Colonel Charles S. Wainwright: 1861-1865* (Boston, MA, 1998), 300; Lance Herdegen & Sherry Murphy, *Four Years With The Iron Brigade: The Civil War Journal of William Ray, Company F, Seventh Wisconsin Volunteers* (Cambridge, MA, 2002), 233. French's message to Humphreys concerning the I Corps is misdated November 9 at 1:15 a.m.

8   OR 29, pt. 2, 436.

trod a mile and a half without encountering any resistance at all. When the first glimmer of light peaked over the horizon at 5:41 a.m. they found themselves inside an abandoned Rebel camp and captors of 38 enemy stragglers. Ball hurriedly sent back word of the enemy's disappearance and noted that the road leading upstream appeared open.[9]

Six miles away at Rappahannock Station, heavy fog denied Federal troops a similar intelligence bonanza. Although hazy conditions didn't prevent Sedgwick from detecting enemy troops on the opposite shore, they did prevent his estimating their numbers or inaugurating the dawn artillery barrage Meade had ordered. Reporting this state of affairs to AOP headquarters in a 6:55 a.m. dispatch, Sedgwick promised to commence his bombardment as soon as the fog lifted.[10]

This news meant little until it arrived at the appropriate command posts; and much to Meade's frustration the dictates of time and distance still hampered Federal communications. It took Col. Ball's message almost two hours to reach French, who promptly passed it up the chain of command along with word that Johnson's division seemed to have withdrawn overnight to Brandy Station and "across Mountain Run." Suspecting that Lee might have ordered a retreat, the left wing commander sensed an opportunity. At 7:40 a.m. he suggested sending Warren to Stevensburg in order to position him for a thrust toward Culpeper Court House, provided Sedgwick had already crossed the river or didn't need further assistance doing so.[11]

It is unclear when Meade received that proposal because he wasn't at his headquarters when French sent it. Impatient for news from the front and wanting to move closer to the scene of impending action, the general and his staff had ridden away from the Carter Farm around 7:30 a.m., headed for Kelly's Ford. The three-mile trip took about an hour, and well before Meade arrived French's troops were already on the move, rendering irrelevant his earlier suggestion.[12]

---

9 Ibid., pt. 1, 563, 577; Boatner, *Civil War Dictionary*, 820. The two regiments were the 122nd and 110th OH Infantry. A company from the 6th MD (US) also took part in the mission. Sykes' official report says he moved at 5 a.m. but a multitude of V Corps' soldier letters and diaries say the march began at 4 a.m.

10 *OR* 51, pt. 1, 1020. Sedgwick's 6:55 Nov. 8 dispatch is mislabeled p.m., but its content leaves no doubt that he wrote it before 7 a.m.

11 *OR* 29, pt. 1, 563, 565 & pt. 2, 436-37. I have derived the time required for Ball and Sedgwick's messages to reach their destinations from the fact that French's dispatch informing Meade of Confederate movements is timed 7:40 a.m. Humphreys writes Sedgwick at 8:30 a.m. seeking news from his front, a clear indication that the latter's 6:55 a.m. dispatch had not reached AOP Headquarters. See *OR* 29, pt. 2, 436-37.

12 Lowe, *Meade's Army*, 63-64. How many of Meade's staff rode with him is uncertain. Lyman certainly did, for he detailed the event in his journal. Provost Marshall Patrick was with Meade

After learning that no Rebels stood in his immediate front, Birney shifted the III Corps from line into column and at 8 a.m. launched it down a road angling northwest toward Providence Church—a small meeting house adjacent to the intersection of two roads, one leading north to Norman's Ford and another running west to the O&A. The junction rested in the shadow of Jamison's Ridge whose heavily fortified northern tip extended to within 400 yards of the Rappahannock and dominated Norman's Ford. Confederate troops had occupied these works throughout yesterday and last night. Carr's division at the head of Birney's column was to push these Rebels out of the way, if they were still there, and open the crossing site for Sedgwick.[13]

The II Corps, on Birney's left flank, advanced simultaneously with the III. After transiting Kelly's Ford near first light, Warren had deployed his troops to the southwest toward last evening's reported position of "Allegheny" Johnson's Rebels. With his 3rd Division in reserve on some high ground close to the river, Warren sent his 1st and 2nd Divisions forward at 8 a.m. Their battle line moved at the double quick, expecting to encounter enemy fire at any moment. Instead, the onrushing Federals quickly confirmed that Johnson had retreated during the night.[14]

A disappointed Warren pushed his men cross country, probing for the enemy and keeping contact with the III Corps until he reached Berry Hill, roughly 2 miles southwest of Kellysville where the II Corps halted.[15]

Atop that elevation's 100-foot high summit Warren established headquarters at the home of Dr. Joseph P. Thom, which had been Ewell's command post only 12 hours ago. Peering westward through binoculars the general spied a large force of

---

when he crossed the Rappahannock some hours later, so he probably accompanied the general as well. Since the Signal Corps had run a telegraph line from Carter's Farm to Kelly's Ford, it is likely that Meade's chief of staff, Maj. Gen. Humphreys, rode to Kelly's Ford as well. At 8:30 a.m. he issued several messages for Meade, but at 1 p.m. sent a signal marked "Kelly's." Apparently, Humphreys initially remained at the Carter Farm and didn't join Meade at Mount Holly until after noon.

13 OR 29, pt. 1, 562-63, 565 & pt. 2, 436-37. Ball commanded the 122nd OH Infantry. Confederate maps label Providence Church as Providence Meeting House.

14 Manley Stacey to Father, Nov. 9, 1863, Manley Stacey Civil War Letters, Historical Society of Oak Park and River Forest, IL, http://martyhackl.net/staceyletters/2009/07/07/november-9-1863-brandy-station/, accessed Aug. 31, 2019. Stacey says that his regiment, the 111th New York in Warren's 3rd Division, crossed the Rappahannock around 7 a.m. The 3rd Division was Warren's rearmost unit.

15 Amos M. Judson, *History of the Eight-Third Regiment Pennsylvania Volunteers, 1861-1865* (Dayton, OH, 1986), 78-79; Byrne, *Haskell of Gettysburg*, 231; Chauncey A. Cronk diary, Nov. 8, 1863, transcript in author's collection; Manley Stacey to Father, Nov. 9, 1863, Manley Stacey Civil War Letters, Historical Society of Oak Park and River Forest, IL, http://martyhackl.net/staceyletters/2009/07/07/november-9-1863-brandy-station/, accessed Aug. 31, 2019.

Rebels hovering four miles away near Brandy Station. Excited by that discovery, he hurriedly sent army headquarters a dispatch reporting the enemy "probably concentrating" near the oft-fought for landmark.[16]

*   *   *

Meade and the leading elements of Sykes' V Corps arrived at Kelly's Ford about 30 minutes after Birney and Warren had started forward. Newton's I Corps reached the area shortly afterwards. His morale heartened by the pleasurable and unusual experience of hearing Union soldiers cheer him as he rode past, the AOP's commander stopped at Mount Holly Church, about a mile from the river. With the sanctuary in use as a field hospital, Meade established an ad hoc command post at a close-by poor house and immediately began issuing orders.[17]

Disregarding the army's wing organization, which officially remained in place, he sent Sykes new instructions. The V Corps' original assignment was to cross the river and move south to Paoli Mills, where the road to Stevensburg crossed Mountain Run. This was a good post for protecting French's left flank, but with the Rebels evidently pulling back toward Brandy Station, Meade decided to situate Sykes for an advance in that direction if needed. New orders directed the V Corps to march beyond Paoli Mills and occupy the intersection of a road linking Brandy Station and Stevensburg. If Sykes could find a route north of Mountain Run that served the same function, Meade authorized him to use it instead.[18]

It took a while for the entire V Corps to get across the Rappahannock—its rearmost brigades didn't start over the pontoon bridges until 10:30 a.m.—and Newton's troops couldn't cross until Sykes' men were out of the way. Nonetheless, the arrival of the I and V Corps along with Sedgwick's two detached brigades brought French's isolation to an end.[19]

---

16 OR 29, pt. 2, 437; Agassiz, *Meade's Headquarters*, 44. Warren referred to Berry Hill as Thom's Hill (misspelled Thorn's Hill in OR). Dr. Thom, a US Army Mexican War veteran and USN Asst. Surgeon from 1853-57, joined the Confederate Army in 1861, was wounded at Kernstown in March 1862, and afterwards served in the Confederate quartermasters dept.

17 Lowe, *Meade's Army*, 63-64; Acken, *Inside the Army of the Potomac*, 393; Goldthwaite, *Four Brothers in Blue*, 363; Nevins, *A Diary of Battle*, 300; Herdegen & Murphy, *Four Years With The Iron Brigade*, 233.

18 OR 29, pt. 2, 436.

19 OR 29, pt. 1, 577; Acken, *Inside the Army of the Potomac*, 393; Goldthwaite, *Four Brothers in Blue*, 363. The tail of Sykes' column got over the river a little after noon.

With most of his command assembled around Kellysville, Meade could stop worrying about facing Lee with a divided army. The VI Corps, however, remained alone and unsupported at Rappahannock Station, and since Sedgwick's 6:55 a.m. dispatch hadn't reached AOP headquarters yet, Meade had no idea what was happening there. A lot depended on the answer to that question and at 8:30 a.m. Humphreys sent Sedgwick a message asking about the "condition of affairs" along his front. The chief of staff also relayed that the Rebels were "retiring toward Stevensburg and Brandy Station" and the III Corps advancing toward Providence Church "to open communication" with the right wing.

That couldn't happen soon enough for George Meade. If the VI Corps remained unsupported, it offered Lee an inviting target. Although the chance of a Confederate attack seemed unlikely given the intelligence arriving at AOP headquarters, the Federals still had no information on A. P. Hill's whereabouts, and Lee's audacity could never be discounted. Meade wouldn't feel completely safe until Sedgwick got south of the river. Only then would the Union army go looking for a fight.

Chapter 10

"Our Chance. . . Is Gone"

Meade's Plan—Action at Fleetwood—Brandy Station Skirmish—Sparring at
Stevensburg—Chapman's Repulse—Spectacular Advance—An Empty Net—Union
Casualties—Missed Opportunity—Rapidan Retreat

MEADE would have been reassured to know that Sedgwick thought everything was under control at Rappahannock Station. Despite the fog hampering his early morning operations, the general felt certain that whatever enemy troops remained in the vicinity would withdraw before long. Such optimism was not misplaced. By 9:05 a.m. he was able to report that Rebel skirmishers were pulling back and his own men moving into abandoned south bank earthworks.[1]

In a second message penned almost two hours later, Sedgwick informed Meade that the III Corps was at Providence Church with its skirmishers atop Jamison's Ridge. More importantly, Col. Spaulding's engineers were close to finishing a pair of bridges—one at Norman's Ford and another upstream at Rappahannock Station, where they were making use of four captured pontoon boats. Wright was already across the river with the VI Corps forward elements and Sedgwick would follow as soon as he received orders from army headquarters.[2]

Dispatches from Rappahannock Station didn't start arriving at Meade's Mount Holly command post until around 9 a.m., and although the lag time in communications caused some confusion, word of Sedgwick's progress undoubtedly eased Meade's mind. With the III Corps at Providence Church and the VI Corps crossing the river, his

1 OR 29, pt. 2, 925.

2 Ibid., 435, 926; Emil & Ruth Rosenblatt, eds., *Hard Marching Every Day: The Civil War Letters of Private Wilbur Fish, 1861-1865* (Lawrence, KS, 1992), 161.

army's two wings had joined hands at last. Now he could concentrate on finding the Rebels.[3]

Although the enemy's exact position wasn't clear, the available sparse intelligence indicated his massing around Brandy Station. Delighted at the Confederate's apparent willingness to accept combat, Meade told Col. Lyman "he meant to pitch right into them." Nonetheless, the general seemed unwilling to commit everything to an attack. He would keep Warren and Sykes in place to shield Kelly's Ford from possible assault while sending Kilpatrick's cavalry towards Stevensburg and the Rapidan to ensure that no surprises lurked to the south. Buford would perform the same function to the west, moving down from Sulphur Springs toward Culpeper Court House as a precaution against Lee slipping around the Federal right to cross the Rappahannock upstream and threaten the Union rear.[4]

For now, that meant the III and VI Corps would constitute the AOP's entire offensive force. Until these units were concentrated, Meade wanted to avoid stumbling into a fight piecemeal and he sent Birney word not to advance beyond the railroad until Sedgwick got all his troops over the river. At that point Birney and Wright would go into line east and west of the railroad respectively and advance on Brandy Station. Newton's I Corps and Warren's 3rd Division would stand ready to offer any needed support. Oddly, Meade didn't designate an overall commander for this southward push, nor did he ride to the O&A and take charge of the operation himself. Instead, the general left his wing organization in place, despite the army's reunification.[5]

This was a peculiar decision given the AOP's current dispositions. Sedgwick's right wing now contained nothing more than his own VI Corps minus two brigades sent to Kelly's Ford and a third detached to guard Rappahannock Station. Likewise, the left wing's mobile force had shrunk to just the III and I Corps. Although Sedgwick was senior to French, Meade left the latter to decide when to call forward Newton's troops or Warren's reserve division near Kelly's Ford.[6]

---

3   OR 29, pt. 2, 437-38; Lowe, *Meade's Army*, 64; Agassiz, *Meade's Headquarters*, 44. It isn't clear whether Sedgwick knew of Meade's relocation or which route couriers travelled between the two headquarters. Humphreys first responded to a Sedgwick message at 9:15 a.m. on November 8. Communication between Sedgwick and Army HQ did speed up as the day went on.

4   Agassiz, *Meade's Headquarters*, 44. Lee had crossed the Rappahannock at Sulphur Springs in October, outflanking Meade's position along the river and forcing his rapid retreat to Centreville.

5   *Report of the Joint Committee on the Conduct of the War at the Second Session of the Thirty-eight Congress*, 4 Vols. (Washington, 1865). Birney's testimony, vol. 4, 372.

6   OR 29, pt. 2, 437.

Perhaps Meade thought his Mount Holly location best suited to coordinating a response to any attack against the army's left flank or shifting Sykes and Warren from their current posts toward Brandy Station or Stevensburg. However logical that decision, it didn't address the absence of an overall commander for the movement on Brandy Station—an oversight that might cause serious trouble at the onset of the major action Meade anticipated.

Regardless of command arrangements, the general had committed his VI and III Corps to going forward in line of battle while searching for the enemy. Organizing such an extended formation and moving it five miles over undulating terrain would be difficult and time consuming. But Meade considered the expenditure of effort essential. Not only would it position his troops for a quick attack once they encountered the Rebels, it would also safeguard against a surprise enemy assault should Lee launch one.

*   *   *

Whatever the general's reasoning, spreading 33,000 men, 92 cannon, dozens of ambulances and as many ordnance wagons across the countryside certainly increased the complexity of Federal operations. The sight of Fitz Lee's cavalry and a section of gray artillery standing two miles away on Fleetwood Heights compounded Union difficulties. Whether Confederate infantry waited in the woods and fields behind Lee's horsemen couldn't be known, but the presence of butternut troopers strongly hinted at trouble ahead.[7]

Obedient to Meade's orders, the III Corps marched for the O&A from Jamison's Ridge shortly after 11 a.m. With Carr's 3rd Division still in the lead, the corps reached the railroad around noon. Swinging his troops into line facing south, Carr directed Col. Joseph W. Keifer's 2nd Brigade to drive off the Rebel cavalry and find out what lurked in its rear.[8]

Keifer was self-confident, aggressive, and ardently anti-slavery. As a field officer in the 3rd Ohio he had taken part in McClellan's victorious 1861 campaign to seize Virginia's western mountains. Promoted to colonel in 1862, the 27-year-old assumed leadership of the 110th Ohio and subsequently served in the lower Shenandoah Valley.

---

7   Ibid., 598; J. Warren Keifer to Eliza, Nov. 9, 1863, J. Warren Keifer papers, LC.

8   OR 29, pt. 1, 563, 573; Robert J. Trout, ed., *Memoirs of the Stuart Horse Artillery Battalion: Moorman's and Hart's Batteries* (Knoxville, TN, 2008), Lewis T. Nunnelee diary, Nov. 8, 1863, 73; Robert J. Trout, *Galloping Thunder: The Stuart Horse Artillery Battalion* (Mechanicsburg, PA, 2002), 388. Keifer preferred to use his middle name, Warren. It is uncertain how much of Lee's division was present, but the best estimate is two brigades.

Keifer had proven his mettle at the Second Battle of Winchester where his boldness helped open an escape route for a portion of the trapped and defeated Federal force. That display of initiative earned him command of a brigade consisting of his own 110th Ohio as well as the 138th Pennsylvania, 122nd Ohio, and 6th Maryland (US).[9]

Dutifully deploying his troops athwart the railroad as per Carr's direction, Keifer estimated he could see some 5,000 or 6,000 enemy cavalrymen lingering around Fleetwood Heights just a half mile away. Unfavorable odds notwithstanding, the colonel was confident that his brigade could flush the Rebels from their position; but as he prepared to go forward, indecision among his superiors suddenly threw everything into disarray. "Orders and counter orders" came tumbling down from Carr and "other generals" as the high command, fearful of provoking a major fight before Meade was fully ready, debated whether to attack or to merely probe Fitz Lee's waiting horsemen.[10]

The initial directive for a brigade assault morphed into sending out a pair of skirmish companies and finally an order to advance just two regiments. A perplexed Keifer did as instructed, assigning the 138th Pennsylvania and 110th Ohio, respectively situated east and west of the railroad tracks, to head for the Rebels. These units had formed in the fall of 1862 but hadn't become part of the AOP until after Gettysburg. Most of their service before then had consisted of guarding Northern railroads; neither had much battlefield experience, although the Ohioans had fought at Second Winchester the preceding June. Colonel Matthew R. McClennan's Pennsylvanians, on the other hand, had yet to see combat—a shortcoming the Confederates soon remedied.[11]

---

9   Eric J. Wittenberg & Scott L. Mingus Sr., *The Second Battle of Winchester: The Confederate Victory that Opened the Door to Gettysburg* (Ed Dorado, CA, 2016), 322-23. Keifer's wartime experiences are detailed in J. Warren Keifer, *Slavery and Four Years of War: A Political History of Slavery in the United States, Together with a Narrative of the Campaigns and Battles of the Civil War in which the Author took part, 1861-1865* (NY, 1900), vol. 2, 56-57. A lawyer before the war, Keifer was a major general at its end. He served in the Ohio Senate from 1868-69 and in the US House of Representatives from 1877-85 and 1905-11, including tenure as Speaker from 1882-84. Recalled to duty as a major general during the Spanish American War, he led the troops who occupied Havana. Keifer died on April 22, 1932. http://bioguide.congress.gov/scripts/biodisplay.pl?index=K000048, accessed Sept. 14, 2019.

10 Keifer to Eliza, Nov. 9, 1863. J. Warren Keifer papers, LC. Keifer's estimate of Rebel strength was off. ANV returns for the end of Oct. 1863 (OR 29, pt. 2, 811) list Fitz Lee's division with 4,108 total effectives on hand. In his letter Keifer refers to the Rebels' holding Miller's Hill, which is a reference to Henry Miller's house, known as Fleetwood, which gave its name to the heights.

11 OR 29, pt. 1, 563; Osceola Lewis, *History of the 138th Regiment of Pennsylvania Volunteer Infantry* (Norristown, PA, 1866), 42-45.

Col. James Warren Keifer
Library of Congress

Watching the bluecoats advance, Chew's gunners selected the 138th as their target, took careful aim, and opened fire. A two-gun bombardment hardly amounted to stout opposition, and nearby veterans cavalierly considered such resistance mere harassment. Nonetheless, to novice combatants Chew's shelling seemed "very severe and seemingly very accurate." Marching in the battle line's rear as a file closer, 1st Lt. Osceola Lewis watched open-mouthed as "shells whizzed over" and through his regiment, tearing up the ground to its front and rear. The sound of humming fragments was even more disconcerting than the sight of solid shot bounding into the air.[12]

McClennan tried to maneuver his command toward safer ground, but with knapsacks and eight days' rations weighing everyone down, the movement barely inconvenienced Rebel artillery. Calmly adjusting their aim, Chew's Virginians exploded a round right in the middle of the Pennsylvania regiment. The shell burst just as it struck Capt. Lazarus C. Andress, "fearfully mangling his hip and thigh" before "carrying off the left arm" of 1st Sgt. Abraham G. Rapp walking directly behind him. The accompanying concussion knocked "several files" of men to the ground, and for a moment confusion gripped the regiment. Officers quickly restored order, however, and the Pennsylvanians shook off the fearful shock of their first casualties, closed ranks like veterans and came on despite losing five more men to enemy shells.[13]

12 Lewis, *History of the 138th*, 43.

13 Ibid, 42-45. Capt. Andress died of his wounds on November 12, 1863, leaving behind a wife and child. American Civil War Research Database, "Lazarus C. Andress," http://www. civilwardata.com/active/hdsquery.dll?SoldierHistory?U&844262 Sgt. Rapp survived but had his arm amputated. Both men were from Company H. The other 5 casualties suffered slight wounds.

The deadly attention paid to the 138th worked to the 110th Ohio's advantage. Momentarily disregarding his role as a brigade commander, Keifer galloped west of the tracks and took personal command of his old regiment's skirmishers, whom he believed would have to do "the real work" of storming the ridge. Bravely (some thought rashly) putting himself between the Rebels and his own troops, Keifer sensed opportunity. The Confederate horsemen appeared irresolute and weren't firing, largely because Fitz Lee had already ordered his brigades to fade back toward Brandy Station.[14]

Thus spared enemy volleys, but also denied worthwhile targets, the 110th's skirmishers—some carrying Henry repeating rifles—moved forward steadily and without firing, their silence allowing the clang and roar of Chew's guns to dominate the field. Suspecting the enemy cannons lacked support, Keifer shouted for his Ohioans to hurry and then spurred his horse to the top of Fleetwood Heights. Cresting the ridge, he found himself a mere 50 feet from limbered-up enemy fieldpieces already pulling away. With his troops just reaching the foot of the hill, the colonel could only draw his revolver and fire a few rounds at the Southern artillerists as they galloped rapidly out of range.[15]

The excitement of firing his weapon in combat for the first time hardly curbed Keifer's frustration as his skirmishers swept onto the ridge only minutes after Chew's escape. Convinced he could have captured the Rebel battery if he had attacked with his entire brigade, Keifer decried the limitations imposed upon him and a lack of artillery support for his assault — a baseless claim, it turned out. At Carr's direction a section of Capt. Frederick M. Edgell's 1st New Hampshire Battery had joined the action just after Keifer moved forward. Unlimbering 2,000 yards from Fleetwood Heights, the gunners opened fire just before the colonel's solo charge. Although Edgell's men hit nothing, the cannoneers believed they had materially assisted the 110th Ohio's attack.

However credible that claim, the New Hampshire battery ceased fire and hurried forward to join Keifer once his men occupied Fleetwood Heights. Like the infantry, these artillerymen arrived too late to accomplish much, and by the time they unlimbered the enemy was already out of sight. Neither Keifer nor Edgell was willing to quit, however, and despite lacking orders to do anything more, they decided to pursue the retiring Confederates.[16]

---

14 Keifer, *Slavery and Four Years of War*, vol. 2, 56-57.

15 Keifer to Eliza, Nov. 9, 1863, Keifer papers, LC; Keifer, *Slavery and Four Years of War*, Vol. 2, 56-57.

16 OR 29, pt. 1, 573; Keifer to Eliza, Nov. 9, 10, 1863, Keifer papers, LC; Keifer, *Slavery and Four Years of War*, Vol. 2, 56-57. Edgell's battery had just 4 guns, all 3-inch Ordnance Rifles.

*   *   *

The antagonists maintained a running skirmish all the way to Brandy Station, which the Yankees reached about 1 p.m. and where Carr ordered Keifer to halt. Fitz Lee's troopers withdrew another 1,500 yards and then turned to make a stand on Kennedy House Hill alongside Chew's gun section and Moorman's horse battery, both of which promptly opened a heavy fire on Keifer's regiments. Knowing the terrain intimately from many previous contests, the Rebel gunners quickly zeroed in on their targets and soon forced the blue infantry to hit the dirt for protection.

Dealing with a more difficult target hardly fazed the Confederates, whose shells were soon bursting over and around the unfortunate Federals, who could only press their bodies close to the earth and take this punishment as long as the Rebels dished it out. Exploding rounds showered dirt onto the prostrate Northerners while whizzing iron fragments stripped the knapsack off one Ohioan's back and ripped away a tin bucket attached to another's belt. Most men endured this onslaught in stoic silence, but not everybody. To the amusement of nearby comrades, a novice soldier "very innocently" asked if solid shot "would hurt a feller if they hit him." The veterans knew the answer of course and eventually one wit hollered that "it was about time to compromise this thing or some of them *would* get hurt."[17]

To support Keifer's immobilized troops, Edgell deployed his guns into woods on either side of the railroad and hurled shells at some exposed Rebel cavalry. Engaging at extreme range and contending with a stiff cross breeze that threw off their aim, the Yankee gunners inflicted little damage and lessened the pressure on their pinned down comrades not at all.[18]

Fortunately, more significant help was on the way as every passing minute brought the AOP's bulk closer to Brandy Station. By the time French sent a 1:17 p.m. dispatch announcing Keifer's capture of the railway stop, Newton's I Corps and Warren's 3rd Division were already hastening towards the O&A with orders to support the drive south. In front of them the VI and III Corps had completed the lengthy task of deploying for battle and were finally moving forward.[19]

The Union advance was a remarkable sight. Culpeper County's gently rolling landscape offered observers an exceptionally rare opportunity to watch 33,000 men

---

17 Keifer to Eliza, Nov. 10, 1863, Keifer papers, LC.

18 OR 29, pt. 1, 564, 573; Trout, *Moorman's and Hart's Batteries*, 73. Edgell's gunners were 1,800 yards from their target. The Rebels slightly wounded two men in the 122nd Ohio; the Yankees hit no one.

19 OR 29, pt. 2, 437.

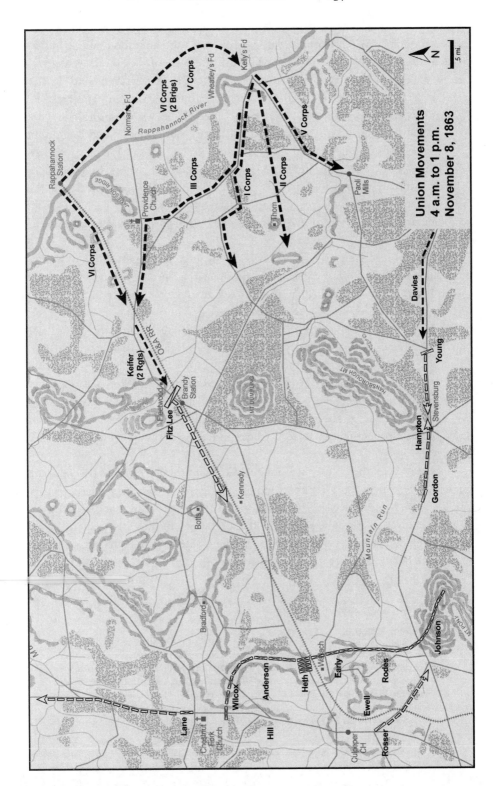

arrayed for action march five miles, flags snapping in the afternoon breeze and the entire formation visible most of the time. Both corps were massed on the center with two of their three infantry divisions striding forward in line, while a third division marched in column on each end of the formation, ready to deal with any flank attack.

Artillery batteries sauntered ahead in the intervals between brigades and along roads to the rear. Spread out at regulation distances, skirmishers flitted beyond the battle line as contingents of cavalry hovered around the edges of the massive force. Guarded by reserve infantry formations, wagons and ambulances trundled along behind the moving wall of soldiers. Col. de Trobriand wrote home that watching this "mass of humanity" heading south in "perfect order, rising and falling gradually according to the undulations of the plain was one of the finest spectacles which could be imagined."[20]

However breathtaking the scene, one sweating infantryman noted that moving in this fashion was "the hardest way in the world" to march." He might have added that it was also "one of the slowest." On mud-free roads an infantry column could cover four or five miles in two hours. Steering a corps cross country in line of battle grossly reduced progress. Every copse of trees, briar patch, creek, ditch, pond, and hill presented difficulties to soldiers trying to keep their place in formation and officers attempting to maintain their alignment. Preserving cadence over uneven ground while burdened with 50–60 pounds of equipment fatigued men quickly. Moreover, the effect of troops bunching together accordion-like to negotiate obstacles subjected units to a halt-shift-hurry-close-up sequence straining both patience and stamina. Commanders had to order frequent pauses to rectify lines and allow everyone a drink from their canteens.[21]

Precisely when the III Corps and the VI Corps' remaining brigades headed south is unclear, certainly it was after noon and maybe closer to 1 p.m. The measured pace resulting from Meade's decision to move forward "in a shape to give or receive battle" meant the advance consumed most of the afternoon. By the time the two corps reached Brandy Station, they had yet to encounter Confederate infantry, which still lay somewhere behind Fitz Lee's bothersome cavalry.[22]

---

20 de Trobriand, *Four Years*, 550.

21 Rosenblatt, *Hard Marching Every Day*, 161.

22 *OR* 51, pt. 1, 1119; Rosenblatt, Hard Marching Every Day, 161. Sedgwick's noon dispatch to Humphreys makes clear that neither the VI nor the III Corps had yet started toward Brandy Station. He also notes that the "last bridge" was "nearly completed." This is probably a reference to the crossing at Rappahannock Station. Access to only one bridge prior to noon would have slowed the VI Corps river crossing. The best guess places the III and VI corps at Brandy Station between 2:30 and 3:00 p.m. (OR 51, pt. 1, 1119).

*　　*　　*

Things were going no better on the Union army's flanks. Kilpatrick's 3rd Cavalry Division had waded the Rappahannock early that morning, with Brig. Gen. Henry Davies' 1st Brigade crossing at Kemper's Ford three miles below Kellysville, and Brig. Gen. George A. Custer's 2nd Brigade at Ellis' Ford, some two miles south of there and close to where the Rapidan flows into the Rappahannock. Davies' destination was Stevensburg, a quaint little place consisting of nothing more than a "few deserted houses with huge chimneys" located six and a half miles from the river. Custer's troopers headed south to guard the army's left flank and scout roads leading to Ely's, Culpeper Mine, and Germanna fords on the Rapidan.[23]

The 1st Brigade's route to Stevensburg pointed almost due west. Well before Davies' three regiments got there, they encountered Col. Thomas J. Lipscomb's 2nd South Carolina Cavalry. Initially outnumbered, the Confederates slowly fell back to a junction with the rest of Young's brigade, which along with Hart's horse artillery had taken up a line blocking Union access to the village. Having found their enemy, Federal troopers deployed to drive him off, and before long a "brisk encounter" was under way. Although a Northern newspaperman characterized the resulting contest as "one of the most spirited and handsomely managed affairs" he had ever seen, the action produced no "severe fighting."[24]

Neither side exhibited much interest in altering that status quo. Knowing they could accomplish their respective missions by maneuver rather than battle, the rival troopers contented themselves with "long range firing and provocative gestures." Stalling for time, Young's Rebels occupied and abandoned a succession of positions while Davies adroitly employed his regiments to threaten the Confederate flanks. These forays occasionally brought on fighting of "short duration" but never really threatened the graycoats, who skillfully retreated until Brig. Gen. James Gordon's

---

23 Elliot W. Hoffman, *History of the First Vermont Cavalry Volunteers in the War of the Rebellion* (Baltimore, MD, 2000), 150. *Wyoming Mirror*, Dec. 6, 1863. The 1st VT was the only non-Michigan unit in Custer's command.

24 Louis Boudrye, *Historic Records of the Fifth New York Cavalry: First Ira Harris Guard* (Albany, NY, 1865), 84; David G. Douglas, *A Boot Full of Memories* (Camden, SC, 2003), 295-96. Merger of the 4th SC Cavalry Battalion and the cavalry battalion of Hampton's South Carolina Legion in the summer of 1862 formed the 2nd SC Cavalry. Lipscomb's strength is uncertain. On November 1, 1863 his regiment received forage for "430 public horses." This would include spare animals, wagons teams, etc. plus mounts for troopers. A receipt covering September 11 to October 31, 1863 lists "511 public horses." Extrapolating from these, the best estimate is between 250 and 300 men. https://www.fold3.com/image/271/77134907 & https://www.fold3.com/image/271/77134976.

North Carolina cavalry brigade arrived to stiffen Confederate defenses just shy of Stevensburg.[25]

Shortly after the Rebel units linked up, what had been a mundane cat and mouse game between mounted forces took on a dramatic air when Maj. Gen. Wade Hampton unexpectedly arrived on the scene. At last fully recovered from his Gettysburg wounds, the famous cavalier's appearance prompted wild cheers from Southern troopers glad to see him back in the field. However inspiring that moment, it was the arrival of Gordon's brigade rather than Hampton's return that swung the advantage near Stevensburg to the Confederates. Suddenly outnumbered eight regiments to three and lacking artillery support, Davies could no longer press the Rebels backwards. Unable to advance, he sullenly held his ground; Hampton happily followed suit, leaving the village in Rebel hands for at least one more night.[26]

* * *

Union troopers on Meade's western flank found themselves equally stymied, but in more sanguinary fashion. Having crossed the upper Rappahannock at Sulphur Springs around dawn, Buford's 1st Cavalry Division had ridden south for the Hazel River and Rixeyville. "Exceedingly" annoyed by "a few" squadrons of Lt. Col. Zachariah S. McGruder's 10th Virginia Cavalry, it took Yankee troopers until noon to traverse the 9 miles separating the two waterways. Leaving Col. Thomas C. Devin's 2nd Brigade to picket nearby fords, Buford continued toward Culpeper Court House. Colonel George H. Chapman's 1st Brigade had the lead, followed by Brig. Gen. Wesley Merritt's Reserve Cavalry Brigade and two batteries of horse artillery.[27]

---

25 Boudrye, *Fifth New York Cavalry*, 84; Leonard Williams to Anna, Nov. 13, 1863, Leonard Williams Letters, Hesburgh Libraries, University of Notre Dame. Williams was a captain in the 2nd SC Cav.

26 Clark, *NC Regts*, Vol. 3, 584. At last fully recovered from his Gettysburg wounds, the dashing South Carolinian had reported for duty in Richmond on November 3. Secretary of War James A. Seddon immediately ordered him to Stuart, who dispatched Hampton to take command of his division within minutes of his arrival at Cavalry Corps headquarters on the morning of November 8.

27 Henry Inch Cowan to Parents, Nov. 11, 1863, Kislak Center for Special Collections, University of Pennsylvania; George Chapman Diary, Nov. 8, 1863, William Henry Smith Memorial Library, Indiana Historical Society (IHS); Hillman Hall, et al., *History of the Sixth New York Cavalry (Second Ira Harris Guard) Second Brigade—First Division—Cavalry Corps, Army of the Potomac: 1861-1865* (Worcester, MA, 1908), 165; Abner Hard, *History of the Eighth Cavalry Regiment Illinois Volunteers, During the Great Rebellion* (Aurora, IL, 1868), 283; Newell Cheney, *History of the Ninth Regiment New York Volunteer Cavalry, War of 1861 to 1865* (Jamestown, NY, 1901), 140; Samuel L. Gracey, *Annals of the Sixth Pennsylvania Cavalry* (Philadelphia, PA, 1868),

Unbeknownst to the Federals, around 1,500 Confederates anxiously awaited them a few miles farther south. In response to an earlier appeal for help from McGruder, Maj. Gen. Wilcox had dispatched Brig. Gen. Henry Lane's five North Carolina regiments and 1st Lt. Andrew B. Johnson's Crenshaw Artillery to blunt Buford's advance. Hurrying forward, Lane got his troops across the bridge over Muddy Run by mid-afternoon and then moved ahead another 1,700 yards to assume an excellent defensive position about six miles from Culpeper Court House. As his infantry deployed into the woods on either side of the road, Johnson's battery unlimbered on a small knoll east of the thoroughfare and sighted its guns in Rixeyville's direction.[28]

Shortly afterwards, a courier reached Lane with word that McGruder's horsemen were "hard pressed" and would soon be "compelled to retire." Such news might have rattled some officers, but it left Henry Lane nonplussed. Although his modest command was several hours' march from any possible assistance, the 30-year old brigadier intuited advantage rather than danger in his circumstances.[29]

An 1854 VMI graduate, Lane had fought in all the army's battles and enjoyed a well-deserved reputation as an able officer. His pre-war career included stints as an assistant professor of tactics at VMI and the North Carolina Military Institute. Two years of battlefield experience had honed that academic expertise to a fine edge, gifting him an ability to calculate military odds. Certain he had deployed into ideal positions blocking the Rixeyville road, Lane told McGruder's messenger to carry back

204-205. Cowan states that the column encountered no opposition until reaching the Hazel River, but Gracey says the 10th VA resisted the Federals from Sulphur Springs to the Hazel. Hill records that the Union column met Rebels in Jeffersonton. Chapman had temporary command of William Gamble's brigade. The 10th VA's colonel (James L. Davis) had been absent since his wounding and capture during the Gettysburg campaign. Hard's history of the 8th Ill. Cav. wrongly lists the date of this advance as November 9. All other sources agree it occurred on November 8. Hard also incorrectly states that Buford was sick and Merritt commanded the division. Buford wrote to Pleasonton on November 7, on November 10 and again on November 11 (OR 29, pt. 2, 430, 445; OR 51, pt. 1, 1121). Buford did not leave his command until November 21, after contracting typhoid fever. He died on December 16, 1863.

28 OR 29, pt. 2, 405, 811; New York Herald, Nov. 11, 1863. Lane's command consisted of the 7th, 18th, 28th, 33rd and 37th North Carolina Infantry regiments. The Crenshaw Artillery had two 12-pounder Napoleons and two 12-pounder field howitzers. Wilcox's four brigade division listed 5,593 men present for duty at the end of October 1863. I have derived Confederate strength by dividing that number by four and adding 100 for Johnson's artillery. Although an imperfect way to calculate a brigade's strength, it's still probably fairly accurate. By the same calculation, Buford's division mustered around 3,666 men, or about 1,200 per brigade.

29 OR Supplement V, pt. 1, 597; Samuel J. B. V. Gilpin Diary, Nov. 8, 1863, E. N. Gilpin, papers, LC; Hard, Eighth Illinois Cavalry, 283. McGruder's strength is unknown. Hampton's Div. numbered 4,000 men on Oct. 31, 1863. That number divided by 12 regiments yields a most unlikely average strength of 333 men. OR 29, pt. 2, 811.

Brig. Gen. James Lane
Valentine Museum, Richmond

instructions for the 10th Virginia Cavalry to retreat "at full speed." The general counted on this sudden withdrawal prompting a headlong Yankee pursuit which would unwittingly impale itself on his hidden battle line. As the courier whirled around and spurred his lathered horse northward, Rebel officers expectantly ordered their men to load and keep under cover.[30]

*   *   *

A mile or so north of Lane's position the 3rd Indiana Cavalry had just pushed McGruder's Virginians past the elegant two-story brick home of Mrs. William Major on Presqu' Isle Plantation. As the vanguard of Chapman's brigade, the Hoosiers had been dueling with McGruder's nettlesome Southerners all morning and although they had hustled their enemies steadily backward it seemed likely the fighting would go on until nightfall. So, it was a jolt when the Federals unexpectedly watched their opponents turn tail and gallop off at high speed.[31]

Major William S. McClure thought this abrupt retreat highly suspicious. Accustomed to Rebel tricks, the 3rd Indiana's 29-year old commander ordered his regiment to dismount and form a skirmish line. The 8th Illinois Cavalry took station as a mounted reserve behind McClure while the rest of Buford's column closed up along the road and halted. Probing forward on foot the Indianans eventually drew fire from a

---

30 OR *Supplement* V, pt. 1, 597; Warner, *Generals in Gray*, 172. The 6th PA Cavalry was better known as Rush's Lancers.

31 Gilpin Diary, Nov. 8, 1863, LC; Hard, *Eighth Illinois Cavalry*, 283; *Editor's Union* Nov. 15, 1863. Mrs. Major's home was located on a 16,000-acre plantation known as Presqu' Isle ("almost an island") which sprawled over the area around the confluence of the Rappahannock and Hazel rivers. Finished in 1815, it was one of the first brick houses in this part of Virginia. The Major family bought the property in 1845 and owned it until 1909. It still exists and has changed little since the war. http://www.presquisle.com/about/ Accessed Sep. 21, 2019.

Col. George Chapman
Library of Congress

patch of woods at the southern end of a sizeable clearing. McClure was sure he'd run into Rebel infantry, and he passed that surmise back to the 8th Illinois, which in turn sent it to Col. Chapman at brigade headquarters. If McClure were correct, Buford's division had gone as far toward Culpeper Court House as it was going to go.[32]

Impatient to keep moving, Chapman hurried forward to see what was going on. The nearsighted, bespectacled 31-year old was a proven fighter and of the restless sort. Massachusetts-born but Indiana-raised, he had served as a midshipman in the US Navy from 1847-50 before becoming in turn a merchant, lawyer, newspaper publisher, and finally assistant clerk to the U.S. House of Representatives—a post he resigned in 1861 to join the cavalry. Transferring to the infantry in 1862 and taking command of a brigade, he saw action in most of the AOP's major battles before returning to the cavalry on the eve of Gettysburg.[33]

Although not as well-known as Custer or Merritt, Chapman shared their belief in aggressively pressing things. Reaching the 6th Indiana Cavalry, he looked over the situation for a bit and discovered no reason for timidity. As far as he could tell, Rebel foot soldiers weren't nearby and it would be illogical for the enemy to have stationed any sizable force so far from Culpeper. He promptly discounted the sound of muskets, observing that some enemy cavalrymen carried infantry weapons.[34]

The 1st Division had been ordered to get as close to Culpeper as possible before dark, and getting there with artillery required using the bridge over Muddy Run. With that objective only a mile and a half away, the colonel wouldn't countenance delay.

32 Gilpin Diary, Nov. 8, 1863, LC; Hard, *Eighth Illinois Cavalry*, 283; *Editor's Union* Nov. 15, 1863; "Colonel William S. McClure," https://www.findagrave.com/memorial/77100680/william-simrall-mcclure Accessed Sep. 21, 2019.

33 Werner, *Generals in Blue*, 80.

34 Gilpin Diary, Nov. 8, 1863, LC; Hard, *Eighth Illinois Cavalry*, 283.

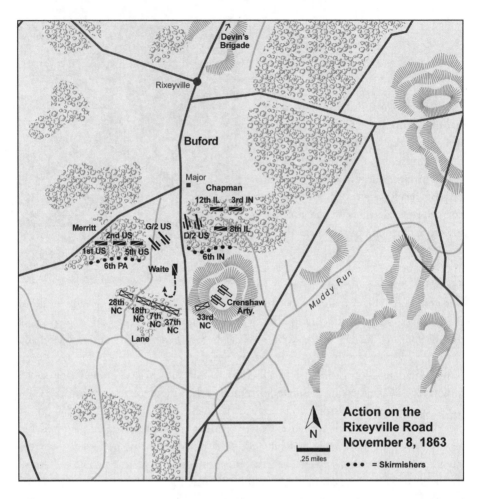

Riding over to the 8th Illinois, Chapman told Maj. John Waite to take his squadron and drive away whatever dismounted Rebel cavalry blocked his path.

A startled Waite—who shared McClure's appraisal of the tactical situation—felt certain his superior didn't fully understand the state of things. Despite having held his current rank for only six days, the newly minted major patiently explained that Confederate infantry lay just to the south and any farther advance would be ill advised. Chapman disagreed, saying he saw nothing to support that claim. Waite assured him it was true, but the colonel was done talking. Frustrated with the Illinoisan's protracted display of caution and unwilling to believe what his own eyes couldn't confirm, Chapman "very peremptorily" repeated the order to attack.[35]

35 Gilpin Diary, Nov. 8, 1863, LC; Hard, *Eighth Illinois Cavalry*, 283; *Editor's Union* Nov. 15, 1863; Clark, NC Regts, Vol. 2, 663; John M. Waite, https://www.findagrave.com/

Left with no choice, Waite led his squadron through the Indiana skirmishers toward the shadowy tree line up ahead. Gamely sweeping forward, the Illinois cavalrymen trotted onto a 500-yard deep plain headed straight for Col. William M. Barbour's concealed 37th North Carolina west of the road. The Tar Heel infantrymen and Johnson's four fieldpieces waited calmly for the Yankees to draw within effective range and then unleashed a "murderous fire" on their front and flank. Within seconds Waite's squadron came apart in blood and confusion. Amidst a shower of Rebel shells, the regiment's frantic officers ordered a retreat back to their starting point.[36]

The decisive Union repulse left two men dead, 12 wounded and numerous horses killed or injured. "They whipped our brigade in about fifteen minutes," one Indiana trooper told his diary, "but the boys didn't know it and we kept on fighting." That was certainly true of the 8th Illinois, which dismounted and continued the contest on foot, albeit from a stationary position beside the 6th Indiana.[37]

Finally facing incontrovertible evidence of Rebel infantry, the Federals deployed their entire force. Chapman ordered the 8th New York Cavalry forward as a mounted reserve, stationing it in a ravine just behind his skirmish line. Buford sent Merritt's Reserve Brigade into the fields on Chapman's right, where the boyish looking brigadier had deployed his 6th Pennsylvania Cavalry as skirmishers. Coming up from the rear, Battery D, 2nd US, unlimbered to support Chapman while Battery G, 2nd US similarly aided Merritt.[38]

Counting eight 12-pounder Napoleons between them, these two commands strenuously tried to silence Lt. Johnson's four pieces, but the resultant "brisk" artillery duel didn't alter the stalemate. Firing from higher ground, the Rebel gunners enjoyed a significant advantage, and a New York trooper recalled that their projectiles "cracked through the trees in a manner more lively than agreeable." Despite many near misses, Buford's cavalrymen suffered few casualties. His cannoneers weren't so fortunate. Rebel shells wounded three men and killed several horses in Battery D and badly mangled the foot of Battery G's Lt. John Butler.[39]

---

36 Hard, *Eighth Illinois Cavalry*, 283; *OR*, 29, pt. 1, 636-37; Clark, *NC Regts*, Vol. 2, 663; *SHSP*, Vol. 31, 275-96.

37 Gilpin Diary, November 8, 1863, LC.

38 Gracey, *Annals of 6th Penns Cavalry*, 205.

39 Ibid.; *OR* 29, pt. 2, 130; *Editor's Union*, Nov. 15, 1863; *NY Herald*, Nov. 11, 1863; *Philadelphia Inquirer*, Nov. 11, 1863; Gracey, *Annals of 6th Penns Cavalry*, 204-205.

Regardless of such losses steady firing went on until nightfall. The 90-minute encounter cost Lane's brigade 3 dead and 12 wounded, while the Crenshaw Artillery counted two men injured. According to a *New York Herald* reporter on the scene, Chapman's brigade lost 5 men killed and "about 25 wounded."[40]

Federal commanders pulled their men back half a mile after dark and went into bivouac. The 18 wounded in 2nd Lt. William C. Hazelton's 1st Brigade ambulance train had farther to go, not stopping until reaching Presqu' Isle Plantation two miles in the rear, where Union doctors had quickly turned Mrs. Major's home into a makeshift hospital. That night surgeons performed "several amputations," including one to remove Lt. Butler's shattered foot. The crippled artilleryman's "heroic endurance" throughout that ordeal deeply impressed Hazelton, who was only a week shy of his 31st birthday and serving as an ambulance chief for the first time.[41]

November 8 marked the Illinois officer's initiation to the reality of caring for wounded at a battlefield aid station. Profoundly moved by that experience, the lieutenant wrote his fiancée: "How I *hated* rebellion that night! How from my inmost soul, I cursed the authors of all the wretchedness that lay around me. The feeling may have been wrong. But he who could have looked on those maimed and bleeding men and *not* feel that way must be something less or more than human."[42]

*   *   *

Though Meade saw none of this, it wasn't necessarily beyond his hearing. Still, as the day wore on, the paucity of dispatches reporting significant enemy contact increasingly called to mind disappointed battle hopes at Williamsport, Front Royal, and Warrenton. At last tired of waiting for news the general gathered his staff and rode forward at 2 p.m. to find out what was going on. Soon after crossing the Rappahannock, Meade encountered a group of soldiers escorting "fresh prisoners" toward Kelly's Ford. Reining up to the captives, Provost Marshal Patrick asked the

40 OR 29, pt. 1, 636; Gilpin Diary, Nov. 8, 1863, LC; *Eighth Ill Cav*, 283; Frederick Phisterer, *NY in War of the Rebellion*, 3rd ed. (Albany, NY, 1912), 6 Vols, Vol. 1, 873; Trout, *After Gettysburg*, 291; Gracey, *Annals of 6th Penns Cavalry*, 205; *NY Herald* Nov. 11, 1863; *SHSP*, Vol. 31, 275-96. In Dobbins, *Grandfather's Journal*, 168. Pvt. Austin Dobbins of the 16th MS, Harris' Brigade, Wilcox Division. lists Confederate losses at 3 killed, 13 wounded, and 11 deserters (1 of whom was under a death sentence).

41 Peter G. Beidler, *Army of the Potomac: The Civil War Letters of William Cross Hazelton of the Eight Illinois Cavalry Regiment* (Seattle, WA, 2013), 154-58.

42 Ibid, 155.

Southerners how they were taken before inquiring, "where is the rest of your army?" The Rebels answered: "All gone last night to the breastworks behind the Rapidan."[43]

Those few words dissipated whatever optimism Union commanders had entertained since November 7. Outwardly Meade took the news in stride. Not so some of his officers. When the general met Warren at his Thom house headquarters a little later, Lyman reported the II Corps commander looking "like a man of disappointed hopes." As he and Meade talked things over, the young major general "gazed around the country" and grumbled out loud "There's nobody here—nobody!" Sadly, Lyman noted, that "was the gist of the matter."[44]

After spending an interval with Warren, Meade and his party rode on to Brandy Station, where sometime around 3 p.m. they met and congratulated Sedgwick on his Rappahannock Station victory. Although two hours of daylight remained before sunset and Fitz Lee's cavalrymen were still visible, the VI, III, and I Corps were going into a happy bivouac. Lyman noted that Federal soldiers were in "fine spirits and yelled and whooped merrily" as they kindled their campfires and prepared to bed down for the night.[45]

There appeared much to celebrate. The Army of the Potomac had won a fine victory and regained almost all the ground lost in October. Its foe had fled, and his winter quarters, four guns, and seven battle flags were in Union hands. The only thing to regret was that the enemy hadn't suffered more.

But everything wasn't as Meade and his troops supposed. Despite what Rebel prisoners said, Lee hadn't yet withdrawn safely behind the Rapidan, nor had his army slipped beyond Meade's reach. In fact, it stood just three miles away, ready to do battle if necessary, even though it occupied a vulnerable position. If Sedgwick and French had continued on for another few miles, they would have found it, perhaps with enough daylight left to entangle the Confederates in a fight from which they couldn't

---

43 Aggassiz, *Meade's Headquarters*, 44-45; Lowe, *Meade's Army*, 63-64; Sparks, *Inside Lincoln's Army*, 304. Meade had moved forward at Falling Waters on July 14, into Manassas Gap toward Front Royal on July 24, and against Warrenton on Oct. 20, 1863 expecting to strike Lee's army only to find no enemy to strike on each occasion. See Hunt, *Meade and Lee After Gettysburg* and *Meade and Lee at Bristoe Station*.

44 Aggassiz, *Meade's Headquarters*, 44-45; Lowe, *Meade's Army*, 63-64; Sparks, *Inside Lincoln's Army*, 304.

45 Lowe, *Meade's Army*, 64; *Report of the Joint Committee*, Vol. 4, 372. Birney claimed in his March 1864 testimony before the committee that the "enemy was in full sight" when the Union advance halted but did not clarify whether he saw Rebel infantry or cavalry. With the ANV's main line still three miles distant, Birney likely saw only cavalry, although Culpeper County's generally open terrain might have allowed Federal troops to catch a long range glimpse of Confederate entrenchments or battle flags.

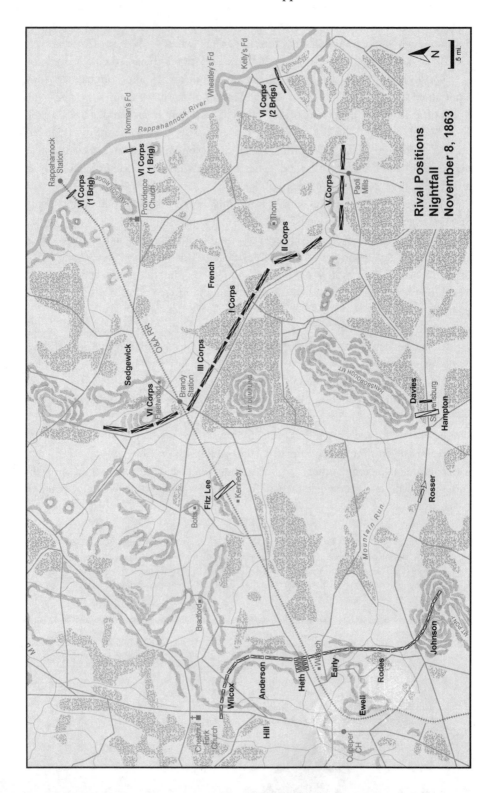

disengage safely. The consequences of such a feat might have led to a major Union victory and acute damage to the Rebel army.[46]

Remarkably, the Federals had little inkling of the opportunity lying just beyond their sight. Having failed to find the enemy where he expected him, Meade simply concluded that Lee had gotten away. As the sun began sinking into the horizon, the Union general and his staff rode north across the Rappahannock, stopping briefly to examine Russell's captured earthworks before heading a few miles farther up the O&A to establish headquarters at the fine brick home of a man named Anderson. It had been a long day, and though Meade was pleased with what his troops had achieved he felt disappointed that the big battle he hoped for hadn't materialized. He was hardly alone in this feeling.[47]

Crossing the Rappahannock had cost the army 539 infantrymen (96 dead, 409 wounded, 11 missing) alongside roughly 35 cavalrymen or gunners, a grand total of 574 casualties. The fight at Kelly's Ford accounted for just 42 souls in that tally (6 killed, 36 wounded). Victory at Rappahannock Station cost a good deal more. Sedgwick reported a combined loss of 476 men, the V Corps suffering 57 casualties (7 killed, 43 wounded and 5 missing) with the VI Corps registering 419 (83 killed, 330 wounded and 6 missing). Russell's division had absorbed most of that punishment losing 327 soldiers of whom 264 belonged to Ellmaker's brigade and 63 to Upton's.[48]

That those casualties hadn't proven the down payment on a major battle disappointed many men who had gone to bed "encouraged and hopeful" after Rappahannock Station. Among these was I Corps artillery chief Col. Charles Wainwright, who confessed mounting frustration to his diary that evening. Believing that hindsight tended to obviate what was invisible when leaders made difficult decisions, the 36-year old New Yorker had always refrained from second guessing his superiors. After this day, however, the colonel "for the first time felt inclined to find fault with General Meade."[49]

---

46 Krick, *Virginia Weather*, 112; Boatner, *Civil War Dictionary*, 820. Sunset on Sunday, Nov. 8, 1863 was 5:07 p.m. total darkness at 5:47 p.m.

47 Lowe, *Meade's Army*, 64.

48 OR 29, pt. 1, 558-61; In Greiner, *A Surgeon's Civil War,* 156, Dr. Holt, the 121st NY's surgeon, says his regiment had 4 killed, 23 wounded and 1 missing; In *With a Flash of His Sword: The Writings of Major Homan S. Melcher, 20th Maine Infantry* (Kearny, NJ 1994), 155-56, Maj. Melcher writes that the 20th ME lost 1 man killed and 7 men wounded at Rappahannock Station. 6th ME regimental casualty analysis at: https://tinyurl.com/y2xckoz4; 5th Wisconsin at: https://tinyurl.com/yxw3hzmk; 119th PA at: https://tinyurl.com/y42gxcyd; all accessed Feb. 1, 2020.

49 Lyman, *Meade's Headquarters*, 45; Nevins, *A Diary of Battle*, 300. Lieutenant Colonel Harris' 6th ME suffered the most, listing 139 casualties including 38 dead and 101 wounded. Six of that

Wainwright thought French's wing should have moved immediately against Culpeper that morning to fix Lee in place until Sedgwick could join the battle. The artilleryman was convinced such a move had been entirely feasible, especially since Meade, operating with fresh troops buoyed by recent success, knew the terrain thoroughly. Instead the general had needlessly sent French to Rappahannock Station, which in turn allowed the Confederates plenty of time "to entrench if they were of a mind to fight" or "get safely across the Rapidan it they weren't. . .." Wainwright dejectedly told his journal "I fear that our chance, whatever it may have been, is now gone."[50]

Gouverneur Warren agreed and later complained that "the whole of November 8 was almost wasted in useless and uncertain movements." Although he avoided assigning responsibility for squandering so much time, the young major general avowed that if Federal forces had advanced "rapidly towards either Culpeper or through Stevensburg" they "should most certainly have cut Lee's army in two."[51]

David Birney likewise believed that Meade had missed a shining opportunity. Convinced by prisoner accounts and contrabands' chatter that the Union offensive had gained "complete surprise" over a foe "scattered for forty miles" in winter camps, the temporary III Corps commander erroneously thought that Lee had massed a mere 30,000 men near Culpeper on November 8. In light of this intelligence, Birney felt certain halting his and Sedgwick's troops at Brandy Station had been a huge mistake. "If I had been permitted to advance," he later told the Joint Committee on the Conduct of the War, "we could have struck the enemy a very severe blow."[52]

Provost Marshall Marsena Patrick agreed. Of all the bitter pills the AOP had swallowed since Gettysburg, this struck him as among the worst. He thought the entire

---

regiment's injured required an amputation, while 8 died of their wounds within two weeks, bringing the total death toll to 46. In contrast, the 5th WS lost 10 dead and 59 wounded (4 of whom died before the end of November), the 49th PA suffered 3 dead and 17 wounded (with at least 1 dying of wounds), while the 119th PA marked 1 missing, 7 killed, 37 wounded—3 of whom died, while 5 had a leg amputated and one lost an eye. In Upton's brigade the 5th ME suffered 7 dead and 28 wounded, the 121st NY 4 killed and 21 wounded, while the 95th and 96th PA each had one man wounded.

50 Nevins, *A Diary of Battle*, 300.

51 *Report of the Joint Committee*, Warren's March 1864 testimony, Vol. 4, 385.

52 *Report of the Joint Committee*, Birney's March 1864 testimony, Vol. 4, 372. David Birney was competent but also ambitious, a man who, in the words of Col. Lyman "looked out for his own interest sharply and knew the mainspring of military advancement." Gen. Warren said that Birney "had no hesitation at time to tell lies." Birney had grievances against Meade dating back to the battles of Fredericksburg and Gettysburg and his testimony was decidedly negative toward the AOP commander. For an excellent account of Birney's testimony, his dispute with Meade and an overview of Birney's character see Hyde, *The Union Generals Speak*, 146-62.

army, or at least its higher ranks, felt "disgusted" by their failure to grasp the tantalizing prospect Rappahannock Station had proffered. Some in the lower ranks echoed their disgruntled leaders' sentiments. One Union soldier mused that the "brilliant opening of the campaign" had been "as much a surprise to the methodical Meade as it was to Lee."[53]

*   *   *

As darkness enveloped the landscape and 80,000 Federals went to bed, the Army of Northern Virginia began its retreat toward the Rapidan. To Robert E. Lee's great relief, Yankee audacity at Rappahannock Station and Kelly's Ford had proven an aberration. Moving with exacting deliberation on November 8, Meade and his subordinates had failed to push hard against the Confederate army's center or right, while allowing Lane to easily repulse Buford's effort on the left. Stuart's cavalry had kept the enemy away from the ANV's vulnerable flanks and at arm's length for most of the day. This not only allowed Lee to avoid a long-odds battle; it gave his trains plenty of time to reach safety and guaranteed the army's unmolested withdrawal behind the Rapidan.

That retrograde movement began shortly after dark and continued throughout the night. Understanding the necessity of celerity in getting over the river before Meade mounted a pursuit, Southern officers pushed their soldiers hard. The hurried pace conspired with "exceedingly cold & windy" weather, a shortage of rations, and lack of rest to produce multitudes of stragglers. Creek crossings and poor roads occasionally caused maddening traffic jams, an inherent consequence of marching through a dark and virtually moonless night. Several units lacking guides or ignorant of their way to the river got lost, forcing more exhausting and time-consuming detours.[54]

Nonetheless, Lee's troops kept going and as the night wore on increasing numbers of them reached the Rapidan. A. P. Hill's corps had the good fortune of using the railroad bridge at Rapidan Station and a "hastily constructed" pontoon bridge at Barnett's Ford near Liberty Mills to get over the river. Ewell's men weren't so lucky: Rodes' and Johnson's brigades crossed at Raccoon Ford while Early's headed for Somerville Ford. Wading through the icy stream was a miserable ordeal. Officers ordered everyone to remove shoes and roll up pant legs before entering the knee-deep

---

53 Sparks, *Inside Lincoln's Army*, 305; Lyman to wife, November 9, 1863, *Meade's Headquarters*, 44-46; Goss, *Recollections of a Private*, 244.

54 Dobbins, *Grandfather's Journal*, 168. The moon was a waning crescent on Nov. 9, 1863. https://www.moongiant.com/phase/11/9/1863; accessed Oct. 1, 2019.

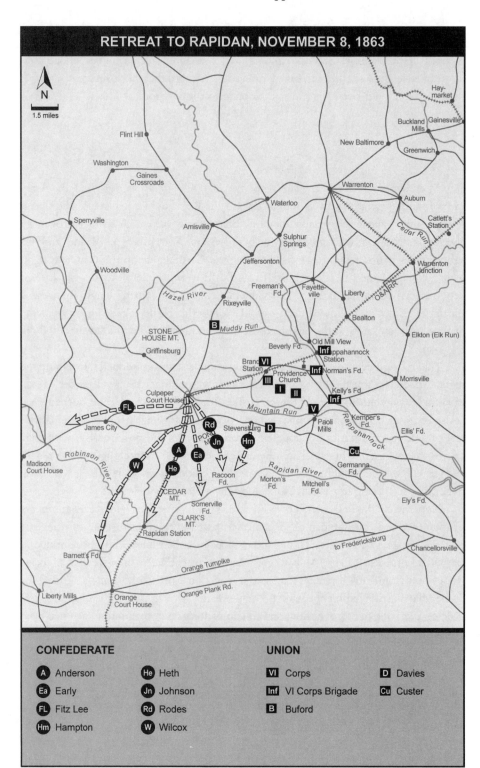

RETREAT TO RAPIDAN, NOVEMBER 8, 1863

N
1.5 miles

Haymarket
Buckland Mills
Gainesville
Flint Hill
New Baltimore
Greenwich
Washington
Gaines Crossroads
Warrenton
Auburn
Catlett's Station
Waterloo
Cedar Run
Sperryville
Amisville
Sulphur Springs
Warrenton Junction
Jeffersonton
Woodville
Freeman's Fd.
Fayetteville
Liberty
Hazel River
Rixeyville
Bealton
Elkton (Elk Run)
STONE HOUSE MT.
B Muddy Run
Griffinsburg
Beverly Fd.
Old Mill View
Inf Rappahannock Station
Branch Station
VI
Providence Church
Inf Norman's Fd.
Morrisville
III
I   **II**
Kelly's Fd.
Culpeper Court House
FL
Inf
Rd Stevensburg **D**
V
Kemper's Fd.
James City
PONY MT.
Jn
Hm
Paoli Mills
Ellis' Fd.
Mountain Run
A **Ea**
Racoon Fd.
Rapidan River
Cu
Germanna Fd.
Rappahannock
Madison Court House
Robinson River
W **He**
Morton's Fd.
Mitchell's Fd.
Ely's Fd.
CEDAR MT.
Somerville Fd.
CLARK'S MT.
Rapidan Station
to Fredericksburg
Chancellorsville
Barnett's Fd.
Orange Turnpike
Liberty Mills
Orange Court House
Orange Plank Rd.

CONFEDERATE

A Anderson   **He** Heth

Ea Early   **Jn** Johnson

FL Fitz Lee   **Rd** Rodes

Hm Hampton   **W** Wilcox

UNION

VI Corps   **D** Davies

Inf VI Corps Brigade   **Cu** Custer

B Buford

river. "As we stepped into the water," Sgt. John Worsham recalled, "it was so cold it felt as if a knife had taken one's foot off; and at each step the depth of the water increased. This feeling continued until we reached the middle of the river, where. . . one felt as if the leg was off from the knee down."[55]

Gaining the opposite shore provided no relief. Men found it impossible to roll down pants or don shoes on their benumbed lower extremities. Determined not to slow the retreat and anxious to fend off illness-generating chills, officers ordered their disheveled formations back onto the road. A brisk mile-long hike restored circulation to half frozen limbs. Thereupon each regiment stepped off into the woods to build "immense fires" around which its troops could rebound to proper marching condition.[56]

Stuart's cavalry buffer and noise-concealing winds helped prevent distant Federal commanders from detecting Lee's withdrawal. By midmorning most Confederate infantrymen were over the Rapidan, Hampton's troopers were slowly retiring toward the river fords, and Fitz Lee's brigades were shifting west on the Sperryville Pike to take station behind Robertson's River on the army's left flank. Just as it had at Falling Waters and at Manassas Gap, the ANV managed to march stealthily away before its enemy could throw a potentially devastating punch. And for the third time in Meade's tenure, Lee had stripped a Yankee victory of its strategic fruit by carrying his army beyond Federal reach.[57]

55 John Worsham, *One of Jackson's Foot Cavalry* (New York, NY, 1912), 184; McDonald, *Make Me A Map*, 183; Jones, *Civil War Memoirs of Capt. Seymour*, 95; Dobbins, *Grandfather's Journal*, 168-69; Julius A. Lineback Diary, Nov. 9, UNC-CH.

56 John Worsham, *One of Jackson's Foot Cavalry*, 184.

57 Lawson Morrisset Diary, November 8, 9, 1863, ACWM; Charles McVicar Diary, Nov. 8, 9, 1863, HRL; Hairsten Diary Nov. 8, 1863, SHC/UNC; Samuel Nunnelee Diary, Nov. 9, 1863, ACWM. A message from French to Meade in *OR* 29, pt. 2, 439 dated November 9 at 1:15 a.m. should be dated November 8 and does not give info relevant to Rebel movements on the night of November 8, but rather conditions just after midnight of November 7. Early's division camped on the north side of Somerville Ford and didn't cross the Rapidan until the morning of November 9.

CHAPTER 11

"Miserable, Miserable Management"

The Afterglow of Success—Russell's Odd Adventure—Offensive Possibilities—Railroad
Repairs—Snow—Rebel Casualties and Reactions—Lee's Problems

GENERAL Lee's successful withdrawal hardly diminished the pride
Meade's soldiers felt in their November 7 victories.
Enthusiastic battle descriptions and praise for everyone who had stormed enemy
earthworks filled soldier letters in the fighting's aftermath. A Maine private who took
part in the Rappahannock Station assault summed up the army's general attitude in
bragging to his parents, "I tell you we boomed 'em good!" The bridgehead attack
inspired even those who didn't participate. A Vermont infantryman allowed that "it
was something to be present at, and in support of, so brilliant an exploit."[1]

The overrunning of Early's entrenchments especially gratified the VI Corps,
whose defeat at Salem Church had gone unredeemed for six months. A 121st New
York soldier proudly exclaimed to his father that Rappahannock Station had
"avenged" the previous May's humiliation. Boasting that he and his comrades had
"marched up to the breastworks as cool and determined as if they were made of steel"
before carrying "everything at the point of the bayonet," he went on to declare that the
entire army attested "that for the numbers engaged it was one of the most brilliant feats
of the war."[2]

---

1 Goss, *Recollections of a Private*, 244; Oliver Norton, *Army Letters 1861-1865* (Chicago, IL,
1903), 188; G. C. Benedict, *Vermont in the Civil War: A History of the Part Taken by the Vermont
Soldiers and Sailors in the War for the Union* (Burlington, VT, 1886), Vol. 1, 405.

2 Delavan Bates to father, Nov. 8, 1863, *The Civil War Letters of Delavan Bates*,
http://www.usgennet.org/usa/ne/topic/military/CW/bates/genbate2.html, accessed Dec.
21, 2019.

Abraham Lincoln certainly hadn't expected the AOP's sudden success and on the evening of November 9, the president telegraphed Meade a message fairly crackling with surprised delight. "I have seen your dispatches about operations on the Rappahannock," he wrote, "and I wish to say *well done!*" That brief dispatch pleased Meade immensely. Having endured three months of subtle but unrelenting administration displeasure and doubts, the general saw vindication in Lincoln's enthusiastic praise.[3]

Passing along the president's sentiments in a congratulatory order to his troops, Meade told them he took "great pleasure in announcing" the chief executive's "satisfaction" with their "recent operations." Proud of his men and pleased with himself, the general forgot all his trepidation about his late offensive. He boasted to Margaret that his victory stemmed from the Rebels "being entirely deceived as to my capacity to move, and to the gallantry of my men." Elated soldiers had cheered him as he rode past on November 8, he noted, and gleefully observed that he was "more popular than ever" with his command.[4]

Headquarters clerk Thomas Carpenter observed that "as of late" Meade "has been gaining the confidence of the troops. . . very rapidly," and that some regiments "now cheer him quite heartily." Watching V Corps veterans "throwing their caps in the air" while "fairly mobbing" the army's commander, Capt. Francis Donaldson overheard enlisted men make "many favorable comments" regarding Meade's "ability to handle them." Even Southern editors begrudgingly admitted that Meade had displayed "wonderful energy" and inflicted a "terrible blow" on the Army of Northern Virginia. The Richmond *Enquirer* remarked that Meade had "returned from his late retreat by no means cowed or evincing any unwillingness to meet Gen. Lee."[5]

Despite these accolades, the general confessed disappointment to Margaret, writing that his desire of "affecting something decisive," and fighting "a great battle" had gone up in smoke when the Rebels gave him the slip. Seeking a silver lining in the setback, he hoped that sundering the Rappahannock line might at least alter

---

3   *OR* 29, pt. 2, 443.

4   *OR* 29, pt. 1, 576, 558, 575-576; Meade, *Life and Letters*, Vol. 2, 155; Meade's was the third congratulatory order the army received. Both French and Sedgwick issued similar pronouncements to their respective wing commands. These orders are found in the *OR* 29, part 1, 575-76.

5   Thomas Carpenter to Phil, Nov. 13, 1863, Carpenter papers, MHS; Acken, *Inside the Army of the Potomac*, 393; Biddle to wife, Nov. 9, 1863, James C. Biddle papers HSP; Lowe, *Meade's Army*, 64; Richmond *Enquirer*, Nov. 10, 1863.

"intelligent" people's opinions of his military skill, which newspapers had maligned so badly after the AOP's recent retreat to Centreville.[6]

Irrespective of public sentiment, Meade wasted little time dwelling over missed chances. He had dissolved the army's ad hoc wing organization at noon on November 9, just as elements of Buford's division rode into Culpeper Court House, and Kilpatrick's troopers started through Stevensburg on their way to seize Pony Mountain. Union infantry didn't follow. Alive to the dangers of occupying the Culpeper 'V', Meade vetoed chasing Rebels to the Rapidan as a pointless exercise. Rather than stick his neck out and invite a repeat of October's misfortunes, he decided to keep his army where it already was.[7]

Following Meade's instruction, Maj. Gen. Humphreys issued a circular directing Sykes to hold his V Corps at Paoli Mills north of Mountain Run and detach a division to guard the pontoon bridges at Kelly's Ford. Warren's II Corps would maintain its position between Sykes and Brandy Station, where French's III Corps would remain in place. Humphreys told Sedgwick to sidle the VI Corps westward to take up a line near Welford's Ford on the Hazel River. Brig. Gen. Hunt would mass the reserve artillery at Rappahannock Station, while John Newton spread his I Corps out to guard the railroad all the way back to Manassas Junction. Pleasonton was ordered to both deploy Buford's cavalry division westward to watch Robinson's River and send Kilpatrick's division to guard the Rapidan fords. Colonel John Taylor's brigade from David Gregg's cavalry division would take station along the upper Rappahannock between Fayetteville and Sulphur Springs while Col. John Irvin Gregg's brigade from the same command spread out north of the Rappahannock to protect the area east of the O&A.[8]

These dispositions gave Meade a relatively secure line from which he could withdraw rapidly if necessary. Pleasonton's horsemen ought to easily detect any threatening enemy movement, while Newton's infantry should suffice to guard the railroad. In this posture the army could mark time until repair crews reconstructed the nine miles of wrecked track between Warrenton Junction and Rappahannock Station, where they would also have to rebuild the burnt railway bridge.

Brigadier General Herman Haupt, chief of construction and transportation for U.S. Military Railroads, pledged to complete those tasks in just 5 days and although that seemed rather ambitious, Haupt usually delivered on his promises. Regardless of the

---

6   Meade, *Life and Letters*, Vol. 2, 155.

7   OR 29, pt. 2, 437-40 & 51, pt. 1, 1121-25.

8   OR 29, pt. 2, 435, 440; Trout, *After Gettysburg*, 293. Sedgwick's detached brigades had returned to the VI Corps.

Union troops inspect the Confederate flags captured at Rappahannock Station. Alfred Waud made this drawing on November 8, 1863. The Federals are standing just downhill from the large redoubt allowing the viewer to get a good idea of the slope leading to the fort and the height of its walls. Note the dead soldier at lower left. *Library of Congress*

railway chief's timetable, any farther advance by the AOP would have to wait for the steady arrival of railway cars in Brandy Station.[9]

Once that happened, Meade thought a campaign across the Rapidan possible if the Rebels didn't strike first—a scenario which remained worryingly possible since he estimated enemy strength at around 80,000 men, and rumors were floating about that Longstreet's Corps had returned to Virginia. Should Lee repeat his October flanking movement, the AOP would have no choice but to scurry back across the Rappahannock to avoid fighting on unfavorable ground. Meade could have little doubt how the Northern press and the Lincoln administration would view another retrograde movement.[10]

At the moment, however, the Federals basked in the afterglow of victory, and such concerns seemed remote. In a November 10 ceremony at army headquarters, Col. Upton and representative companies from the regiments that had overrun Rappahannock Station presented seven captured Rebel flags to Meade. The general followed with a fine speech commending everyone for their accomplishment and

9   OR 29, pt. 2, 832.

10 Ibid., 326, 328, 380, Sparks, *Inside Lincoln's Army*, 310. The report of Longstreet's return came from Rebel deserters.

reminding them more trials lay ahead. Then he asked Brig. Gen. Russell to personally deliver the army's new trophies to the War Department.[11]

*   *   *

Still nursing his Rappahannock Station foot wound, Russell entrained for Washington the next day accompanied by Sgt. Otis Roberts, whose November 7 exploits had merited a Medal of Honor. Once in the capital, the general sent a message to Stanton, asking when the secretary would find it convenient to receive the captured flags? After vainly waiting most of the day for a reply, the AOP representatives began worrying that their message might have gone astray. Impatient to complete his mission, Russell decided to pursue a personal meeting with the cabinet minister.

The wounded officer limped into the recently renovated four-story brick building housing the War Department, gave his name to a clerk, and requested an audience with the secretary. The man disappeared into the building's bustling interior only to return a few moments later bearing word that Stanton was busy and couldn't see the brigadier. Following this "interesting if unsatisfactory" experience, Russell forwarded the captured flags to the war department via courier and returned to the army.[12]

No one ever explained why Stanton didn't meet Russell. A well-known workaholic, the secretary spent the first hour of every day with supplicants pressing business upon his department. After that he retired to the burdens and attendant political complications of administering the Union's massive military machine, usually working late into the night and sometimes sleeping in his office. He might have considered Russell's purpose more appropriate to each morning's public audience or

---

11 Lowe, *Meade's Army*, 66; McMahon, "From Gettysburg to the Coming of Grant," B&L, Vol. 4, 87-88n. *New York Herald*, Nov. 12, 1863 has the text of Meade's speech. An honor guard consisting of Col. Upton, the New Jersey Brigade band and one company from each regiment that participated in the attack presented the flags to Meade. The flags belonged to the 6th, 54th, and 57th North Carolina regiments, and the 8th, 5th, and 9th LA and the LA Guard Artillery. It will be recalled that the 6th Louisiana's flag was saved and successfully hidden by its color bearer, while the 7th LA's color bearer burned his flag in a campfire on the night of Nov. 7 while a prisoner of war. The Federals also presented Meade with that regiment's flag staff.

12 McMahon, "From Gettysburg to the Coming of Grant" *B&L*, Vol. 4, 87-88n. http://www.mrlincolnswhitehouse.org/washington/the-war-effort/war-effort-war-departm ent/, Accessed Dec. 29, 2019. Originally constructed in 1819, the War Department's building stood about 400 yards northwest of the White House. A row of Ionic columns graced the portico at the main entrance, which faced north toward Pennsylvania Avenue. To accommodate the agency's vastly increased wartime staff the Government added two stories to the building in 1862 (and to the Navy Department building next door). Today the Dwight Eisenhower Executive Office Building occupies the footprint of the Civil War era War and Navy Department structures.

he may really have been too busy to deal with the New Yorker. Either way, some VI Corps officers perceived a purposeful insult in Stanton's breach of protocol, suspecting he had snubbed Russell to signal dissatisfaction with Meade's failure to follow up his November 7 triumph.[13]

If the war secretary appeared indifferent to the AOP's conquests, Northern newspapers had a different attitude. The *New York Times* hailed Sedgwick's "fine victory" at Rappahannock Station and lauded French's equally "handsome operation" at Kelly's Ford. Although it couldn't resist taking a swipe at what it saw as post-Gettysburg lethargy, *Harper's Weekly* joyfully proclaimed that the army had, "after a long period of ease," finally "commenced a forward movement" which had not only proven "remarkably successful" but entitled Meade "to high praise as a commander." Mocking Lee for refusing "to take up the gauge of battle" which his counterpart had so "urgently pressed upon" him, *Harper's* sighed that the Army of the Potomac would have to "bear with what grace it may the disappointment of its desire to bring about a decisive engagement."[14]

Whether the AOP might attempt to realize that yearning before winter set in wasn't clear. At the moment Meade held the initiative, but Christmas was just 46 days away and the certainty of worsening weather called into question any ability to exploit his latest success. The season's first snow had fallen just 48 hours after Meade breached the Rappahannock, leaving "a winding sheet of spotless white" coating the countryside on the morning of November 10 and ice standing in roadside puddles.[15]

Happily for the troops, this cold spell didn't last long and the snow melted away "quicker than it came." Temperatures rebounded into the low 70s within a few days and hovered between there and the mid-50s for several weeks. Nonetheless, the brief spasm of wintry precipitation reminded everyone that time was running out for combat

---

13 Margaret Leech, *Reveille in Washington: 1861-1865* (New York, 1989), 175-78. Stanton had sharply criticized Meade for failing to prevent Lee's crossing of the Potomac after Gettysburg and snidely remarked in September on the general's seeming unwillingness to attack an ANV weakened by the transfer of Longstreet's corps to Georgia and South Carolina. Whenever Meade visited Washington, however, the secretary was always supportive, kind and cordial and throughout 1864 treated Meade in similar fashion both in person and in writing, including securing his promotion to Maj. Gen. in the Regular Army.

14 *New York Times*, Nov. 9, 1863; *Harper's Weekly*, Nov. 21 & 28, 1863.

15 Kirkpatrick diary, Nov. 9, 1863, UT; George Patch to Parents, Nov. 10, 1863, George Patch papers, VHS; Charles W. Cowtan, *Services of the Tenth New York Volunteers (National Zouaves) in the War of the Rebellion* (New York, NY, 1882), 226; Martha Derby Perry, *Letters from a Surgeon of the Civil War* (Boston, MA, 1906), 123.

operations. If the Army of the Potomac still had ambitions toward producing a post-Gettysburg showdown the calendar was no longer its ally.[16]

*   *   *

Taking advantage of this "Indian summer," Haupt's repair crews descended on the O&A. By November 12 these hard-working men had laid five miles of new track and reestablished train service as far south as Bealton Station. Meade anticipated that they would need just a few more days to get the railroad running all the way to Brandy Station. The Federal high command hadn't yet decided what it would do with the AOP once that happened, but the question was very much on the mind of Meade, Halleck, and Lincoln.[17]

It was also on the mind of Robert E. Lee, who found himself saddled with an enlarged set of difficulties after his abandonment of Culpeper County. Some problems were new and others seemingly perpetual, but all of them complicated an already unpleasant situation. Certainly, the sour taste of a second embarrassing defeat within a little over three weeks nullified whatever satisfaction Confederates drew from their successful, albeit inelegant, escape behind the Rapidan.

November 7 and 8 had cost the ANV 21 known dead, 181 confirmed wounded and 1,939 missing, almost all of who were captured. The fighting around Kelly's Ford contributed 385 men (11 dead, 79 wounded, 295 missing) to that tally while skirmishing on the army's flanks added 15 soldiers from A. P. Hill's corps (3 dead, 12 wounded) and 13 troopers (1 killed, 12 injured) from Stuart's cavalry. The battle at Rappahannock Station accounted for the remaining dead and wounded as well as 1,630 of the unaccounted for. Since the enemy held the field no one could calculate the number of slain or injured among the absent, but the virtual annihilation of two brigades and a battery was beyond doubt.

Hays reported a loss of 702 men (2 dead, 16 wounded, 684 missing). Hoke's brigade listed 928 casualties (3 killed, 19 wounded, 906 missing). Lieutenant Green's Louisiana Guard Artillery came away from Rappahannock Station with only 28 men and 9 horses, having lost virtually all its equipment, 45 horses, and 42 gunners including one known dead and two wounded, both of who were captured. The Rockbridge Artillery had one man killed.

---

16 Krick, *Civil War Weather*, 112; George Patch to Parents, Nov. 10, 1863, George Patch letters, VHS.

17 OR 29, pt. 2, 437-38; OR 51, pt. 1, 1120. Meade had cautioned Halleck on the evening of November 8 that the AOP couldn't advance very far without repairing the O&A all the way to Rappahannock Station.

Some Confederates insisted that most of Early's missing had fallen killed or wounded amid intense combat. Such an Alamo-like defense, they comforted themselves, surely inflicted significant enemy losses and proved that Southern troops hadn't been distressingly eager to surrender. Unfortunately, such assertions ran afoul of Federal claims to have taken 1,600 prisoners in the bridgehead, meaning that only 30 missing Rebels had died.

Precise figures aside no one could mistake what Lee's Rappahannock strategy had cost the Confederacy. The loss of four cannons with their limbers and caissons plus seven battle flags was humiliating enough, but the subtraction of veteran manpower hurt far worse. On November 10, fewer than 500 men mustered in Hays' brigade and just 286 in Hoke's command. Only one officer, a captain, remained in the 5th Louisiana.[18]

If not for the sizable number of troops gathering firewood and building materials when the Federals attacked, both brigades might have shriveled to the point of disbandment. As it was, they would likely never be the same. One Louisianan described Hays' command as a mere "skeleton" whose strength "cannot be swelled again." He predicted that one or two more charges would finish off the survivors, leaving only "ghosts" to fill its ranks. A distressed Richmond newspaper reflected that the brigade had been worth its "weight in gold to the army" and wondered where the South would find material to replace it.[19]

Rebel officials in Richmond were similarly distraught. Gen. Josiah Gorgas, chief of the Confederate ordnance bureau, voiced a widely-held view in his diary that "it is very strange how little success has attended the movement of Lee's army since the death of Jackson." Noting that the ANV's recent losses had "greatly exceeded" those it had inflicted, a War Department clerk confessed that Southern affairs looked "very

18 Previous paragraphs based on OR 29, pt. 1, 561, 607, 616-617, 624-52, 629-32, 635 & pt. 2, 576. Ewell's losses were concentrated in the 2nd and 30th North Carolina, while Hill's were in Lane's brigade. The LA Guard Artillery listed 1 man killed and 41 missing. Postwar analysis of individual service records from Hoke's regiments on www.civilwardata.com shows named losses of 932 men—6 killed, 17 wounded, 10 missing, and 899 (including 16 wounded) captured. The 10 missing likely died trying to cross the river. The 54th NC lost 2 dead, 1 wounded, 4 missing, and 307 (including 2 wounded) captured. The 57th NC suffered 2 killed, 6 wounded and captured and 271 unwounded captured (no missing). The 6th NC lost 2 dead, 10 wounded, 8 wounded and captured, 6 missing, and 307 unwounded prisoners. Interestingly, the 6th NC suffered a great many leg wounds. The final tally of survivors in Hoke's brigade was 290. The majority of Hays' remaining troops were from the 6th, 8th, and 9th LA. The War Department reassigned the LA Guard Artillery's survivors to Richmond's defenses.

19 Jones, Lee's Tigers, 185; Daniel Barfoot, General Robert F. Hoke: Lee's Modest Warrior (Winston-Salem, NC, 1996), 102-103. The Federals released 500 Louisiana Tigers in a March 1864 prisoner exchange and many of Hoke's men some months later in another exchange.

gloomy," while another bureaucrat observed that "not a few are despondent from the recent disasters to our arms."[20]

The lamentable outcome at Rappahannock Station stung all the more because it came hard on the heels of A. P. Hill's Bristoe Station calamity three weeks earlier. Colonel Taylor thought the combination of these two battles "the saddest chapter" in the army's history. Major Sandie Pendleton of Ewell's staff felt "personally disgraced" by the campaign's "absolutely sickening" outcome and imagined the entire ANV felt the same.[21]

As if to prove that supposition editors and troops lashed out at what Taylor called the "miserable, miserable management" behind the November 7 defeat. The question everyone wanted answered was how Hoke's and Hays' brigades had become "so completely isolated" that it had proven impossible to withdraw or reinforce them before disaster struck. Answering this query dispassionately required after action reports, which Lee promptly called for. Many, however, reached conclusions without awaiting official documentation.[22]

Although some shrugged off the defeat as "one of those surprises that will at times occur" in war, few were prone to similar objectivity. Since no one doubted the valor of the bridgehead's defenders most writers blamed the catastrophe on a gross failure of leadership. Reflecting on the decision that placed his unit in such a vulnerable a position, one of Hoke's soldiers sarcastically observed that the "wisdom" of such generalship was "not apparent." War department officials and Richmond newspapers agreed, citing "bad management" and "leniency to duty" as the defeat's chief components.[23]

Despite a popular consensus favoring that verdict, efforts at finding scapegoats elicited divergent views. Brigade and division leaders were the logical suspects and each endured considerable censure. Forgetting that Hoke was in North Carolina, a

---

20 Edward Younger, ed., *Inside the Confederate Government: The Diary of Robert Garlick Hill Kean* (Baton Rouge, LA, 1993), 111-12; John B. Jones, *A Rebel War Clerk's Diary* (Philadelphia, PA, 1866) Vol. 2, 93; Wiggins, Sarah Woolfolk, ed., *The Journals of Josiah Gorgas, 1857-1878* (Tuscaloosa, AL, 1995), 85.

21 Taylor to Bettie, Nov. 7, 1863, *Lee's Adjutant*, 82; Sandie Pendleton to William Pendleton, Nov. 10, 1863 in Susan P. Lee, *Memoirs of William Nelson Pendleton, d.d. Rector of Latimer Parish, Lexington, Virginia: Brigadier-General C. S. A.; Chief of Artillery, Army of Northern Virginia.* (Philadelphia, PA, 1893), 305; Freeman, R.E. *Lee*, Vol. 3, 192-93.

22 Taylor to Bettie, Nov. 7, 1863, *Lee's Adjutant*, 82; Freeman, *R.E. Lee*, Vol. 3, 192-93; Jones, *Lee's Tigers*, 186; Richmond *Enquirer*, Nov. 10 & 14, 1863.

23 Flemming Saunders to Mother, Nov. 21, 1863, Saunders Family Papers, VHS; Casler, *Four Years in the Stonewall Brigade*, 196; Clark, *NC Regts*, Vol. 1, 320; Richmond *Enquirer*, Nov. 10 & 14, 1863.

judgmental Richmond *Enquirer* demanded that both he and Hays lose their commands. The Memphis *Daily Appeal* aimed its ire at Jubal Early, saying it was incumbent upon him to account for how the enemy had caught his division napping.[24]

Lee's performance earned its own share of criticism. Early's aide, Peter Hairston, recorded in his diary that the prevailing "impression" within "the army seems to be that Gen'l Lee is responsible as he was there and saw what was going on." An appalled Capt. Henry Watkins, echoing Hairston, cast aspersions on every general at Rappahannock Station. Admitting that Meade's offensive had surprised officers and enlisted men alike, he nonetheless chided his superiors for taking so long "to comprehend" what the enemy was doing and then failing to react wisely despite "timely warning" of their movements. That included the army's commander, who had neglected to "awake from his reverie" until after disaster had struck. Lieutenant Robert Hubbard, Jr. joined Watkin's critique, calling Rappahannock Station "the greatest military blunder Lee ever committed."[25]

Some tempered their assessment of Marse Robert by concluding that "like a chess player when highly excited [Lee] had become so intent upon his own plan, he didn't watch the movement of his adversary with sufficient care." Many men felt that the army's commander was more sinned-against than sinner, however. *Enquirer* editors, for example, hoped there were "good and sufficient reasons" for the "strange circumstances" that led to the mishap and that "upon investigation" Lee would be "satisfied" he hadn't lost two brigades through negligence or stupidity.[26]

*   *   *

Whatever explained the ANV's latest setback, Richmond newspapers urged immediate retribution against Meade's "bold and daring insult" to Southern arms. Although willing to credit the Pennsylvanian for landing a surprise blow at Rappahannock Station, the *Enquirer* felt certain the Union general would "quietly settle down at the first good place for winter quarters," rather than risk his laurels by continuing to advance. Whether Lee would let the Yankees go into hibernation without a fight remained an open question. Conceding that whatever the great warrior decided to do would be "readily accepted as right and proper," the paper declared that "if the

---

24 Richmond *Enquirer*, November 10, 1863; Memphis *Daily Appeal*, November 16, 1863.

25 Hairston Diary Nov. 12, 1863, SHC/UNC; Richard Watkins to Mary, Nov. 11, 1863, Richard Henry Watkins papers, VHS; Thomas P. Nanzig, ed., *The Civil War Memoirs of a Virginia Cavalryman: Lt. Robert T. Hubbard, Jr.* (Tuscaloosa, AL, 2007), 113; Richmond *Enquirer* Nov. 14, 1863.

26 Nanzig, *Civil War Memoirs of a Virginia Cavalryman*, 113; Richmond *Enquirer* Nov. 14, 1863.

wishes of the people could influence him, they would like to see the punishment fall swift and heavy."[27]

Many Rebel soldiers felt the same, and few doubted their chief shared that desire. Believing Lee eager to "wipe out the advantage Meade has gained & teach him a lesson," Maj. Jedediah Hotchkiss, chief topographical engineer on Ewell's staff, predicted the ANV would "fight again this year." Having collaborated closely with its commander on several occasions, the talented cartographer most likely appraised his subject correctly. Past campaigns had certainly proven Lee's combative inclinations and he had struck something of an aggressive tone while commiserating with Harry Hays about the "sad affair" at Rappahannock Station. When the brigadier expressed dismay at losing so many men, Lee empathized, remarking that the "only thing" to do now was "try to get even" with the enemy tomorrow.[28]

Regrettably, serious hurdles confronted any attempt to fulfill that desire by offensive action. Among these were Yankee intentions, which Lee hadn't yet fully developed, as well as the weather, which could snarl any plan. The third and by far the most inhibiting was the intractable problem of supply. In mid-October Lee had abandoned his goal of holding Meade near the Potomac because he lacked faith in Richmond's ability to feed and clothe his troops that far north. The ANV's logistical difficulties had continued despite its return to Culpeper County, and Lee worried that even backing up another 20 miles to the Rapidan wouldn't help much.

Reading November 10's snowfall as the harbinger of a difficult winter, he wrote Secretary of War James A. Seddon to remind him that large numbers of barefooted soldiers manned the Rapidan front. Crediting recent shoe shipments for relieving "much hardship" as well as increasing the army's "efficiency," Lee stressed the necessity of maintaining a steady flow of warm clothing and footwear to his troops.

The question of shoes paled in comparison to a scarcity of forage for the army's mules and horses—another matter giving Lee "great anxiety." Informing Seddon that "corn for our animals comes in very slowly," the general warned that if Richmond didn't hasten deliveries and increase quantity, much of the army's livestock would perish that winter. Although these difficulties hobbled Lee's ability to move, let alone fight, the general couldn't do anything more than "beg" Seddon to urge "great diligence and activity" upon those departments responsible for meeting the army's needs.[29]

---

27 Richmond *Enquirer*, November 10, 1863.

28 Jedediah Hotchkiss to Sara, Nov. 9, 1863 http://valley.lib.virginia.edu/papers/A4058; Hotchkiss to Wife, Nov. 11, 1863, http://valley.lib.virginia.edu/papers/A4059, both accessed Feb. 2, 2020; Jones, *Lee's Tigers*, 187. Often identified as a captain or major, Hotchkiss actually never received an official commission.

29 *OR* 29, pt. 2, 830.

Intelligence received over the next 48 hours sharpened the urgency of Lee's request. Alert scouts kept ANV headquarters so well apprised of Union affairs, that Lee could inform Jefferson Davis of Federal trains running to Bealton a day before Meade announced that fact to Halleck. Recent movements of enemy artillery, wagons, and spare horses suggested another AOP advance. If Lee estimated Yankee intentions correctly, Meade would move against the army's right flank by crossing the Rapidan at Germanna and Ely's fords. The bluecoats would then probably march southeast to cut the railroad connecting Fredericksburg to Richmond. If so, Meade surely planned to abandon the O&A as a supply line and move his base to Aquia Creek or perhaps to Fredericksburg itself.[30]

Should his opponent employ that strategy Lee promised to pursue and engage the enemy as rapidly as possible. But he confessed he could do so only with "the greatest difficulty" given chronic supply shortages. Central Virginia's countryside was barren, and the ANV's commissariat had "no forage on hand and very little prospect of getting any." Lee feared his horses would die in "great numbers" without grain and confessed he didn't "know how they will survive two or three days' march without food." Expressing hope that "every effort will be made" to get forage to the army, he suggested that President Davis "stop the transportation of everything on the railroad excepting military supplies."[31]

Lee recognized that his logistical difficulties stemmed as much from the Virginia Central Railroad's poor condition as from bureaucratic problems in Richmond. Primarily built to move cotton to coastal ports, the Southern railway system began the war ill-suited to meet martial needs, and its capabilities had steadily deteriorated since the war began. Lack of spare parts, insufficient manufacturing capacity, too few skilled laborers, and a shortage of iron caused by the Union naval blockade increasingly plagued maintenance of rolling stock and track. The Confederacy was thus forced to cannibalize abandoned or less strategic lines for replacement rails and crossties. Indeed, Lee had risked igniting a battle in late October to reclaim track near Rappahannock Station, and a similar Rebel effort north of Fredericksburg had startled George Meade briefly in early November.

---

30 Ibid., 832.

31 Ibid. Lee also passed along rumors that the Federals were assembling a large number horses in anticipation of launching a raid to free thousands of Union prisoners held around Richmond. This was the first indication Southern intelligence operatives had passed along regarding what would become the famous Kilpatrick-Dahlgren raid in February 1864—an endeavor which ended disastrously for the Northern cause. For this and "many reasons" Lee recommended removing the Yankee POWs from Richmond "as soon as practicable."

Salvage operations couldn't meet the ever-expanding need for replacement track, of course, and the South's industrial base struggled to deal with hundreds of broken rails every month. The Confederacy's sparse telegraph system prevented train crews from learning about bad spots on the road until they ran into them, which was often too late to forestall an accident. To lessen the risk, locomotives reduced their standard operating speed from 25 miles per hour in 1861 to a mere 10 in 1863. Although necessary, this measure significantly slowed the movement of supplies.

The Virginia Central, which connected Lee's army to Richmond and the Shenandoah Valley, wasn't spared these difficulties, and on November 12 the general told Seddon that the line's condition seemed "worse every day." Frequent derailments caused by worn out rails and crossties were thoroughly disrupting a steady flow of necessities to the ANV. Lee asked the secretary to "consult" with the president and the railroad's superintendent about "what measures can be taken for its repair" before winter set in.

Cautioning that it was impossible to detach men from his army for such work, Lee suggested that if the railroad company couldn't get the job done, engineer troops currently maintaining Richmond's fortifications ought to undertake the task. Either way, the general minced no words in pressing the issue. If the Virginia Central couldn't be "relied on for the regular transportation" of supplies, he would have no alternative but to "fall back nearer Richmond." That meant evacuating the Rapidan line, leaving the "richest portion" of Virginia to "the mercy of the enemy," and severing ties between the Shenandoah Valley and Confederate capital.[32]

In the weeks that followed government authorities made many promises to Lee assuring him they would remedy the logistical situation. But the problem persisted, leaving the ANV to live hand to mouth, receiving only slightly more supplies each day than it consumed. What that would mean if the Yankees came looking for a fight was unknowable, but Lee warned that the results might be catastrophic.

---

32 Previous paragraphs based on *OR* 29, pt. 2, 832-833; https://www.battlefields.org/learn/articles/railroads-confederacy accessed Feb. 5, 2020. In 1863 one quarter of all Southern locomotives required serious maintenance.

Chapter 12

"The Appearance of an Advance"

Culpeper Again—Meade Visits Washington—Reactions and
Overreactions—Skirmishing at the Fords—Hampton's Raid—Uncertain Plans

A sense of déjà vu hovered over Meade's headquarters as it settled in near Fleetwood Heights. With mid-November approaching, Union troops once again stood inside Culpeper's 'V'. No one wearing blue could overlook the familiarity of their surroundings or their circumstances. All or part of the AOP had crossed the Rappahannock going in one direction or another six times in the last 100 days. During that same period it had taken or lost Brandy Station five times, rebuilt the Rappahannock Station railway bridge once, burned it once, and was again about to rebuild it.[1]

If all the back-and-forth these gyrations entailed frustrated Federal troops, having to confront the same conundrum he had faced since late July exasperated George Meade. His army's current position was just a few miles south of where it had been on August 1 and in almost exactly the same spot it had occupied on September 16. Now, as then, he found himself tied to an extended, vulnerable supply line while opposing an enemy ensconced in stout fortifications behind a challenging river. Now, as then, the Union army occupied a position easily outflanked and also devoid of good defensive ground. And now, as then, government policy compelled Meade to operate on an axis he considered highly disadvantageous.

Nonetheless, Union morale was riding high. The aura of invincibility once surrounding the Army of Northern Virginia was gone—its chastening at Gettysburg

---

1 Lowe, *Meade's Army*, 66; Emily Jennings, "Ceremony Honors Historic Church Site" https://www.starexponent.com/news/ceremony-honors-historic-church-site-brandy-station -dead/article_bce96ba3-7df6-50db-9d48-bc902421a2ba.html ; accessed Feb. 7, 2019. Meade's HQ was located in the woods near Saint James Church.

accentuated by Bristoe Station, Kelly's Ford, and Rappahannock Station. Lee and his men were hardly any less capable or dangerous, of course, but it was refreshing to hear people talking about competent Federal generalship for a change.

However positive Northern moods, a sober consideration of the strategic picture wasn't heartening. Four months after Gettysburg the eastern theater remained deadlocked around Culpeper Court House. The last few weeks had more than validated all Meade's arguments against operating in this area, but that hadn't altered Lincoln's or Halleck's determination to fight it out along the O&A line.

Ironically, the AOP's triumphant assault across the Rappahannock undercut Meade's insistence on the impropriety of trying to assail Lee's strong position astride the Rapidan. After all, if Union troops could storm Rebel breastworks north of Culpeper, why couldn't they do the same south of there? The Confederate failure to stand and fight between the rivers had disappointed Meade, but from a military perspective he understood Lee's decision well. Inside Washington's offices and Northern press rooms, however, the enemy's retreat suggested weakness rather than strategy, and that viewpoint intensified expectations that Meade would press his newly-won advantage and spark a major battle.

The general realized this and despite announcing his intention to delay any movement pending full restoration of O&A operations to Brandy Station, Meade knew he couldn't avoid undertaking some sort of offensive before winter immobilized both armies. However, after a late summer and fall of asking for either unambiguous direction or strategic flexibility, and gaining neither, he wouldn't risk launching a risky offensive without getting some sort of buy-in from his superiors.

With that purpose in mind he telegraphed Halleck on November 13. After noting the army's current position and updating his boss on the status of railroad repairs, Meade asked permission to visit Washington and confer with the general-in-chief and secretary of war. Replying that a "consultation is desirable," Halleck told his subordinate to come ahead.[2]

Foreseeing at least a two-night stay in the capital Meade wired Margaret an invitation to hop a train in Philadelphia and join him for a brief reunion. Naturally, she accepted. Maj. James C. Biddle would accompany Meade along with fellow staff officers Capts. Robert W. Mitchell and George Meade, the general's son and aide-de-camp. Following his chief's lead, Biddle (who had married just the past December) also arranged a rendezvous with his young bride in the capital.[3]

---

2   OR 29, pt. 2, 449.

3   Lyman, *Meade's Headquarters*, 48; Lowe, *Meade's Army*, 67. Biddle married Gertrude Gouverneur Meredith on December 27, 1862.

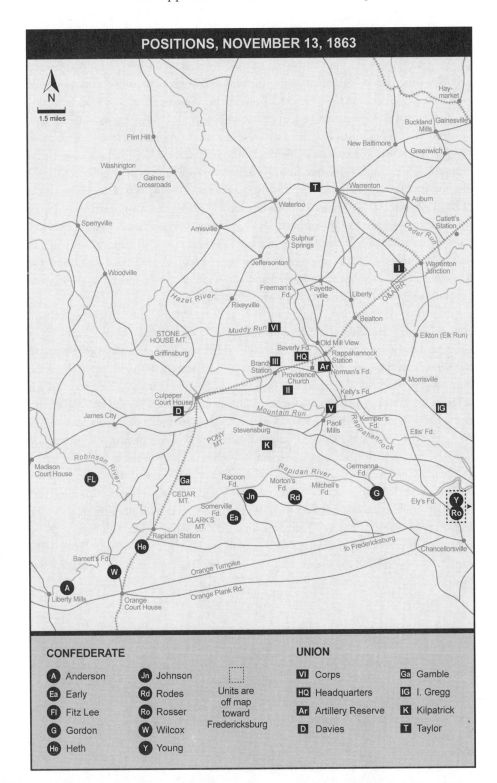

POSITIONS, NOVEMBER 13, 1863

N
1.5 miles

CONFEDERATE

- (A) Anderson
- (Ea) Early
- (Fl) Fitz Lee
- (G) Gordon
- (He) Heth
- (Jn) Johnson
- (Rd) Rodes
- (Ro) Rosser
- (W) Wilcox
- (Y) Young

Units are off map toward Fredericksburg

UNION

- (VI) Corps
- (HQ) Headquarters
- (Ar) Artillery Reserve
- (D) Davies
- (Ga) Gamble
- (IG) I. Gregg
- (K) Kilpatrick
- (T) Taylor

*   *   *

While the Union high command planned discussions, both armies remained wide awake for any hint of enemy mischief. Confederate infantry and artillery stood watch in the fortifications carved out behind the Rapidan. A. P. Hill's troops held the line between Liberty Mills and Rapidan Station with Anderson's division standing guard at the former while Wilcox's and Heth's commands camped around Orange Court House. Ewell defended the river from Somerville to Morton's fords, deploying Early's division at Somerville, Johnson's troops at Raccoon Ford, and Rodes' men near Morton's Ford. Fitz Lee's cavalry looked after the ANV's left flank with one brigade stationed in Madison County picketing Robertson's River and two brigades below the Rapidan to Hill's left. Wade Hampton's division monitored the army's right. James Gordon's North Carolina regiments spread out between Mitchell's Ford and the Rapidan's confluence with the Rappahannock, while Young's and Rosser's brigades covered the lower Rappahannock towards Fredericksburg.[4] 1

North of the Rapidan, Yankee infantry maintained the line Meade laid out on November 9. Pleasonton's cavalry, on the other hand, continued its never-ending effort to fix the outlines of Rebel defenses and detect any signs of enemy activity. Kilpatrick's command based around Stevensburg watched the Rapidan between Morton's and Raccoon fords, with its 1st Vermont Cavalry scattered along the river for seven miles. Buford's division encamped a little south of Culpeper Court House, with its 1st Brigade (once again under Col. William Gamble) maintaining an outpost line on the old Cedar Mountain battlefield in the direction of Rapidan Station and Somerville Ford. Davies' 2nd Brigade kept an eye on Robertson's River to the west.

Major General David Gregg's 2nd Cavalry Division remained widely dispersed. Its 1st Brigade under Col. John Taylor bivouacked around Warrenton and along the upper Rappahannock at Sulphur Springs and Waterloo charged with keeping tabs on the AOP's right flank and rear. The division's 2nd Brigade under Col. Irvin Gregg scrutinized the upper Rappahannock's east bank as well as the area between Morrisville and Hartwood Church, both of which lay on the Bealeton Station-Fredericksburg road.[5]

4   McDonald, *Make Me A Map*, 182-83; Jones, *Civil War Memoirs*, 95; Trout, *After Gettysburg*, 298; Swank, *Sabres, Saddles and Spurs*, 101; Dozier, *A Gunner in Lee's Army*.

5   OR 29, pt. 2, 446; Hoffman, *History of the First Vermont Cavalry*, 150; Samuel Gilpin Diary, Nov. 10 & 12, 1863, E. N. Gilpin, papers, LC; Swank, *Sabres, Saddles and Spurs*, 101; Trout, *After Gettysburg*, 293-96; Samuel M. Blackwell, Jr., *In the First Line of Battle: The 12th Illinois Cavalry in the Civil War* (DeKalb, Ill., 2002), 126-27. Col. Chapman returned to the 3rd Indiana Cavalry upon Gamble's resumption of command. Gambles' brigade lost one of its four regiments on Nov. 1

As usual the zone between Stuart's and Pleasonton's troopers existed as a murky no-man's land in which each side sought to blind its opponent and uncover his intentions. The James City area halfway between Culpeper Court House and Robertson's River was particularly volatile. Northern forays or Confederate foraging expeditions churned through the sector almost daily. Occasionally rival horsemen bumped into each other and fought brief, exciting encounters that seldom caused any casualties.[6]

It was more dangerous above the Rappahannock where Mosby's partisans constantly harassed Federal troops. Acknowledging that those gray raiders "rule the roost" from the Blue Ridge to Chesapeake Bay, Capt. Walter S. Newhall said that the Rebel "wretches" had become such "a scourge" that anything smaller than a platoon straying beyond the army's lines was vulnerable to attack.[7]

With the luxury of choosing the time and place for their exploits, the guerrillas usually operated in small bands relying on thunderclap surprise and daring to achieve their aims. They were "the worst kind of enemies to contend with," one frustrated New Jersey soldier wrote, "for we cannot tell where to find them." Despite constant effort Gregg's troopers met with little success against the Southern marauders, but this was true of every Yankee unit that had confronted them. Capt. Newhall, who likened pursuing Mosby's riders to chasing ghosts, wasn't surprised. His understanding of them rested "on these facts," he wrote, "Nobody ever saw one; they leave no tracks, and they come down upon you when you least expect them."[8]

Annoying as Mosby's incursions were, the only price they extracted was an irritatingly large number of animals, wagons, and captives, including a few careless sutlers. Nevertheless, the presence of Newton's I Corps and Gregg's cavalry along the O&A prevented Mosby from doing anything that might tangibly affect the course of events. Closer to the Rapidan, however, the goals and concerns of each side's high command created an atmosphere where even routine activity could instigate a battle.

---

when the 12th Ill. Cavalry, having reenlisted, went home to reorganize as a "Veteran" unit and recruit.

6   Newell, *Ninth Regiment New York Volunteer Cavalry*, 140; Hard, *Eighth Cavalry Regiment Illinois Volunteers*, 283. Troopers from Devin's brigade swept through the region on November 11. The next day cavalrymen from Brig. Gen. William C. Wickham's Virginia brigade scrounged through the district and obtained four wagonloads of corn.

7   David Smith to Elizabeth, Aug. 8, 1863, David Smith letters, GLI; Walter S. Newhall, *A Memoir* (Philadelphia, PA, 1864), 123-24. While serving with the 3rd PA Cavalry Newhall had distinguished himself at Gettysburg on July 3, 1863. Five months later, on Dec. 18, 1863 he suffered a fatal accident when his horse slipped and fell on him while attempting to ford the Rappahannock. The Captain was traveling home on Christmas furlough.

8   Newhall, *A Memoir*, 123-24.

*   *   *

On November 13, Lt. Col. Otto Harhaus led the picket reserve of his 2nd New York Cavalry (Davies' brigade, Kilpatrick's division) on a reconnaissance toward Lee's right flank. Taking half his force to Morton's Ford, he sent the other half eastward under Capt. Obadiah J. Downing to scout Mitchell's and Sission's fords. Harhaus discovered a "pretty strong" enemy force at Morton's, while Downing uncovered a battalion of Rebel cavalry near Sission's and plenty of Confederate infantry at Mitchell's Ford. Enemy artillery opened fire wherever the Federals showed themselves and for a time the cannonading was "pretty lively." By 3 p.m., however, the shooting had nearly died off, and the Yankees were headed back to camp.[9]

That same day Irvin Gregg sent a regiment to Hartwood Church on a routine relief of picket posts. Although for Pleasonton's troopers none of this amounted to more than another hard ride, the effect south of the Rapidan was stirring. Lee had already forecast Meade's next move as an attempt to skirt the ANV's right flank by crossing the Rapidan at Germanna Ford or points farther east, followed by an effort to interpose the AOP between Richmond and the Rebel army. Acutely aware that derailing such an offensive depended on an early and speedy response, Southern leaders maintained a keen lookout for the initial maneuvers sure to initiate such a scheme.

In this hyper-alert state, they interpreted Federal cavalry marching on Hartwood Church and Harhaus's probe as evidence Meade's expected offensive had begun. Fearful that the Yankees were moving on Fredericksburg, Rodes' division left its camps behind Morton's Ford and made for Chancellorsville "as if on a race for life." The gray column's pace didn't slacken until near sunset when its officers learned that the supposed danger had passed and put everyone into bivouac. As the weary troops prepared dinner after a taxing seven-mile march, no one could have guessed that their fruitless hike was about to inspire 48 hours of intense anxiety at AOP headquarters.[10]

*   *   *

Meade and his party departed Brandy Station for Washington at 6 a.m. on November 14. Just as they crossed the Rappahannock a worrisome report landed on the desk of Henry Davies, whose brigade picketed the Rapidan near Morton's Ford.

---

9   OR 29, pt. 2, 451-52.

10 McDonald, *Make Me A Map*, 183; Munson, *Confederate Correspondent*, 104-05; James R. Montgomery diary, Nov. 14, 1863, Eleanor S. Brockenbrough Library, American Civil War Museum, Richmond, VA. Rodes' camps lay only an eighth of a mile south of Morton's Ford.

The dispatch originated at a Union outpost that had heard "considerable noise"—a mix of rumbling wagons and men shouting "as [if] on a march"— emanating from the crossing's south bank around 11 p.m. the prior evening. These suspicious omens were followed by enemy musicians sounding reveille at 3 a.m. on the morning of the fourteenth—an odd hour to awaken a supposedly supine army.[11]

Curious and concerned, Davies rode out to look things over. At first glance everything seemed serene. Rebel sentries displayed "less animosity" than usual, and as best he could tell, the graycoats weren't as numerous as they had been the day before. In and of themselves these observations weren't especially disquieting, but upon closer consideration Davies realized that cavalrymen had replaced enemy infantry pickets on the opposite shore. This suggested that Rebel foot soldiers were on the move and "inclined" the 27-year old New Yorker to believe the Confederates had "withdrawn their main force from the river." Whether this signaled an enemy advance or a retreat the brigadier couldn't say. But recalling how the last Rebel offensive had begun, he quickly relayed word of these developments up the chain of command.[12]

Davies' report went to Maj. Gen. Pleasonton at Cavalry Corps headquarters, and he forwarded it promptly to Army HQ. Meade had asked John Sedgwick to come over and take temporary command of the AOP in his absence, but he hadn't arrived yet and therefore it was Maj. Gen. Humphreys who received Davies' alert. The army's chief of staff wasn't unduly concerned. No other part of the line was sending in similar observations and what Davies' troopers had heard might be nothing more than the ordinary shifting about of enemy units. Refusing to take alarm, Humphreys busied himself with routine and the arrival of four English army officers who had come down from Washington to get a look at the American war.[13]

The general's nonchalance dissipated later that evening when a trio of runaway slaves and a Rebel deserter arrived at army headquarters amidst a "drenching" thunderstorm. The runaways had crossed the Rapidan earlier that day, while the disaffected Confederate had abandoned his regiment 24 hours ago. Each of them corroborated Davies' sense that something was brewing along the Rapidan. By themselves none of these tidbits would have stirred much concern. Together they were mutually supportive and disconcerting.

By 11 p.m. a now-apprehensive Humphreys sent Meade a cautionary telegram. He relayed Davies' earlier report and noted that the three runaways had overheard their master warning friends to move all valuable property southward because the

11 OR 29, pt. 2, 451.

12 Ibid., 453.

13 Ibid., 453-54; Lowe, Meade's Army, 67.

Confederate "army is falling back," and its troops had already abandoned Morton's and Mitchell's fords. Specifically, the contrabands reported their former owner saying Rodes' division had gone toward Orange Court House. In partial support of the ex-slaves' story, Humphreys noted that according to the North Carolina deserter, Southern cavalry had replaced infantry at Morton's Ford before Rodes' troops pulled back either to Spotsylvania or Orange Court House.

There was no way to confirm any of this. None of Col. Sharpe's spies had returned recently from behind enemy lines, and hazy atmospherics prevented the Pony Mountain signal station from observing Rebel movements. Until he knew more Humphreys wouldn't hazard a guess at enemy intentions. The signs might point to an advance or to a retreat. But if Lee had decided to take up a position farther south, the staff chief conjectured, he had done so as a strategic choice and not in response to anything the Union army had done. Of course, it was just as likely the crafty Rebel was reprising his October offensive and looking to swoop down on the AOP from an unexpected direction.

Leaving nothing to chance, Humphreys carefully instructed the army's corps commanders to hold their troops ready to move at "very short notice." He also directed Sharpe to send more agents below the Rapidan and Pleasonton to "push reconnaissance close in on enemy" at daylight, November 15. Kilpatrick's troopers would probe the Rapidan from Raccoon to Germanna fords while Buford checked on Rapidan Station and reconnoitered Robertson's River. Concurrently Gregg would send a "strong scouting party" to check out the area between Hartwood Church and U.S. Ford on the lower Rappahannock. Humphreys assured Meade that if the enemy were advancing, the army's flanks had been "looked after."[14]

* * *

Federal horsemen rode out of camp early on the morning of November 15 despite 38-degree temperatures and high winds lashing a cold rain into their backs. With Kilpatrick away on court-martial duty, George Custer had command of the 3rd Cavalry Division and as always he was energetic. Sending Davies' brigade to examine Mitchell's and Germanna fords, he ordered part of his own brigade (temporarily under Col. Charles H. Town) to scout Raccoon Ford while he led the remainder of his force and Capt. Alexander C. M. Pennington's Battery M, 2nd US to test Confederate strength at Morton's Ford.

---

14 Previous paragraphs from *OR* 29, pt. 2, 454. The deserter was from the 15th NC Infantry, part of Cooke's brigade in Heth's division. The regiment had suffered heavy casualties at Bristoe Station on October 14, 1863.

It didn't take the Michigan brigadier long to discover a large contingent of Southerners manning the latter crossing's extensive breastworks, from which at least six Rebel guns opened a "brisk cannonade" at the first appearance of blue uniforms. Although the rain-swollen Rapidan prevented Union troopers from fording the river, Pennington swung his battery into action and engaged the enemy cannons. Unable to restrain himself, Custer dismounted to personally aim a few of the Federal fieldpieces. An aide said the general did some fine shooting before resuming his primary duties.[15]

The artillery duel went on for some time, its echoes putting troops on edge up and down the river. The firing also brought a surge of Rebel reinforcements rushing up to Morton's Ford. For Custer it looked like an entire Confederate division held the crossing. The enemy seemed equally numerous at Raccoon Ford where a "strong infantry force" occupied fortified heights alongside a battery which fired a few rounds to keep the Federals at bay. Custer's personal inspection of the river between the two fords uncovered more south bank Rebel artillery, some of which repaid his curiosity by lobbing shells in his direction.[16]

Having learned what Pleasonton wanted to know, Custer ordered his soaked troopers back to camp. Henry Davies turned his men toward home about the same time. When the muddy brigadier returned to Stevensburg he confirmed that Rebel infantry held Mitchell's Ford in "strong force." Although the mounted contingent sent to Germanna Ford hadn't yet returned, Custer considered his mission complete. At noon he informed Cavalry Corps HQ that he'd seen no mounted Rebels between Raccoon and Mitchell's fords but abundant enemy infantry defending the river below Somerville Ford.[17]

Unlike Custer, John Buford got off to an uncharacteristically poor start that morning. In fact, he seemed genuinely perturbed by Pleasonton's directive to send men out in dreadful weather to scout a front line they had canvassed many times already. In an 8:25 a.m. dispatch the Kentuckian brusquely implied that such a reconnaissance wasn't necessary. He felt certain no enemy infantry was north of the river save a small picket post at Rapidan Station, while the Rebel cavalry maintained their previous positions.[18]

---

15 OR 29, pt. 2, 462; Krick, *Civil War Weather*, 112; Sandy Barnard, ed., *An Aide to Custer: The Civil War Letters of Lt. Edward G. Granger* (Norman, OK, 2018), 143-45.

16 OR 29, pt. 2, 462; Edwin Weist diary, Nov. 15, 1863, www.civilwarhome.com/ weistdiary.htm, accessed Mar. 12, 2020). Although Custer didn't report the battery's location it was most likely at Stringfellow Ford

17 OR 29, pt. 2, 462.

18 Ibid., 461. Buford was a no-nonsense kind of officer. His attitude on the morning of November 15 might have resulted from irritation at what he considered needless orders. On

Sedgwick had taken up his temporary post in Meade's stead by this time, and after reading the message he concluded Buford wasn't aware of recent intelligence that validated his current orders. The ersatz army commander told Pleasonton to explain the purpose of Buford's mission and make sure he grasped exactly what HQ wanted to find out. Finally prodded into action, the 1st Cavalry Division's troopers quickly confirmed much of what their commander already avowed. Rebel infantry in slightly larger numbers than before remained entrenched north of Rapidan Station with plenty of gray foot soldiers and guns on the southern bank. Nothing but enemy cavalry lurked along Robertson's River, although admittedly in considerable strength. The only other news Buford shared came from an unidentified source who claimed that a brigade of Southern horsemen had been in James City on November 14.

A little before 1 p.m. Humphreys wired Meade that Pleasonton's reconnaissance efforts were producing minor skirmishing and had revealed significant numbers of enemy infantry at Morton's and Raccoon fords. Somewhat better weather had restored limited visibility to Pony Mountain's signal station which could see campfire smoke near Orange Court House and around some of the river crossings, but little else. Beyond these nuggets of information, the chief of staff reported that repair crews had just completed the Rappahannock Station railroad bridge and should finish laying the last track to the river before nightfall.

Additional reports to army headquarters over the next 90 minutes enabled Humphreys to send Meade a more detailed telegram at 2:30 p.m. Union signal stations could discern no telltale campfire smoke on either of the army's flanks. Gregg's scout toward U.S. Ford had detected no enemy presence whatsoever. Custer was positive Rebel infantry still held the Rapidan crossings while Buford had found no trace of Southern troops east of Robertson's River. Thus informed, Humphreys promised his chief that the Confederates had "not withdrawn from the Rapidan." Unfortunately, however, he had received additional information to dampen his reassuring tone. Signalmen on Pony Mountain were reporting that Rebel "wagons and infantry in double columns"—probably part of Rodes' division returning to camp—had been passing westward behind Raccoon Ford for more than an hour. There also remained Buford's claim of an entire brigade of enemy cavalry hovering about James City 24 hours ago.

Meade didn't see this message until 6:40 p.m., having presumably spent the day in meetings with Halleck and Stanton. Responding to his chief of staff's last telegram, the AOP's commander concurred that Lee hadn't withdrawn from the Rapidan. But

---

the other hand, his impatience may have stemmed from ill health. The general would leave the army with a fatal case of typhoid fever on November 21. He died in Washington, DC on December 16, 1863 at the age of 37.

Meade didn't like reports of Rebel cavalry in James City or large-scale movement of enemy infantry at Raccoon Ford, both reminiscent of earlier Confederate maneuvers inaugurating the Bristoe campaign. "This has the appearance of an advance," he told Humphreys. Although Meade planned to leave the capital at 9 a.m. the next morning, which would put him back at headquarters around noon on November 16, he promised to leave immediately if "later intelligence" suggested a Confederate offensive. Meade asked Humphreys to respond at once to his wire.[19]

Telegraph operators took an hour to transmit the general's message, but much to his relief Humphreys immediately confirmed that additional intelligence forwarded that afternoon indicated "the enemy is not advancing." Pony Mountain's signalmen said that the movement of Confederate infantry had stopped not long after first reported. Southern cavalry near James City had turned out to be a reconnaissance patrol, and Pleasanton's horsemen had established that Lee's infantry remained along the Rapidan. Davies' earlier warning and the stories told by runaways or deserters had grown out of enemy responses to Union cavalry probes, nothing more. There was no need for Meade to hasten his return.[20]

*   *   *

Nonetheless, when the AOP's commander boarded a train for Brandy Station on the morning of November 16 his army remained ensconced in a jittery twilight zone. Nobody, from private to general, felt confident in predicting what might happen next. Moderate weather pointed toward the possibility of another campaign, but the certainty of December rain and mud counseled a halt to active operations. A headquarters circular issued upon Meade's return directing each corps maintain its readiness to move on "short notice" hardly clarified things. Such an order might presage a Federal offensive or be nothing more than prudent precaution against Rebel adventurism.[21]

Living with uncertainty was hardly novel for the soldiers. Despite swirling rumors and a cascade of predictions, all a man could really do was arrange his current circumstances as comfortably as possible. Regiments not lucky enough to inherit "good log shanties" abandoned by the Confederates wielded axes and once again began building winter quarters. The arrival of paymasters at least enabled more pleasant distractions. "You can scarcely imagine what a rage there is for playing cards as

---

19 Previous four paragraphs ibid., 459, 460, 461.

20 Ibid.; Carter, *Four Brothers in Blue*, 366.

21 *OR* 29, pt. 2, 471.

soon as greenbacks arrive," marveled a Massachusetts officer, noting that "the boys are gambling high to-night."[22]

With greater freedom, more pay and ready access to alcohol, commanders found alleviating the miseries of military life much easier than their enlisted men did. With the war at a standstill, men wearing shoulder straps had ample time to engage in "fun and festivity." Army headquarters wasn't immune to revelry, and Col. Lyman's journal recorded several instances of heavy drinking by staff officers and generals alike.[23]

A III Corps review on the morning of November 16 engendered an especially infamous bout of overindulgence. During a post-ceremony luncheon hosted by Gen. French, an abstaining Col. Lyman remarked that it had been a long while since he had seen "so many people" get drunk at the same time—among them Gen. Pleasonton who reduced himself to such a "decidedly boozy condition" he could barely ride back to his headquarters. Lyman concluded that "some active operations would highly benefit the army; for whiskey drinking is taken to as a defense against nothing to do," and he noted that the "great strength of the liquor" had an unsavory effect on everyone who imbibed it. However personally demeaning such behavior might be, Lyman thought it affected the rank and file far more grievously. "Nothing can be worse for the men," he wrote, "than to be deprived of drink themselves yet see their officers with too much!"[24]

Meade's reappearance at Brandy Station curbed the excess drinking while simultaneously breathing life into rumors of forthcoming "active operations." Naturally, not everyone welcomed the possibility of a year-end fight, and most troops dreaded the prospect. Meade's insistence on keeping everything keyed up and ready increased his troops' apprehensions. Few of them relished tempting fate just weeks before bad weather ended 1863's "harvest of death." Although willingly dutiful, the majority of soldiers eagerly anticipated winter quarters and the virtually guaranteed five months of life it promised, especially in regiments whose enlistments were due to expire before the 1864 spring campaign began.[25]

Little wonder then that newspaper demands for an offensive and the probability that Meade contemplated one stressed already taunt nerves. With everyone edgy even well wishes from home provoked unlikely responses. When he received a letter expressing hope for continued mild weather so that the troops might be more

22 Meier, *Memoirs of a Swiss Officer*, 132; Carter, *Four Brothers in Blue*, 366; Lewis, *Battery E, 1st Rhode Island Light Artillery*, 243.

23 McMahon, *B&L*, Vol. 4, 88; Meier, *Memoirs of a Swiss Officer*, 132.

24 Lowe, *Meade's Army*, 67.

25 Carter, *Four Brothers in Blue*, 366.

comfortable, Massachusetts infantryman George Patch reacted the way most of his comrades would have. "You say you don't want the snow to come on account of the soldiers. Now we are praying for it to come so that it will hasten us to winter quarters." Patch continued sarcastically, writing "I suppose I am not self-denying enough for my country's sake, yet the way things are conducted. . . is enough to cool the hottest patriot's adore [sic]."[26]

*   *   *

South of the Rapidan hopes for a season's repose competed with the desire to punish the Yankees for Rappahannock Station. Few Rebels believed the campaign over. Writing home from the 13th Virginia, Stanley Russell predicted that "Meade will be forced by the Yankee Administration to give us another battle this winter." Like his comrades and many other Southerners, the infantryman welcomed the possibility, certain that Lee "would gain a decisive victory, and perhaps drive" the enemy "beyond the Rappahannock." As it occurred, Jeb Stuart's cavalry chose not to await a Union advance before retaliating.[27]

Happy to be back in the field after a lengthy recovery from his Gettysburg wounds, Maj. Gen. Wade Hampton III was in a fighting mood. Although the South's wealthiest man and probably its largest slave holder, he had opposed secession until it became fact. He then threw himself and his fortune into the Confederate cause. Enlisting as a private before accepting a colonel's commission, he had raised and equipped with his own money a mixed force of cavalry, infantry, and artillery known as Hampton's Legion. Without prior military experience, the 45-year old South Carolinian soon proved himself a natural soldier. Arriving at First Manassas by train he had marched his infantry straight from its boxcars into the fight—a first in military history. His unit played a key role in the battle, earning bountiful praise for its troops and their commander, who suffered a slight head wound in the action.[28]

Promoted to brigadier in May 1862 Hampton quickly justified his new rank with a gritty performance at Seven Pines, where he refused to leave the field after taking a bullet in the foot. Though still mounted and under fire, the general instructed a surgeon to extract the round without using anesthesia, and sat motionless on his horse while the doctor dug out the projectile. That injury sidelined Hampton through June, and he missed the Seven Days battles before transferring to the cavalry in July. The general

26 George Patch to Parents, Nov. 15, 1863 George Patch Letters, VHS.

27 Carroll, *Letters of F. Stanley Russell*, 36-37; Dobbins, *Grandfathers Journal*, 169

28 Tagg, *Generals of Gettysburg*, 359-62.

Maj. Gen. Wade Hampton III
Library of Congress

found his true calling at the head of a mounted brigade and quickly earned a stellar reputation for bravery, resourcefulness, and daring. Elevated to major general in September 1863 and given command of a division in Stuart's newly created cavalry corps, the powerfully-built, luxuriously bearded cavalier approached war with somber earnestness, seeing it as an unpleasant job rather than a grand adventure.[29]

His dramatic return to the field on November 8 had bolstered troop morale, and the combative South Carolinian was eager to build on that foundation. With Stuart's permission to launch a raid across the Rapidan, Hampton issued a call for 500 volunteers from each of his three brigades—Rosser's, Young's and Gordon's—instructing everyone to assemble near Chancellorsville after dark on November 17. A little after midnight, the general led 1,500 riders toward Ely's Ford. Shortly before dawn Rebel troopers splashed across the narrow waterway and headed northwest toward Stevensburg and Kilpatrick's 3rd Cavalry Division, which remained under Custer's temporary command.[30]

The 18th Pennsylvania Cavalry's camp, located at a crossroads linking Stevensburg to Germanna and Ely's fords, lay directly in the path of the approaching Confederates. And this morning the Keystone State troopers were destined for some terrible luck. About the same time Hampton crossed Ely's Ford, the regiment, complying with Custer's order, dispatched 60 men to escort division staff officer Lt. Edward W. Whittaker in reconnoitering Germanna and Ely's fords. The detachment's original route led to Ely's from which it would then ride west to Germanna Ford. A last-minute

---

29 Hampton's Legion was broken up in 1862, the artillery becoming Hart's Battery of Horse Artillery and its cavalry companies the 2nd SC Cavalry regiment. The infantry retained Hampton's Legion name. "Hampton's Legion" https://civilwartalk.com/threads/hamptons-legion.146452/, accessed Mar.13, 2020.

30 *OR*, 29, pt. 1, 656-67; William N. McDonald, *A History of the Laurel Brigade* (Baltimore, MD, 1907), 203.

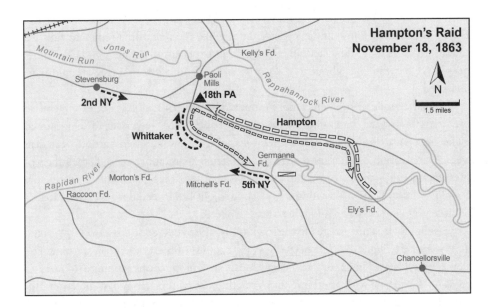

change of plans, however, reversed this itinerary and sent the troopers to Germanna Ford before swinging east to Ely's. This slight deviation launched the little contingent of Federals in the opposite direction of Hampton's oncoming cavalcade. Though that would ultimately redound to the benefit of Whittaker and his escort, it denied the remainder of the 18th Pennsylvania even accidental advance warning of impending danger.[31]

As the lieutenant and his support rode away, most of the regiment's 90 remaining men busied themselves with breakfast. Their commander, Capt. Marshall S. Kingsland, had turned everyone out early enough to have the horses saddled before any cooking was allowed. With one quarter of his strength headed toward Germanna Ford, Kingsland knew he was out on a limb. Although a squadron from the 5th New York stood watch at Germanna and there was nothing to fret about in that direction, no Federal troops picketed Ely's Ford and the possibility of an enemy movement in that sector couldn't be ignored.[32]

Fortunately, Brig. Gen. Davies knew this too, and he had directed Kingsland to pull back closer to Stevensburg as soon as his men finished breakfast. Ill disposed to taking chances, Kingsland deployed the usual vedettes and picket reserve astride the

31 OR, 29, pt. 1, 655-57; Theophilus F. Rodenbough, et al *History of the Eighteenth Regiment of Cavalry Pennsylvania Volunteers (163rd Regiment of the Line) 1862-1865* (New York, NY, 1909), 99-100; *New York Times*, Nov. 21, 1863. The regiment's camp was about 7 miles from Ely's Ford and 3 miles from Germanna Ford.

32 *OR*, 29, pt. 1, 656-57.

Ely's Ford road to sound any necessary alarm while the rest of the regiment finished eating, struck tents, and packed up. The captain's expectations of his sentinels weren't misplaced, but fate was about to cast those troopers into a scenario few could have imagined.[33]

A quarter-mile or so from camp, a mounted handful of Union vedettes shivered in pre-dawn 46-degree temperatures despite wearing wool overcoats. The mounted picket reserve of approximately 20 men standing a few hundred yards to the rear weren't comfortable either, perhaps less so because its members could smell the hot breakfast wafting over from camp. All these men had performed this kind of duty countless times. Watchful waiting was always tedious but imperative given Jeb Stuart's habit of showing up when and where least expected.[34]

As the single sentry posted in the road to Ely's Ford peered southward through the dim morning twilight, he unexpectedly saw a column of men riding toward him. The alert Pennsylvanian instantly grew suspicious. No Union troops stood guard at Ely's crossing, so no one with good intentions ought to be coming from that direction. But recalling that Lt. Whittaker's detachment had ridden out not long ago, and seeing oncoming strangers in blue overcoats, the Yankee picket hesitated a handful of seconds about what to do. His true situation didn't crystalize until the mysterious horsemen broke into a gallop. Suddenly grasping what was happening, the soldier quickly fired a shot or two then turned his horse and raced for the rear, the enemy close behind and gaining fast.[35]

Both the vedette and the pursuing Rebels were on top of the picket reserve before it knew what was happening, and it fled without offering even token resistance. Before the handful of blue troopers could reach their regiment, Hampton's vanguard caught up with them, the fleeing Yankees and pursuing Rebels merging together in a tumultuous galloping mêlée; the entire mixed mass tumbling down the road toward the 18th Pennsylvania's bivouac.[36]

Despite its brevity, that lone vedette's stand fulfilled the essential mission of warning Kingsland. At the first sound of gunfire the captain ordered his startled men to mount up. Dropping tin cups and skillets, most of the Northerners managed to leap into their saddles just as the surviving blue pickets came tearing into camp amid a tsunami of charging Confederates screeching the Rebel yell.

---

33 Ibid.

34 Ibid.; Krick, *Civil War Weather*, 112.

35 *OR*, 29, pt. 1, 656-57.

36 Ibid.

Within seconds the leading edge of 1,500 gray cavalrymen smashed into Kingsland's Pennsylvanians. What happened next was confusing and chaotic. It is unclear whether the Federals had managed to form a battle line or if the Rebel vanguard attacked in a column of fours or squadrons. But what resulted once the two forces collided is beyond doubt. A brief instant of hand-to-hand combat swirled across the intersection as at least some Yankees crossed sabers with the enemy and others hastily fired weapons into the mass of butternut uniforms. Kingsland, at the forefront of the fight, suffered a saber cut to his ear and the left side of his face before receiving another slashing blow on his back as he turned to retreat.[37]

Outnumbered more than ten to one, Federal resistance quickly buckled, and those who could spurred their horses and ran for dear life, some on foot and others on unsaddled mounts. A few fled without having time to put on their boots, while at least one unfortunate soul caught using the latrine didn't even find time to pull up his pants before skedaddling with his "shirt tail out." Only a few brutal moments sent what survived of Kingsland's command scurrying toward Stevensburg, with volunteers from Rosser's brigade hotly pursuing for a short distance.[38]

Unfortunately for the 18th Pennsylvania, its travails were hardly over. Upon hearing firing from the regiment's camp, now nearly two miles away, Lt. Whittaker and his 60-man escort riding toward Germanna Ford immediately turned around and retraced their steps. Moving with all the speed they could muster they couldn't escape the sinking feeling that something very bad must have happened. Nearing their destination, the blue troopers spotted a line of Rebel cavalrymen Hampton had positioned just west of the road to safeguard against Yankee intervention from Germanna Ford.[39]

Surprised to find the enemy in "regimental strength" and waiting with drawn sabers, some of Whittaker's men opened an ineffectual "random" fire which only drew Rebel attention and incited a charge. In the face of this onslaught, the Pennsylvanians "resorted to the only means left them" by scattering into the woods east of the road, where most of them eluded capture.[40]

---

37 Ibid.; *New York Times*, Nov. 21, 1863.Besides Kingsland's wounds, Pvt. Daniel Carbaugh received a saber cut on the head and Sgt. Charles P. Sheafe a pistol gunshot in the right arm.

38 McDonald, *Laurel Brigade*, 204; Richard M. Coffman, *Going Back the Way They Came: The Phillip's Legion Cavalry Battalion* (Macon, GA, 2011), 61. Civil War armies referred to latrines as sinks.

39 *OR*, 29, pt. 1, 656-57; *New York Times*, Nov. 21, 1863.

40 *OR*, 29, pt. 1, 656-57; Clark, *NC Regts*, Vol. 3, 585; *New York Times*, Nov. 21, 1863. Not all the Yankees got away. Thirty-two-year old Second Lieutenant Roseberry Sellers of Company A, 18th PA CAV took a bullet through the head. He survived long enough to be placed in an

The fighting closed with that retreat. Darkness and surprise had enabled the Rebels to execute a masterful stroke. Now they turned to reaping its rewards, gathering up prisoners and spoils prior to carrying their loot behind the Rapidan. Hampton, however, wasn't quite done. To foil mischance he had ordered a "considerable force" of cavalry and three guns to assemble on Germanna Ford's south bank. From all indications, the general wouldn't need these troopers north of the river, but they still might help him gobble up whatever Yankees guarded the crossing on his way home.[41]

*   *   *

Kingsland had no idea of Rebel intentions as he pushed his battered command toward Stevensburg. To his relief, the enemy had abandoned pursuit a short distance from the captured camp. Because they might renew the chase at any moment, the captain rode on, hoping to alert Custer's division as soon as possible.

Happily, help was already on the way. A couple of miles above its lost bivouac, Kingsland's column encountered Lt. Col. Harhaus's 2nd New York Cavalry heading south. Davies had sent it out earlier that morning to escort the Eighteenth to a more secure campground nearer Stevensburg. Learning what had just happened to the disheveled Pennsylvanians, and undaunted by their accounts of Rebel numbers, Harhaus decided to press on and confront the enemy. Capt. Kingsland and his troopers, hungry for revenge, agreed to go along.[42]

Much to their disappointment, although undoubtedly also to their profit, the Yankees found only a small Rebel rearguard lingering in the Eighteenth's ransacked camp. The other raiders had long gone; Hampton having split his force in two, sending one column with the captured vehicles to Ely's Ford and another to Germanna Ford, where he hoped to destroy whatever enemy formation picketed the crossing. Unfortunately for these aspirations Capt. Luke McGuinn's 5th New York squadron at the ford didn't surprise easily. Noticing the concentrating enemy strength across the river and learning what had happened to the 18th Pennsylvania from Whittaker's

---

ambulance but soon died of his wounds without regaining consciousness. Sellers had just passed his 10th wedding anniversary on November 1. His 33-year old wife, Mary, was left alone to care for three children—two boys ages 9 and 7 and one girl, age 6. She applied for and the US Government granted her a $15 a month pension in 1864. Civil War Widows pensions on Fold3.com https://www.fold3.com/image/263331865, accessed Mar. 28, 2020.

41 McDonald, *Laurel Brigade*, 204; Clark, *NC Regts*, Vol. 3, 585.

42 *OR*, 29, pt. 1, 656-57; Rodenbough, *Eighteenth Regiment of Cavalry Pennsylvania Volunteers*, 99-100; *New York Times*, Jan. 23, 1864.

fugitive escort, the 32-year old officer decided to pull his men away from the Rapidan and what looked like certain trouble.[43]

The wisdom of that move soon became apparent when Wade Hampton came sweeping down on Germanna Ford with hundreds of gray cavalrymen. Disappointed that his target had flown, Hampton led his men over the river. By 10:30 a.m. the attackers were south of the Rapidan and reveling in their adventure. Having lost only one man killed and two wounded, the Rebels had slain one Federal, wounded three others, and captured something like 40 men, among them an assistant surgeon and a paymaster holding a satchel full of Union greenbacks. In addition to the money, which Southern troopers divided among themselves, the Confederates had made off with 83 horses, 10 mules, and an ambulance, a hospital wagon, an army wagon, a forge, assorted tents and other baggage, plus the Pennsylvanians' national and regimental colors. Hampton sent the latter to Richmond for display in the Virginia State House.[44]

For Federal cavalrymen it had been a highly embarrassing episode, occurring just a day shy of the one-month anniversary of Kilpatrick's October debacle at Buckland Mills. Most Northern newspapers took little note of the incident, but Pleasonton demanded an explanation for what had gone wrong. Both Davies and Custer produced written reports on the very day the action took place. The former found no fault with the 18th Pennsylvania or Capt. Kingsland, blaming their defeat on the scattered nature of his regiment.[45]

Custer tried to put a brighter face on the affair, claiming Harhaus's 2nd New York had "closely pursued" the withdrawing Confederates and "driven" them back over the Rapidan. That was nonsense. Union troopers hadn't chased Hampton in any meaningful sense and he had escaped with all his booty. Pleasonton chided Custer for drawing Whittaker's escort from a regiment assigned outpost duty but otherwise let the matter drop, no doubt happy to have it receive as little attention as possible.[46]

*   *   *

---

43 OR, 29, pt. 1, 655-57.

44 Ibid., 656-57; Ulysses R. Brooks, *Stories of the Confederacy* (Columbia, SC, 1912), 213; Clark, *NC Regts*, Vol. 3, 585.

45 Hunt, *Meade and Lee at Bristoe Station*, 397-428 is a full account of the October 19, 1863 fight at Buckland Mills (or Buckland Races).

46 OR, 29, pt. 1, 655-57. On November 21, 1863 *New York Times* carried an article on the fight which called Hampton's Raid a "most miserably conducted" affair because it failed to capture the entire 18th PA.

Beyond its bountiful capture of animals and other supplies Hampton's foray amplified tensions along the Rapidan front. Raid participant Pvt. John T. Swan of the Phillip's Legion Cavalry (Young's brigade) declared that the expedition had "stirred up the whole army." With picket fighting "happening almost every day," he believed another campaign more likely than ever.[47]

Northern editors saw things differently. Meade's failure to follow up his Rappahannock Station victory had resurrected familiar complaints about the general's perceived lethargy. *Harper's Weekly* bemoaned a lack of AOP action despite Federal troops being in "good spirits and eager for a fight." Yankee correspondents reported that Meade's command was "very large—as large as it was at Gettysburg," and passed along rumors that while some officers estimated Lee's strength at 70,000 others thought it "less than half" that number. And yet the Army of the Potomac, which hadn't moved for ten days, appeared "once more stuck in the mud—in which unhappy state it has spent a large portion of its existence."[48]

This sentiment didn't prevail between the Rappahannock and the Rapidan, however. Talkative aides and officers privy to pieces of the strategic debate between Meade and Washington speculated openly about pending plans, often citing outdated or incomplete information. Although many enlisted men still believed winter quarters nigh, Meade's staff suspected he wasn't yet ready to settle down to year end slumbers. Headquarters clerk Thomas Carpenter noted gossip claiming the general had said "that when he gets ready to move he will compel [the Rebels] to abandon their works without a battle."[49]

Brigadier General Patrick had heard such talk too, though unlike Carpenter, he had an incontrovertible informant. In his diary on November 19, he reported that Meade "says we will strike out very soon and he rather thinks we will cut loose from this line entirely." But the fiery 52-year old New Yorker didn't quite believe his old Academy classmate:

> I cannot make out his plans because he cannot make them out himself. He does not want to move until he knows everything. Without a shadow of proof, he insists that Lee has 80,000 troops, when even in Richmond, Lee's force is not put beyond 40,000 and we have every reason to believe that to be 5,000, 10,000 or even 15,000 too large an estimate.[50]

47 Coffman, *Going Back the Way They Came*, 61.

48 *Harper's Weekly*, December 5, 1863; *New York Times*, Nov. 21, 1863.

49 Thomas Carpenter to "Phil," Nov. 13, 1863, Carpenter Letters, MHS.

50 Sparks, *Inside Lincoln's Army*, 310; OR 29, pt. 2, 866. The ANV's returns on December 10 showed 57,418 men present; 42,000 were infantry.

Although Patrick's assessment of Confederate strength was inaccurate—in early December the ANV recorded 57,000 men present for duty—his criticisms weren't groundless. At the climax of Lee's October offensive, Meade claimed he had faced 80,000 Rebels, to which Halleck retorted that intelligence reports from Richmond credited Lee with only 55,000 men. In the face of the general-in-chief's remarkably precise count, the AOP's commander refused to alter his appraisal of enemy strength. Perhaps this resulted from his own reluctance to launch an operation without a clear numerical advantage and his inability to envision Lee acting otherwise.[51]

Whatever his logic, Meade understood that in initiating a campaign meant assuming the tactical offensive against a foe he felt sure would fight from behind earthworks. Even with only 55,000 Rebels south of the Rapidan, the general didn't think the AOP's 95,455 men provided the kind of infantry superiority needed for "offensive moves against strong positions." Together with Meade's concern over dwindling Union manpower and his doubts that the draft could replenish it, his viewpoint demanded he prepare for every eventuality before committing troops to battle. Having to operate on an axis of advance he disapproved only stiffened his resolve. If he were going to fight despite these obstacles, Meade insisted on putting in place anything that might empower his army to achieve something decisive and justify the heavy losses sure to accompany a major engagement.[52]

Accomplishing this required thorough and time-consuming preparation. Meade knew others would interpret all this as unwillingness to fight or a reluctance to run risks, but he didn't care. The army would move when everything was ready and its chance for success maximized, not a minute sooner. Just what it would do once it advanced he had not firmly decided. He was nonetheless committed to launching an offensive at the first practicable moment, even if his definition of practicable wasn't uniformly accepted.

Until such time Meade would not share his plans with anyone who didn't need to know. With no official word from headquarters, the bulk of the army's troops slipped into routine camp life. Unaffected by the cavalry's daily scuffles, they continued constructing winter quarters or fixing up captured Confederate cabins. As always drill, roll calls, and fatigue duty consumed much of the day. Occasional rain and a spate of grand reviews broke the monotony. French had held one such event on November 16 and Warren another two days later. Sedgwick followed suit on November 20 with an impressive VI Corps display attended by Gen. Meade and accompanied by a

---

51 OR 29, pt. 2, 326, 328.

52 Aggassiz, Meade's Army, 38-40.

"sumptuous lunch" replete with a "huge amount of champagne and punch" afterwards.[53]

Returning to his headquarters from these festivities a little before noon, Meade sat down to write a telegram updating Halleck on the state of things in Culpeper County. Lee's army remained behind the Rapidan, its right flank at Germanna Ford and its left near Orange Court House. The Confederates had strongly fortified all the river crossings and held each with plentiful force. Meade suspected that Lee had ordered Hampton's recent raid to ascertain whether the AOP was moving against the Rebel right, which Meade incorrectly reported as near Germanna, not Morton's Ford.

About the timing and nature of his upcoming offensive, the general said he needed to tie up logistical lose ends and receive additional reconnaissance reports before moving. Although repair crews had finished rebuilding the O&A on November 9, heavy rains five days later had washed out sections of track. Consequently, the railway was "not yet in good working order." Meade expected completion of additional repairs within a day or two, by which time his cavalry should have concluded its final examination of the Rapidan.

"As soon as the army is fully supplied, I shall move forward," Meade promised, "turning either the right or left flank of the enemy." He strongly leaned toward attacking the eastern end of Lee's line since a thrust in that direction would not "uncover my rear or communications and in the case of failure enables the withdrawal of the army without difficulty." That meant moving by Germanna and Ely's fords, both of which Pleasonton's troopers were currently scouting. Once Meade had their reports and railroad repairs allowed Union quartermasters to fill their coffers, he would "decide which movement to make and at once proceed to its execution."

A few hours later George Custer reported on the crossings in question. No Rebel troops occupied either site, both of which were fordable. Equally important, the roads leading to and from the river were "in excellent condition." With this news Meade could finally see an unopposed way around Lee's flank. That same day O&A repair crews completed their work, and locomotives shifted the last boxcars of supplies from Warrenton Junction to Brandy Station.[54]

With all its requirements in place the AOP was finally ready to move. Despite the wistful hopes of soldiers on both sides, yet one more campaign remained before 1863 faded into 1864. What would happen when Meade threw his men across the Rapidan was of course unknown, but with Lee having already predicted his foe's intentions, a battle was almost inevitable.

53 Ibid., 405; Lowe, *Meade's Army*, 38, 69.

54 *OR* 29, pt. 2, 474-75.

On Saturday, November 21, a day-long storm dumped nearly an inch of water on central Virginia. The troops, as ever, suffered through the downpour as best they could. The superstitious discerned ill tidings in the rain, however, which came down "red, as if it were blood." Although easily explained as red soil born aloft by some distant wind and now brought to earth by precipitation, the crimson downpour was an unnerving sight nonetheless. "If I believed in omens, I would be frightened," one Confederate confided to his diary.[55]

Dread was justified. In the four months since Gettysburg neither Lee nor Meade had gained a meaningful advantage in their long running chess match. But if the final weeks of 1863 offered a chance for one more fight, both stood ready to take it, Lee to avenge his string of minor defeats since Gettysburg and Meade to finish what he had started there. Within the week something far worse than auburn rain would wash across Virginia's already blood soaked soil.

55 Krick, *Civil War Weather*, 112 (like the temperature readings, the precipitation records in Krick's book were measured at Georgetown); Dobbins, *Grandfather's Journal*, 169.

Chapter 13

"Too Great a Reliance"

Official Reports—Explaining Rappahannock Station—Lee's Generalship—Sedgwick's
Successful Failure—Unexploited Victory—Meade's Generalship

LIKE George Meade, Robert E. Lee spent part of November 20 writing to his boss. Rather than muse about an upcoming offensive, however, he faced the distasteful task of finishing his account of Rappahannock Station for Jefferson Davis. The general's November 10 preliminary report had delivered a basic outline, but once his officers' official statements came to hand Lee had constructed a lengthier postmortem.[1]

The reports written by Capt. Massie, Col. Stallings, and Capt. John C. McMillian thoroughly explained the encounter at Kelly's Ford. In his overview Rodes lauded the 2nd North Carolina for its stubborn defense while noting that the 30th North Carolina hadn't sustained "its reputation." The division commander refrained from blaming Lt. Col. Sillers for his regiment's performance and graciously offered no judgement about the dead leader's dubious decision to reinforce Kellysville.[2]

---

1 OR 29, pt. 1, 610-17. Ewell, Early, Rodes, Hays and Tate (writing for Hoke's brigade) each submitted statements on the action, all of which were at Army HQ by November 11 or 12. Capt. Jason M. Carrington, commanding Jones' Artillery Battalion submitted a statistical account of the LA Guard Artillery's role in the battle on November 21. The only regimental reports in the OR are from the 2nd (McMillian) and 30th NC (Stallings). Lee's account of Rappahannock Station was twice as long as his report on the entire Bristoe Station campaign.

2 Ibid., 630-33, 636; OR Supplement V, Pt. 1, 609-12. Capt. McMillian assumed command of the 30th NC Infantry after Lt. Col. Seller's death and wrote the regiment's report on Kelly's Ford.

Hays provided a forthright account of Rappahannock Station in which he stressed the good conduct of his troops. Postulating that they had inflicted heavy loss on the enemy, he explained their defeat by comparing his command's small size with the "20,000 to 25,000" Federals sent against it. As the ranking survivor in Hoke's brigade, Col. Tate wrote just three paragraphs, mostly chronicling the 6th and 57th North Carolina's final stand under Col. Godwin. He said nothing about that officer's refusal to attempt a breakout toward the pontoon bridge. Although Tate offered no cause for the bridgehead's loss, he strongly implied that his men weren't responsible for its fate, since they had barely deployed into the trenches when the action began.[3]

Predictably, Early's report ran long—eight pages in the postwar official records as compared to Lee's four pages. After giving an extremely detailed, almost minute-by-minute version of his division's part in the battle, as well as his own movements, the general spent an entire page expounding upon the defeat's origins. Declaring that he and his men had done everything possible to win the day, Early blamed the bridgehead's capture on its poorly designed earthworks, a failure to employ more artillery along the Rapidan's south shore, reliance on a single pontoon bridge to support the position, and assigning too few defenders to the post.

Summoning his pre-war talents as a prosecuting attorney, Early subtly tried shifting some culpability from his shoulders. Pointing out that he had complained about the bridgehead's shortcomings before the battle, he also noted that Lee, although on the scene, hadn't intervened in the conduct of operations. Early correctly maintained that his superior had no more foreseen the Federal assault than he had, going on to write, "I must candidly confess that I did concur in the opinion of the commanding general that the enemy did not have enterprise enough to attempt any serious attack after dark." But having obliquely questioned Lee's judgment, Early deftly sidestepped actual condemnation, saying he didn't believe any alternate appraisal of Yankee intentions would have prevented the catastrophe.[4]

Richard Ewell allowed his subordinates' detailed reports to document Second Corps actions on November 7. The general penned a single covering paragraph when he forwarded Early's manuscript explaining that with Lee and Early both at Rappahannock Station, he had turned his "whole attention" to the Yankee crossing at Kelly's Ford. Ewell rejected the alleged inadequacy of the earthworks as a contributing factor to the bridgehead debacle. Noting that he had "paid frequent visits" to the position upon whose fortifications "much labor had been bestowed," the general

3   OR 29, pt. 2, 626-30.

4   Previous paragraphs based on OR 29, pt. 2, 618-26. Most officers at Ewell's and Early's HQ cited poorly designed earthworks as the reason for their defeat. None of them ever explained why they hadn't seen or corrected those deficiencies before the battle.

implied he hadn't found its defenses wanting. Ewell also contested Early's assertion that more south bank artillery would have made a difference. Remarking that darkness and terrain had rendered the guns already on site of "little use during the final attack," he argued that additional fieldpieces saddled with the same impediments would not have altered the battle's result.

Lee let these accounts stand as the official version of events and incorporated them into his own report, adding only some strategic context to the fighting. He agreed with his officers that their troops had performed beyond reproach, and observed that darkness, noise-cancelling winds, and topographic features all contributed to the enemy's success. Refusing to discount Early's critique of the bridgehead defenses or echo Ewell's implied approval of their construction, Lee said that though the works were "slight," he thought them adequate to their purpose. His only overt criticism was the failure of Hays and Godwin to maintain an early-warning line of sharpshooters in front of the breastworks—an erroneous assessment given the battle's actual evolution.[5]

Those hoping Lee's official report would assign blame for Rappahannock Station were disappointed. The general had never envisioned holding the bridgehead against overwhelming force but rather expected its defenders to fall back under covering fire from south bank artillery if so confronted. Since he had witnessed the fighting, any failure to reinforce or withdraw the garrison ultimately rested on his shoulders, and Lee "rather intimated" to his staff that blame for the defeat "must attach" to him.[6]

*   *   *

Shouldering responsibility as befitted an army commander was admirable, but it didn't answer the principal question hanging in the air after Rappahannock Station: was the disaster preventable? Early maintained that poorly designed earthworks meant "inevitable" Federal success once they decided to attack. If this were true, faulty engineering alongside command failure to recognize and correct the resulting weaknesses had planted the seeds of defeat long before November 7. Harry Hays thought overwhelming odds, not deficient fortifications, had brought the ANV's misfortune. Theoretically Lee and Early should have recognized both those threats and withdrawn the garrison before the Federal attack.

But is that supposition accurate? Abatis, defensive ditches, higher parapets, better-constructed gun emplacements, and properly-sited rifle pits undoubtedly would

5   Ibid., p. 1, 611-16, 618.

6   Ibid., 613; Hotchkiss, *Make Me A Map*, 181-82.

have made Rappahannock Station much more difficult to overrun. Some or all these features might have dissuaded the Yankees from even attempting an assault. Additional batteries on the Rapidan's southern shore would have likely been ineffectual against a dusk attack, but extra guns and another regiment or two inside the works might have boosted its defense immeasurably. A wall of canister fire to break up any probable assault or an infantry reserve to immediately plug ruptures in the bridgehead's perimeter could have redressed the balance of forces. It is intriguing to speculate about how the presence of Brig. Gen. Hoke and his missing regiment might have changed the result on November 7.[7]

Most of Early's critiques were valid. Those who thought the Confederates should have reinforced the bridgehead more robustly or ordered up more artillery advanced reasonable arguments. But did the high command's failure to do these things doom the position? Evidently not, at least in the precise way it was lost.

The ANV's dogged supply challenges cancelled any chance of getting additional artillery to Rappahannock Station on November 7. The pastures around Brandy Station barely sufficed to feed quartermaster livestock and the horses of the three batteries under Dance, Graham, and Moore kept near the river. With the O&A straining to bring up rations, tasking the railroad with large shipments of fodder beyond Culpeper Court House was out of the question. Hence Lee's positioning Stuart's main cavalry force near the town and Ewell's five artillery battalions several miles south of there on the old Cedar Mountain battlefield.[8]

While this simplified feeding animals and distributing whatever grain the trains brought, it also meant ANV guns would need five or six hours to reach the Rappahannock. Ewell had summoned his batteries soon after the Yankees launched their Kelly's Ford assault, but the time required to relay that message and get the fieldpieces on the road meant French was already laying pontoon bridges before the cannons rolled out of camp. It was almost 8 p.m. when they reached Stevensburg at the end of their 11-mile march. With Cedar Mountain 18 miles distant from

---

7 Gen. Hoke and his 21st NC had been detached home in September 1863 to round up deserters and enforce conscription. Note that putting another battery in the works would have precluded additional infantry, since there was only so much space along the perimeter for units to occupy. Likewise, the shallowness of the bridgehead restricted how many troops could camp inside the perimeter, limiting the size of its garrison and the number of additional units that could squeeze into the position.

8 Agassiz, *Meade's Headquarters*, 46-47. A. P. Hill's guns bivouacked close to the Third Corps infantry northwest of Culpeper. In a Nov. 13, 1863 letter home Col. Lyman remarked that "there isn't a thing to eat" in the "desolate" area between Culpeper Court House and the Rappahannock, noting that an army operating in such a "desert region" had to haul in by rail "every pound of meat and quart of oats" it consumed (citation in above).

Rappahannock Station, the clock would have struck 10 p.m. or even later before any batteries neared there, far too late to take part in the battle. Hill's artillery would have needed almost as much time to reach the field.[9]

Might better fortifications have altered the battle's result? Although the entrenchments did have flaws, Lee correctly appraised their defects as not necessarily fatal. Sedgwick, Wright, and Sykes judged the works and the approach to them daunting enough to discourage assault—an opinion Wright abandoned only at Russell's urging and when darkness rendered such an effort nearly impossible. Doubtless Rappahannock Station's breastworks were at least as stout as the field fortifications soldiers on both sides employed to slaughter attackers on other occasions during the war. Despite lack of defensive ditches or other such features, Hays' Louisianans stopped the 6th Maine's initial assault while Capt. Fish's New Yorkers managed a lodgment only where roads broke up the perimeter trenches.

The arrival of follow-on assault waves and the unplanned charge of V Corps skirmishers had tipped the battle in favor of the Federals, though admittedly the deficiencies catalogued by Gen. Early made their job easier. Since attackers didn't outnumber defenders, the success of these additional assault troops depended almost entirely on deepening nightfall and the psychological impact Sedgwick's ostentatious deployment of two corps made upon the Confederates earlier that day.

Twilight prevented Rebel troops from accurately assessing how many Yankees attacked the bridgehead. This, along with the speed and breadth of the assault across the entire center and right of the bridgehead, kept Hays and Godwin—both without reserves—from mounting a meaningful counterattack and undermined the morale of those regiments not directly engaged. Dimly witnessing multiple formations of attackers charging the large fort plus knowing that 20,000 more Yankees were nearby, the defenders assumed resistance futile in the face of an enemy using his immense strength to hurl overwhelming numbers against the bridgehead. This resulted in the quick surrender or collapse of units holding the position's flanks once the large redoubt fell.[10]

If the Federals had attacked in daylight with the same force using the same tactics, the Confederates could have correctly judged the nature of the assault and likely beaten it back. General Russell's decision to strike at dusk laid the foundation for Union success, both by shielding the small size of his attacking force and undermining the

---

9 Dozier, ed., *A Gunner in Lee's Army*, 216; Runge, ed., *Four Years in the Confederate Artillery*, 60.

10 Agassiz, *Meade's Headquarters*, 46. Col. Lyman heard first-hand accounts of the Rappahannock Station attack and emphasized the role morale played in the battle. Referencing the bridgehead's fortifications he wrote "we took part of them and scared [the Rebels] out of the rest." (See above citation.)

defenders' confidence by conjuring visions of endless Yankee hordes. Neither the garrison's size nor defects in its fortifications determined the struggle's outcome. Rather, the twilight assault in successive waves, with the unintended participation of V Corps skirmishers, against an enemy already rattled by Sedgwick's display of immense strength, led to Federal victory despite even odds and the failure of Russell's initial attack wave.

*   *   *

Still it is impossible to argue against the proposition that Rebel commanders left Rappahannock Station more vulnerable than it need have been and thus diluted the attackers' challenges. Confederate engineers could have implemented at least some of the defensive improvements Early recommended as well as others he didn't, such as chevaux-de-friese, gabions, or similar mobile devices to obstruct roads piercing the perimeter. If engineers weren't available, men from regiments occupying the bridgehead could have done the work. Certainly by this point in the war, Southern soldiers had acquired enough expertise constructing fieldworks that improving Rappahannock Station's earthen defenses didn't require special engineer details.[11]

It can be easily surmised that units assigned to the bridgehead didn't carry out defensive renovations because they spent only a week at a time in the position, and most of them spent that interval deployed well in front of the fortifications. Given Ewell's rotation of brigades between Johnson's and Early's divisions, once a command had occupied the works it wouldn't have another turn in the emplacements for two months or more. No brigade, then, could have felt ownership of the bridgehead or seen improving its defenses as vital to its own safety.

Only general officers had the authority to overcome these complications, yet Confederate leaders seem to have taken a laissez faire attitude toward the post despite its importance in their overall strategy. Notwithstanding his self-reported complaints to engineers supervising bridgehead construction, Early never claimed to have pushed the issue with his superiors. As commander of the corps charged with defending the bridgehead, Ewell had primary responsibility for ensuring its readiness to repel assault.

---

11 Unfortunately, the historical record has yet to produce any clues about who built the fortifications, who supervised the work, whether additional construction had been planned, when the project began, or when it ended. Therefore, we have no way to discern the reasoning behind what was done or left undone, the resources and time available to erect the entrenchments, or possible responses to Early's complaints about their inadequacy. Rebel engineers might have planned to do some of this work but if so, they didn't accomplish it before the battle. There is nothing yet found in the historical record to confirm or deny this possibility.

He admitted visiting the site often, observing the immense amount of labor expended upon the position, and finding no fault with its results.[12]

That left Lee as the only person who might have noticed shortfalls in the earthworks and ordered them corrected. However, no record of his inspecting the fortifications exists. Poor health in the form of serious back pain, loosely diagnosed as "rheumatism," probably accounts for this uncharacteristically lackadaisical approach. It had forced him to ride in an ambulance for the first couple of days of his October offensive. Even after returning to horseback, he had suffered great pain with every movement.

We don't know how long that condition persisted; at some point the affliction became bearable. When Lee ate dinner with his son Robert on October 20, the young enlisted cannoneer thought his father looked well. Six days later the commanding general noted his earlier indisposition in a letter to Longstreet, stressing that though he felt "rather better now" he was "still suffering." That Lee's back issues vigorously returned during the first four days of November is certain. Indeed, they rendered him incapable of even mounting a horse, let alone riding miles to scrutinize Rappahannock Station personally. Whether or not this represented a missed opportunity can't be certain, but one can hardly blame Lee for relying on Ewell to ensure the position maintained a proper defensive posture.[13]

*   *   *

Nevertheless, the overall strategy for holding and using the bridgehead belonged to Lee alone, and his operational concept was quite clear. The north shore earthworks existed to pose a continual threat to Meade's communications if he tried moving southeast to Fredericksburg or assaulted the Rappahannock line. Correctly expecting his opponent to choose assault over maneuver by crossing at Kelly's Ford, Lee anticipated Meade's deploying a considerable force to mask the bridgehead, dividing his command in the process. Once a significant part of the Union army forded the river near Kellysville, Lee intended to throw almost his entire weight against whichever half of Meade's army offered the best target.

The Virginian leaned toward striking at Kelly's Ford. One of his favorite stratagems throughout the war was attempting to use waterways to isolate portions of enemy armies and then annihilate them with overpowering numbers. He had first employed this tactic at Gaines's Mill in June 1862 and would famously try it again along

12 OR 29, pt. 1, 618.

13 OR 52, pt. 2, 549-50; Robert E. Lee, Jr., *Recollections and Letters*, 114.

the North Anna River in late May 1864. Driving a beaten enemy against a river and endeavoring to destroy him there was a strategy staple for Civil War generals, and one Virginia's geography encouraged Lee to pursue several times, albeit never successfully.[14]

Beyond doubt, the ANV's commander was prepared to employ this tactic near Kelly's Ford. On October 20 he and Ewell spent the morning examining the area and formulating defensive plans. Lee referred several times in his official report to pre-plotted positions, intentions and counter-movements for responding to a possible Federal thrust near Kellysville. The swift Confederate reaction to French's attack on November 7—Rodes occupying a selected line some miles from the river, the rapid shift of Johnson's division to his aid, Ewell's assuming overall direction of the defense—bespoke implementation of a well-plotted contingency operation.[15]

Confederate movements at Rappahannock Station don't leave the same impression. Of the two divisions that responded to Sedgwick's advance, Early's and Anderson's, neither deployed its full strength along the river. After detailing single brigades to defend Norman's and Beverly fords, most of their troops retired several miles and went into bivouac. The movement of Hoke's (Godwin's) regiments into the bridgehead was the sole reinforcement Hays received, and even that maneuver surprised Lee, who clearly hadn't decided by late afternoon how vigorously to defend his north bank bastion.

At first glance all this suggests indecision. But that was hardly the case. Unlike Kelly's Ford, where Federal movements were highly predictable and the response to them readily planned, the enemy had a lot more options near Rappahannock Station. Correctly deducing Meade's intention was fundamental to Lee's strategy and explains why he rode north to the bridgehead instead of east to Kelly's Ford where both he and Meade expected the real battle.

The presence of two Yankee corps at Rappahannock Station meant that Lee's bridgehead gambit had forced Meade to divide his army as anticipated. The Rebel aim now was to keep Sedgwick's wing in place with minimal force, while the rest of the army attacked French near Kellysville. Time meant everything in pursuing that goal. Meade wouldn't keep his army separated indefinitely, and once most of it concentrated south of the river, Lee's chances of winning whatever fight developed would markedly decrease. In short, the Rebels, with a narrow interval in which to act, widened their opening the longer they pinned down half the AOP at Rappahannock Station.

---

14 Lee had endeavored to destroy significant parts of the AOP in this fashion at Chancellorsville and Salem Church.

15 *OR* 29, pt. 1, 612, 615-16: McDonald, *Make Me a Map*, 179.

Doing this required Lee to assume the role of military wizard: ostensibly confronting the enemy everywhere but in reality, just distracting him at one place while hammering him at another. Unable to launch an offensive out of the bridgehead against two Union corps and resolutely refusing to fight a hopeless battle to hold the position, Lee still had to appear threatening enough there to immobilize Sedgwick's force. In this regard the cautious, time-consuming Yankee approach to Rappahannock Station proved most helpful to the Rebels. Sedgwick's decision to merely shove Hays' skirmishers inside their earthworks before trying to shell the Rebels out of their trenches was everything Confederate generals could have asked for, and it shored up Lee's confidence about maintaining his north bank ruse until at least sometime after sunset. Once night fell, he could decide exactly how to assail Meade's army. This strategy set up a bold, dangerous game that relied on Lee's ability to seize the initiative and his confidence in Northern generals being too slow or careful to derail his plans.

Up until the moment Russell's assault destroyed the bridgehead and its threat to Meade's army, Lee's gamble played out almost exactly according to plan. The scheme's what-might-have-beens are irrelevant of course, but the Confederate plan had a reasonable chance of success if the ANV moved faster than the AOP and Southern attackers prevailed against their foes. Of course, Lee's decision to fight at the northern edge of the Culpeper 'V' courted risk, but he had taken far greater risks at Chancellorsville and on the Peninsula in June 1862. Both had paid off spectacularly. By comparison, his Rappahannock strategy was only a couple of rungs above routine.

*   *   *

Given the above it is hard to criticize Lee's performance on November 7. He had anticipated the Federal campaign and developed a typically bold program to defeat it. Although the timing of Meade's offensive came as something of a surprise, its character did not. After an initial scramble to meet the foe's unexpected appearance, everything went mostly as Lee desired. Rodes, Johnson, and Ewell swiftly implemented a pre-planned response at Kellysville, while Lee scrutinized events at Rappahannock Station, preserving his army's flexibility while gauging his opponent's intentions.

Right up until Yankee troops shattered the bridgehead's perimeter, Lee had every reason to believe his foes were behaving exactly as he expected. Given Meade's angst about attacking across the Rappahannock, and Sedgwick's reluctance to assault the bridgehead, it is difficult to argue that Lee underestimated his opponents. Indeed, every Yankee officer confronting Early's fortifications except Albion Howe and David Russell viewed them as virtually impregnable. It wasn't Meade's audacity that Lee and his commanders misjudged on November 7 but, rather, that of Russell and Horatio Wright.[16]

Their twilight attack pulled the rug out from under everything the ANV was trying to achieve, not only upending Lee's strategy but negating all he had accomplished so far to produce the kind of battle he wanted. By converting a promising situation into a forced retreat, the Yankees added Rappahannock Station to a growing list of Rebel defeats and barred its inscription on the honor roll of Lee's triumphs.

Since the Confederates apparently did everything right until the 6th Maine and its adjacent units charged, the only remaining question is whether someone in Rebel leadership should have foreseen such a threat and better prepared to meet it. In his post-war memoirs Early claimed that Southern commanders had placed "too great [a] reliance" on the enemy's lack of "audacity" and "want of enterprise" at Rappahannock Station—an echo of his wartime belief that the enemy didn't "have enterprise enough to attempt any serious attack after dark."[17]

Indeed, as evening fell on November 7, 1863, hardly anyone in gray anticipated a Federal attack, especially since the Yankees had done nothing that afternoon but displace some skirmishers and seize ground for Union artillery. Sedgwick's failure to strike despite punishing numerical superiority strongly suggested he wouldn't attack. Under such circumstances, any Rebel concerns about a possible twilight assault conducted by one brigade would have seemed ridiculous to a rational observer.[18]

To their surprise, however, that is exactly what the enemy did. Lee didn't blame his subordinates for the stunning defeat that ensued because they hadn't done anything fundamentally wrong. Despite intimating to his staff that responsibility for the defeat was his, Lee didn't really appear to think he had failed either, despite feeling the loss of two brigades and the sting of defeat most acutely. What happened at the bridgehead resulted from a unique confluence of circumstances that first undermined the defenders' morale and then enabled enterprising Union officers to launch a well-executed attack at an unexpected time, in an environment that cloaked their thrust from all but those actually facing it. Excellent leadership, hard fighting, good tactics, guile, courage, a little luck, and defects in the Rebel earthworks did the rest.[19]

---

16 OR 29, pt. 1, 586. Howe was the first officer to suggest the bridgehead vulnerable to attack, but when he begged permission to launch an assault, Wright had turned him down.

17 Ibid., 625; Early, *Autobiographical Sketch and Narrative*, 316.

18 Hays' and Godwin's troops remained alert and, though momentarily surprised by the attack, recovered quickly enough to stop the 6th ME's first effort at entering the works.

19 Flemming Saunders to Mother, Nov. 21, 1863, Saunders Family Papers, VHS.

Notwithstanding the setback, the Confederate response to their bridgehead's fall was impressive. Lee reacted decisively, holding his troops in place long enough to get his wagons packed and on their way before shifting the army to a new line above Culpeper Court House. Quartermasters and teamsters did an outstanding job of quickly loading and hauling off vital supplies. Despite unexpected orders to retreat, Rebel troops and their officers conducted an orderly withdrawal and speedily constructed a serviceable line of entrenchments before the Union army had even begun a pursuit.

Aided by Meade's decision making, Stuart's horsemen adroitly kept the enemy away from the ANV's main line long enough to significantly reduce any possibility of a Yankee attack on November 8, while Brig. Gen. Lane's infantry and supporting artillery bloodied Federal noses near Rixeyville. After offering battle for an entire day, the Confederates conducted a disciplined retreat to the Rapidan which they swiftly deployed to defend. The nighttime withdrawal wasn't without its confusions or hardships, but at least it wasn't as chaotic as that of the army's supply trains, which had retreated with unseemly but necessary haste. Nonetheless, Lee's soldiers proved once again that they could march hard and move fast whenever need arose. The successful Rebel redeployment robbed Meade's Rappahannock victories of strategic significance. That was hardly a pre-ordained outcome, however, and it is fair to ask whether Federal commanders could have done anything to produce a different result.

*   *   *

While Confederates had a defeat to dissect, Federals had a victory to celebrate and much to applaud. Meade had breached the Rappahannock and his advance had succeeded handily, indeed surprisingly so in the eyes of many. As army commander he had organized the effort, assigned officers to its key tasks, allocated resources, and laid down a basic plan. He had shown remarkable competence performing these tasks, especially since he undertook the movement against his better judgment, and in lieu of a preferred strategy that Lincoln and Halleck had rejected. Another leader in similar circumstances might have lost heart, found excuses not to act, or succumbed to resentment and gone forward so half-heartedly as to all but guarantee defeat. George Meade was a far better man than that. Despite his own doubts, he hewed to performance of his duty and did everything possible to assure success. His subordinates rewarded that investment with victory.

The III Corps assault on Kelly's Ford had been a textbook operation. In contrast to his halting performance at Manassas Gap the previous July, French had deployed his troops well, taken maximum advantage of favorable terrain, and brought concentrated force to bear before making a timely, vigorous strike against his objective. Keeping army headquarters thoroughly informed, he had promptly followed up Maj. Gen.

David Birney's tactical triumph. If Meade entertained doubts about William French's ability to handle a corps, November 7 might have eased them a bit.

John Sedgwick's success seemed even more stunning. Northerners thrilled to his twilight attack and conquest of a fortified position. That the VI Corps had destroyed Lee's famous Louisiana Tigers simply sweetened the Federal victory. Unquestionably, David Russell deserved most of the credit for this success. Willing to attack when almost everyone else thought the idea foolhardy, he had concocted a daring scheme, won approval for it, and carried it out with a deft medley of tactics, battlefield conditions, soldierly instinct, energy, and courage. Attacking Union troops also had performed commendably, exhibiting a willingness to engage in hand-to-hand combat that demonstrated grit and bravery. Likewise, Yankee tactical leadership had proven exemplary.

Nonetheless, Rappahannock Station was a flawed operational success and far from a perfect tactical masterpiece. However valiant, Union efforts there still represented a missed opportunity for the AOP and a prime example of the pivotal role chance played on the battlefield. Lost in all the tributes heaped upon the Yankee right wing was the fact that its victory had come too late in the day to permit any chance of exploiting the success.

Responsibility for that outcome belonged to John Sedgwick. Duly impressed by Meade's musings about potentially unassailable earthworks and contingency plans for shifting most of the army's right wing to Kelly's Ford, he had approached Lee's bridgehead as if its field fortifications were the permanent defenses of Richmond. This was hardly required, for given his vast numerical superiority vis-à-vis Harry Hays' Louisianans, Sedgwick could have overrun the Rebel earthworks at almost any moment. Instead he spent hours deploying two entire corps before sending forward a skirmish line backed by a single division on either side of the O&A. And that movement's purpose was not an attack but rather to seal off the position and gain ground for deploying Union artillery.

Failing to discern Rebel weakness when his troops displaced Confederate skirmishers with ease, Sedgwick seemed as concerned with bracing for a possible counterattack as destroying the bridgehead. When Brig. Gen. Albion Howe pleaded for permission to charge Hays' earthworks after his division's almost effortless occupation of the ridge overlooking Rappahannock Station, Maj. Gen. Wright denied the request; ostensibly fearful that south bank Rebel artillery would pulverize any assault. But since no enemy guns were in place to do that, Wright's real reason for declining the proposal was most likely his belief that an attack on the fortifications would prove a "hopeless" undertaking.[20]

20 *OR* 29, pt. 1, 585.

Sedgwick apparently agreed, for rather than hurl his enormous force against the bridgehead in one decisive blow, he invested two hours of quickly fading sunlight trying to induce a Confederate retreat with harassing fire from Federal skirmishers and artillery. At no time, apparently, did Sedgwick, Wright, or George Sykes contemplate using their immense preponderance of men to swamp the Rebel breastworks with a massive attack.

Indeed, Sedgwick didn't even advance four of his six divisions beyond the spot of their initial deployment until Col. Godwin's brigade reinforced the bridgehead—yet another indicator that the Yankees were as focused on mounting a defense as launching an assault. No evidence indicates that the right wing commander ever pushed his subordinates to strike Jubal Early's fortifications. From all indications, Sedgwick seems to have taken a hands-off approach, passing along authority for Wright to attack if he wished, something the temporary VI Corps leader readily characterized himself as reluctant to do. If not for David Russell's last-minute plea to attack, it is virtually certain that the Federals would have made no attempt on the bridgehead before nightfall.[21]

That failure would have undermined Meade's entire strategy. Yet, despite fully understanding the AOP's need to unite quickly by rapid success at Rappahannock Station, Sedgwick held back until Russell altered the course of events. When one recalls Meade's explicit instructions that, upon reaching its objective, the right wing should attack "at once" and "if practicable" drive the Rebels south of the river, it is hard to understand Sedgwick's (and his ranking subordinates') reluctance to strike Lee's bridgehead long before sundown.[22]

Perhaps they thought pushing enemy skirmishers into the bridgehead and opening an artillery bombardment satisfied the dictate to attack "at once." Or maybe they didn't deem an assault "practicable." Then again, their hesitancy might have arisen from the unfamiliar responsibilities so many of them shouldered on November 7: Wright stepping up to corps command, for example, while several other men were leading brigades, regiments, or divisions in combat for the first time. Sedgwick, of course, had previous experience in the Chancellorsville campaign directing a two-corps wing. But his defeat at Salem Church in that capacity might have urged more caution than aggressiveness in an encore opportunity. For whatever reason, methodical caution gripped Union efforts at Rappahannock Station for most of the afternoon.

---

21 See Appendix Two.

22 *OR* 29, pt. 2, 427. "If practicable" was an oft-used phrase in Civil War orders. Although its logic is self-evident, it granted commanders enormous discretion and often allowed an unenthusiastic subordinate to evade tough decisions or to eschew risk if so inclined.

*   *   *

That changed when Russell got Wright's permission to attack. But despite the New York brigadier's daring plan, good timing, and clever tactics, he too failed to apply decisive force against the enemy. Although he led a division, Russell chose to strike with a single brigade. No one ever asked him to explain that decision, but it probably stemmed from his mistaken belief that the Rebels held their earthworks with only a strong skirmish line. It is also possible that unfamiliarity with division command left him thinking like a brigadier.

Either way, his assault would have probably failed if conducted strictly as designed. Despite the advantages of an advance at dusk and the novel use of a doubled skirmish line to lead the way, Russell succeeded in large part because units on his flanks lent him unexpected support by charging alongside the 6th Maine without orders or any pre-directed role in the action whatsoever. Absent the V Corps' skirmishers engaging the 9th and 6th Louisiana in addition to overrunning the small redoubt, and Capt. Fish's reinforced company hitting the earthwork's weakest sector and capturing 127 defenders, Harry Hays might easily have assembled enough troops to hold the large fort and repel the Yankee assault.

Luckily for Russell those aggressively-minded captains and majors on his flanks were eager to assist the Union attack. Their troops absorbed so much Rebel attention that the 8th Louisiana had to defend the large fort mostly alone, successfully stopping the 6th Maine but giving way to rapid follow-on strikes by the 5th Wisconsin and the rest of Ellmaker's brigade. That success gave Russell time to realize he'd underestimated enemy numbers and call for reinforcements. However, the general again declined using maximum power and asked Upton to bring forward only two regiments.

Russell's decisions gave his men no better than even odds during the fight and without the unintended participation of Sykes' and Fish's skirmishers, the Yankees would have been outnumbered and probably fatally so. Certainly, Russell's failure to use more of his available troops made Rappahannock Station a riskier, bloodier battle than it might otherwise have been.

Fortunately for the Federals, darkness not only cloaked their small numbers; it also vastly magnified the morale-deflating effect Confederates suffered after seeing two Union corps array against them earlier that afternoon—a circumstance vital to Union success and likely Sedgwick's greatest contribution to ultimate victory. These factors, Russell's decision making and the force he committed to his dusk charge, along with its serendipitous supports, carried the bridgehead.

Although this success mitigated Sedgwick's failure to quickly overrun Rappahannock Station earlier in the day, it didn't recoup the opportunity he had lost by not doing so. If the Federal right wing had attacked energetically upon reaching its target, the strength of even one of its divisions would have been enough to force Hays' lone brigade to evacuate the bridgehead. Such a withdrawal might have allowed Sedgwick to get a significant force over the river before nightfall—which would have potentially positioned the V and VI corps to split the ANV next day and put most of Ewell's divisions between the AOP's two wings.

Tactically speaking the only impact of such a success on November 7 would have been to free Meade from having to shift the V Corps to Kelly's Ford and compel Lee to deploy units to confront whatever troops Sedgwick got over the river. Circumstances would still have forced a Confederate withdrawal to a line north of Culpeper Court House that night and a stand there the next day to give Lee's supply trains time to get away.[23]

Since Sedgwick, like French, couldn't have crossed more than a fraction of his force over the river before nightfall, the real significance of an expedited Federal triumph at the bridgehead would have manifested itself the next day. With at least part of the Union right wing south of the Rappahannock at dawn, Sedgwick could have moved toward Brandy Station almost a half day earlier than he did. With the V Corps on hand to support the VI, Meade could have either concentrated more of his army on the railroad or swung French's units through Stevensburg toward Culpeper Court House, thus endangering the rear of any Confederates facing the army's right wing.

Even if most of the left wing had stayed behind to shield Kelly's Ford, Sedgwick would have had six hours or so of daylight left to continue operations after driving Fitz Lee's cavalry from Brandy Station. Those extra hours should have allowed Meade to find Lee three miles beyond the railway stop and bring him to battle. The Rebel general's ability to extricate his army from such a fight and safely retreat to the Rapidan is at least questionable. Thus, Meade might have gotten the contest he hoped for, though perhaps a day later, on November 9.

*   *   *

Sedgwick's inability to cross the river on November 7 renders the foregoing scenario a historical "might have been." But did that failure irrecoverably deny Meade the opportunity for a major engagement? Some prominent Union officers certainly didn't think so. Indeed, they believed the general's chances of forcing a fight remained high, and he only failed to provoke one by moving too cautiously.

---

23 Ironically, an earlier Union success at Rappahannock Station wouldn't have been without some unseen benefit for Lee and his army. It would have given its quartermasters several extra hours of daylight to pack up their stores—perhaps allowing them to save considerably more material than they actually did.

That view has merit: Meade might have operated more aggressively in a number of ways on the morning of November 8. By leaving the V Corps with Sedgwick and putting the III Corps in motion for Brandy Station at dawn, he would have had Union troops at the railway stop several hours earlier than they were. Directing Warren to Stevensburg instead of deploying him around Kelly's Ford would have brought the AOP's II Corps within striking distance of Culpeper Court House at midday. By summoning Brig. Gen. Henry Hunt's Reserve Artillery across the river to protect Kelly's Ford, Meade might even have sent Newton's I Corps to assist Warren.

These moves would have put Northern troops on every major route Lee could use to strike at Kelly's Ford, and though that meant committing the Union army to the offensive, attacking offered as good a way to defend the vital river crossing as any other. More importantly, these maneuvers would have closed the distance between Meade's command and Lee's actual battle line relatively swiftly, leaving plenty of daylight available for a Yankee push past Brandy Station in search of Rebels.[24]

Of course, Meade did none of these things, instead sticking to his original plan by focusing on getting over the river, uniting the army, and guarding against a Rebel counterattack before embarking on any kind of offensive action. In hindsight that seems unduly cautious, but at the time it was hardly an illogical stance. After all, Meade had to lay his plans for November 8 based on the information he had on the night of November 7, and that intelligence wasn't especially enlightening.

Meade knew that despite flattening Early's bridgehead, Sedgwick had failed to cross the river or drive enemy troops from its southern shore. French had the III Corps over the Rappahannock with Warren's three divisions massed on the north bank ready to cross the river at daybreak. Newton's two divisions were under orders to move from Morrisville to Kelly's Ford at first light and follow Warren over the stream. Nevertheless, dawn would find but a single Union corps south of the Rappahannock and that force was vulnerable to an overwhelming counterattack. Only Sykes' V Corps remained uncommitted and available for Meade's use.

Details on the enemy were sparser. French's skirmishers reported a strong Rebel force blocking the road to Brandy Station and another enemy formation extending the

---

24 Krick, *Civil War Weather*, 112; Boatner, "Sunrise, Sunset," *Civil War Dictionary*, 820-21. Official sunrise on Sunday, November 8, 1863 was at 6:53 a.m. and sunset at 5:07 p.m. Morning nautical twilight—when there is enough light to see objects 400 yards distant—arrived around 5:40 a.m., however, with evening nautical twilight coming at 5:47 p.m. Since the weather was clear, the AOP had roughly 12 hours of useable light to work with as it searched for Lee. As events happened III Corps troops didn't encounter Rebel cavalry on Fleetwood Heights until around noon and didn't take Brandy Station until 1 p.m. When Meade and his staff reached there at 3 p.m. Federal troops were already going into bivouac. The Union army took 7 hours to cover the 5 miles separating the Rappahannock River from Brandy Station, and then stopped for the night with nearly 3 hours of daylight remaining.

Confederate front southward toward Stevensburg. All the prisoners taken that day belonged to Ewell's Corps. A. P. Hill's whereabouts were unknown and worrisome. His missing corps might be assuming defensive positions against Sedgwick or maneuvering to attack either wing of the Union army. Bitter experience had taught Union commanders to beware the unexpected from Lee and Meade could hardly dismiss the possibility of his foe assuming the offensive.

With so little hard intelligence to go on, neither Meade's continued anticipation of a battle near Kelly's Ford nor his wariness that the Confederates would launch an attack were illogical. From that perspective, shifting Sykes' V Corps and part of the VI Corps to Kelly's Ford made sense, as did ordering the III Corps to force its way to Rappahannock Station. Birney's dawn reconnaissance reports indicating that the situation had changed didn't reach army or wing headquarters in time to make any last-minute changes to Meade's plan. And even if they had, it is doubtful that the army's commander would have felt their revelations illuminating enough to change his program.

Thus, the first hours of November 8 unfolded according to script. But as the day wore on, Meade's decisions became cloudier—and harder to understand, while his army's operations seemed to grow increasingly languid. Although a steady lack of firm intelligence explained some of the general's determinations, he had only himself to blame for that difficulty.

By deploying Pleasonton's cavalry on his army's flanks, Meade crippled his own capacity to track Rebel movements and react swiftly to changing circumstances. Buford's three-brigade foray from Sulphur Springs simply confirmed that Lee wasn't reprising his October maneuver to leap the Rappahannock and threaten the Union rear. Splitting Kilpatrick's division by sending Custer to scout toward the Rapidan while Davies' weak brigade rode to Stevensburg didn't help either. On the other side, Lee used his cavalry to far greater effect, posting only a single regiment to tend the ANV's far left while concentrating Stuart's two divisions athwart the primary avenues Meade must use to threaten the Southern army.[25]

Federal strategy would have benefited from copying these Rebel dispositions. Rather than deploying his mounted units as mere flank guards, Meade might have detailed most of Buford's division to spearhead Sedgwick's drive down the O&A while

---

25 Pleasonton also had Maj. Gen. David Gregg's 2nd Cavalry Division at hand, of course, but thanks to Mosby and other guerrilla leaders' relentless activities, Meade consigned Gregg's troopers to guarding the army's supply trains, reserve artillery, and O&A lifeline from Confederate raiders. Lee wasn't required to protect his rear and could deploy Stuart's entire corps as a shield for the ANV—a pointed reminder of Meade's arguments against using the O&A as his line of communication and the effectiveness of Rebel partisans in keeping a third of the AOP's cavalry off the battlefield on November 8.

massing the bulk of Kilpatrick's command to lead a Stevensburg push. With cavalry at their front, Union infantry advancing from Rappahannock Station might have marched in time-saving columns rather than maneuvering across country in ponderous lines of battle. Pleasonton's troopers could have facilitated driving Stuart's horsemen back on Lee's main line by early afternoon, thus buying time for Union foot soldiers to engage the Rebel army well before sunset.

If Meade's conservative cavalry deployments on November 8 stymied his cause, some of his other decisions defied easy explanation. First was the weight he lent to spotty intelligence asserting a Rebel concentration at Brandy Station. Other than his mistaken belief that the ANV numbered 80,000 men and Warren's distant sighting of enemy troops along the O&A, no reason existed to suspect Lee had chosen that location to make a stand. This is especially so given Meade's knowledge of Culpeper County after the AOP's 15-day sojourn there in September. He surely understood that an attacker could outflank any position near the railway stop and potentially cut off its defenders' retreat. Indeed, the general had appraised this ground so poorly last month that he had refused to fight there. Why he thought Lee would behave differently once Union forces had eliminated the Rappahannock Station bridgehead is perplexing.

Moreover, if Meade really intended to "pitch into" the Rebels on November 8 and expected to fight them at Brandy Station, why did he direct only two of his five corps toward that point, one of which (the VI) lacked the equivalent of an entire division because a pair of its brigades had been dispatched to protect Kelly's Ford and another pair detailed to stay at Rappahannock Station and Norman's Ford. And exactly what enemy threat were the latter outfits guarding against? Even if Lee had been willing to give battle at Brandy Station, sending only two corps against the center of the entire Rebel army hardly augured inevitable success. The relative weakness of Meade's assault force becomes even more confounding given his incessant worry that the enemy would surely fight from behind entrenchments in the next battle. And why did Meade maintain the AOP's wing structure after he reunited his army, and Sedgwick's "wing" had shriveled to nothing more than a weakened VI Corps? Why didn't Meade assign either Sedgwick or French overall command of the drive down the O&A, or go there himself to take charge of a movement he hoped and expected would generate a battle?

The biggest question of all, however, is why Meade allowed the III and VI Corps to go into camp between 2 and 3 p.m. rather than continue their advance on November 8. Even if he had done nothing differently that morning, the general could have certainly provoked some sort of late afternoon fight with Lee by directing that those two corps keep moving after they reached Brandy Station. A march of just another three miles would have located the Rebels north of Culpeper Court House and created at least a fleeting opportunity to strike the enemy before nightfall.

Of course, the chances of that assault succeeding were slim. With dusk approaching rapidly, Federal troops would have had time for only the most rudimentary reconnaissance before launching a frontal attack on entrenched Confederates. That attack's almost certain failure might have done more than lengthen causality lists, however, for it would have presented Lee with a thorny problem. Yankee proximity to the ANV in such a fight's aftermath would have offered him only two unpalatable options. He could remain in place and give battle on marginal ground or stage a nighttime withdrawal knowing he was unlikely to get his entire army over the Rapidan before pursuing Federals caught up with him. Choosing to stand and fight risked a potentially devastating flank attack that could cut off any retreat and lead to his army's substantial destruction. Retiring toward the river was hardly less hazardous. Should Meade pursue closely, Lee would be forced to assign some part of his army to fight a desperate rearguard action in hope of protecting the main body of his command as it funneled over the river fords. Meade would have perforce found a good opening to maul at least some part of Lee's army. By allowing the VI and III Corps to go into camp while nearly three hours of daylight remained, Meade foreclosed these enticing opportunities.

The general never justified that decision, nor did anyone ever ask him to. But accounts left behind by Brigadier Patrick and Col. Lyman make it abundantly clear Meade had given up hope of an engagement well before he met Sedgwick along the O&A. And for what reason? Primarily because he chose to believe enemy prisoners claiming that the ANV had fled behind the Rapidan during the previous night. Why these stories affected the general so profoundly is puzzling. He was far too experienced to believe without skepticism stories told by Rebel captives. Moreover, his own familiarity with this part of Virginia must have suggested that the enemy couldn't have gotten completely beyond his reach. In October it had taken the AOP almost 24 hours to evacuate Culpeper County even though most Federal units started their retreat no farther south than the courthouse, just 12 miles from the Rappahannock. Why did Meade think Lee could escape Culpeper so much faster when most of his troops stood nearer the county's northern border at the start of their 20-mile withdrawal to the Rapidan?

*   *   *

Meade never seems to have grasped how thoroughly he had wrested the initiative from Lee at Rappahannock Station. At no time on November 8 did the Union army behave as though it was pursuing a disadvantaged foe. Indeed, the leading elements of Meade's command marched only 6 miles from the river that day and most of the AOP covered even less. This tepid advance strongly implies that Meade had no offensive intent beyond accomplishing the mission he had laid out on November 7: get the army over the Rappahannock, unite its left and right wings at Brandy Station, and stand ready to receive a Confederate attack.

Having experienced great apprehension about his ability to accomplish even this much, the general appears not to have perceived his chance to do more. After failing to find the enemy waiting at Brandy Station, Meade rested on his laurels. Shunning additional risks and believing the foe had already escaped, he encamped his army, ordered Brig. Gen. Herman Haupt to begin rebuilding the last few miles of destroyed O&A track and told Pleasonton's cavalry to ride south next day to confirm Lee's presence behind the Rapidan.

Although officers like Marsena Patrick, Gouverneur Warren, David Birney, and Charles Wainwright bemoaned the AOP's failure to exploit its November 7 victories, Meade didn't share their chagrin. Despite his disappointment that no battle had come off, it appeared that he was mostly disappointed that no fight had occurred according to his expectations or terms. Indeed, Meade seemed oblivious to the idea that he had fumbled away any opportunities after Rappahannock Station.

When curmudgeonly Culpeper Unionist John Minor Botts visited army headquarters on November 12, he angrily lashed out at Meade for failing to chase the Rebels more vigorously four days earlier. Botts pointed out that Confederate wagons hadn't begun creeping past his Brandy Station home until midnight on November 7, while the last of Early's infantry hadn't marched by until 10 a.m. the next morning. By implication a spirited Union pursuit might have caught the Rebels on the move, and Botts implied that only mismanagement or incompetence explained Meade's failure to do so.[26]

Colonel Lyman heard this broadside leveled at his chief. While agreeing that "a shade more mercury in the feet of some of our commanders might do no harm," he otherwise felt Botts' critique unjustified. Lyman thought the general had "every

---

26 John Minor Botts, 63, had a well-deserved reputation as a contrarian. He served in the Virginia legislature from 1833–38 when he joined the Whig Party despite opposing some of its core positions. Blaming the financial panic of 1837 on Democratic policies, he developed a life-long hatred of Democrats, although in several instances he supported various articles of their agenda. Botts served in the U.S. House of Representatives from 1839-43 and 1847-49, before becoming a delegate to Virginia's constitutional convention of 1850-51, where he played a prominent role. Although a slaveholder, he opposed slavery in the Kansas Territory, to the disgust and execration of Virginia Democrats. An effort to nominate Botts for the presidency as a "unification" candidate in 1860 failed. He opposed secession and blamed the Democratic party for undermining compromises that might have prevented the Civil War. Briefly arrested and imprisoned by Confederate authorities in March 1862, he left Richmond and moved to his Culpeper County estate near Brandy Station. Here he welcomed both Union and Confederate generals as dinner guests and sold supplies to both armies even while bedeviling them with grievances for their treatment of his property. After the war he became a Radical Republican but failed to win election to public office thereafter. He died on January 8, 1869 at his Culpeper County home. Janet L. Koryell, "John Minor Botts," Union or Secession: Virginians Decide; https://edu.lva.virginia.gov/online_classroom/union; accessed Sept. 12, 2020.

reason" to believe Lee would fight at Brandy Station, and that any "premature hurrying forward of a portion of the troops would have" been ruinous. Meade's aide concluded that the army had conducted the campaign as "scientifically" as possible and therefore won victory with little loss of life. As for failing to do more, he called to mind something Lt. Col. Frederick T. Locke had told him: "If we were omniscient, omnipresent, and omnipotent, we might, with care, get a very pretty fight out of the Rebs!"[27]

Though an intelligent and a keen observer, Lyman was still a military novice who had been in uniform for only three months and still hadn't experienced a major battle. At this point he tended to see events through the prism of prevailing opinion at army headquarters and to accept its conventional wisdom uncritically. His writings reflected that viewpoint. They also attested that many of the army's senior leaders felt quite satisfied with what had been accomplished and were doubtful that more could have been done without needlessly endangering the army.

Meade apparently belonged firmly in that camp and hardly entertained the thought that he had missed any opportunities. Boasting of his success to Margaret, he compared his October maneuvers, mischaracterized by so many as a "retreat," to Lee's recent withdrawal, noting that it was the Rebel army "attacked in front" and not an outflanked AOP, which had truly avoided battle. Stressing that he had expected Lee to fight, Meade confided that he could only "account for his not doing so on the ground that he was deceived as to my strength and construed my sudden and bold advance [as] evidence that I had been strongly reinforced and greatly outnumbered him."[28]

That passage says far more about George Meade than it does about Robert E. Lee, illustrating the Union general's faulty estimation of relative Union and Confederate strength, as well as the foundation of his strategic thinking. Meade had greatly outnumbered Lee since early September. If he supposed his enemy interpreted a "sudden and bold advance" as proof that Washington had significantly reinforced the AOP, then surely Meade must have viewed Lee's October offensive as evidence that Richmond had vastly strengthened the ANV—a conclusion Meade doggedly held onto despite plentiful intelligence it wasn't true.[29]

Consequently, Meade regarded offensive action as a risky endeavor, even absent the need to fight his way over a river. By that logic, acting too audaciously after crossing

27 Aggassiz, *Meade's Headquarters*, 46-47; Lowe, *Meade's Army*, 27, 67. Locke was the V Corps AAG.

28 Meade, *Life and Letters*, Meade to Margaret, Oct. 30 and Nov. 9, 1863, Vol. 2, 154-56. Meade explained that in October he had been maneuvering to "get into proper position to offer battle," rather than retreating.

29 *OR* 29, pt. 2, 326, 328; Sparks, *Inside Lincoln's Army*, 310.

the Rappahannock might have exposed his army to a shattering counterattack. He had therefore moved prudently, carefully positioning his force to meet an assault before seeking out a foe unexpectedly reluctant to join battle. In Meade's eyes, the only reason that fight hadn't come off was that his aggression had scared the Confederates into retreat. Although this misread what really happened, the general's performance and interpretation of events during early November's brief campaign was an excellent example of his mindset.

Meade's generalship is probably best described as deliberate. Approaching war as science rather than art, he tackled military problems with the mathematical precision of an engineer intent on laying down a firm foundation before building his edifice. Preferring not to act until thoroughly prepared and fully informed on enemy strength and dispositions, Meade believed that concentration of force before unleashing a heavy blow to achieve decisive results was far superior to attempting a daring, risky maneuver without guarantee of reward. Fighting bloody battles to gain ground or accomplish goals that maneuver could obtain at little cost was pointless. His worries about the North's ability to replenish casualty-depleted Union ranks beset by disease and expiring enlistments only reinforced his guiding tenets.

For those inclined to disagree, the general could point to the AOP's long, unfortunate history whenever it had violated those principles. As Meade practiced them, however, he operated at a one-step-at-a-time tempo that struck many as overly cautious or needlessly methodical, thus reinforcing Lincoln's and Halleck's perception that their general lacked the killer instinct necessary to win and then ruthlessly exploit victory. Fairly or not, many considered Meade's nearly five-month long tenure at the head of the AOP ample evidence to support this impression.

*   *   *

The Union victories at Rappahannock Station and Kelly's Ford ultimately accomplished little more than restoring the Virginia stalemate to its early August location. Meade had recovered the ground lost in October, provided a morale boost for his troops, and inflicted a highly embarrassing defeat on the Rebels. But he might have done more. After getting over the Rappahannock, he had within his grasp a chance to engage Lee on some of the most disadvantageous ground that the Rebel army had ever occupied. For numerous reasons, good and bad, the AOP's commander failed to pursue his opportunity aggressively. Having with much trepidation undertaken a hazardous operation, Meade had played for limited stakes, been content to collect his winnings, and walked away without attempting to push his luck.[30]

Robert E. Lee had gambled more audaciously and come within a whisker of the bigger prize he sought—a chance to wreck a sizable portion of the Union army. Whether that wager would have paid off we cannot know, for David Russell's boldness and, to a slightly lesser extent, that of Horatio Wright, undercut the Confederate general's plans at the last minute and forced his retreat after inflicting a mournful wound. Despite finding itself in unanticipated peril, the ANV made a day-long stand near Culpeper Court House lest the Yankees press their advantage. Of course, Meade failed to act, not only allowing Lee to withdraw behind the Rapidan unmolested but also divest the Yankee triumphs along the Rappahannock of meaningful strategic fruit.

In the 48 hours encompassing November 7 and 8 both commanding generals had missed opportunities, but for different reasons. Lee had fallen victim to the ancient axiom that battlefield outcomes often depended more on the common solider and his lower level leaders than on the decisions of highly-ranked commanders. Meade on the other hand was the architect of his own missed chance.

However justifiable his caution during the early morning hours of November 8, the general failed to intuit the significance of his changed strategic circumstances and the opening they created. Unable to abandon his preconceived notions of a battle near Brandy Station and the imagined fruits of victory there, Meade demonstrated neither the flexibility nor daring necessary to turn an initial success into something more. Precisely when a Jackson or Lee would have pressed hard after the enemy, intent on gutting him before he could escape, Meade had put his troops into bivouac convinced he had already accomplished what he could.

In October 1862, George Meade—then just a division commander—had critiqued Maj. Gen. George B. McClellan's performance following Antietam, musing that he "errs on the side of prudence and caution" before concluding "that a little more rashness on his part would improve his generalship." Ironically, Meade's subordinates could level the same charge against him in the wake of Rappahannock Station. History is silent on whether Meade's own experience in command of the Army of the Potomac tempered his opinion of McClellan's leadership. But it is intriguing to wonder what might have happened if Meade had taken his own advice and incorporated "a little more rashness" into his generalship. Maybe the battles of November 7, 1863 would

---

30 Jones, *Lee's Tigers*, 193-94. Some of that damage proved ephemeral since 500 of Hays' Louisiana Tigers would return to the ANV in March 1864 via prisoner exchange.

have become the gateway to something far more significant than pushing Robert E. Lee behind the Rapidan.[31]

---

31 Meade, *Life and Letters*, Meade to Margaret, Oct. 12, 1862, Vol. 1, 318.

Deciphering the Rappahannock
Station Battlefield

ONE of the most interesting challenges in writing this volume was developing an accurate understanding of the Rappahannock Station battlefield. The primary scene of action no longer exists in original form. During the late 19th century the town of Rappahannock Station, today known as Remington, began growing west of the O&A and by the 1970s it covered the entire valley across which Union troops attacked the Confederate bridgehead, as well as the high ground occupied by Federal artillery and the area around the small Rebel redoubt. A large farmhouse and silo occupied the location of the large fort. The ridge along which the rest of the Confederate defenses were situated and about 100 yards of ground to their front was still unmarred by development when I first visited the site in 2014, but efforts to preserve this historic ground proved unsuccessful and a subdivision took over the sector around 2018. In sharp contrast to the mostly barren nature of the area during the war, heavy woods cover the region today.

The only unsullied parts of the battlefield are the sloping ground leading to the Rappahannock behind the Rebel earthworks and the fields east of the railroad tracks, which remain farmland. Additionally, several fortifications south of the river are extant. The American Battlefield Trust has managed to save some of them and is working to rescue more as this book goes to print. Nonetheless, it is no longer possible to walk the ground and try to catch a glimpse of its topography as the combatants saw it on November 7, 1863.

Consequently, I had to rely on the historical record to gain an understanding of the battlefield. Interestingly, no map of the action accompanied any official report written by a Federal officer engaged at Rappahannock Station. Fortunately, Robert E. Lee included a map with his battle report, and it provides an outline of the Rebel defensive

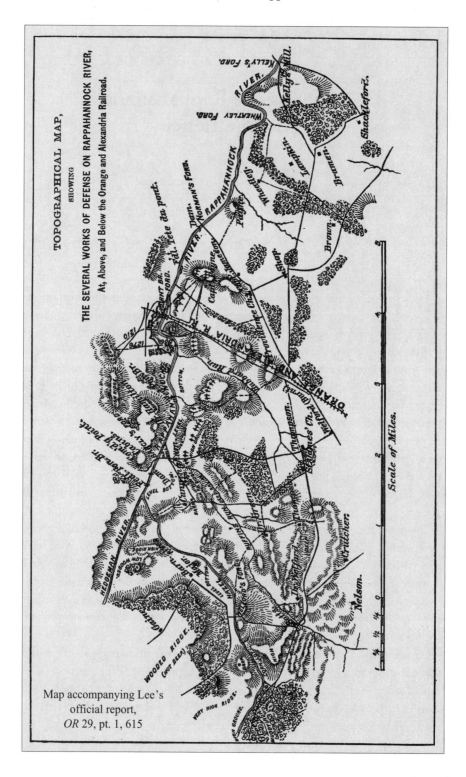

TOPOGRAPHICAL MAP,
SHOWING
THE SEVERAL WORKS OF DEFENSE ON RAPPAHANNOCK RIVER,
At, Above, and Below the Orange and Alexandria Railroad.

Scale of Miles.

Map accompanying Lee's
official report,
OR 29, pt. 1, 615

works and the topography on either side of the Rappahannock. However, it fails to show any troop positions.

Although Lee's map provides the only official visual representation of the Rappahannock Station contest, Union and Confederate after-action reports, soldier letters, newspapers accounts, and regimental histories offer a remarkable amount of written detail on the field and the nature of the bridgehead's fortifications. There is also a rich treasure trove of area photographs taken by Timothy O'Sullivan in August 1862 and a host of sketches by Edwin Forbes and Alfred Waud made during the fall of 1863. These include many drawings of the O&A Railroad Bridge, its surrounding topography, and Federal pontoon bridges laid down in the vicinity during September and October 1863.

Supplementing these vital visual aids are Forbes' drawings of the August 1862 fight at Rappahannock Station, the onsite sketch he created while watching the November 7 Union attack from a position east of the railroad, and another he made showing Northern troops standing in front of the large redoubt examining captured Confederate flags. A post-battle drawing depicting Upton's attack on the bridgehead (although somewhat fanciful from a tactical perspective) provides a good look at the nature of the Southern fortifications, the placement of the Rebel pontoon bridge, the terrain behind the earthworks and, the relationship of the two forts and the bridge to one another. Most of these drawings are included in this book, and taken together they allow the viewer to form an excellent idea of the key features of the Rebel position as well as some notion of how it appeared to Federal attackers.

Another invaluable set of source material I discovered during my research were two maps, both drawn by participants just after the battle. The first of these, (see page 279) in the archives of the Gilder Lehrman Institute of American History, is the work of Adam Clark Baum, a 31-year old assistant surgeon in the 50th New York Engineers who frequently drew maps detailing engagements in which his unit participated. The second map (see page 278) resides in the New York Public Library and is part of its online digital collection. Although the cartographer is unknown, the map is of wartime origin. Neither map includes a scale and they differ in some respects, but both display abundant information on terrain, woods, roads, creeks, troop positions, and more. These maps were critical to understanding the battle and placing the many written descriptions of the field and the fight in context.[1]

Additional detail is found in *Reports on Riflepits and Earthworks thrown up at Rapphk. St. and Beverly Ford* written on June 12, 1863 by Lt. Washington Roebling for

---

1   Baum's map is at https://www.gilderlehrman.org/collection/glc0601303, accessed Oct. 14, 2019. For the NY Public Library map, see https://digitalcollections.nypl.org/items/fc521570-f81b-0132-b187-58d385a7bbd0, accessed Sep. 8, 2019.

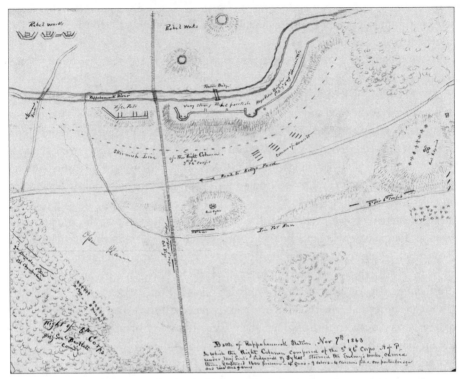

Battle of Rappahannock Station Map, author unknown, *NYSPL*

Gouverneur Warren, then the AOP's chief engineer. Housed in the Manuscripts and Special Collections Division of the New York State Library, it contains an in-depth analysis of the terrain Lee's troops would occupy during the Rappahannock Station fight as well as some nearby fords. The area sketch Roebling incorporated into his report includes such important details as the height of hills on which all the Confederate fortifications were sited and the distance between the heights on the south and north banks. Roebling's manuscript is invaluable for understanding the action on November 7, 1863.

All these sources were vital in creating my account of the battle. In developing my map of the bridgehead and its surrounding terrain, I have interwoven the material discussed above, carefully searching for corroborating evidence to verify each feature of the field. Lee's map, Baum's map, Capt. John Fish's description of the Rebels' "serrated line of rifle pits", and Alfred Waud's drawing of Upton's assault all confirm that salients jutted out from the bridgehead's perimeter—a feature absent from every modern map or account of the battle. Verification of these salients shines a new light on Upton's account of the engagement and those written by his men. Placing these

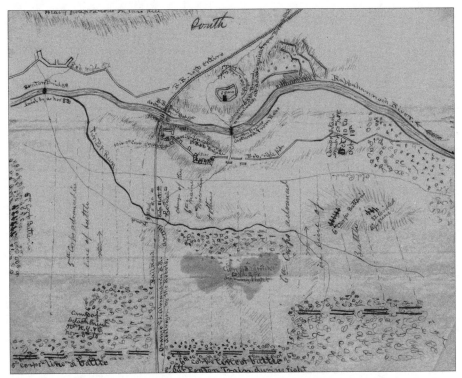

Map of Rappahannock Station drawn by Surgeon Alfred Baum, 50th NY ENG.
Gilder Lehrman Institute of American History

words beside an accurate map of the bridgehead's fortifications dramatically alters our understanding of the direction of Upton's attack and how it unfolded.

Another significant revelation about Rebel fortifications came from Baum's map, which depicts gaps in the earthworks where a road coming up from the Rappahannock exited the bridgehead. Previously ignored, this feature of the Confederate defenses conforms to wartime military manuals which always depict an opening for a roadway in a téte-de-pont (bridgehead), a phrase Lee routinely used in his official report. More importantly, the staggered earthworks shown on Baum's map support Capt. Fish's claim of encountering two lines of enemy works and help explain the success of his small contingent of attackers and their ability to capture 127 Rebels so quickly.

Ordering the
Rappahannock Station Attack

DECADES after the war, Sedgwick's assistant adjutant general, Lt. Col. Martin T. McMahon, recalled the issuance of orders to attack Rappahannock Station's earthworks in his article "From Gettysburg to the Coming of Grant" eventually contained in *Battles and Leaders of the Civil War*. His account differs radically from Horatio Wright's and David Russell's post-battle reports. McMahon attests that Sedgwick rode forward to Wright and asked him if an infantry assault stood any chance of success. Wright responded: "Just as you say, General." Sedgwick then asked Wright "What does Russell think." Seeing Russell riding up, Wright responded "Here comes Russell; he can speak for himself." When the brigadier

arrived, Sedgwick asked "Can you carry those works with your division?" When Russell replied, "I think I can sir." Sedgwick told him "Go ahead and do it."

McMahon was hardly a fabulist. He held a Master's Degree and a Doctor of Laws Degree from St. John's College, Fordham and would receive a brevet promotion to Maj. General of Volunteers in 1866 as well as an 1891 Medal of Honor for burning an abandoned supply train while under enemy fire on June 30,

Col. Martin McMahon
Library of Congress

1862 at the Battle of White Oak Swamp. Before taking up the post of VI Corps Assistant Adjutant General in January 1863, McMahon had served as an aide-de-camp for Maj. Gens. George B. McClellan and William B. Franklin. He was at Sedgwick's side when a Rebel sharpshooter killed the general on May 9, 1864 at the Battle of Spotsylvania Court House. Sedgwick died in the colonel's arms, and his account of the event became famous. His *In Memoriam Maj. Gen. John Sedgwick* was published in 1885.

Despite this sterling reputation, I have rejected his account of Rappahannock Station for a number of reasons. Although Sedgwick and Wright did ride forward together to examine the Confederate fortifications, they did so alone. No aides or staff officers accompanied them, and their reconnaissance took place several hours prior to dusk, well before Russell's division moved forward from its initial position. Moreover, both Russell and Wright in their after-action reports provided detailed accounts of how they decided to assault. They specified the officers carrying messages back and forth but never referred to Sedgwick.

At some point Sedgwick and Wright doubtless discussed their tactical problem at Rappahannock Station. And it is certainly possible that McMahon may have been present for a conversation where the right wing commander asked his subordinate about the odds of a successful assault. However, nothing in the wartime record supports McMahon's version of events.

McMahon's recollection doesn't square with the timing of the attack or Russell's movements recorded in several regimental histories and memoirs. Moreover, Russell and Wright filed their official reports within 9 days and 5 weeks of the battle, respectively, when memories remained fresh. McMahon penned his version of events long after the war. The colonel's life-long dedication to his former chief, aided by imprecise memory, possibly led him to embellish Sedgwick's role in that officer's greatest triumph.

Emory Upton and
Rappahannock Station's Legacy

ALTHOUGH Brigadier General David A. Russell was the architect of Union victory at Rappahannock Station, Emory Upton is most often associated with the battle in historical memory. That distinction stems from his role at the Battle of Spotsylvania Court House in May 1864, as well as Upton's postwar status as one of the U.S. Army's foremost tactical theorists and reformers.

After the horrific Battle of the Wilderness inaugurated what historians label the Overland Campaign, Lt. Gen. Ulysses S. Grant ordered Maj. Gen. George Meade's Army of the Potomac to sidestep Gen. Robert E. Lee's Army of Northern Virginia to attempt getting between the Rebels and Richmond. The Confederates anticipated the move and managed (barely) to thwart the Union maneuver by reaching Spotsylvania Court House just ahead of the Yankees. Following the practice initiated during the Mine Run campaign (November 24-December 3, 1863) the Southerners rapidly dug in and erected a line of formidable earthworks. Those entrenchments, however, had a potentially fatal flaw: a huge salient in the center of the Rebel position that troops nicknamed "the Muleshoe."

As the AOP deployed against Lee's line on May 9 a Southern sharpshooter killed Maj. Gen. John Sedgwick in one of the war's most famous incidents. Horatio Wright then assumed command of the VI Corps, leaving David Russell to take charge of Wright's division which included Upton's brigade. Thus, by bloody happenstance, the senior officers responsible for the attack on Rappahannock Station got a chance to reprise the roles they had played six months earlier.[1]

---

1 Gordon Rhea, *The Battles for Spotsylvania Court House and the Road to Yellow Tavern: May 7-12. 1864.* (Baton Rouge, LA, 1997), 94-96. The popular VI Corps commander was chiding some of

Lt. Gen. Ulysses S. Grant
Library of Congress

Yankee commanders planned a full-scale assault against the Rebels' Spotsylvania defenses for May 10. During a conference attended by Grant, Meade, and Wright the latter argued, as Upton had been doing, against using traditional battle lines to assail fortified enemy positions. The young colonel insisted that the proper method to attack earthworks was to strike them with a dense formation that would advance rapidly on the enemy without pausing to fire and rely on the bayonet to tear open a breach in the Rebels' line. Fast moving follow-on units could convert that gap into a true breakthrough. If the attackers made their move by surprise, so much the better. It is doubtful that Grant knew much about the previous November's Rappahannock Station affair, but Wright and Meade certainly did, and they must have recognized its inspiration in Upton's scheme.

Grant liked the idea and incorporated it as part of his grand effort. Meade assigned Wright's VI Corps to assail the Muleshoe using Upton's suggested tactics. Engineer Captain Ranald S. Mackenzie of Meade's staff would select a propitious spot for the VI Corps attack, while Wright handpicked a force of 12 assault regiments. The II, V, and IX Corps would strike Lee's defensive flanks to tie down the bulk of the ANV and prevent the enemy from shifting troops to counter Wright's expected breakthrough. A II Corps division under Brig. Gen. Gershom Mott would charge the enemy defenses on Wright's left and exploit his anticipated success.

No doubt recalling Rappahannock Station, Wright gave David Russell the task of selecting the attack force and overseeing its operation. Predictably, he chose Upton to

his men for dodging enemy bullets, quipping that "They couldn't hit an elephant at this distance," when a fatal round struck him below his left eye.

lead the effort and included among his specially chosen command all the VI Corps regiments that had overrun Lee's bridgehead last November, plus five additional regiments. When VI Corps staff officer Lt. Col. McMahon gave Upton this list of units he told the ambitious colonel that he would receive a promotion to brigadier if he succeeded in breaking the Rebel line. Thrilled at having such "splendid" regiments placed under his leadership—the "best men in the army" he thought—Upton promised to carry the enemy line or die trying.[2]

Not only were the troops and officers slated for the assault the same men who had stormed Rappahannock Station; the operational circumstances were similar as well. Brigadier General George Dole's Georgia brigade, supported by a four-gun battery, held the breastworks that Capt. Mackenzie selected as Upton's target. This part of Lee's line bulged out of the Muleshoe slightly, giving it the same sort of semicircular perimeter that Brig. Gen. Harry Hays and Col. Archibald Godwin had defended the previous November. The assault would originate in a heavy wood just 200 yards from the Rebel earthworks—the exact same distance from which Col. Harrison's 6th Maine launched the leading wave of Russell's attack last year—and army headquarters scheduled the movement to begin two hours before sunset at 5 p.m.

What the Federals had faced in November 1863 wasn't what they would face in May 1864, however. Most notably the Spotsylvania entrenchments were stouter than those of the bridgehead battle. Not only had the enemy built an abatis in front of their breastworks; those fortifications sported head logs which allowed defenders to fire while virtually avoiding exposure. More importantly, no unfordable river flowed behind Doles' brigade, nor was that command isolated from the rest of Lee' army, which could send in reinforcements rapidly to counterattack any force penetrating its line. Nor had the unexpected appearance of a large, irresistible Union host undermined Southern morale.

Our scope precludes fully discussing Grant's attack, which failed for a variety of reasons including poor coordination, disrupted time schedules, and robust Confederate resistance. Upton's assault, launched an hour and half late—it went forward only 30 minutes before sunset—used four succeeding lines of three regiments each and managed to break the enemy line in a flurry of hand-to-hand combat despite failing to surprise the Rebels and having to overcome abatis and well-constructed earthworks. These facts refute the thesis that poorly built fortifications primarily caused the Confederate defeat at Rappahannock Station.[3]

---

2   The 121st NY, 5th ME, 6th ME, 5th WS, 49th and 119th PA plus the 43rd and 77th NY, 96th PA, 2nd, 5th and 6th VT comprised the assault force.

3   Previous paragraphs based on Rhea, *The Battles for Spotsylvania Court House*, 161-76.

Upton at Spotsylvania by Alfred Waud. *Library of Congress*

Although Upton's men made a lodgment inside Doles' works and fought with desperate fury to maintain what they had won, Lt. Gen. Richard Ewell orchestrated a violent Confederate counterattack that drove the Yankees back to their starting point within an hour of the assault's start. Upton had proven that his tactics worked well enough to breach a fortified line, but they couldn't do more unless a large, well-led reserve stormed speedily into the breach to expand and capitalize on initial success. Grant recognized this immediately and supposedly said after Upton's repulse, "A brigade today, we'll try a corps tomorrow." He also saw to it that Emory Upton received his brigadier's star.[4]

On May 12, Grant hurled Maj. Gen. Winfield S. Hancock's II Corps at the Muleshoe in a dawn assault. Employing Upton's tactics and benefiting from a Confederate error that removed all their artillery from the point under attack, the Yankees smashed a huge hole in Lee's line. The Rebels managed to contain the breach and launch a lethal counterattack that produced some of the most vicious close-quarters combat of the entire war. The location of this fight would go down in the record books as the Bloody Angle, and Upton's tangential connection to that

---

4   Lumen H. Tenney, *War Diary of Lummen Harris Tenney, 1861-1865.*

episode as well as the success of his tactics gained the new brigadier a reputation as one of the North's more innovative generals.

That standing served Upton well after the war. Carrying a regular army rank of lieutenant colonel and eventually colonel, he became famous as a military reformer and theorist, serving on an 1866 board to develop a new system of infantry tactics before becoming commandant of West Point from 1870–75 where he also served as an instructor in infantry, artillery, and cavalry tactics. Following Germany's stunning defeat of France in the Franco-Prussian War (1870-71), General William T. Sherman (then commanding the U.S. Army) sent Upton to study the military forces of Europe and Asia with a special emphasis on the Prussians. Upon returning Upton presented a series of recommendations to make the American army a more professional force, including the creation of a general staff, establishing schools for advanced military studies and an overhaul of the army's personnel system.

Although some proposals were as controversial as they were influential, all Upton's ideas attracted a great deal of attention. Whenever contemporaries or historians sought to understand Upton's thinking or the origins of his ideas, they always revisited Spotsylvania Court House and they never failed to link his attack there to his participation in the Battle of Rappahannock Station. With both Russell and Sedgwick killed in action during the war, Upton became the best-known surviving actor in that drama. General Wright faded into the background despite outliving Upton and attaining higher rank in the postwar army.

Eventually, this quirk of historical focus seemed to erase David Russell's role at Rappahannock Station almost entirely. Gordon Rhea, the preeminent historian of Grant's Overland campaign, provided an excellent example of how Upton's repute had pervaded Civil War literature in his book on Spotsylvania. Rhea noted that Upton's "success in capturing seemingly invulnerable positions gave his ideas a ring of authority. In early November, 1863 he had stormed a formidable Confederate bridgehead at Rappahannock Station and had carried it."[5]

Emory Upton undoubtedly played a significant role at Rappahannock Station. His actions on that field were courageous, decisive, and agile. Moreover, the colonel's quick thinking allowed him to exploit Confederate confusion in the bridgehead and prevented his men suffering heavy losses. What Upton didn't do on November 7, 1863 was employ radical new tactics, nor did he plan the attack or take part in the assault that broke the enemy line. Upton led a follow-on force that adroitly exploited the initial success of David Russell's assault, and it is the latter, not the former, who history should remember as the brains behind Union victory at Rappahannock Station.

---

5 Rhea, *The Battles for Spotsylvania Court House*, 161-63.

Confederate Uniforms At
Rappahannock Station and Kelly's Ford

IN his *History of the 1st New Jersey Cavalry*, (1871), regimental chaplain Henry Pyne notes that the Rebel prisoners his regiment escorted rearward on November 7 were "warmly clothed, some wearing overcoats of English frieze, whose materials had run the blockade," while most of their uniforms were made of "common, homespun Negro-cloth, dyed with the juice of the butternut," better known to students of Confederate uniforms as "jean cloth." Pyne said that none of the clothing appeared old, although it "looked weather-beaten and shabby, the coloring matter rapidly fading into a dingy, dirty hue." Many of the Southerners carried "pieces of rag-carpeting" instead of blankets, although all appeared "well shod." Pyne thought that "man for man, they weren't equal" to Union troops, but he acknowledged that the Rebels "were generally effective-looking soldiers" and supposed that in an equal fight the two sides would be "so nearly matched, that accident would give either party the superiority."

Colonel Lyman recorded his impression of the Confederate prisoners who passed Meade's Mount Holly command post near Kelly's Ford on November 8. To the general's aide the captives, dressed in clothes "of a gray cloth," seemed "very thin, but still healthy looking." He had "seen none with overcoats, but most have a blanket, and a good proportion, excellent English shoes." (Lowe, *Meade's Army*).

Thomas M. Arliskas in *Cadet Gray and Butternut Brown: Notes on Confederate Uniforms* (2006) incorrectly states that Hays' and Hoke's brigades were wearing imported dark gray uniforms. Arliskas' source is Frank Rauscher's memoir of service in the 114th PA, *Music on the March 1862-'65*, (1892). This describes the uniforms of North Carolina troops captured at Kelly's Ford, not at Rappahannock Station.

Troops Engaged at Rappahannock Station

Confederate

Early's Division
Maj. Gen. Jubal A. Early

Hay's Brigade
Brig. Gen. Henry Hays
5th Louisiana
6th Louisiana
7th Louisiana
8th Louisiana
9th Louisiana
Hoke's Brigade
Col. Archibald Godwin
6th North Carolina
54th North Carolina
57th North Carolina
Gordon's Brigade
Brig. Gen. John B. Gordon
13th Georgia
26th Georgia
31st Georgia
38th Georgia
60th Georgia
61st Georgia
Pegram's Brigade
Brig. Gen John Pegram
13th Virginia
31st Virginia
49th Virginia
52nd Virginia
58th Virginia
Artillery
Powhatan Artillery
Rockbridge Artillery
Louisiana Guard Artillery

Union

V Corps
Maj. Gen. George Sykes

First Division
Brig. Gen. Joseph J. Bartlett
1st Brigade
Col. Joseph Hayes
18th Massachusetts
22nd Massachusetts
1st Michigan
118th Pennsylvania
2nd Brigade
Col. Jacob B. Sweitzer
9th Massachusetts
32nd Massachusetts
4th Michigan
62nd Pennsylvania
3rd Brigade
Col. Joshua L. Chamberlain
20th Maine
16th Michigan
44th New York
83rd Pennsylvania

VI Corps
Brig. Gen. Horatio G. Wright
1st Division
Brig. Gen. David A. Russell
1st Brigade
Brig. Gen. Alfred T. A. Torbert
1st New Jersey
2nd New Jersey
3rd New Jersey
4th New Jersey
15th New Jersey
2nd Brigade
Col. Emory Upton
5th Maine
121st New York
95th Pennsylvania
96th Pennsylvania
3rd Brigade
Col. Peter Ellmaker
6th Maine
49th Pennsylvania
119th Pennsylvania
5th Wisconsin

Second Division
Brig. Gen. Albion P. Howe
2nd Brigade ("Vermont Brigade")
Col. Lewis A. Grant
2nd Vermont
3rd Vermont
4th Vermont
5th Vermont
6th Vermont
3rd Brigade
Brig. Gen. Thomas H. Neill
7th Maine
43rd New York
49th New York
77th New York
61st Pennsylvania
Third Division
Brig. Gen. Henry D. Terry
1st Brigade
Brig. Gen. Alexander Shaler
65th New York
67th New York
122nd New York
23rd Pennsylvania
82nd Pennsylvania
2nd Brigade
Brig. Gen. Henry L. Eustis
7th Massachusetts
10th Massachusetts
2nd Rhode Island
3rd Brigade
Brig. Gen. Frank Wheaton
62nd New York
93rd Pennsylvania
98th Pennsylvania
102nd Pennsylvania
139th Pennsylvania
Artillery
1st Rhode Island Light Battery C
5th Massachusetts Battery E
5th US Battery D
5th US Battery F
5th New York Battery

Troops Engaged at Kelly's Ford

Confederate

Rodes' Division
Maj. Gen. Robert Rodes
Daniel's Brigade
Brig. Gen. Junius Daniel
32nd North Carolina
43rd North Carolina
45th North Carolina
53rd North Carolina
2nd North Carolina Battalion
Ramseur's Brigade
Col. William R. Cox
2nd North Carolina
4th North Carolina
14th North Carolina
30th North Carolina
Doles' Brigade
Brig. Gen. George Doles
4th Georgia
12th Georgia
21st Georgia
44th Georgia
Battle's Brigade
Brig. Gen. Cullen Battle
3rd Alabama
5th Alabama
6th Alabama
12th Alabama
26th Alabama

Johnston's Brigade
Col. Thomas Garrett
5th North Carolina
12th North Carolina
20th North Carolina
23rd North Carolina
Artillery
Fluvanna Artillery

Union

III Corps
Maj. Gen. David B. Birney
First Division
Brig. Gen. John Henry Hobart Ward
1st Brigade
Col. Charles H. T. Collis
57th Pennsylvania
63rd Pennsylvania
68th Pennsylvania
105th Pennsylvania
114th Pennsylvania
141st Pennsylvania
2nd Brigade
Col. Hiram Berdan
3rd Maine
4th Maine
86th New York
124th New York
99th Pennsylvania
2nd US Sharpshooters
3rd Brigade
Col. Régis de Trobriand
17th Maine
3rd Michigan
5th Michigan
40th New York
110th Pennsylvania
1st US Sharpshooters

Second Division
Brig. Gen. Henry Prince
1st Brigade
Col. Robert McAllister
11th Massachusetts
16th Massachusetts
11th New Jersey
26th Pennsylvania
84th Pennsylvania

2nd Brigade ("Excelsior Brigade")
Col. William R. Brewster
70th New York
71st New York
72nd New York
73rd New York
74th New York
120th New York
3rd Brigade
Brig. Gen. Gershom Mott
5th New Jersey
6th New Jersey
7th New Jersey
8th New Jersey
115th Pennsylvania
Third Division
Brig. Gen. Joseph B. Carr
1st Brigade
Brig. Gen. William H. Morris
14th New Jersey
151st New York
10th Vermont
2nd Brigade
Col. Joseph W. Keifer
6th Maryland
110th Ohio
122d Ohio
138th Pennsylvania
3rd Brigade
Col. Benjamin F. Smith
106th New York
126th Ohio
67th Pennsylvania
87th Pennsylvania
Artillery
10th Massachusetts Light Battery
1st Rhode Island Light, Battery E
1st Connecticut, Battery M

Primary Sources

Unpublished Manuscripts

Albert H. Small Special Collections Library, University of Virginia, Charlottesville, VA
    Brand, William Francis. Letters
    Woods, Micajah. Papers
Dolph Briscoe Center for American History, University of Texas, Austin, TX
    Kirkpatrick, James. Diary
    Smith, William Adolphus. Letters
Duke University Special Collections Library, Durham, NC
    Hancock, Winfield Scott. Papers
Eleanor S. Brockenbrough Library, American Civil War Museum, Richmond, VA
    Montgomery, James R. Diary
    Morrisett, Algernon S. Diary
    Morissett, Lawson. Diary
    Myers, Robert Pooler. Diary
    _____. Letter Copy Book
    Nunnelee, Lewis T. Memoir
Fondren Library, Rice University, Houston, TX
    Wilber, Escek G. Letters
Fredericksburg-Spotsylvania National Military Park, Fredericksburg, VA
    Justice, Benjamin W. Letter, Nov. 11, 1863
Gettysburg National Military Park, Gettysburg, PA
    Bailey, Thomas. "The Life and Times of Thomas Bailey: A Civil War Diary."
Gilder Lehrman Institute of American History, New York, NY
    Baum, Adam Clark. Map of the Battle of Rappahannock Station, Nov. 1863
    Bope, Abraham. Letters
    Smith, David letters
    Tate, Jeremiah. Letters
Hesburgh Libraries, Department of Special Collections, University of Notre Dame
    Williams, Leonard. Letters
Historical Society of Pennsylvania, Philadelphia, PA
    Biddle, James Cornell. Letters, 1861-1865
    Meade, George G. Papers
Indiana Historical Society, William Henry Smith Memorial Library, Indianapolis, IN
    Chapman, George. Diary

Van Dyke, Augustus M. Papers
Indiana State Library, Indianapolis, IN
    Bellamy, F. J. Diary
Library of Congress, Washington, DC
    Burbank, Sidney. Diary
    Galwey, Thomas Francis. Diary
    Gilpin, E. N. Diary
    Hatton, John William Ford. Memoir
    Keifer, J. Warren. Papers
    Long-Breckinridge Papers, Long, William S. "Reminiscences"
    Rose, Luther A. Diary
Library of Virginia, Richmond, VA
    Gibson Family Papers
Milne Special Collections and Archives, University of New Hampshire Library, Durham, NH
    Cheney, Thomas Carleton. Papers
Missouri Historical Society, Columbia, MO
    Carpenter, Thomas. Letters
National Archives, Washington, DC
    Bureau of Military Information File
New York State Library, Manuscripts and Special Collections Division, Albany, NY
    Baum, Adam Clark. Letters.
    Roebling, Washington. Map Memoir, June 12, 1863, Reports on Riflepits and Earthworks thrown up at Rapphk. St. and Beverly Ford
    Unknown. Map. Battle of Rappahannock Station, Nov. 7th 1863
    Warren, Gouverneur K. Letters
North Carolina State Archives, Raleigh, NC
    Anthony, Whit Hill. "Personal Sketch and Reminiscences."
    Cowles, William H. Sketch.
    Foard, Noah. Memoirs.
Ohio Historical Society, Columbus, OH
    Powell Manuscript, "Campaign on the Rappahannock"
Pearce Museum, Navarro College, Corsicana, TX
    Edwards, Clark S. Papers
    Northway, Delos. Letters
Rauner Special Collections Library, Dartmouth College, Hanover, NH.
    Mather, Andrew E. and Mather, A. Dan. Letters
Southern Historical Collection, University of North Carolina. Chapel Hill, NC
    Hairston, Peter Wilson. Diary and Papers
    Lineback, Julius A. Diary
    Malone, Bartlett Yancey. Diary
The Handley Regional Library, Steward Bell Jr. Archive, Winchester, VA
    McVicar, Charles W. Diary
United Daughters of the Confederacy Memorial Library, Richmond, VA
    Francois Bienvenu Cire Memorandum Book
United States Civil War Collection, Western Michigan University, Kalamazoo, MI
    Harrington, George. Diary

University of Virginia, Charlottesville, VA
    Lee, H. C. Papers
    Micajah Woods. Papers
US Army Center for Military History, Fort McNair, Washington, DC
    Blackford, Eugene. Diary
Frank, Abner. Diary
    Walker, Edward A. Letter & Diary
US Military History Institute, Carlisle, PA
    Click, Jacob. Letters
Virginia Historical Society, Richmond, VA
    Johnson, Elijah S. Diary
    Patch, George H. Papers
    Saunders, Flemming. Papers
    Sneden, Robert Knox. Diary
    Stuart, James E. B. Papers
    Watkins, Richard Henry. Papers
Virginia Military Institute, Lexington, VA
    Garibaldi, John. Letters
Western Reserve Historical Society, Cleveland, OH
    Bushnell, Wells A. "Sixth Regiment Ohio Volunteer Cavalry Memoir, 1861-1865"
        typescript
Winchester-Frederick County Historical Society, Handley Regional Library, Winchester, VA
    Russell, Stanley F. Letters
Wisconsin Historical Society, Madison, WS
    Quiner, Edwin B. Scrapbook: Correspondences of the Wisconsin Volunteers.

Published Primary Sources

"A Confederate." *The Grayjackets and How They Lived, Fought and Died for Dixie. With Incidents & Sketches of Life in the Confederacy*. Richmond, VA: Jones Brothers & Co., 1867.

Acken, J. Gregory, ed. *Inside the Army of the Potomac: The Civil War Experience of Captain Francis Adams Donaldson*. Mechanicsburg, PA: Stackpole Books, 1998.

Aggassiz, George R., ed. *Meade's Headquarters 1863-1865: Letters of Colonel Theodore Lyman*. Boston, MA: The Atlantic Monthly Press, 1922.

Aldrich, Thomas M. *The History of Battery A First Regiment Rhode Island Light Artillery in the War to Preserve the Union 1861-1865*. Providence, RI: Snow & Farnham, 1904.

Avery, James Henry. *Under Custer's Command: The Civil War Journal of James Henry Avery*. Washington, DC: Brassey's, 2000.

Barber, Raymond G. & Gary E. Swinson, ed. *The Civil War Letters of Charles Barber, Private, 104th New York Volunteer Infantry*. Torrance, CA: Gary E. Swinson, 1991.

Bartlett, A. W. *History of the Twelfth Regiment New Hampshire Volunteers in the War of the Rebellion*. Concord, NH: Ira C. Evans, Printer, 1897

Barnard, Sandy ed. *An Aide to Custer: The Civil War Letters of Lt. Edward G. Granger*. Norman, OK: University of Oklahoma Press, 2018.

Bassett, M.H. *From Bull Run to Bristow Station*. St. Paul, MN: North Central Publishing Co, 1962.

Baylor, George. *From Bull Run to Bull Run; or, Four Years in the Army of Northern Virginia.* Richmond, VA: B.F. Johnson Publishing Company, 1900.

Beale, George W. *A Lieutenant of Cavalry in Lee's Army.* Boston, MA: The Gorham Press, 1918.

Beale, R. *History of the Ninth Virginia Cavalry in the War Between the States.* Richmond, VA: B.F. Johnson Publishing Co., 1899.

Bean, William. *Stonewall's Man: Sandie Pendleton.* Chapel Hill, NC: University of North Carolina Press, 1959.

Beidler, Peter G. *Army of the Potomac: The Civil War Letters of William Cross Hazelton of the Eight Illinois Cavalry Regiment.* Seattle, WA: Epicenter Press, 2013.

Benjamin, Charles F. "Hooker's Appointment and Removal," *Battles and Leaders of the Civil War,* Vol. 3. New York: Castle Books, 1956.

Bennett, Edwin C. *Musket and Sword, or The Camp, March and Firing Line in the Army of the Potomac.* Boston, MA: Coburn Publishing Co., 1900.

Best, Isaac O. *History of the 121st New York State Infantry.* Chicago: Self-published.

Billings, John D. *The History of the Tenth Massachusetts Battery of Light Artillery in the War of the Rebellion, 1862-1865.* Boston, MA: Hall & Whiting, Publishers, 1881.

Birdsong, James, ed. *Brief Sketches of the North Carolina State Troops in the War Between the States.* Raleigh, NC: Josephus Daniels, State Printer and Binder, 1894.

Blackford, Charles Minor III, ed. *Letters from Lee's Army.* Lincoln: University of Nebraska Press, 1998.

Blackford, W.W. *War Years with Jeb Stuart.* Baton Rouge: Louisiana State University Press, 1993.

Blake, Henry N. *Three Years in the Army of the Potomac.* Boston: Lee and Shepard, 1866.

Bowen, James L. *History of the Thirty-Seventh Regiment Massachusetts Volunteers.* New York: Clark W. Bryan & Co., 1884.

Boudrye, Louis. *Historic Records of the Fifth New York Cavalry: First Ira Harris Guard.* Albany, NY: S.R. Gray, 1865.

Brock, Heros Von. *Memoirs of the Confederate War for Independence.* 2 vols. Edinburgh, UK: William Blackford & Sons, 1866.

Brooks, U.R., ed. *Stories of the Confederacy.* Columbia, SC: The State Company, 1912.

Bruce, George A. *The Twentieth Regiment of Massachusetts Volunteer Infantry, 1861-1865.* Boston: Houghton, Mifflin and Company, 1906.

Bryan, Charles Jr. and Lankford Nelson, eds. *Eye of the Storm.* New York: Simon & Schuster, 2000.

_____. *Images from the Storm.* New York: The Free Press, 2001.

Buck, Samuel. *With the Old Confeds: Actual Experiences of a Captain in the Line.* Baltimore, MD: H. E. Houck, 1925.

Byrne, Frank. *Haskell of Gettysburg: His Life and Civil War Papers.* Kent, OH: Kent State University Press, 1989.

Caldwell, J.F.J. *The History of a Brigade of South Carolinians.* Dayton, OH: Morningside Press, 1984.

Carroll, Douglas, ed. *The Letters of F. Stanley Russell: The Movements of Company H Thirteenth Virginia Regiment.* Baltimore, MD: Paul M. Harrod Company, 1963.

Carter, Robert G. *Four Brothers in Blue.* Austin: University of Texas Press, 1978.

Casler, John Overton. *Four Years in the Stonewall Brigade.* Marietta, GA: Continental Book Co., 1951.

Cassedy, Edward K. *Dear Friends at Home: The Civil War Letters of Sergeant Charles T. Bowen, Twelfth United States Infantry, First Battalion, 1861-1865.* Baltimore, MD: Butternut & Blue, 2001.

Chapman, Sarah Bahnson, ed. *Bright and Gloomy Days: The Civil War Correspondence of Captain Charles Frederic Bahnson, a Moravian Confederate*. Knoxville: University of Tennessee Press, 2003.

Cheney, Newell. *History of the Ninth Regiment New York Volunteer Cavalry, War of 1861 to 1865*. Jamestown, NY: Martin Mere & son, 1901.

Clark, Charles A. *Campaigning with the Sixth Maine*. Des Moines: The Kenyon Press, 1897.

Coltrane, Daniel. *The Memoirs of Daniel Branson Coltrane, Co. I, 63rd Regiment, N.C. Cavalry C.S.A.* Raleigh, NC: Edwards & Broughton Company, 1956.

Cooke, John Esten. *Wearing of the Gray; Personal Portraits, Scenes and Adventures of the War*. New York: E. B. Treat & Co., 1867.

Corson, Blake W. Jr., ed. *My Dear Jennie*. Richmond, VA: Dietz Press Inc., 1982.

Cockrell, Monroe, ed. *Gunner with Stonewall: Reminiscences of William Thomas Poague*. Wilmington, NC: Broadfoot Publishing, 1987.

Cockrell, Thomas D. *A Mississippi Rebel in the Army of Northern Virginia: The Civil War Memoirs of Private David Holt*. Baton Rouge: Louisiana State University Press, 2005.

Cowtan, Charles W. *Services of the Tenth New York Volunteers (National Zouaves) in the War of the Rebellion*. New York: Charles H. Ludwig, Printer, 1882.

Craft, David. *History of the One Hundred Forty-First Regiment Pennsylvania Volunteers, 1862-1865*. Towanda, PA: Reporter-Journal Printing Company, 1885.

Crowninshield, Benjamin. *A History of the First Regiment of Massachusetts Cavalry Volunteers*. Cambridge, MA: The Riverside Press, 1899.

Cutrer, Thomas W. & Parrish, T. Michael eds., *Brothers in Gray: The Civil War Letters of the Pierson Family*. Baton Rouge: Louisiana State University Press, 1997.

David, James A., ed., *"Bully for the Band!" The Civil War Letters and Diary of Four Brothers in the 10th Vermont Infantry Band*. Jefferson, NC: McFarland & Company, 2012.

Denison, Frederic. *Sabres and Spurs: The First Regiment Rhode Island Cavalry in the Civil War, 1861-1865*. Central Falls, RI: The First Rhode Island Cavalry Veteran Association, 1876.

de Trobriand, Regis. *Four Years with the Army of the Potomac*. Gaithersburg, MD: Ron R. Van Sickle Military Books, 1988.

Dobbins, Austin, ed. *Grandfather's Journal*. Dayton, OH: Morningside Press, 1988.

Doster William E., *Lincoln and Episodes of the Civil War,* New York: G. P. Putnam's Sons, 1915.

Dougherty, Michael. *Diary of a Civil War Hero*. New York: Pyramid Books, 1960.

Dowdy, Clifford and Louis Manarin, eds. *The Wartime Papers of Robert E. Lee*. New York: Bramhall House, 1961.

Dozier, Graham, *A Gunner in Lee's Army: The Civil War Letters of Thomas Henry Carter*. Chapel Hill, NC: University of North Carolina Press, 2014.

Durkin, Joseph T., ed. *Confederate Chaplain: Rev. James B. Sheeran, C.S.S.R. 14th Louisiana, C.S.A.* Milwaukee, WI: The Bruce Publishing Company, 1960.

Early, Jubal. *Lieutenant General Jubal Anderson Early, C.S.A. Autobiographical Sketch and Narrative of the War Between the States*. New York: Konecy & Konecy, 1994.

Eggleston, George Cary. *A Rebel's Recollections*. New York: G. P. Putnam's Sons, 1905.

Eidler, Peter G. *Army of the Potomac: The Civil War Letters of William Cross Hazelton of the Eighth Illinois Cavalry Regiment*. Seattle, WA: Coffeetown Press, 2013.

Favill, Josiah Marshall. *The Diary of a Young Officer*. Chicago, IL: R.R. Donnelley & Sons Company, 1909.

Floyd, Dale E. *"Dear Folks at Home . . ." The Letters and Diary of Thomas James Owen, Fiftieth New York Volunteer Engineer Regiment, During the Civil War.* Washington, DC: US Government Printing Office, 1985.

Ford, Andrew E. *The Story of the Fifteenth Regiment Massachusetts Volunteer Infantry in the Civil War, 1861-1864.* Clinton, MA: Press of W. J. Coulter, 1898.

Fremantle, Arthur L. *Three Months in the Southern States: April-June 1863.* New York: John Bradburn, 1864.

Galwey, Thomas Francis. *The Valiant Hours: An Irishman in the Civil War.* Harrisburg, PA: The Stackpole Company, 1961.

Gibbon, John. *Recollections of the Civil War.* New York: G. P. Putnam's Sons, 1890.

Gienapp, William E. and Erica L. Gienapp, eds., *The Civil War Diary of Gideon Welles: Lincoln's Secretary of the Navy,* Urbana: University of Illinois Press, 2014.

Glazier, Willard. *Three Years in the Federal Cavalry.* New York: R. H. Ferguson & Co., 1870.

Goss, Warren. *Recollections of a Private.* New York: Thomas Y. Crowell & Co., 1890.

Gracey, Samuel L. *Annals of the Sixth Pennsylvania Cavalry.* E. H. Butler & Co., 1868.

Graham, Dozier T., ed. *A Gunner in Lee's Army: The Wartime Letters of Thomas Henry Carter.* Chapel Hill: University of North Carolina Press, 2004.

Greiner, James M. *Subdued by the Sword: A Line Officer in the 121st New York Volunteers.* Albany, NY: State University of New York Press, 2003.

Greiner, James M., Coryell, Janet L. and Smither, James R., eds., A Surgeon's Civil War: The Letters and Diary of Daniel M. Holt, M.D. Kent, OH: Kent State University Press, 1994.

Griffin, Richard, ed. *Three Years a Soldier: The Diary and Newspaper Correspondence of Private George Perkins, Sixth New York Independent Battery, 1861-1864.* Knoxville: University of Tennessee Press, 2006.

Grimsley, Daniel. *Battles in Culpeper County, Virginia, 1861-1865 and other articles by Major Daniel A. Grimsley, of the Sixth Virginia Cavalry.* Culpeper, VA: Exponent Printing Office, 1900.

Hall, Hillman, et al. *History of the Sixth New York Cavalry (Second Ira Harris Guard) Second Brigade—First Division—Cavalry Corps, Army of the Potomac: 1861-1865.* Worcester, MA: The Blanchard Press, 1908.

Hamilton, J. G. DeRoulhac ed. *The Diary of Bartlett Yancey Malone.* Chapel Hill: University of North Carolina, 1919.

Handerson, Henry. *Yankee in Gray: The Civil War Memoirs of Henry E. Handerson.* Cleveland, OH: Western Reserve University Press, 1962.

Hard, Abner. *History of the Eighth Cavalry Regiment Illinois Volunteers, During the Great Rebellion.* Aurora, IL: Self-published, 1868.

Harden, M. D. *History of the Twelfth Regiment Pennsylvania Reserve Volunteer Corps.* New York: Self-published, 1890. Harris, Samuel. *Personal Reminiscences of Samuel Harris.* Chicago, IL: The Rogerson Press, 1897.

Haupt, Herman. *Reminiscences of General Herman Haupt.* Milwaukee, WI: Wright & Joys Co., 1901.

Haynes, Edwin M. *A History of the Tenth Regiment Vermont Volunteers.* Lewiston, ME: Journal Steam Press, 1870.

Hennessy, John, ed. *Fighting with the 18th Massachusetts: The Civil War Memoir of Thomas H. Mann.* Baton Rouge: Louisiana State University Press, 2000.

Herdegen, Lance and Murphy Sherry, eds. *Four Years with The Iron Brigade: The Civil War Journal of William Ray, Company F, 7th Wisconsin Infantry.* Cambridge, MA: De Capo Press, 2002.

Hewett, Janet, Suderow, Bryce, and Trudeau, Noah Andre, eds. *Supplement to the Official Records of the Union and Confederate Armies.* 100 Volumes. Wilmington, NC: Broadfoot Publishing Co., 1995.

Hoffman, Elliott W. *History of the First Vermont Cavalry Volunteers In the War of the Great Rebellion.* Baltimore, MD: Butternut & Blue, 2000.

Hood, John Bell. *Advance and Retreat: Personal Experiences in the United States and Confederate States Armies.* New Orleans, LA: Hood Orphan Memorial Fund, 1880.

Hopkins, Luther. *From Bull Run to Appomattox.* Baltimore, MD: Fleet-McGinley Co., 1914.

Howard, McHenry. *Recollections of a Maryland Confederate Soldier and Staff Officer.* Baltimore, MD: Williams & Wilkins, 1914.

Howard, Oliver Otis. *Autobiography of Oliver Otis Howard, Major General, United States Army.* New York: The Baker & Taylor Company, 1907.

Humphreys, Andrew. *From Gettysburg to the Rapidan—The Army of the Potomac, July, 1863 to April, 1864.* New York: Charles Scribner's Sons, 1883.

Hyndman, William. *History of a Cavalry Company: A Complete Record of Company A, 4th Penn'a Cavalry.* Philadelphia, PA: Jas. B. Rodgers Co, Printers, 1870.

Jones, J. William. *Christ in the Camp: Religion in Lee's Army.* Richmond, VA: B. F. Johnson Company, 1887.

Jones, John B. *A Rebel War Clerk's Diary.* 2 Vols. Philadelphia, PA: J.B. Lippincott & Co., 1866.

Jones, Terry, ed. *Campbell Brown's Civil War: With Ewell and The Army of Northern Virginia.* Baton Rouge: Louisiana State University Press, 2001.

_____. *The Civil War Memoirs of Captain William J. Seymour: Reminiscences of a Louisiana Tiger.* Baton Rouge: Louisiana State University Press, 1991.

Judson, Amos M. *History of the Eight-Third Regiment Pennsylvania Volunteers, 1861-1865,* Dayton, OH: Morningside Press, 1986.

Kidd, James. *Personal Recollections of a Cavalryman.* Ionia, MI: Sentinel Printing Company, 1908.

Keifer, Joseph Warren. *Slavery and Four Years of War: a Political History of Slavery in the United States, Together With a Narrative of the Campaigns and Battles of the Civil War in Which the Author Took Part, 1861-1865.* 2 Vols. New York: G. P. Putnam's Sons, 1900.

Lane, James H. "History of Lane's North Carolina Brigade" *Southern Historical Society Papers.* Vol. 9. January-December 1881. Richmond, VA: Wm Ellis Jones, Printer.

Lane, Mills. *Dear Mother, Don't Grieve About Me, If I Get Killed, I'll Only Be Dead: Letters from Georgia Soldiers in the Civil War.* Savannah, GA: Beehive Press, 1977.

Lee, Robert E. Jr., *Recollections and Letters of General Robert E. Lee.* New York, NY: Doubleday, Page & Co., 1904.

Lee, Susan P., ed. *Memoirs of William Nelson Pendleton, d.d. Rector of Latimer Parish, Lexington, Virginia: Brigadier-General C. S. A.; Chief of Artillery, Army of Northern Virginia.* Philadelphia, PA: J.B. Lippincott Co., 1893.

Lewis, George. *Battery E First Rhode Island Light Artillery 1861-1865.* Providence, RI: Snow & Farnham, 1892.

Lewis, Osceola. *History of the 138th Regiment of Pennsylvania Volunteer Infantry.* Norristown, PA: Wills, Iredell & Jenkins, 1866.

Livermore, Thomas. *Days & Events 1860-1866.* Boston, MA: Houghton Mifflin Co., 1920.

Lloyd, William. *History of the First Regiment Pennsylvania Reserve Cavalry.* Philadelphia: King & Baird, 1864.

Long, A. L. *Memoirs of Robert E. Lee.* Secaucus, NJ: The Blue and Gray Press, 1983.

Longstreet, James. *From Manassas to Appomattox*. Secaucus, NJ: Blue & Gray Press, 1984.

Longstreet, James. "Lee in Pennsylvania," *The Annals of the War Written by Leading Participants North and South*. New York: De Capo Press, 1994.

Lowe, David, ed. *Meade's Army: The Private Notebooks of Lt. Col. Theodore Lyman*. Kent, OH: Kent State University Press, 2007.

MacNamara, Daniel G. *History of the Ninth Regiment Massachusetts Volunteer Infantry*, Boston, MA: E. B. Stillings & Co., Printers, 1899.

Martin, James, et al. *History of the Fifty-Seventh Regiment Pennsylvania Volunteer Infantry*. Meadville, PA: McCoy & Calvin, n.d.

McClellan, Henry B. *I Rode with Jeb Stuart: The Life and Campaigns of Major General J. E. B. Stuart*. Bloomington: Indiana University Press, 1958.

McDonald, Archie P., ed. *Jedediah Hotchkiss: Make Me a Map of the Valley: The Civil War Journal of Stonewall Jackson's Topographer*. Dallas, TX: Southern Methodist University Press, 1973.

McDonald, William N. *A History of the Laurel Brigade*. Baltimore, MD: Sun Job Printing Office, 1907.

McKim, Randolph, *A Soldier's Recollections: Leaves from the Diary of a Young Confederate*. New York: Longmans, Green and Co., 1910.

McKinney, Edward P. *Life in Tent, Camp and Field, 1861-1865*. Boston, MA: Badger, 1922.

McMahon, Martin. "From Gettysburg to the Coming of Grant." *Battles and Leaders of the Civil War*. Vol. 4. New York: Castle Books, 1956.

McMullen, Glenn, ed. *A Surgeon with Stonewall Jackson: The Civil War Letters of Dr. Harvey Black*. Baltimore, MD: Butternut and Blue, 1995.

McNamara, M. "Lt. Charlie Pierce's Daring Attempts to Escape from Johnson's Island" *Southern Historical Society Papers*. Volume 8. 1880.

McSwain, Eleanor ed., *Crumbling Defenses or Memoirs and Reminiscences of John Logan Black, Colonel C.S.A.* Macon, GA: The J. W. Burke Company, 1960.

Meade, George. *Life and Letters of George Gordon Meade*. 2 Volumes. New York: Charles Scribner's Sons, 1913.

Michie, Peter. *The Life and Letters of Emory Upton*. New York: D. Appleton and Company, 1885.

Meir, Heinz K., ed. *Memoirs of a Swiss Officer in the American Civil War*. Frankfurt, Germany: Peter Lang AG, International Publishing House of Sciences, 1972.

Merrington, Marguerite, ed. *The Custer Story, The Life and Intimate Letters of General George A. Custer and His Wife Elizabeth*. New York: Devin-Adair, 1950.

Meyer, Henry C. *Civil War Experiences under Bayard, Gregg, Kilpatrick, Custer, Raulston, and Newberry: 1862, 1863, 1864*. New York: The Knickerbocker Press, 1911.

Moore, Edward. *The Story of a Cannoneer Under Stonewall Jackson*. New York: Neale Publishing, 1907.

Moore, Frank, ed. *The Rebellion Record: A Diary of American Events with Documents, Narratives, Illustrative Incidents, Poetry, Etc.,* 12 Volumes. New York: D. Van Nostrand, Publisher, 1864.

Moore, John W. *Roster of North Carolina Troops in the War Between the States,* 18 Volumes. Ashe & Gatling State Printers: Raleigh, NC, 1882.

Morse, Frances W., *Personal Experiences in the War of the Rebellion: From December 1862 to July 1865*. Albany, NY: Unpublished. Printed, 1866.

Morse, J. T., ed. *Diary of Gideon Welles*. 3 Volumes. Boston: Houghton Mifflin Co., 1952.

Moyer, H. P. *History of the Seventeenth Regiment Pennsylvania Volunteer Cavalry*. Lebanon, PA: Sowers Printing Co., 1911.

Muffly, Joseph. *The Story of Our Regiment: A History of the 148th Pennsylvania Volunteers.* Des Moines, IA: Kenyon Printing & Mfg. Co., 1904.

Mulholland, St. Clair. *The Story of the 116th Regiment Pennsylvania Infantry: War of Secession, 1862-1865.* Philadelphia, PA: F. McManus Jr. & Co., 1899.

Munson, E. B., ed. Confederate Correspondent: The Civil War Reports of Jacob Nathaniel Raymer, Fourth North Carolina. Jefferson, NC: McFarland & Company, Inc. Publishers, 2009.

Nanzig, Thomas P., ed. The Civil War Memoirs of a Virginia Cavalryman: Lt. Robert T. Hubard, Jr. Tuscaloosa: The University of Alabama Press, 2007.

Nash, Eugene A. A History of the Forty-fourth Regiment New York Volunteer Infantry in the Civil War 1861-1865. Chicago, IL: R. R. Donnelley & Sons Company, 1911.

Neese, George M. Three Years in the Confederate Horse Artillery. New York: The Neale Publishing Company, 1911.

Nevins, Allan., ed. A Diary of Battle: The Personal Journals of Colonel Charles S. Wainwright, 1861-1865. New York: Da Capo Press, 1998.

Newhall, Walter S. A Memoir. Philadelphia, PA: C. Sherman Son & Company, 1864.

Nichols, George. A Soldier's Story of His Regiment (61st Georgia) and Incidentally of the Lawton-Gordon-Evens Brigade, Army of Northern Virginia. Tuscaloosa: The University of Alabama Press, 2011.

Norton, Henry. Deeds of Daring or a History of the Eighth N.Y. Volunteer Cavalry. Norwich, NY: Chenango Telegraph Printing House, 1889.

Norton, Oliver. Army Letters 1861-1865. Chicago, IL: O. L. Deming, 1903.

Page, Charles. History of the Fourteenth Regiment Connecticut Vol. Infantry. Meriden, CT: Horton Printing Co., 1906.

Park, Robert Emory. "War Diary of Captain Robert Emory Park." Southern Historical Society Papers. Vol. 24. Richmond, VA: Wm Ellis Jones, Printer.

Perry, Martha Derby. Letters from a Surgeon of the Civil War. Boston, MA: Little, Brown and Company, 1906.

Phisterer, Frederick. New York in the War of the Rebellion, 3rd edition. Albany, NY: J.B. Lyon Company, 1912.

Pickerill, W. N. History of the Third Indiana Cavalry. Indianapolis, IN, 1906.

Porter, Horace, Campaigning with Grant, New York: Century, 1897.

Preston, N.D. History of the Tenth Regiment of Cavalry New York State Volunteers. New York: D. Appleton & Co., 1892.

Pyne, Henry. History of the First New Jersey Cavalry. Trenton, NJ: J.A. Beecher, 1871.

Rawle, William Brooke, et al. History of the Third Pennsylvania Cavalry 1861-1865. Philadelphia, PA: Franklin Printing Co., 1905.

Regimental Association Publication Committee. History of the Eighteenth Regiment of Cavalry Pennsylvania Volunteers, 1862-1865. New York: Winkoop, Hallenbeck, Crawford Co., 1909.

Regimental History Committee. History of the Third Pennsylvania Cavalry, Sixtieth Regiment Pennsylvania Volunteers in the American Civil War, 1861-1865. Philadelphia, PA: Franklin Printing Company, 1905.

Reichardt, Theodore. Diary of Battery A, First Regiment Rhode Island Light Artillery. Providence, RI: N. Bangs Williams, Publisher, 1865.

Rhodes, John H. The History of Battery B, First Regiment Rhode Island Light Artillery in the War to Preserve the Union, 1861-1865. Providence, RI: Snow Farnham Printers, 1894.

Rodenbough, Theophilus F. et al. History of the Eighteenth Regiment of Cavalry Pennsylvania Volunteers (163rd Regiment of the Line) 1862-1865. New York: Wynkoop Hallenbeck Crawford Company, 1909.

Roe, Alfred S. The Thirty-Ninth Massachusetts Volunteers 1862-1865. Worcester, MA: Regimental Veteran Association, 1914.

Rosenblatt, Ruth & Emil ed. Hard Marching Every Day: The Civil War Letters of Private Wilbur Fish, 1861-1865. Lawrence, KS: University of Kansas Press, 1992.

Runge, William H., ed. Four Years in the Confederate Artillery: The Diary of Private Henry Robinson Berkeley. Richmond: Virginia Historical Society, 1991.

Schultz, Jane E. ed. This Birth Place of Souls: The Civil War Diary of Harriet Eaton. New York: Oxford University Press, 2011.

Scott, Robert Garth, ed. Fallen Leaves: The Civil War Letters of Major Henry Livermore Abbott. Kent, OH: The Kent State University Press, 1991.

Silliker, Ruth L., The Rebel Yell & the Yankee Hurrah: The Civil War Journal of a Maine Volunteer. Camden, ME: Down East Books, 1985.

Simons, Ezra. A Regimental History. The One Hundred and Twenty-Fifth New York State Volunteers. New York: Ezra D. Simons, 1888.

Sloan, John A. Reminiscences of the Guilford Grays, Co. B, 27th N.C. Regiment. Washington, DC: R. O. Polkinhorn, Printer, 1883.

Smith, John L. History of the Corn Exchange Regiment, 118th Pennsylvania Volunteers. Philadelphia, PA: J. L. Smith, Publisher, 1888.

Smith, William A. The Anson Guards: History of Company C, 14th Regiment, N.C.V., Army of Northern Virginia. Charlotte, VA: Stone Publishing Co., 1914.

Sparks, David. Inside Lincoln's Army: The Diary of Marsena Rudolph Patrick, Provost Marshal General, Army of the Potomac. New York: Thomas Yoseloff, 1964.

Spencer, Carrie Esther & Samuels, Bernard. A Civil Marriage in Virginia: Reminiscences and Letters. Boyce, VA: Carr Publishing Co., 1956.

Stevens, Charles. Berdan's United States Sharpshooters in the Army of the Potomac. St. Paul, MN: Price-McGill Company, 1892.

Stevens, George. Three Years in the Sixth Corps. New York: D. Van Nostrand, Publisher, 1870.

Stewart, Robert L. History of the One Hundred Fortieth Regiment Pennsylvania Volunteers. Philadelphia, PA: The Regimental Association, 1912.

Stiles, Robert. Four Years Under Marse Robert. New York, NY: Neale Publishing Co., 1903.

Styple, William B. With A Flash of His Sword: The Writings of Major Homan S. Melcher, 20th Maine Infantry. Kearny, NJ: Belle Grove Publishing, 1994.

Survivors' Association. History of the 121st Regiment Pennsylvania Volunteers: An Account from the Ranks. Philadelphia: Catholic Standard and Times, 1906.

Swank, Walbrook D., ed. Sabres, Saddles and Spurs: Lieutenant Colonel William R. Carter, CSA. Shippensburg, PA: Burd Street Press, 1998.

_____. The Civil War Diary of John William Peyton. Shippensburg, PA: Burd Street Press, 2003.

Taylor, Michael, ed. To Drive the Enemy from Southern Soil: The Letters of Col. Francis Marion Parker and the History of the 30th Regiment North Carolina Troops. Dayton, OH: Morningside Press, 1988.

Tenney, Lumen H. *War Diary of Lummen Harris Tenney, 1861-1865*. Oberlin, OH: Frances Andrews Tenney, 1914.

Tobie, Edward. *History of the First Maine Cavalry, 1861-1865*. Boston: Press of Emery & Hughes, 1887.

Tower, R. Lockwood, ed., *Lee's Adjutant: The Wartime Letters of Colonel Walter Herron Taylor, 1862-1865*. Columbia: University of South Carolina Press, 1995.

Trout, Robert, ed. *Memoirs of the Stuart Horse Artillery Battalion: Moorman's and Hart's Batteries*. Knoxville: University of Tennessee Press, 1998.

_____. *Memoirs of the Stuart Horse Artillery Battalion, Volume 2: Breathed's and McGregor's Batteries*. Knoxville: University of Tennessee Press, 2010.

Turner, Charles W., ed. *Ted Barclay, Liberty Hall Volunteers: Letters from the Stonewall Brigade (1861-1865)*. Natural Bridge Station, VA: Rockbridge Publishing Company, 1992.

Urban, John W. *My Experiences Mid Shot and Shell and in the Rebel Den*. Lancaster, PA: Hubbard Brothers, 1882.

Van Santvoord, C., *The One Hundred and Twentieth Regiment New York State Volunteers. A Narrative of its Services in the War for the Union*. Rondout, NY: Press of the Kingston Freeman, 1894.

Von Brock, Heros *Memoirs of the Confederate War for Independence*, 2 Vols. Edinburg, England: William Blackwood & Sons, 1866.

Walker, Francis. *History of the Second Army Corps*. New York: Charles Scribner's Sons, 1887.

Wallace, Lew. *Lew Wallace, An Autobiography*, New York: Harper and Brothers, 1906.

Walters, John. *Norfolk Blues: The Civil War Diary of the Norfolk Light Artillery Blues*. Shippensburg, PA: Burd Street Press, 1997.

Ward, Joseph R.C. *History of the One Hundred Sixth Regiment Pennsylvania Volunteers 2nd Brigade, 2nd Division, 2nd Corps*. Philadelphia, PA: Grant, Faires and Rodgers, 1883.

Wells, Cheryl, ed. *A Surgeon in the Army of the Potomac*. Montreal: McGill Queens University Press, 2008.

Westbrook, Robert S. *History of the 49th Pennsylvania Volunteers*. Altoona, PA: Altoona Times Print, 1898.

Wiggins, Sarah Woolfolk, ed. *The Journals of Josiah Gorgas, 1857-1878*. Tuscaloosa, AL: University of Alabama Press, 1995.

Williams, Edward B., ed. *Rebel Brothers: The Civil War Letters of the Truehearts*. College Station: Texas A&M University Press, 1995.

Wittenberg, Eric, ed. *One of Custer's Wolverines: The Civil War Letters of Brevet Brigadier General James H. Kidd, 6th Michigan Cavalry*. Kent, OH: Kent State University Press, 2000.

_____. *Under Custer's Command: The Civil War Journal of James Henry Avery*. Compiled by Karla Jean Husby. Washington, DC: Brassey's, 2000.

_____. *"We Have It Damn Hard Out Here: The Civil War Letters of Sergeant Thomas W. Smith, 6th Pennsylvania Cavalry."* Kent, OH: Kent State University Press, 1999.

Worsham, John. *One of Jackson's Foot Cavalry*. New York: Neale Publishing Co., 1912.

Woodward, E. M., *Our Campaigns; or the Marches, Bivouacs, Battles, Incidents of Camp Life and History of Our Regiment During Its Three Years Term of Service*. Philadelphia: John E. Potter, 1865.

Wright, James A. *No More Gallant a Deed: A Civil War Memoir of the First Minnesota Volunteers*. St. Paul: Minnesota Historical Society Press, 2001.

Younger, Edward, ed. *Inside the Confederate Government: The Diary of Robert Garlick Hill Kean*. Baton Rouge: Louisiana State University Press, 1993.

Online Primary Sources

"Albert L. Peel Diary," http://freepages.rootsweb.com/~peel/family/peelnov.html

Anderson, James S, "The Battle of Rappahannock Station" in Proceedings at the Annual Meeting of the Association of Fifth Wisconsin Volunteer Infantry, (Milwaukee, WI, 1901), https://babel.hathitrust.org/ cgi/pt?id=mdp.39015078124883;view=1up;seq=1

Civil War Voices—Soldier Studies, "Soldier Profile, Bates, Delavan." http://www. soldierstudies.org/ index.php?action=soldier_profile&Soldier=12.

Civil War Letters of George Bolton of New York. http://www.canton.org/ canton/Civil%20War%20Letters%20of%20George%20Bolton%20of%20New%20York .htm.

Hathi Trust Digital Library. "Letters of Fredrick C. Winkler, 1862-1865." https://catalog.hathitrust.org/ Record/009628680

Historical Society of Oak Park and River Forest, Ill, "Manley Stacey Civil War Letters." http://martyhackl.net/ staceyletters/2009/07/07/november-9-1863-brandy-station/

Howard, Wiley C. "Sketch of Cobb Legion Cavalry and Some Incidents and Scenes Remembered." http:// docsouth.unc.edu/fpn/howard/howard.html

Morse, Charles F. Civil War Letters of Charles F. Morse: 1861-1865. www.bigbytebooks.com, 2014.

New York State Military Museum and Veterans Center. "1st Artillery Regiment, Light, Battery L, George Breck Columns, Chapter xxi, 'An Army of Observation' All Quiet On The Rappahannock, July 28, 1863–Oct. 7, 1863."http://dmna.ny.gov/historic/reghist/civil/ artillery/1stArtLt/1stArtLtBatLBreckChap21Observation. htm.

_____. "5th Regiment Cavalry, New York Volunteers." https://dmna.ny.gov/historic/ reghist/civil/ cavalry/5thCav/5thCavCWN.htm.

_____. "43rd Infantry Regiment, New York Volunteers" https://dmna.ny.gov/historic/ reghist/civil/infantry/ 43rdInf/43rdInfCWN3.pdf

Shotgun's Home of the American Civil War. "The Diary of Edwin B. Weist." www. civilwarhome. com/weistdiary.htm

Sillers-Homes Family Correspondence, Manuscripts of the American Civil War, University of Notre Dame. https://rarebooks.nd.edu/digital/civil_war/letters/sillers-holmes/ 5025-15.shtml

The Civil War Letters of Charles Engle. 137th New York Volunteer Infantry. http:// www.sugarfoottales.org/.

The Civil War Letters of Delavan Bates. http://www.usgennet.org/usa/ne/ topic/military/CW/ bates/genbate2.html

"The Civil War Letters of Thompson, Connecticut's Henry Washington Brown, 21st Massachusetts Volunteer Regiment, 1861-1865." https://www.thompsonhistorical.org/pdf/Private%20Henry%20W%20Brown% 20Letters.pdf..

"The year 1863 from the diary of Alonzo Clapp." http://web.cortland.edu/woosterk/genweb/ alonzoclapp/alonzoclapp1863.html.

The 126th Ohio Volunteer Infantry. "Letters of First Lieutenant Rufus Ricksecker." http://www. frontierfamilies.net/family/Rickpt1.htm

The Valley of the Shadow. "Hotchkiss Family Letters—the War Years." http:// valley.lib.virginia. edu/VoS/personalpapers/documents/augusta/p2hotchkissletters.html

Wikitree. "John   Dominque   Vautier   (1843-1912)"   www.wikitree.com/wiki/
        Vautier-28#Transcript_of_ John.27s_ Civil_War_Diary

Newspapers

Alexandria [VA] *Gazette*
Burlington [VT] *Daily Free Press*
Brookville [PA] *Republican*
Charleston [SC] *Mercury*
Columbia Democrat [Bloomsburg, PA]
Daily Morning Chronicle [Washington, DC]
Daily National Republican [Washington, DC]
Harper's Weekly [New York, NY]
Illustrated London News [London, England]
Lamoille News Dealer [Hyde Park, VT]
Memphis [TN] *Daily Appeal*
National Intelligencer [Washington, D.C]
Orleans Independent Standard [Irasburgh, VT]
Philadelphia Evening Bulletin [Philadelphia, PA]
Providence Evening Press [Providence, RI]
Republican & *Sentinel* [Youngstown, OH]
Richmond [VA] *Dispatch*
Richmond [VA] *Whig*
Southern Watchman [Athens, GA]
The Abingdon [VA] *Virginian*
The Anderson Intelligencer [Anderson, SC]
The Evening Star [Washington, DC]
The Gettysburg [PA] *Compiler*
The Daily Intelligencer [Wheeling, WV]
The National Tribune [Washington, DC]
The New York Daily Tribune
The New York [NY] *Herald*
The New York [NY] *Times*
The Peoples Press [Selma, NC]
The Philadelphia [PA] *Inquirer*
The Press [Philadelphia, PA]
The Republican Standard [New Bedford, MA]
The Richmond [VA] Enquirer
The Richmond [VA] *Examiner*
The [NY] *Sun*
The [NY] *World*
Wyoming Mirror [Warsaw, NY]

Government Documents

Commonwealth of Virginia Dept. of Transportation, *State Highway Commission Plan and Profile of Proposed State Highway, Fauquier and Culpeper Counties from 0.02 Mi. N. of S.C.L. of Remington to 0.667 Mi. South*. Sheets 1-5, October 24, 1927.

Report of the Joint Committee on the Conduct of the War at the Second Session of the Thirty-eighth Congress, Vol. 4. Washington: Government Printing Office, 1865.

The War of the Rebellion: A Compilation of the Official Records of the Union and Confederate Armies. 128 Volumes. Washington, DC: Government Printing Office, 1880-1901.

Secondary Sources

Books

Ambrose, Stephen E. *Halleck: Lincoln's Chief of Staff*. Baton Rouge: Louisiana State University Press, 1996.

Andrews, Cutler. *The South Reports the Civil War*. Princeton, NJ: Princeton University Press, 1970.

Bache, Richard Meade. *Life of General George Gordon Meade Commander of the Army of the Potomac*. Philadelphia, PA: Henry T. Coates and Company, 1897.

Backus, Bill and Orrison, Robert. *A Want of Vigilance: The Bristoe Station Campaign, October 9-19, 1863*. El Dorado, CA: Savas Beatie, 2015.

Barfoot, Daniel. *General Robert F. Hoke: Lee's Modest Warrior*. Winston-Salem, NC: John F. Blair, 1996.

Benedict, G. C. *Vermont in the Civil War: A History of the Part Taken by the Vermont Soldiers and Sailors in the War for the Union*. Burlington, VT: The Free Press Association, 1886.

Best, Isaac O. *History of the 121st New York State Infantry*. Chicago, IL: Jas. H. Smith, 1921.

Black, Robert C. III. *The Railroads of the Confederacy*. Chapel Hill, NC: University of North Carolina Press, 1998.

Blackwell, Samuel M. Jr. *In the First Line of Battle: The 12th Illinois Cavalry in the Civil War*. DeKalb, IL: Northern Illinois University Press, 2002.

Boatner, Mark III. *The Civil War Dictionary*. New York: David McKay Company, 1959.

Burns, Vincent L. *The Fifth New York Cavalry in the Civil War*. Jefferson, NC: McFarland & Co., Inc., 2014.

Bushong, Millard and Dean. *Fightin' Tom Rosser, C.S.A*. Shippensburg, PA: Beidel Printing House, Inc., 1983.

Callaham, Donald. *The Rappahannock Canal*. Fredericksburg, VA: R. A. Hodge, 1969.

Cilella, Salvatore G. Jr. *Upton's Regulars: The 121st New York Infantry in the Civil War*. Lawrence: University Press of Kansas, 2008.

Clark, Walter, ed. *Histories of the Several Regiments and Battalions from North Carolina in the Great War 1861-1865*. 5 Volumes. Goldsboro, NC: Nash Brothers, 1901.

Cleaves, Freeman. *Meade of Gettysburg*. Norman: University of Oklahoma Press, 1960.

Coffman, Richard M. *Going Back the Way They Came: The Phillips Legion Cavalry Battalion*. Macon, GA: Mercer University Press, 2011.

Collea, Joseph D., Jr. *The First Vermont Cavalry in the Civil War*. Jefferson, NC: McFarland & Company Inc., 2010.

Collins, Darrell L. *Major General Robert E. Rodes of the Army of Northern Virginia: A Biography*. El Dorado Hills, CA: Savas Beatie, 2008

Davis, George B. et al., *The Official Military Atlas of the Civil War*. Washington, DC: Government Printing Office, 1891.

Davis, William C. *Jefferson Davis: The Man and His Hour, A Biography*. New York: Harper Perennial, 1992.

Douglas, David. *A Boot Full of Memories: Captain Leonard Williams, 2nd S.C. Cavalry*. Lexington, SC: Palmetto Books, 2003.

Ellis, Edward S. *The Campfires of General Lee from the Peninsula to Appomattox Court-house*. Philadelphia, PA: Henry Harrison & Co., 1885.

Ent, Uzal W. *The Pennsylvania Reserves in the Civil War: A Comprehensive History*. Jefferson, NC: McFarland & Company, Inc., 2012.

Faust, Patricia, ed. *Historical Times Illustrated Encyclopedia of the Civil War*. New York: Harper & Row, 1986.

Freeman, Douglas Southall. *Lee's Lieutenants*. 3 Volumes. New York: Charles Scribner's Sons, 1944.

_____. *R. E. Lee*. 4 Volumes. New York: Charles Scribner's Sons, 1935.

Fyre, Dennis. *The Second Virginia Cavalry*. Lynchburg, VA: H.E. Howard, 1984.

_____. *The Twelfth Virginia Cavalry*. Lynchburg VA: H.E. Howard, 1988.

Gallagher, Gary. *Lee & His Army in Confederate History*. Chapel Hill, NC: University of North Carolina Press, 2001.

_____. *Lee the Soldier*. Lincoln: University of Nebraska Press, 1996.

_____. *Stephen Dodson Ramseur: Lee's Gallant General*. Chapel Hill: University of North Carolina Press, 1985.

Gottfried, Bradley M. *Brigades of Gettysburg: The Union and Confederate Brigades at the Battle of Gettysburg*. Cambridge, MA: Da Capo Press, 2002.

_____. *Stopping Pickett: The History of the Philadelphia Brigade*. Shippensburg, PA: White Mane Books, 1999.

Graham, Martin and Skoch, George. *Mine Run: A Campaign of Lost Opportunities. October 21, 1863–May 1, 1864*. Lynchburg, VA: H. E. Howard, 1987.

Hand, Harold, Jr. *One Good Regiment: The 13th Pennsylvania Cavalry in the Civil War, 1861-1865*. Victoria, British Columbia, Canada: Trafford Publishing, 2000.

Harrell, Roger. *The Second North Carolina Cavalry*. Jefferson, NC: McFarland & Company Inc., Publisher, 2004.

Hartley, Chris. *Stuart's Tarheels: James B. Gordon and His North Carolina Cavalry in the Civil War*. Jefferson, NC: McFarland & Company, Inc., 2011.

Hattaway, Herman and Jones, Archer. *How the North Won*. Chicago: University of Illinois Press, 1983.

Henry, Robert S. *The Story of the Confederacy*. New York: Grosset & Dunlap, 1936.

Hess, Earl J. *Braxton Bragg: The Most Hated Man of the Confederacy*. Chapel Hill: University of North Carolina Press, 2016.

Holland, Lynwood. *Pierce M. B. Young: The Warwick of the South*. Athens: University of Georgia Press, 1964.

Humphreys, Henry. *Andrew Atkinson Humphreys–A Biography*. Gaithersburg, MD: Ron R. Van Sickle Military Books, 1988.

Hunt, Jeffrey Wm. *Meade and Lee After Gettysburg: The Forgotten Final Stage of the Gettysburg Campaign, From Falling Waters to Culpeper Court House, July 14-31, 1863.* El Dorado Hills, CA: Savas Beatie, 2017.

_____. Meade and Lee at Bristoe Station: The Problems of Command and Strategy After Gettysburg, From Brandy Station to the Buckland Races, August 1 to October 31, 1863. El Dorado Hills, CA: Savas Beatie, 2019.

Hyde, Bill. *The Union Generals Speak: The Meade Hearings on the Battle of Gettysburg.* Baton Rouge, LA: Louisiana State University Press, 2003.

Jones, Terry. *Lee's Tigers: The Louisiana Infantry in the Army of Northern Virginia.* Baton Rouge: Louisiana State University Press, 1987.

_____. *Lee's Tigers Revisited: The Louisiana Infantry in the Army of Northern Virginia.* Baton Rouge: Louisiana State University Press, 2017.

Jordon, David M. *Happiness Is Not My Companion: The Life of General G.K. Warren.* Bloomington: Indiana University Press, 2001.

Kreiser, Lawrence, Jr. *Defeating Lee: A History of the Second Corps, Army of the Potomac.* Bloomington: Indiana University Press, 2011.

Krick, Robert. *Civil War Weather in Virginia.* Tuscaloosa: The University of Alabama Press, 2007.

_____. *Ninth Virginia Cavalry.* Lynchburg, VA: H. E. Howard, 1982.

_____. *Staff Officers in Gray: A Biographical Register of the Staff Officers in the Army of Northern Virginia.* Chapel Hill: University of North Carolina Press, 2003.

Laine, J. Gary and Penny, Morris M. *Law's Alabama Brigade in the War Between the Union and the Confederacy.* Shippensburg, PA: White Mane Publishing Co., Inc., 1996.

Leech, Margaret. *Reveille in Washington: 1861-1865.* New York: Harper & Row, 1989.

Longacre, Edward G. *Lee's Cavalrymen: A History of the Mounted Forces of the Army of Northern Virginia.* Mechanicsburg, PA: Stackpole Books, 2002.

_____. *Lincoln's Cavalrymen: A History of the Mounted Forces of the Army of the Potomac.* Mechanicsburg, PA: Stackpole Books, 2000.

_____. *To Gettysburg and Beyond: The Twelfth New Jersey Volunteer Infantry, II Corps, Army of the Potomac, 1862-1865.* Highstown, NJ: Longstreet House, 1988.

Mackowski, Chris and White, Kristopher D. *Chancellorsville's Forgotten Front: The Battles of Second Fredericksburg and Salem Church, May 3, 1863.* El Dorado Hills, CA: Savas Beatie, 2013.

Mahood, Wayne. *Alexander "Fighting Elleck" Hays: The Life of a Civil War General From West Point to the Wilderness.* Jefferson, NC: McFarland & Company, Inc., Publishers, 2005.

Martin, Samuel. *Kill Cavalry: The Life of Union General Hugh Judson Kilpatrick.* Mechanicsburg, PA: Stackpole Books, 2000.

Matteson, Ron. *Civil War Campaigns of the 10th New York Cavalry, With One Soldier's Personal Correspondence.* Self-published, Lulu.com, 2007.

McElfresh, Earl B. *Maps and Mapmakers of the Civil War.* New York: Henry N. Abrams, Inc., Publishers, 1999.

Mesic, Harriet Bey. *Cobb's Legion: A History and Roster of the 9th Georgia Volunteers in the Civil War.* Jefferson, NC: McFarland & Co, Inc., 2011.

Miller, Richard F. ed. *States at War*, 6 volumes. Hanover, PA: University Press of New England 2014.

Nicholas, Richard & Servis, Joseph. *Powhaten, Salem and Courtney Henrico Artillery.* Lynchburg, VA: H.E. Howard, 1997.

O'Reilly, Francis Augustín. *The Fredericksburg Campaign: Winter War on the Rappahannock.* Baton Rouge: Louisiana State University Press, 2003.

Osborne Charles C. *Jubal: The Life and Times of General Jubal A. Early.* Chapel Hill: University of North Carolina Press, 1992.

Pennypacker, Isaac R. *General Meade.* New York: D. Appleton and Co., 1901.

Pfanz, Donald. *Richard S. Ewell: A Soldier's Life.* Chapel Hill: University of North Carolina Press, 1998.

Pullen, John J. *The Twentieth Maine: A Volunteer Regiment in the Civil War.* Dayton, OH: Morningside Press, 1984.

Rafuse, Ethan S. *George Gordon Meade and the War in the East.* Abilene, TX: McWhiney Foundation Press, 2003.

Ray, Fred. *Shock Troops of the Confederacy: The Sharpshooter Battalions of the Army of Northern Virginia.* Asheville, NC: CFS Press, 2006.

Rhea, Gordon. *The Battles for Spotsylvania Court House and the Road to Yellow Tavern: May 7-12, 1864.* Baton Rouge: Louisiana State University Press, 1997.

Robertson, James. *General A.P. Hill: The Story of a Confederate Warrior.* New York: Random House, 1987.

Roberts, Bobby L. *Portraits of Conflict: A Photographic History of Louisiana in the Civil War.* Fayetteville: University of Arkansas Press, 1998.

Sandburg, Carl. *Abraham Lincoln: The War Years.* 4 Volumes. New York: Harcourt, Brace & World, 1939.

Scheel, Eugene. *The Civil War in Fauquier County Virginia.* Warrenton, VA: The Fauquier National Bank, 1995.

Sears, Stephen W. *Lincoln's Lieutenants: The High Command of the Army of the Potomac.* New York: Houghton Mifflin Harcourt, 2017.

Starr, Stephen Z. *The Union Cavalry in the Civil War: The War in the East, From Gettysburg to Appomattox, 1863-1865.* Baton Rouge: Louisiana State University Press, 1981.

Styple, William B. *Generals in Bronze: Interviewing the Commanders of the Civil War.* Kearny, NJ: Belle Grove Publishing Company, 2005.

Sutherland, Daniel E. *Seasons of War: The Ordeal of a Confederate Community, 1861-1865.* New York: The Free Press, 1995.

Tagg, Larry. *The Generals of Gettysburg: The Leaders of America's Greatest Battle.* Campbell, CA: Savas Publishing Company, 1998.

Thomas, Emory. *Bold Dragoon: The Life of J. E. B. Stuart.* New York: Harper Row, 1986.

Trout, Robert. *After Gettysburg: Cavalry Operations in the Eastern Theater, July 14, 1863 to December 31, 1863.* Hamilton, MT: Eagle Editions Ltd, 2012.

_____. *Galloping Thunder: The Stuart Horse Artillery Battalion.* Mechanicsburg, PA: Stackpole Books, 2002.

Tsouras, Peter G. *Major General George H. Sharpe and the Creation of American Military Intelligence in the Civil War,* Philadelphia, PA: Casemate Publishers, 2018.

Urwin, Gregory. *Custer Victorious: The Civil War Battles of General George Armstrong Custer.* Edison, NJ: The Blue & Gray Press, 1983.

Warner, Ezra. *Generals in Blue: The Lives of the Union Commanders.* Baton Rouge: Louisiana State University Press, 1964.

_____. *Generals in Gray: The Lives of Confederate Commanders.* Baton Rouge: Louisiana State University Press, 1959.

Wittenberg, Eric. *Rush's Lancers: The Sixth Pennsylvania Cavalry in the Civil War*. Yardley, PA: Westholme Publishing, 2007.

Wise, Jennings. *The Long Arm of Lee: The History of the Artillery of the Army of Northern Virginia*. New York: Oxford University Press, 1959.

Woodward, Harold R, Jr. *Defender of the Valley: Brigadier General John Daniel Imboden, C.S.A.* Shenandoah Valley. Berryville, VA: Rockbridge Publishing Co, 1996.

_____. *For Home and Honor: The Story of Madison County, Virginia During the War Between the States*. Madison, VA: Skyline Services, 1990.

Peiodical Articles

Robertson, James, ed., "An Indiana Soldier in Love and War: The Civil War Letters of John V. Hadley," *Indiana Magazine of History*, Vol. 59, Sept. 1963.

Toler, J. T. "One of Fauquier's Historic Treasures: Rappahannock River Canal, 1816-60," *News and Notes from the Fauquier Historical Society*, Vol. 16, 1994.

Wilson, John S. "Captain Fish and the 121st New York Volunteers at Rappahannock Station, Virginia" *Military Collector & Historian: Journal of the Company of Military Historians*, Vol. 48, Fall 1996, Washington, DC.

Newspaper Articles

"Rappahannock," *National Tribune*, Dec. 25, 1884.

"The Sixth Maine's Superb Gallantry at Rappahannock Station," *National Tribune*, July 28, 1887.

"The 6th Maine," *National Tribune*, March 15, 1888.

"The 6th Maine at Rappahannock Station," *National Tribune*, June 14, 1888.

"A Daring Lieutenant," The *Anderson* [SC] *Intelligencer*, April 22, 1880

Online Secondary Sources

Hall, Clark B. "Upper Rappahannock River Front: The Dare Mark Line." http://www.brandystation foundation.com/places/Rappahannock%20Front.pdf

"Culpeper County During the Civil War," Encyclopedia Virginia, https://www.encyclopedia virginia.org/ Culpeper_County_During_the_Civil_War#start_entry

"Godwin, Archibald Campbell, Biography" https://www.ncpedia.org/biography/godwin-archibald-campbell

"Officers of Berdan's Sharpshooter Regiments" http://berdansharpshooter.org/officers.htm

"Remington, Virginia History" https://www.remingtonva.com/history "Railroads of the Confederacy" https://www.battlefields.org/learn/articles/railroads-confederacy

"Rappahannock Station" http://thenewoanda.weebly.com/blog/rappahannock-station

"The Upper Rappahannock Mapping Project: The Civil War in Culpeper and Fauquier Counties 1862-1864." https://issuu.com/culpeperhistory/docs/final_cffc_report_oct_20_2013

"Topographic Map of Fauquier County" https://en-us.topographic-map.com/ maps/s0np/Fauquier-County/

Note: Three helpful websites used in researching this book were www.fold3.com, www.civilwardata.com, and www.findagrave.com. All require annual memberships but are reasonably priced with memberships that can be cancelled at any time. Fold3 has digitized the Civil War service records collected at the National Archives. They are searchable by unit and name. Civil War Data aggregates information on individual regiments and soldiers from a wide variety of sources. Searchable by unit or name, it lists engagements and casualties sustained in each action including the names and some biographic information of the men killed, wounded, or missing. The findagrave.com site provides much-harder-to-locate information about individual soldiers.

Index

Jeffrey William Hunt is Director of the Texas Military Forces Museum, the official museum of the Texas National Guard, located at Camp Mabry in Austin, Texas, and an Adjunct Professor of History at Austin Community College, where he has taught since 1988. Prior to taking the post at the Texas Military Forces Museum, he was the Curator of Collections and Director of the Living History Program at the Admiral Nimitz National Museum of the Pacific War in Fredericksburg, Texas for 11 years.

Jeff holds a Bachelors Degree in Government and a Masters Degree in History, both from the University of Texas at Austin. In 2013, he was appointed an honorary Admiral in the Texas Navy by Governor Rick Perry, in recognition of his efforts to tell the story of the Texas naval forces at the Texas Military Forces Museum. He is a frequent speaker for a wide variety of organizations as well as documentaries and news programs. He is also the author of *The Last Battle of the Civil War: Palmetto Ranch*, and has contributed to *Essential Civil War Curriculum*, the *Revised Handbook of Texas*, and the *Gale Library of Daily Life: American Civil War*.

Jeff's first two books in this series were: *Meade and Lee after Gettysburg: The Forgotten Final Stage of the Gettysburg Campaign, from Falling Waters to Culpeper Court House, July 14-31, 1863* (Savas Beatie, 2017), which was awarded the Gettysburg Civil War Round Table's 2017 Distinguished Book Award, and *Meade and Lee at Bristoe Station: The Problems of Command and Strategy after Gettysburg, from Brandy Station to the Buckland Races, August 1 to October 31, 1863* (Savas Beatie, 2018).